Adirondack Mountain Club

High Peaks Trails

Fourteenth Edition
Forest Preserve Series (4th ed.), Volume 1

Editors, Tony Goodwin and David Thomas-Train

Adirondack Mountain Club, Inc.
Lake George, New York

Published by the Adirondack Mountain Club, Inc.
814 Goggins Road, Lake George, NY 12845-4117
www.adk.org

The Adirondack Mountain Club (ADK) is dedicated to the protection and responsible recreational use of the New York State Forest Preserve and other parks, wild lands, and waters vital to our members and chapters. The Club, founded in 1922, is a member-directed organization committed to public service and stewardship. ADK employs a balanced approach to outdoor recreation, advocacy, environmental education, and natural resource conservation.
ADK encourages the involvement of all people in its mission and activities; its goal is to be a community that is comfortable, inviting, and accessible.

Library of Congress Cataloging-in-Publication Data

Adirondack mountain club high peaks trails / editors, Tony Goodwin and David Thomas-Train.—Fourteenth ed.
      p. cm.— (Forest preserve series (4th ed.), volume 1)
   Rev. ed. of Adirondack Trails: High Peaks Region (13th ed.), 2004.
   Includes index.
   ISBN 978-1-931951-13-5 (guidebook alone)—ISBN 978-1-931951-25-8 (high peaks trails & map pack) 1. Hiking—New York (State)—Adirondack Park—Guidebooks. 2. Trails—New York (State)—Adirondack Park—Guidebooks. 3. Adirondack Park (N.Y.)—Guidebooks. I. Goodwin, Tony, 1949– II. Thomas-Train, David, 1951–
   GV199.42.N652A343 2012
   917.47'5—dc23
                                         2012027470
ISBN: 978-1-931951-13-5   Printed in the United States of America
24 23 22 21 20 19 18 17 16 15   4 5 6 7 8 9 10 11 12

James A. Goodwin (1910–2011)

This edition of *Adirondack Mountain Club High Peaks Trails* is dedicated to my father, who had a hand in the preparation of every edition of this guide from the sixth in 1956 to the eleventh in 1985. Additionally, he initiated the original contour map for the High Peaks guide. His dedication to sharing his knowledge of the mountains with other hikers has been my inspiration to produce this and three previous editions of this guide. I therefore humbly continue the family tradition so the current generation of hikers can continue to safely and responsibly enjoy the mountains my father loved so much.

—*Tony Goodwin*

Adirondack
ADK
Mountain Club

WE WELCOME YOUR COMMENTS

Use of the information in this book is at the sole discretion and risk of the hiker. ADK makes every effort to keep its guidebooks up-to-date; however, trail conditions are always changing.

In addition to reviewing the material in this book, hikers should assess their ability, physical condition, and preparation, as well as likely weather conditions, before a trip. For more information on preparation, equipment, and how to address emergencies, see the introduction.

If you note a discrepancy in this book or wish to forward a suggestion, we welcome your comments. Please cite book title, year of most recent copyright and printing (see copyright page), trail, page number, and date of your observation. Thanks for your help!

Please address your comments to:
Publications
Adirondack Mountain Club
814 Goggins Road
Lake George, NY 12845-4117
518-668-4447
pubs@adk.org

24-HOUR EMERGENCY CONTACTS

In-town and roadside: **911**

Backcountry emergencies in the Adirondacks: DEC dispatch, **518-891-0235**

Emergencies elsewhere: **518-408-5850**, or toll-free, **877-457-5680**

(See page 25 for more information)

Contents

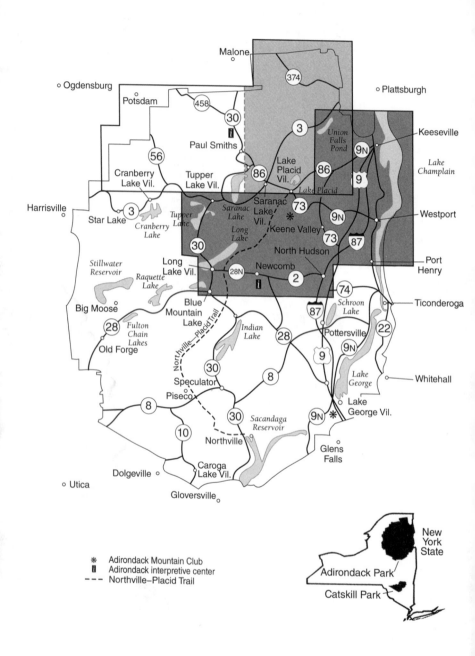

*   Adirondack Mountain Club
🛈   Adirondack interpretive center
- - -   Northville–Placid Trail

Preface

Since the publication of the thirteenth edition of this guidebook in 2004, there have been enough changes to warrant bringing out a new edition. The most significant changes include new trail systems in Wilmington and Lake Placid plus major changes in land ownership in the southern part of the region. New trail construction has added a system of walking trails just south of the village of Lake Placid in an area known as Henrys Woods. In Wilmington near The Flume, a system of mountain bike trails also provides marked access to Flume Knob and to the Wilmington Trail to Whiteface Mt. The transfer of land from the Open Space Institute to the State of New York brings another 6,800 acres into the Forest Preserve. This now provides public access to Henderson Lake, the Preston Ponds, and the direct route to Santanoni Peak. There will be further changes as public access is gradually granted to the former Finch Pruyn lands currently owned by the Nature Conservancy. The latter, in particular, has the potential to affect approaches to Allen Mt. and may permit access to the Boreas Ponds.

Of lesser significance, but still important to users of this guide, the regulations regarding the High Peaks Wilderness Area have been refined so that there is no longer the requirement to carry a self-issuing permit for either day hikes or camping trips. Ongoing experience with failed bear "hangs" has lead to new regulations requiring the use of bear-resistant canisters. Lean-tos at Lake Colden have been relocated, and additional campsites have been designated. The herd paths to the Dix Range and Gray Peak have been designated and are on Trails Illustrated Map 742. Additionally, the renaming of roads to implement E-911 service in this area appears to be complete, so trailhead directions should not be changing for the foreseeable future.

What has remained unchanged is the popularity of the High Peaks Region for hikers. The regulations and ongoing maintenance work have been successful in preventing or even reversing deterioration of this resource, but only continued adherence to posted regulations will allow this trend to continue. All users should also consider contributing to ongoing maintenance efforts—either monetarily or by volunteering. Also consider exploring lesser-known areas of both this region and other regions of the Adirondack Park. Plan to do popular climbs at off-peak times and try something new on peak weekends. If taken, the above suggestions will help prevent any degradation of this precious resource and reduce the need for any additional restrictive regulations.

—*Tony Goodwin*
Keene, New York
June 2012

Great Range from Basin. Carl Heilman II

Introduction

The Adirondack Mountain Club
Forest Preserve Series

The Forest Preserve Series of guides to Adirondack and Catskill trails covers hiking opportunities on the approximately 2.6 million acres of Forest Preserve (public) land within the Adirondack Park and nearly 300,000 acres in the Catskill Park. The Adirondack Mountain Club (ADK) published its first guidebook, covering the High Peaks and parts of the Northville-Placid Trail, in 1934. In the early 1980s, coinciding with the decade-long centennial celebration of the enactment of the Forest Preserve legislation in 1885, ADK set out to achieve its long-time goal of completing a series of guides that would cover the two parks. This series now includes the following guidebooks:

1 Adirondack Mountain Club High Peaks Trails
2 Adirondack Mountain Club Eastern Trails
3 Adirondack Mountain Club Central Trails
4 Adirondack Mountain Club Western Trails
5 Adirondack Mountain Club Northville–Placid Trail
6 Adirondack Mountain Club Catskill Trails

The public lands that constitute the Forest Preserve are unique among all other wild public lands in the United States because they enjoy constitutional protection against sale or development. The story of this unique protection begins in the 1800s and continues today as groups such as ADK strive to guard it. This responsibility also rests with the public, who are expected not to degrade the Forest Preserve in any way while enjoying its wonders. The Forest Preserve Series of trail guides seeks not only to show hikers, skiers, and snowshoers where to enjoy their activities, but also to offer guidelines whereby users can minimize their impact on the land.

THE ADIRONDACKS
The Adirondack region of northern New York is unique in many ways. It contains the only mountains in the eastern United States that are not geologically Appalachian. In the late 1800s it was the first forested area in the nation to benefit from enlightened conservation measures. At roughly the same time it was also the most prestigious resort area in the country. In the twentieth century, the Adirondacks became the only place in the Western Hemisphere to host two winter Olympiads. In the 1970s the region was the first of significant size in the nation to be subjected to comprehensive land use controls. The Adirondack Forest Preserve (see below) is part of the only wild lands preserve in the nation whose fate lies in the hands of the voters of the entire state in which it is located.

Geologically, the Adirondacks are a southern appendage of the Canadian Shield. In the United States the Shield bedrock, which is over one billion years old, mostly lies concealed under younger rock, but it is well exposed in a few regions. Upward doming of the Adirondack mass in the past few million years—a process that is still going on, resulting in the mountains rising a few millimeters every century—is responsible for erosional stripping of the younger rock cover. The stream-carved topography has been extensively modified by the sculpting of glaciers, which, on at least four widely separated occasions during the Ice Age, completely covered the mountains.

Ecologically, the Adirondacks are part of a vegetation transition zone, with the northern, largely coniferous boreal forest (from the Greek god Boreas, owner of the north wind, whose name can be found on a mountain peak and series of ponds in the High Peaks region) and the southern deciduous forest, exemplified by beech-maple stands, intermingling to present a pleasing array of forest tree species. Different vegetation zones are also encountered as one ascends the higher mountains in the Adirondacks; the tops of the highest peaks are truly arctic, with mosses and lichens that are common hundreds of miles to the north.

A rugged and heavily forested region, the Adirondacks were generally not hospitable to Native Americans, who used the region principally for hunting. Remnants of ancient campgrounds have been found in some locations. The native legacy survives principally in place names.

The first European to see the Adirondacks was likely the French explorer Jacques Cartier, who on his first trip up the St. Lawrence River in 1535 stood on top of Mont Royal (now within the city of Montreal) and discerned high ground to the south. Closer looks were had by Samuel de Champlain and Henry Hudson, who came from the north and south, respectively, within a few weeks of each other in 1609.

For the next two centuries the Champlain Valley to the east of the Adirondacks was a battleground. Iroquois, Algonquin, French, British, and eventually American fighters struggled for control over the valley and with it supremacy over the continent. Settlers slowly filled the St. Lawrence Valley to the north, the Mohawk Valley to the south, and somewhat later, the Black River Valley to the west. Meanwhile the vast, rolling forests of the interior slumbered in virtual isolation, disturbed only by an occasional hunter, timber cruiser, or wanderer.

With the coming of the nineteenth century, people discovered the Adirondacks. Virtually unknown as late as the 1830s (the source of the Nile River was located before the source of the Hudson), by 1850 the Adirondacks made New York the leading timber-producing state in the nation. This distinction did not last for long, though, as the supply of timber was quickly brought close to extinction. Meanwhile, mineral resources, particularly iron, were being exploited.

After the Civil War, people began to look toward the Adirondacks for recreation. At the same time, resource conservation and wilderness preservation ideas began to take hold, sometimes conflicting with the newfound recreational interests. Conservation and preservation concepts were given legal standing in 1885, when the New York State legislature created the Adirondack Forest Preserve and directed that

Dix Mt. from Noonmark Mt. Hardie Truesdale

"the lands now or hereafter constituting the Forest Preserve shall be forever kept as wild forest lands." This action marked the first time a state government had set aside a significant piece of wilderness for reasons other than its scenic uniqueness.

In 1892, the legislature created the Adirondack State Park, consisting of Adirondack Forest Preserve land plus all privately owned land within a somewhat arbitrary boundary surrounding the Adirondacks, known as the "blue line" because it was drawn in blue on a large state map when it was first established. In 1894, in response to continuing abuses of the Forest Preserve law, the state's voters approved the inclusion of the "forever wild" portion of that law in the constitution of New York State, thus creating the only preserve in the nation that has constitutional protection. Today the Forest Preserve (the lands owned by the people of the State of New York) includes 2.5 million acres within the 6-million-acre Adirondack Park, the largest park in the nation outside of Alaska.

After World War I, tourism gradually took over as the primary industry in the Adirondacks. The growth of the second-home industry spurred implementation of land use plans and an Adirondack Park Agency to manage them. While the plans and the Agency have remained controversial, they indicate the need to address the issues facing the Adirondacks boldly and innovatively.

STATE LAND UNITS AND CLASSIFICATIONS

Since 1972, most Forest Preserve lands in the Adirondacks have been classified as Wilderness, Primitive, or Wild Forest, depending on the size of the unit and the types of use thought to be desirable for it. The largest and most remote units are generally Wilderness, with only foot travel permitted and minimum facilities, such as lean-tos.

Primitive areas are similar, but with a nonconforming "structure" such as a fire tower, road, or private inholding. Wild Forest areas are generally smaller but potentially more intensively used, with snowmobiles and mountain bikes permitted on designated trails. Management of each unit is prescribed in a unit management plan (UMP), which determines what facilities, such as trails or shelters, will be built and maintained as well as any special regulations needed to manage each unit effectively.

Use of all units covered by this book is governed by general Forest Preserve regulations. Additionally, with the completion and implementation of its UMP, there are now special regulations for use of the High Peaks Wilderness Area. These regulations govern day and camping group size, campfires, and the leashing of dogs. The UMPs for the Dix Mountain and Giant Mountain wilderness areas have recommended additional regulations that may be implemented in the future. See pp. 21–24 for details.

Trails described in this volume are located in the following units:
- Wilderness Areas: Dix Mountain, Giant Mountain, High Peaks, Jay Mountain, McKenzie Mountain, Sentinel Range, Hurricane Mountain
- Primitive Areas: Ampersand, Johns Brook
- Wild Forest Areas: Hammond Pond, Saranac Lakes, Taylor Pond, Wilmington

PARKING LIMITS AND FEES

Increased use of the High Peaks in recent years has often resulted in parking areas at some popular trailheads reaching capacity on weekends. There are currently no plans to increase parking capacity at these trailheads because the High Peaks Unit Management Plan has accepted parking limits at popular trailheads as a legitimate method to control peak use of the area.

In particular, the Garden in Keene Valley usually reaches capacity late Friday or early Saturday on Victoria Day and Memorial Day in May plus all weekends between July 4 and late October. To help control this situation, there is now a shuttle bus from an overflow parking lot and a fee for parking. (See Keene Valley section, p. 29.) To date, ADK's parking area, which is also subject to a fee, reaches capacity mostly on long holiday weekends. At both the Garden and ADK's Heart Lake Property, the public road that approaches the parking area is posted against parking—both to avoid conflict with adjacent private homeowners and to restrict overuse of the area. When any parking lot is full, one must either find a legal parking area and walk to the trailhead or try another hike where parking is still available.

LEAVE NO TRACE

ADK supports the seven principles of the Leave No Trace program:

1. *Plan Ahead and Prepare*
   Know the regulations and special considerations for the area you'll visit.
   Prepare for extreme weather, hazards, and emergencies.
   Travel in groups of less than ten people to minimize impacts.

2. *Travel and Camp on Durable Surfaces*
   Hike in the middle of the trail; stay off of vegetation.
   Camp in designated sites where possible.
   In other areas, don't camp within 150 feet of water or a trail.

3. *Dispose of Waste Properly*
   Pack out all trash (including toilet paper), leftover food, and litter.
   Use existing privies, or dig a cat hole five to six inches deep, then cover hole.
   Wash yourself and dishes at least 150 feet from water.

4. *Leave What You Find*
   Leave rocks, plants, and other natural objects as you find them.
   Let photos, drawings, or journals help to capture your memories.
   Do not build structures or furniture or dig trenches.

5. *Minimize Campfire Impacts*
   Use a portable stove to avoid the lasting impact of a campfire.
   Where fires are permitted, use existing fire rings and only collect downed wood.
   Burn all fires to ash, put out campfires completely, then hide traces of fire.

6. *Respect Wildlife*
   Observe wildlife from a distance.
   Avoid wildlife during mating, nesting, and other sensitive times.
   Control pets at all times, and clean up after them.

7. *Be Considerate of Other Visitors*
   Respect other visitors and protect the quality of their experience.
   Let natural sounds prevail; avoid loud sounds and voices.
   Be courteous and yield to other users on the trail.

For further information on Leave No Trace principles
log on to www.lnt.org.

ALPINE ZONES

The actual land area above timberline in the Adirondacks is a very small part of the Forest Preserve, but it is one of the most unique and precious natural resources in the state. The alpine vegetation of moss, grasses, lichens, and rare flowers is very sensitive to human interference, and any damage is extremely slow to heal.

Hikers are therefore urged to stay on the designated trails and in all cases to walk only on solid rock. Even exposed dirt and gravel must be avoided because these areas may grow back again if left undisturbed.

Because of the precious and irreplaceable nature of these alpine areas, ADK and the Nature Conservancy, in cooperation with the DEC, have funded a Summit Steward program to put naturalists on Mt. Marcy, Algonquin Peak, and occasionally other summits for the purpose of educating the hiking public about the importance of protecting this fragile resource. For these reasons, camping above four thousand feet is now forbidden any time of year, and camping between thirty-five hundred and four thousand feet is permitted only at designated campsites.

USING THIS GUIDEBOOK

The trails described in this book are all in the High Peaks region of the Adirondacks, which derives its name from the fact that it contains all of the Adirondack peaks with elevations over four thousand feet, as well as numerous other mountains under four thousand feet. The region is located in the northeastern quadrant of the Adirondack State Park (see p. 6) and includes the villages of Lake Placid, Saranac Lake, Keene, Keene Valley, and Newcomb. The private holdings and roads within this area divide the public Forest Preserve lands into separate areas or "units"; users must be aware that there are different regulations governing use of different land units. (See p. 12 for details.)

Like all volumes in the Adirondack Mountain Club Forest Preserve Series of guides to Adirondack and Catskill trails, this book is intended to be both a reference tool for planning trips and a field guide to carry on the trail. All introductory material should be read carefully; it contains important information regarding current camping and hiking regulations as well as numerous suggestions for safe and proper travel by foot in the Adirondacks.

The guide is divided into geographic sections (Keene Valley, St. Huberts, Heart Lake, Northern, Eastern, Southern, and now Champlain). The introduction to each of these sections gives hikers an idea of the opportunities available in that area as well as information on facilities and regulations common to that section. Each section's introduction also provides recommended hikes in the "short," "moderate," and "harder" categories. Many of these recommended hikes incorporate lesser-used trails in an attempt to make hikers aware of the many beautiful and seldom-visited places aside from the most popular hiking, climbing, and camping areas.

Boardwalk on final approach to Mt. Marcy. ADK Archives

ABBREVIATIONS AND CONVENTIONS

In each of the books in the Forest Preserve Series, R and L, with periods omitted, are used for right and left. The R and L banks of a stream are determined by looking downstream. Likewise, the R fork of a stream is on the R when one faces downstream. N, S, E, and W, again without periods, are used for north, south, east, and west. Compass bearings are given in degrees. N is 0 degrees, E is 90 degrees, S is 180 degrees, and W is 270 degrees.

The following abbreviations are used in the text and on the maps:

ADK Adirondack Mountain Club
AMR Adirondack Mountain Reserve
APA Adirondack Park Agency
ATIS Adirondack Trail Improvement Society
ATV All-terrain vehicle
DEC New York State Department of Environmental Conservation
GPS Global Positioning System
JBL Johns Brook Lodge
N-P Northville-Placid (Trail)
PBM Permanent Bench Mark
USGS United States Geological Survey
4WD Four-wheel-drive vehicle
ft foot or feet
jct. junction
km kilometer or kilometers
m meter or meters
mi mile or miles
yd yard or yards

LEGEND

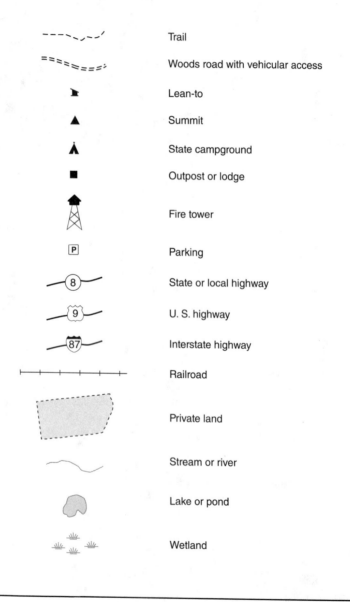

----~-,-~'	Trail
========'	Woods road with vehicular access
▶	Lean-to
▲	Summit
⋀	State campground
■	Outpost or lodge
🔥	Fire tower
P	Parking
8	State or local highway
9	U. S. highway
87	Interstate highway
+-+-+-+-+-+	Railroad
	Private land
	Stream or river
	Lake or pond
	Wetland

MAPS

Users now have a choice of maps to accompany this guide. Waterproof, durable, and tear-resistant, these maps are available from ADK.

ADK's Trails of the Adirondack High Peaks. This newly published (2015) map is a composite of USGS metric maps with a scale of 1:62,500 and a 10 meter contour interval. The map has updated overlays of trails, shelters, campsites, and private land boundaries. Trail marker color and distances between junctions are also shown. This map includes all 46 High Peaks, but does not include most of the trails described in the Champlain Valley Section or outlying trails to the N and W.

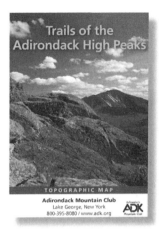

In addition to UTM grid lines, this map is letter-number coded, with letters running across the top and bottom of the map, and numbers running vertically on the sides. Each trail's coordinate (example: A4) appears with the corresponding description in this book, and each trail is numbered on the map and in this book. These numbers are not used on any signs on the trails.

The map also shows the boundary between the Eastern and Western Zones of the High Peaks Wilderness Area, an important distinction because there are different regulations for each zone. Additional important symbols are those showing junctions with private trails and roads. These serve both as landmarks with which to locate one's position and as a reminder that hikers are not to use private roads or trails.

National Geographic Trails Illustrated Maps 742 and 746. Together, these two maps include all trails described in this guide. Their scale is 1:75,000 with a 50 foot contour interval. Map 742 shows all of the High Peaks except for Whiteface and Esther Mts., which are shown on Map 746.

Trails Illustrated maps show trail number, trail marker color, and distances between junctions. Lean-tos, parking areas, and other recreational activities including boating and rock climbing are shown. Campsites are not shown. These maps have letter-number grids as well as UTM grid lines. Private land boundaries and the boundary between the Eastern and Western Zones of the High Peaks Wilderness are also shown.

ADK's Forest Preserve Series and Corresponding Maps

Every guidebook in this series matches trail information provided on National Geographic Trails Illustrated maps for the Adirondack and Catskill Parks. These large, two-sided waterproof maps were created in partnership with ADK. See ADK's Web site (adk.org/category.php?pname=books-maps-adk) for Forest Preserve

Series guides and the corresponding maps, including T.I. Map 736: Northville–Placid Trail.

TRAIL SIGNS AND MARKERS

Marked and maintained DEC trails for Adirondack hikers, cross-country skiers, snowshoers, and snowmobilers tend to have signs posted at trailheads and major trail junctions. Trail signs usually give the distance to named locations on the trail. Trail markers are plastic disks placed on trees or posts along the trails themselves and on the signs at trailheads and junctions. The color and type of marker used on a trail is included in the descriptions in this book. (Painted blazes on trees generally indicate property boundaries and should not be confused with trail markers.)

With normal alertness to one's surroundings and exceptions made for lightly traveled trails, most marked trails are easy to follow. Although this guidebook does mention particularly tricky turns or trails that might pose special difficulties, each hiker must remain alert at all times for changes of direction. Group leaders have a particular responsibility not to let inexperienced members of their party travel by themselves. A trail that seems obvious to a more experienced person may not be that way at all to an inexperienced member of the group.

It should go without saying that one should never remove any sign or marker. Hikers noticing damaged or missing signs should report this to the DEC.

All trails described in this guide are on public land or public rights-of-way that cross private land. The continued goodwill of public-spirited Adirondack landowners is directly dependent upon the manner in which the public uses this land. The "posted" signs occasionally found on rights-of-way are usually intended to remind hikers that they are on private land over which the owner has granted permission for hikers to pass. In most cases, leaving the trail, camping, fishing, and hunting are not permitted on these lands. Hikers should respect the owner's wishes.

DISTANCE AND TIME

Trails in this guidebook have been measured with a professional surveyor's wheel. Distances are expressed to the nearest tenth of a mile. Shorter distances are expressed as yards.

At the start of each section of this guide, there is a list of trails in the region, the mileage unique to the trail, and the page on which the trail description begins. All mileages given in the trail description are cumulative, the beginning of the trail being the 0.0-mile point. A distance summary is given at the end of each description, with a total distance expressed in kilometers as well as in miles. If a trail has climbed significantly over its course, its total ascent in both feet and meters is provided.

To the inexperienced hiker, distances are likely to seem longer on the trail given the often rough nature of the trails described in this guide. Steep ascents and descents also contribute to the significant difference between "sidewalk miles" and "trail miles."

No attempt has been made to estimate travel time for these trails. A conservative rule to follow in estimating time is to allow an hour for every one and one-half miles, plus one half hour for each one thousand feet of ascent, letting experience indicate how close the individual hiker is to this standard. Most day hikers will probably go a little faster than this, but backpackers will probably find they go somewhat slower. Some quickening of pace usually occurs when descending, though this may not be true on steep descents.

MINIMUM MAINTENANCE TRAILS, PEAKS WITHOUT MAINTAINED TRAILS, AND UNMARKED PATHS

In recent years, a number of new hiking routes have been created that fall somewhere between a formal, DEC-marked trail and a pure bushwhack. The most significant change has been the "designation" of certain herd paths on the twenty remaining "trailless" peaks climbed by the Adirondack Forty-Sixers. This designation effort comes in response to recommendations in the High Peaks Wilderness Area Unit Management Plan. The goals in this ongoing effort are to designate a route that can better withstand use without deteriorating and to consolidate multiple routes into one, thereby preserving the terrain around the one route.

Designation has been accomplished by selective blowdown removal and the "brushing off" of undesirable routes so the vast majority of hikers will be able to stay on the path. Except for an occasional rock cairn, however, no markers are used and hikers absolutely should not add any markers such as colored flagging or blazes.

This guide describes in some detail paths that have been officially designated, or defined, because these routes are not likely to change significantly. Those routes not yet designated will continue to be described only in general terms, including the usual starting point and the basic terrain followed.

SO WHAT IF IT'S NOT MAINTAINED?

Frequent hikers in the Adirondacks sometimes describe a moment of insight in which they understand why they should have paid more attention to the nuances of route terminology. With any luck, the epiphany doesn't coincide with being lost, or worse, lost without map and compass.

A formal, DEC-marked trail and a bushwhack form the bookends of hiking possibilities in the Adirondacks—with lots more range in between than most hikers expect. Unmaintained trails, unmarked trails, "trailless" routes, or herd paths have two things in common: They are unmarked paths, lacking official DEC signs and markers, and they may necessitate advanced orientation skills.

Unmarked paths can range from reasonably well-trodden, well-defined routes with cairns to a whisper of a track with no discernible tread. A hiker's experience with one kind of unmarked path doesn't necessarily assist him or her on another. Hikers should carry a map and compass and know how to use them. They shouldn't let past experience inspire false confidence or tempt them to forgo packing a map and compass.

In addition to the designated herd paths, other old trail systems have been revived with minimal marking and maintenance while other informal routes have become plain enough and appear to be permanent enough to warrant being shown on the map. All such routes that are shown on the map are identified in this guide as unmarked paths. Consult the guidebook description for the condition and marking of these lesser routes.

Use of any of these unmarked paths requires good route-finding and tracking skills. They are not for the inexperienced. (See sidebar.)

Warning: The DEC considers the unauthorized placement of flagging to mark a trail to be littering. The blazing or painting of trees or rocks is considered defacing state property. Both actions are subject to prosecution and resulting significant fines.

WEATHER IN THE HIGH PEAKS

The High Peaks region presents an abundance of extremely steep terrain as well as exposed alpine environments. On these exposed summits, one must be prepared for a sudden loss of visibility, a rapid drop in temperature, or both, even in the summer. Hikers should always carry extra clothing when traveling above timberline and also should pay close attention to their location in the event that visibility is suddenly reduced. Summer hikers must also watch the sky and be prepared to descend quickly to timberline if lightning becomes a threat. Winter hikers should be aware that a sudden storm can produce near-arctic conditions above timberline.

Summer temperatures in the High Peaks can drop below freezing at night, particularly in late August, and snow or ice, though rare, is not unknown on the summits in any month of the year.

Mt. Emmons, Seward Range. Joanne Kennedy

CELL PHONES

Cell phones should not be relied upon in case of emergency. Despite several highly publicized stories, their use in the mountains is limited by terrain, distance from communication towers, and other factors. Those who carry them should, out of consideration for their fellow backcountry users, use them only when necessary—and should have alternative plans for handling emergencies in case they do not operate.

From early September through the end of May, hikers should always consider the possibility of considerable snow or freezing temperatures on the summits. True winter conditions can commence in early November and last until May. During the winter, weather conditions in the lowlands can be relatively benign while at higher elevations, and especially above timberline, conditions may be so severe that a single miscue or a momentary lapse of concentration could prove fatal. In winter it is recommended that persons travel in groups of not less than four and be outfitted properly. Be advised that the DEC requires High Peaks users to have snowshoes or skis when there is more than eight inches of snow on the ground.

For more information on winter travel, see the Adirondack Mountain Club publication *Winterwise* by John Dunn.

DAY HIKING AND WILDERNESS CAMPING

The information presented below is not intended as a how-to manual on wilderness travel, but is meant to explain those regulations currently in force in the areas covered by this guide. Users who intend to hike or camp for the first time are urged to consult a current book on the subject, attend one of the many workshops or training sessions available, or at least join a group led by someone with experience. The ability to camp comfortably in any weather without causing any undue impact on the environment is not as simple as it might at first appear; but every user—from novice to experienced—has a responsibility to camp properly so that the resource is in no way degraded for those who follow.

The following pages detail the specific regulations that apply in the region covered by this guide. Although more restrictive than in the past, the regulations regarding tenting and the use of shelters are relatively unrestrictive when compared to those found in other popular backpacking areas in this country and Canada. The current regulations should be seen as the minimum standard hikers and campers must meet to responsibly use the region. As of 2012, the general regulations for the use of the Forest Preserve still apply in the Giant Mt. and Dix Mt. Wilderness Areas. The Unit Management Plans approved in 2003 for these two areas recommend stricter regulations similar to those that apply to the High Peaks Wilderness Area. Users should thus be aware that stricter regulations may be implemented in future.

SPECIAL REGULATIONS
for the High Peaks Wilderness Area—Eastern and Western Zones:
The boundary between the Eastern and Western zones of the High Peaks Wilderness can be seen on p. 259, which also shows the Adirondack Canoe Route Zone.

Day-Hiking Regulations in the High Peaks Wilderness Area.
1. Day groups are limited to fifteen people in both the Eastern and Western zones of the High Peaks Wilderness. *Affiliated groups whose total size exceeds group limits must maintain a separation distance of at least 1 mile (1.6 kilometers) throughout the duration of their visit to comply with the above regulations.*
2. Pets must be leashed in most areas (see below).
3. Skis or snowshoes must be worn when there is more than eight inches of snow on the ground. (The use of crampons may be necessary when the trail is hard-packed and icy, but snowshoes should still be carried and used if the crust no longer supports one's weight.)

Camping Regulations in the High Peaks Wilderness Area
Be sure to review the general camping regulations that follow.

Group Size
Camping groups are limited to eight in the Eastern and Western Zones of the High Peaks Wilderness Area. Also see general regulations on group size below.

Campsites
At-large camping under the provisions below is still permitted in the High Peaks Wilderness Area. In the South Meadow–Flowed Lands corridor, however, current practice in the field restricts all camping to designated sites only.

Fires
Fires are not allowed for any purpose in the Eastern High Peaks.

Bear Canisters
Approved bear-resistant canisters must be used in the Eastern High Peaks between April 1 and November 30.

REGULATIONS FOR PETS
in the High Peaks Wilderness Area
1.Must be leashed:
On marked trails (Eastern Zone, High Peaks Wilderness only)
At campsites and lean-tos
Above four thousand feet
At areas where the public has congregated
2. No pet may be left unattended.

3. All pets must be under the complete control of the owner or handler at all times.
4. Proof of a valid and current rabies inoculation is required for dogs.

CAMPING REGULATIONS
for the General Forest Preserve

The following are the most important regulations all campers must obey when camping in the Adirondack Forest Preserve. Note that special regulations apply in the Eastern and Western zones of the High Peaks Wilderness (See pp. 22–23.)

Group Size

1. Camping groups are limited to nine throughout the Forest Preserve. (See significant exceptions above.)
2. In the Adirondack Canoe Zone of the High Peaks Wilderness Area and in most other areas of the Park, groups of up to twelve are allowed—but only with a permit from the DEC forest ranger in whose district the trip starts. (One should contact the ranger by mail either directly or through DEC Headquarters in Ray Brook several weeks in advance. Telephone contact is not guaranteed given rangers' unpredictable schedules. Remember that in most cases one is calling a private home when trying to contact a forest ranger by telephone.)

Affiliated groups whose total size exceeds group size limits must maintain a separation distance of at least 1 mile (1.6 kilometers) when either camping or day hiking to comply with the above regulations.

Campsites

1. Designated sites marked with an official marker are defined as an area within fifteen feet (five meters) of the marker.
2. Pristine or at-large sites must be located at least 150 feet (46 meters) from roads, trails, or water sources. Also see Campsites, p. 22.
3. No camping is permitted above 4000 feet (1219 meters) at any time of the year.
4. Camping between 3500 and 4000 feet (1067 and 1219 meters) is allowed at designated sites only. Currently Sno-Bird, Lake Arnold, and Mary Louise Pond are the only designated sites found between these elevations.

Lean-tos

1. Must be shared by groups up to the capacity (eight persons) of the shelter.
2. No plastic may be used to close off the front of the shelter.
3. No nails or other permanent fastener may be used to affix a tarp. Rope, however, may be used to tie a nylon or canvas tarp to a lean-to.
4. No tent may be pitched inside a lean-to.
5. No tent may be pitched next to a lean-to to increase capacity.

Campfires

1. Campfires are allowed at designated campsites and legal at-large sites only. (Also see Fires, p. 22.) Only dead and down wood may be used for fires.

2. Build fires only on nonflammable surfaces such as rock, sand, or mineral soil. The organic matter and soil typical of Adirondack forests is highly flammable and will burn long after the campfire is supposedly out. (A major fire on Noonmark Mt. started this way in 1999.)

OTHER REGULATIONS
1. Do not use soap or detergent in any water source.
2. Do not dispose of food scraps in any water source. (Compliance with numbers 1 and 2 requires that all dishwashing or bathing be done at least 150 feet from any water source.)
3. Glass containers are prohibited.
4. Quiet must be observed from 10 PM to 7 AM.
5. Audio devices must not be audible outside the immediate campsite.
6. All trash must be packed out.
7. All human waste must be disposed of properly. Use privies where available; otherwise bury waste six to eight inches below the surface and 150 feet from any trail or water source.
8. Do not feed any animals.
9. Store food properly to keep it away from animals—particularly bears.

DRINKING WATER
For many years, hikers could trust almost any water source in the Adirondacks to be pure and safe to drink. Unfortunately, as in many other mountain areas, some Adirondack water sources have become contaminated with a parasite known as *Giardia lamblia*.

This intestinal parasite causes a disease known as giardiasis—often called "beaver fever." Although any warm-blooded mammal can spread this parasite when infected feces wash into the water; beavers are prime agents in transferring this parasite because they spend so much of their time in and near water. Hikers themselves have also become primary agents in spreading giardiasis owing to improper backwoods toileting.

Prevention: Follow the guidelines for the disposal of human excrement as stated in Other Regulations, above. Equally important, make sure that every member of your group is aware of the problem and follows the guidelines as well. The health of a fellow hiker may depend on your consideration.

Water Treatment: No water source can be guaranteed to be safe. Boil all water for 2 to 3 minutes, utilize an iodine-based chemical purifier (available at camping supply stores and some drug and department stores), or use a commercial filter designed specifically for giardiasis prevention. If after returning from a trip you experience recurrent intestinal problems, consult your physician and explain your potential problem.

HUNTING SEASONS

Unlike the national park system, public lands within the Adirondack and Catskill state parks are open to sport hunting. There are separate rules and seasons for each type of hunting (small game, waterfowl, and big game), but it is the big-game season, i.e. deer and bear, that is most likely to concern hikers.

During any of these open seasons, wear a bright-colored outer garment for safety; orange is recommended. The chance of encountering hunters on mountain trails in this region is relatively small because the game being pursued do not favor the steeper mountain slopes.

Big-game seasons in the Adirondacks are usually as follows:
• Early Bear Season: Begins the first Saturday after the second Monday in September and continues for four weeks.
• Archery Season (deer and bear): September 27 to opening of the regular season.
• Muzzle-loading Season (deer and bear): The seven days prior to the opening of regular season.
• Regular Season: Next-to-last Saturday in October through the first Sunday in December.

EMERGENCY PROCEDURES

All backcountry emergency assistance, including help from the local ranger, is dispatched from the following hotline. Make sure the person going for help has the telephone number as well as a complete written description of the type and exact location of the accident. A location marked on the map or UTM grid coordinates can be very helpful. If possible, leave a call-back number in the event those responding to the incident require additional information.

• **For all backcountry emergencies in the Adirondacks, call the DEC 24-hour hotline: 518-891-0235.**

• **For emergencies elsewhere, call 518-408-5850; or toll-free, 877-457-5680; or 911**

Calling the DEC hotline is preferable to calling 911. At the DEC emergency number, the caller is usually able to speak directly with someone who is knowledgeable about the area where the accident has occurred. Cell phone callers are especially prone to problems because the call may be picked up by a distant tower in a neighboring jurisdiction (or even a different state) with the message then having to be relayed through several agencies.

Other DEC Region 5, Ray Brook contacts:
General information: 518-897-1200; Rangers: 518-897-1300;
Environmental conservation officers: 518-897-1326

On occasion, special situations require DEC to modify the usual dates of hunting seasons.

The Adirondack Mountain Club does not promote hunting as one of its organized activities, but it does recognize that sport hunting, when carried out in compliance with the game laws administered by the DEC, is a legitimate sporting activity.

BEAR SAFETY

Most wildlife in the Adirondacks and Catskills can be a minor nuisance around the campsite. Generally, the larger the animal the more timid it is in the presence of humans. The exception is the bear, which can be emboldened by the aroma of food.

The following tips will reduce the likelihood of an encounter with a bear.

- Never keep food in your tent or lean-to.
- Use bear-resistant canisters. DEC requires campers to use bear-resistant canisters in the Eastern Zone of the High Peaks Wilderness between April 1 and November 30. In other areas, use a canister or hang food at least fifteen feet off the ground from a rope strung between two trees that are at least fifteen feet apart and one hundred feet from the campsite. (Hangs using a branch have a high failure rate.) Using dark-colored rope tied off five or more feet above the ground makes it less likely that a foraging bear will see the line or find it while sniffing along the ground.
- Wrap aromatic foods well.
- Through careful planning, keep trash and leftovers to a minimum. Wrap in sealed containers such as large Ziploc bags, and hang or place in canister.
- Hang your pack, along with clothing worn during cooking.

BEAR CANISTERS

Bears in many parts of the High Peaks have figured out the long-popular campers' technique of hanging food from a rope strung between two trees. Thus the DEC recommends—in some cases requires—the use of bear-resistant, food-storage canisters.

Note that bear canisters are required in the Eastern High Peaks Wilderness from April 1 through November 30.

Canisters can be obtained from outdoor retailers, borrowed from many ADK chapters, or rented or purchased from the High Peaks Information Center at ADK's Heart Lake Program Center. The canisters also protect food from many smaller forest creatures.

The DEC's current management goal with respect to bears is to educate campers about proper food storage. Bears unable to get food from campers will, it is hoped, return to their natural diet. Thus campers play an important role in helping to restore the natural balance between bears and humans. Losing one's food to a bear should be recognized as a critical failure in achieving this goal.

- Keep a garbage-free fire pit, preferably away from your camping area.
- Should a bear appear, do not provoke it by throwing objects or approaching it. Bang pots, blow a whistle, shout, or otherwise try to drive it off with sharp noises. Should this fail, leave the scene.
- Report bear encounters to a forest ranger.

RABIES ALERT

Rabies infestation has been moving north through New York State. Although it is most often associated with raccoons, any warm-blooded mammal can be a carrier.

Although direct contact with a rabid animal in the forest is not likely, some precautions are advisable:

- Do not feed or pet any wild animals, under any circumstances.
- Particularly avoid any wild animals that seem to be behaving strangely.
- If bitten by a wild animal, seek medical attention immediately.

BUG-BORNE DISEASES

Although not unique to the Adirondacks and Catskills, two insects found in these areas carry potentially lethal diseases. Deer ticks can spread Lyme disease, and mosquitoes can transmit West Nile virus. These are issues of particular concern in the Catskills.

In both instances, protection is advisable. Wear long pants and long-sleeved shirts and apply an insect repellent with the recommended percentage of N, N-diethyl-meta-toluamide (commonly known as DEET); treating clothing with a permethrin product is a safe preventive measure. On returning home, thoroughly inspect yourself, and wash yourself and your clothing immediately. Seek immediate attention if any early symptoms (rash, headache, fever) arise.

View from Little Porter Mt. David Hough

Keene Valley Section

 Keene Valley has long been popular as the starting point for hikes to Mt. Marcy, the Great Range, and many shorter destinations. This well-deserved popularity, however, has for over 25 years caused periodic parking problems at the main trailhead—"the Garden." When the Garden is full (see Parking Limits and Fees, p. 12), the only legal parking for overnight users is the parking lot S of the village on NY 73. Day parking only is tolerated on some streets near the village, but the school and church parking lots on Market St. may not be used as that might interfere with their primary use.

Since 1999, the Town of Keene has charged a fee for parking ($7 as of 2012) at the Garden from early May to late October. An attendant is on duty during weekends to control parking. A shuttle bus ($4 round-trip as of 2012) is available on weekends to bring hikers from an overflow lot located at Marcy Field, 2 mi north of Keene Valley.

Keene Valley is located on NY 73, 12 mi N of Exit 30 on I-87 (the Adirondack Northway) or approximately 28 mi S of Exit 34 via NY 9N and NY 73. There is daily bus service through Keene Valley on Adirondack Trailways, starting from Albany to the S or from Canton to the N. In the village are a grocery store, mountaineering store, and several restaurants. Overnight accommodations are available at several local inns.

ADK's Johns Brook Lodge (JBL), 3.5 mi up the Phelps Trail to Mt. Marcy, offers overnight accommodations from mid-June through Labor Day and is open on a caretaker basis Memorial Day Weekend until late June and the weekend after Labor Day until Columbus Day. (See also p. 263.) Staying at JBL before climbing Marcy is perhaps the easiest way to ascend this peak because it is only 5.5 mi from JBL to the summit, compared with over 7 mi or more from any trailhead.

Trails in winter: Unless otherwise noted, trails in this section are not suitable for skiing. Winter ascents of the higher peaks usually require crampons, perhaps the use of an ice ax, and possibly a rope, in addition, of course, to snowshoes.

The following are some suggested hikes among the many excellent possibilities:

SHORT HIKES

Baxter Mt. from NY 9N on Spruce Hill: 2.6-mi (4.4 km) round-trip. Mostly easy to moderate grades lead to a series of blueberry-covered ledges with nice views of Keene Valley, the Great Range, and Mt. Marcy. See trail 20.

Blueberry Mt.: 4.8-mi (7.7 km) round-trip. This trail, though steep in spots, offers great rewards as it ascends to a bald summit via a series of ledges. Good views commence after 1.5 mi with steadily improving views of Keene Valley, Giant Mt., and the Great Range from that point to the summit. This aptly named peak offers extensive blueberries in season, and parking is plentiful at the trailhead. See trail 17.

MODERATE HIKES

Porter Mt. from the Garden with return via Ridge Trail to Marcy Airfield: 8.4 mi (13.5 km) point to point. An ascent with relatively easy grades and a nice view from Little Porter Mt., with a return via the Ridge Trail and its many views, including the ledges on aptly named Blueberry Mt. The weekend shuttle service allows one to ride to the start and then hike back to one's car. See trails 16 and 17.

Big Slide Mt. via The Brothers with return via Slide Mt. Brook Trail and Phelps Trail: 9.5 mi (15.3 km) round-trip. An ascent over three summits with good views, culminating in a spectacular view from Big Slide Mt. Return down pretty Slide Mt. Brook and the Phelps Trail. See trails 1, 13, and 15.

HARDER HIKES

Gothics via ADK Range Trail: 14.7 mi (23.7 km) round-trip. A rugged loop including two peaks before Gothics' spectacular summit, followed by an even more spectacular descent of the W face. See trails 1, 4, and 8.

Haystack Mt.: 17.7 mi (28.6 km) round-trip. Too many hikers come to the Adirondacks to climb Mt. Marcy and don't realize that it is far better to sit in relative solitude on what many consider the finest summit in all of the Adirondacks and gaze at Marcy. See trails 1 and 10.

	Trail Described	*Total Miles* (one way)	*Page*
1	Johns Brook Lodge and Mt. Marcy via Phelps Trail	9.1 (14.7 km)	32
2	Mt. Marcy via Hopkins Trail	4.0 (6.5 km)	35
3	Southside Trail to Johns Brook Lodge	3.5 (5.6 km)	35
4	ADK Range Trail to Upper Wolf Jaw Mt., Armstrong Mt., and Gothics	4.8 (7.7 km)	37
5	Lower Wolf Jaw Mt.	0.5 (0.8 km)	39
6	Woodsfall Trail	1.1 (1.8 km)	39
7	Short Job	0.7 (1.1 km)	40
8	Gothics via Orebed Brook Trail	3.7 (6.0 km)	40
9	State Range Trail to Saddleback Mt., Basin Mt., Mt. Haystack, and Mt. Marcy	3.4 (5.5 km)	41
10	Mt. Haystack from State Range Trail	0.6 (1.0 km)	43
11	Shorey Short Cut from State Range Trail to Phelps Trail	1.1 (1.8 km)	44
	Mt. Marcy from Keene Valley via the complete Great Range	13.5 (21.8 km)	44
12	Klondike Notch Trail to South Meadow	5.3 (8.5 km)	46
13	Big Slide Mt. via Slide Mt. Brook Trail	2.4 (3.9 km)	47
14	Big Slide Mt. via Yard Mt.	2.7 (4.4 km)	47
15	Big Slide Mt. via The Brothers	3.9 (6.3 km)	48
16	Porter Mt. from the Garden	3.8 (6.1 km)	49

Skiing toward Gothics North Face. **Mark Meschinelli**

1 Johns Brook Lodge and Mt. Marcy via Phelps Trail

ADK High Peaks Map: F8–E9 | Trails Illustrated Map 742: Z25

This route to Mt. Marcy was established by Ed Phelps, son of the famous Keene Valley guide Old Mountain Phelps. The trail is also called the Johns Brook Trail, Northside Trail, or in its upper sections, Slant Rock Trail. This approach to Marcy leads up the Johns Brook Valley past ADK's Johns Brook Lodge, which offers the closest overnight accommodations to the summit of Marcy. It is also the best to use if one is traveling by public transportation, because the bus route through Keene Valley is only 1.6 mi from the trailhead, as compared to 5 mi or more from all other Marcy trailheads.

▶ Trailhead: The trail starts at the Garden parking lot W of Keene Valley. ◀

From the center of Keene Valley at the DEC sign, "Trail to the High Peaks," follow yellow markers along a paved road, going straight at 0.3 mi onto Johns Brook Ln. At 0.6 mi the road turns sharp R across a bridge over Johns Brook. The road now begins a steady climb, bearing L at the two jcts. with other paved roads. At 1.3 mi the road surface becomes gravel and ends at the Garden at 1.6 mi, where there is parking for about 60 cars.

On busy weekends this parking lot can be full, and hikers should be aware that parking is not permitted on the private land next to the road. (See p. 29 for information on parking fees and shuttle service.) In winter, the Town of Keene plows the final narrow section of road to the Garden—but only after other town roads have been plowed. There may, therefore, be times in winter when one cannot reach the Garden. As in the summer, parking is not permitted along the road; if one cannot make it to the Garden, one must park in Keene Valley, because even one car parked in the wrong place will prevent the large snowplows from turning around. In this instance especially, the threat to tow cars away is not an idle one.

Leaving the register at the far end of the Garden (0.0 mi), the trail, which has yellow DEC disks, crosses a small stream and begins a moderate climb for a few hundred yards. Easing off, it dips to cross a small stream and then continues mostly on the level to a jct. at 0.5 mi with the Southside Trail (trail 3), an alternate route to Johns Brook Lodge. Bearing R, the Phelps Trail continues mostly on the level, crossing one brook and then crossing Bear Brook just before reaching the former site of Bear Brook Lean-to at 0.9 mi. Still mostly on the level, the trail continues to Deer Brook Lean-to, located 200 yd up to the R at 1.3 mi. Just beyond, the trail dips down, crosses Deer Brook on two bridges, and climbs steeply up the far bank. Again mostly on the level, the trail passes three large boulders on the R and comes to a small stream at 1.5 mi.

The trail now begins a steady, moderate climb that eases at 2 mi. Proceeding mostly on the flat and crossing several small brooks, the trail reaches the relocated Howard Lean-to on the L with a designated campsite on the R at 3 mi before dropping down to a jct. and trail register just above the DEC Interior Outpost at 3.1 mi. (Trail L leads 50 yd to the DEC Interior Outpost and 200 yd to a suspension bridge over Johns Brook and a connection to the Southside Trail, trail 3; ADK Range Trail, trail 4; and the Orebed Brook Trail, trail 8.)

Turning R, the trail passes the former site of Howard Memorial Lean-to on the L before crossing Slide Mt. Brook (high-water bridge located 100 yd upstream) with a jct. just beyond at 3.2 mi. (Trail R with red DEC markers leads 2.4 mi to Big Slide Mt., trail 13.) Continuing on the flat, the trail soon passes a private bridge leading L across Johns Brook to ADK's Camp Peggy O'Brien (formerly Winter Camp) and Grace Camp—both camps part of Johns Brook Lodge. Continuing past this bridge, the trail crosses a bridge over Black Brook at 3.4 mi and reaches Johns Brook Lodge at 3.5 mi. Johns Brook Lodge is owned and operated by the Adirondack Mountain Club and offers overnight accommodations, meals, candy, drinks, and information to hikers. For further information, call ADK at 518-523-3441.

Just past JBL is a jct. and signpost. Trail L is the State Range Trail (trail 9) with blue DEC markers leading to Gothics and the upper Great Range as well as the Woodsfall Trail (trail 6), which connects with the ADK Range Trail (trail 4). Trail R is the Klondike Trail (trail 12) leading to South Meadows near Lake Placid and also connecting with the trail to Big Slide Mt. via Yard Mt. (trail 14).

Going straight at the signpost, the Phelps Trail to Marcy proceeds on the level, with some designated campsites on the R (N) side of the trail at 3.6 mi. Past this point the trail continues at an easy grade near the L bank of Johns Brook to the former site of Hogback Lean-to at 4.5 mi. Crossing Hogback Brook just beyond, the trail climbs a steep ridge known as a hogback, the remnant of a lateral moraine of a valley glacier that came down the Johns Brook Valley for a short time after the last ice age.

The steep climbing eases at 4.6 mi and the trail continues at easier grades. At 5 mi a vague spur trail L leads very steeply down for 250 yd to the base of Bushnell Falls. This was a favorite spot for Rev. Horace Bushnell, a respected nineteenth-century theologian from Hartford, Connecticut. He spent many summers in the Adirondacks, and the falls was named in his honor by the Keene Valley guides as he was a very well-liked summer resident of the valley.

About 50 yd beyond the jct. with the spur trail is another jct. at the former site of the first Bushnell Falls lean-to (now located 200 yd up the Hopkins Trail). The yellow markers continue to the R on the Hopkins Trail (trail 2). Turning L and now with red DEC markers, the Phelps Trail descends at a moderate grade to Johns Brook at 5.2 mi. The trail crosses on the rocks to the far bank just above the confluence of Chicken Coop Brook. Another lean-to is located just beyond. The high-water bridge upstream is no longer serviceable.

From the upper Bushnell Falls lean-to, the trail swings away from Johns Brook at a moderate grade near the L bank of Chicken Coop Brook. Swinging R and away from Chicken Coop Brook, the grade moderates at 5.8 mi and crosses Basin Brook at 6.4 mi. Now mostly on the level, the trail comes to Johns Brook again, with Slant Rock just beyond at 6.8 mi. This large rock, which forms a natural shelter, was a famous early camping spot. Just past the rock, a trail leads R and up for 300 yd to a lean-to. Other camping in this area is generally limited to sites on the side of the trail away from the brook.

Swinging L just past Slant Rock, the Phelps Trail follows close to the L bank of Johns Brook to a jct. at 6.9 mi. (Trail L with yellow markers is the Shorey Short Cut, trail 11, leading 1.1 mi to the State Range Trail between Basin Mt. and Mt. Haystack.) Past this jct., the climbing becomes steep in spots, with a last crossing of Johns Brook at 7.4 mi. This is followed by moderate grades with some steep pitches to a jct. with the State Range Trail (trail 9) at the top of the pass between Mts. Marcy and Haystack at 7.8 mi. The Phelps Trail bears R and continues to climb steeply to a jct. at 8.5 mi with the Van Hoevenberg Trail from Heart Lake (trail 61).

Bearing L with blue markers, the trail climbs a few yards to some bare rocks with a first view of the summit. (This point marks the beginning of the arctic-alpine zone where hikers must walk only on the marked trail or bare rock to preserve the fragile alpine vegetation.) After dipping down and crossing a beautiful high-altitude bog on a series of bridges, the trail climbs onto another rocky shoulder at 8.7 mi.

From this point the trail is on open rock to the summit. It is marked with cairns and yellow paint blazes, and care is needed to follow it in fog. After passing over a slightly lower eastern summit, the trail reaches the summit rock with a plaque commemorating the first ascent of the peak at 9.1 mi. A trail continues over the summit and down the SW side toward Lake Tear to connect with the Elk Lake–Marcy Trail and the trail to Lake Colden and Upper Works near Tahawus. (See Southern Section, pp. 181 and 188.) On most days in the summer and fall a Summit Steward is on duty at the summit, both to ensure that hikers stay off the alpine vegetation and to provide additional information and interpretation.

❄ Trail in winter: Suitable for skiing as far as JBL with a foot of snow cover, although the bridges are narrow and a few brook crossings may require removing one's skis.

🏃 Distances: Garden parking lot to DEC Interior Outpost, 3.1 mi; to Johns Brook Lodge, 3.5 mi; to Bushnell Falls Lean-to and jct. with Hopkins Trail, 5.1 mi; to Slant Rock, 6.8 mi; to jct. with State Range Trail, 7.8 mi; to jct. with Van Hoevenberg Trail, 8.5 mi; to summit of Marcy, 9.1 mi (14.7 km). Ascent from the Garden, 3821 ft (1165 m). Elevation, 5344 ft (1629 m). Order of height, 1.

New slide on Saddleback Mt. **David Hough**

2 Mt. Marcy via Hopkins Trail

ADK High Peaks Map: E9 | Trails Illustrated Map 742: Y24

This trail was laid out by Arthur S. Hopkins, former director of Lands and Forests for the Conservation Department, as a short cut for his crews during the survey of some major land acquisitions in 1920.

▶ Locator: The trail leads from a point 5.1 mi SW on the Phelps Trail at Bushnell Falls (trail 1) to the Van Hoevenberg Trail (trail 61) and offers an alternate route for those heading between the Johns Brook valley and Heart Lake. The trail is, however, much rougher than the Phelps Trail because it has not received the same degree of maintenance in recent years. The upper end is generally very wet. ◀

Leaving the Phelps Trail at Bushnell Falls (0.0 mi), the Hopkins Trail, with yellow markers, ascends at an easy grade to a descent across a small ravine at 0.4 mi. After a short, steep climb up the far bank, the trail levels out until it dips to cross another brook at 0.9 mi. After another steep climb, the grades are easy to moderate until the trail comes to the L bank of the L fork of Johns Brook at 1.5 mi. Now the climbing increases as the trail remains near the L bank of the brook before finally crossing it at 2.1 mi. Shortly after this crossing, the grade moderates and then levels out through some swampy terrain at 2.8 mi. After a few more short climbs and some more wet areas, the trail joins the Van Hoevenberg Trail (trail 61) with blue markers at 2.8 mi.

🚶🚶 Distances: Bushnell Falls to Van Hoevenberg Trail, 2.8 mi; to summit of Mt. Marcy, 4 mi (6.5 km). (From JBL, 5.5 mi or 8.9 km. From the Garden parking lot, 9.1 mi or 14.7 km. Ascents are the same as for the Phelps Trail.)

3 Southside Trail to Johns Brook Lodge

ADK High Peaks Map: F8–E9 | Trails Illustrated Map 742: Z25

▶ Locator: This trail offers an alternate route to Johns Brook Lodge (JBL) and the Range trails. Departing from the lower Phelps Trail, it follows an old tote road along the R bank of Johns Brook, offering many views of this characteristic mountain stream.

The grades on this trail are easy throughout, but overall it is a more difficult approach to JBL because it can be very wet in spots. Additionally, flood damage in 2011 altered the stretch of rock-hopping next to the brook to the extent that the better choice of route is to remain on the road that goes steeply up and L at 1.6 mi. The crossing of Johns Brook near the Garden can also be quite difficult in times of high water. Though this trail is still passable, as of 2013 a DEC sign announces that maintenance has been discontinued on it owing to washouts. ◀

From the Garden (0.0 mi), follow the Phelps Trail (trail 1) 0.5 mi to the jct. with the Southside Trail. Turning L with ADK markers, the trail descends a steep hogback and then turns sharp R and down off the hogback at the second flat area. From the bottom of the hogback, the trail is level to Johns Brook at 0.7 mi, which is crossed on stones. Some care is needed to find the trail on the far side. Climbing the bank, the trail comes to the old tote road at 0.8 mi, now a rough tractor and ATV road that sees occasional motorized use by owners of the several private inholdings along Johns Brook. (*Note:* This turn is easy to miss coming down the trail; watch for it shortly after crossing a large tributary and climbing a short, steep grade.)

Turning R, the trail follows the road, drops down across a large tributary, and turns L at the far side. Now at an easy grade, the trail follows the road until 1.6 mi, where the road goes up and L and is now the better route owing to flood damage on the trail that continues straight ahead. After 250 yd of moderate climbing, the grade eases, crosses Rock Cut Brook at 2 mi, and descends to the level of the brook at 2.1 mi, where the

Johns Brook Lodge.

marked trail rejoins the road. Swinging L and again near Johns Brook, 100 yd later a side trail leads R and down to some beautiful flat rocks with good swimming holes called Tenderfoot Pools.

Continuing at easy grades and swinging away from Johns Brook, the trail crosses the wide, rocky mouth of Bennies Brook at 2.4 mi, followed by Wolf Jaw Brook, and then comes to a jct. at 2.9 mi with the ADK Range Trail (trail 4) leading to Wolf Jaws Lean-to and the Great Range. Beyond this jct., the road branches L shortly before the trail comes to the suspension bridge and a jct. at 3 mi. Trail L with blue markers is the Orebed Brook Trail to Gothics (trail 8). Crossing the bridge, the trail reaches the DEC Interior Outpost at 3.1 mi. Just beyond, it rejoins the Phelps Trail from the Garden. Continuing straight ahead, Johns Brook Lodge is at 3.5 mi.

❄ Trail in winter: The descent to and crossing of Johns Brook is usually too difficult to make this a better alternative than the Phelps Trail. If one does choose to ski this route, stay on the bulldozed road around the washout even though it involves a little extra climbing.

🐾 Distances: The Garden to jct. with Southside Trail, 0.5 mi; to ADK Range Trail, 2.9 mi; to DEC Interior Outpost, 3.1 mi; to JBL, 3.5 mi (5.6 km).

4 ADK Range Trail to Upper Wolf Jaw Mt., Armstrong Mt., and Gothics

ADK High Peaks Map: E9 | Trails Illustrated Map 742: Z25

See Gothics via Orebed Brook Trail (trail 8) for information on the naming of this peak. Information on the naming of Wolf Jaws is found with the Wedge Brook Trail (trail 33) description. Armstrong Mt. was named for Thomas Armstrong, a prominent lumberman in Plattsburgh, who with his partner Almon Thomas in 1866 acquired title to Township 48, Totten and Crossfield Purchase, a parcel that included much of the Great Range and Mt. Marcy. In 1887 they sold it to the Adirondack Mountain Reserve, which still owns the part near the Ausable lakes (see St. Huberts section, p. 57).

▶ Locator: This ADK-maintained Range Trail leads from Johns Brook by the DEC Interior Outpost over Upper Wolf Jaw Mt., Armstrong Mt., and Gothics, with a side trail leading to Lower Wolf Jaw Mt. ◀

From the DEC Interior Outpost (0.0 mi), head E and down a slight grade through the open field to the suspension bridge across Johns Brook. At the far side of the bridge, turn L and follow the Southside Trail to a jct. at 0.2 mi. Southside Trail (trail 3) leads straight ahead 2.9 mi to the Garden. (See trail 3 for changes.) Turning R, the Range Trail, marked with red DEC markers, climbs at a moderate grade past two designated campsites on the R at 0.4 mi and 0.6 mi before coming to some recent slide debris on the L bank of Wolf Jaws Brook at 0.7 mi. The trail swings back, away from the brook, and then climbs steadily to the new (2012) location of Wolf Jaws Lean-to at 0.9 mi. One hundred yards beyond, the trail crosses a new (2011) slide followed by a jct. with the Woodsfall Trail (trail 6) at 1.1 mi. Wolf Jaws Lean-to (scheduled to be moved to the new location in 2012) is about 50 yd. past this jct. on the L.

From this jct., the trail continues at a steady, moderate climb to another new slide at 1.4 mi. After the second of two small tributaries at 1.7 mi, the grade steepens until the jct. at the top of the pass is reached at 2 mi. Trail L, marked with yellow DEC trail markers, leads to Lower Wolf Jaw (trail 5). Turning R, with yellow DEC trail markers, the trail begins a steep to very steep climb, switchbacking up through many ledges. At 2.3 mi there is a good view of Big Slide and Whiteface Mts., with the trail reaching the lesser summit of Upper Wolf Jaw at 2.5 mi. From here, the trail descends easily to a col and then ascends to a jct. at 2.9 mi with a spur trail R leading 20 yd to the summit lookout.

From the summit there are good views to the S and E. A vague trail leads NW from the summit a few yards to another ledge with good views of Johns Brook Valley.

Upper Wolf Jaw ascent from DEC Interior Outpost, 2000 ft (610 m). Elevation, 4185 ft (1276 m). Order of height, 29.

The ADK Range Trail continues straight ahead from the jct. with the spur trail and drops to a col at 3.1 mi, after which it climbs over an intermediate bump before descending to the base of Armstrong Mt. at 3.4 mi. A long ladder takes the trail up over some steep ledges, after which the climbing remains steep nearly to the summit at 3.9 mi (6.3 km). A large ledge on the R offers views of the Johns Brook Valley and the upper Great Range.

Armstrong Mt. total ascent from DEC Interior Outpost, 2500 ft (762 m). Elevation, 4400 ft (1342 m). Order of height, 22.

Continuing on, the trail descends over a few steep ledges to a col and then climbs to the S peak of Armstrong at 4.2 mi. Here the trail swings R and descends to a jct. at 4.3 mi with the blue-marked Beaver Meadow Trail to the Lake Rd. Trail and St. Huberts (trail 34). Continuing with yellow markers, the trail is level for a few yards before it climbs steeply to the E peak of Gothics, where the grade moderates. (This is the beginning of the arctic-alpine zone where one must walk only on the trail or bare rock to protect this unique resource.)

ALPINE ALERT
See page 14

The trail then reaches the summit of Gothics at 4.8 mi (7.7 km). The view is unobstructed, with about 30 major peaks discernible. The boathouse at Lower Ausable Lake can be seen, but to see any of Upper Ausable Lake one must proceed past the summit 0.1 mi to the blue-marked trail over Pyramid and go L on this trail a few yards to a wide ledge with views to the S and W. Gothics total ascent from DEC Interior Outpost, 3000 ft (915 m). Elevation, 4736 ft (1444 m). Order of height, 10.

The trail continues over the summit and along the ridge to the W peak of Gothics and then down the very steep and open W face with two cables to aid passage. At the bottom of this face, the trail joins the Orebed Brook Trail (trail 8) at 5.4 mi.

🥾 Distances: DEC Interior Outpost to jct. with Woodsfall Trail, 1.1 mi; to jct. with trail to Lower Wolf Jaw Mt., 2 mi; to summit of Upper Wolf Jaw Mt., 2.9 mi; to summit of Armstrong Mt., 3.9 mi; to summit of Gothics, 4.8 mi; to Orebed Brook Trail jct., 5.4 mi (8.7 km).

Slide at Lower Wolf Jaw created by Tropical Storm Irene.
David Hough

5 Lower Wolf Jaw Mt.

ADK High Peaks Map: E–F9 | Trails Illustrated Map 742: Y25

▶ Locator: From Wolf Jaws Notch, a branch of the ADK Range Trail (trail 4) leads to the summit of Lower Wolf Jaw Mt. and connects with the W. A. White Trail (trail 32) to St. Huberts or Keene Valley. ◀

From the notch (0.0 mi), the trail heads E on the flat for 50 yd to a jct. with the cut-off to the Wedge Brook Trail (trail 33), which goes R. Turning L, the trail begins to climb steeply to a jct. at 0.2 mi, where the main Wedge Brook Trail comes in from the R. From this jct., the trail continues to climb to the summit at 0.5 mi, where there are good views from the lookout on the L. Trail straight ahead is the W. A. White Trail (trail 32) to St. Huberts with connections to Keene Valley via Hedgehog and Rooster Comb.

🚶 Distances: DEC Interior Outpost to Wolf Jaws Notch, 2 mi; to summit of Lower Wolf Jaw Mt., 2.5 mi (4 km). Ascent, 2000 ft (610 m). Elevation, 4175 ft (1273 m). Order of height, 30.

Looking down slide on Wolf Jaw.
David Hough

6 Woodsfall Trail

ADK High Peaks Map: E9 | Trails Illustrated Map 742: Y25

▶ Locator: This ADK-maintained trail offers the most direct approach from Johns Brook Lodge to the Wolf Jaws and the ADK Range Trail (trail 4). For the first 0.3 mi this route coincides with the blue-marked approach to the State Range Trail (trail 9). ◀

From the signpost at JBL (0.0 mi), the trail descends and crosses Johns Brook on stones. Turning R and then immediately L on the far bank, the trail leads up over two small ridges to Orebed Brook at 0.2 mi. Climbing the far bank in two steep pitches with some wooden steps, the trail reaches a five-way jct. at 0.3 mi. Trail sharp R and sharp L is the blue-marked Orebed Brook Trail (trail 8) leading from the DEC Interior Outpost to Gothics and the upper Great Range. Trail nearly straight ahead at 110° is the ADK trail to Short Job (trail 7).

The Woodsfall Trail bears slightly R with yellow DEC markers, heading away from this jct. at 170° on an easy to moderate grade. Crossing several small brooks, it reaches a height of land at 0.9 mi and descends gradually, crossing two brooks and a new (2011) slide before joining the ADK Range Trail (trail 4) near Wolf Jaws Lean-to at 1.1 mi. This lean-to may soon (2012) be relocated 0.2 mi down the trail to the L.

🚶 Distances: Johns Brook Lodge to jct. with Orebed Brook Trail, 0.3 mi; to jct. with ADK Range Trail, 1.1 mi (1.8 km).

7 Short Job

ADK High Peaks Map: E9 | Trails Illustrated Map 742: Y25

This small knoll across the valley from Johns Brook Lodge offers some interesting views for a short hike.

▶ Locator: From JBL (0.0 mi), follow the Woodsfall Trail description (trail 6) to the five-way jct. at 0.3 mi. ◀

From the five-way jct., take the trail heading at 110°, which climbs gradually at first but then up more steeply to the first lookout toward the Great Range at 0.7 mi. The trail continues with a slight descent to a lookout over the Johns Brook valley at 0.7 mi.

🏃 Distances: Johns Brook Lodge to Orebed Brook Trail at five-way jct., 0.3 mi; to end of trail at second lookout, 0.7 mi (1.1 km).

8 Gothics via Orebed Brook Trail

ADK High Peaks Map: E9 | Trails Illustrated Map 742: Z25

According to legend, the arched peaks of this triple-crested mountain, with their great slides and bare rock, suggested Gothic architecture to Frederick Perkins and Old Mountain Phelps one day in 1857 when they sat on the top of Mt. Marcy and christened Mt. Skylight, Basin Mt., Saddleback Mt., and Gothics with characteristic names. More recent evidence contained in a poem written by a minister from North Elba (Lake Placid), however, has surfaced to indicate that Gothics had been named as early as 1850.

▶ Locator: The Orebed Brook Trail is the most direct route to Gothics from the Johns Brook valley. It connects at Gothics Col with the State Range Trail to Saddleback Mt., Basin Mt., and Mt. Haystack (trail 9). Like the ADK Range Trail (trail 4), the shortest approach to this trail from the Phelps Trail (trail 1) is from the DEC Interior Outpost, but one can also approach from Johns Brook Lodge via the Woodsfall Trail (trail 6). ◀

From the DEC Interior Outpost (0.0 mi), the trail goes E and down gradually through an open field a few yards to a suspension bridge over Johns Brook. On the far side of the brook at 0.1 mi there is a jct. with the Southside Trail (trail 3). The blue-marked Orebed Brook Trail leads R and up steeply to a rough road. Turning R on an easy grade, the Orebed Brook Trail soon swings L, away from the road (be alert; this turn is not well marked), and continues to climb on an older tote road to a five-way jct. at 0.6 mi. Woodsfall Trail (trail 6) goes R to JBL and L to the Wolf Jaws while Short Job Trail (trail 7) goes sharp L.

Continuing straight ahead on the old tote road at an easy grade, the Orebed Brook Trail crosses a large brook at 1.2 mi, with Orebed Brook Lean-to just beyond to the L of the trail. There are some designated campsites down and to the R at this point as well. Continuing at an easy grade, the trail passes a huge boulder on the R at 1.5 mi and passes two small brooks before descending to cross a larger brook at 1.8 mi. The trail climbs a steep bank on the far side and then continues at moderate grades along the R bank of the main branch of Orebed Brook. At 2.3 mi the trail comes to an old slide coming down off the small peak to the L.

The trail is now close to the R bank of Orebed Brook and soon comes to the base of a large new (2011) slide that has necessitated a reroute.

The climbing soon becomes much steeper and a very steep pitch with wooden stairs commences at 2.7 mi. The trail then continues to climb on bare rock with a steep open slide just to the R offering some views back to Johns Brook Valley. The grade eases slightly as the trail veers L and traverses across the sidehill. The grade finally eases back to moderate at 3 mi at the base of a small slide with a view of the W peak of Gothics and the summit beyond. The jct. at Gothics Col is reached at 3.1 mi. Trail R is the State Range Trail (trail 9).

Turning L and now with yellow markers, the trail climbs quite steeply up the mostly bare W ridge of Gothics. The first of two cables fastened to the rocks is reached at 3.2 mi, and above the second cable the trail continues to climb steeply around to the L of a final steep step to gain the W summit at 3.4 mi, where there are good views. (This is the beginning of the arctic-alpine zone where one must walk only on the trail or bare rock to protect this unique resource.) Crossing over this summit, the trail descends slightly and then climbs to a jct. at 3.6 mi with the blue-marked trail to Lower Ausable Lake via Pyramid (trail 35). From here, the trail continues mostly on the flat to the summit of Gothics at 3.7 mi. See ADK Range Trail (trail 4) for notes on views.

🚶 Distances: DEC Interior Outpost to five-way jct., 0.6 mi; to Orebed Brook Lean-to, 1.3 mi; to Gothics Col and State Range Trail, 3.1 mi; to summit of Gothics, 3.7 mi (6 km). Ascent from Johns Brook, 2360 ft (720 m). Elevation, 4736 ft (1444 m). Order of height, 10.

9   State Range Trail to Saddleback Mt., Basin Mt., Mt. Haystack, and Mt. Marcy

ADK High Peaks Map: E10 | Trails Illustrated Map 742: Y25

This section of trail is perhaps the most spectacular of any in the Adirondacks as it goes over the bare summits of Saddleback and Basin Mts. and connects to the spur trail to Mt. Haystack. It is also a very rugged trail and is a serious undertaking, especially with backpacks. There are many sections of steep rock, particularly on the W sides of Basin and Saddleback, which can be very uncomfortable to negotiate with a heavy pack. Day trips are suggested for those wishing to climb these peaks.

Backpackers may want to consider hiking this trail in reverse direction so as to ascend, rather than descend, the most precipitous and dangerous sections.

► Locator: The State Range Trail (and blue markers) start at JBL. This description starts from the Orebed Brook Trail (trail 8) at Gothics Col (0.0 mi). ◄

The trail climbs steeply up the E side of Saddleback Mt. with many good views back at the spectacular slides on Gothics. At 0.3 mi the grade eases on the E peak of Saddleback, after which the trail dips to the "saddle" at 0.4 mi with a side trail L to a good view just beyond. The trail then climbs two rock steps to the summit at 0.5 mi (0.8 km), where a broad ledge offers good views.

Saddleback ascent from Johns Brook, 2200 ft (671 m). Elevation, 4515 ft (1377 m). Order of height, 17.

The trail turns sharp R at the summit and follows along a ledge marked with yellow paint blazes. Turning L at the end of the ledge, the trail descends precipitously over ledges where extreme caution is needed. The trail reaches the bottom of the col at 0.8 mi, after which it begins a moderate ascent through open firs with views back at Saddleback. The grade becomes progressively steeper and remains steep until it eases on a shoulder of Basin Mt. at 1.1 mi. The trail descends gradually to a col and then begins steep climbing again at 1.3 mi. At 1.4 mi, the trail crosses a spectacular narrow ledge and then turns L and up. (This is the beginning of the arctic-alpine zone. One must walk only on the trail or bare rock to protect this unique resource.)

After a short steep scramble the trail reaches the summit of Basin at 1.5 mi. Here in the rock is embedded the bolt placed by Verplanck Colvin during the Adirondack Survey in 1876. The view is unobstructed in all directions except to the S, but with a little walking around one can see this view as well. Gothics to the E, Mt. Marcy to the W, and Mt. Haystack to the SW are the most prominent peaks visible, with Upper Ausable Lake to the S and the valley to the SE forming an almost perfect basin from which the peak got its name.

Basin total ascent from Johns Brook, 2870 ft (875 m). Elevation, 4827 ft (1472 m). Order of height, 9.

The trail goes straight over the summit, turns L at the base of the summit rocks (this is the other border of the arctic-alpine zone), and then descends generally easy to moderate grades along a SW shoulder to the top of a ledge at 1.9 mi. Going R to bypass this ledge, the trail then descends very steeply for 75 yd to a second ledge with a ladder to aid the descent. After descending this pitch, the trail levels out for a few hundred yards before descending steeply to a jct. at 2.3 mi with the Shorey Short Cut (trail 11) to the Phelps Trail.

The State Range Trail continues its steep descent for another 100 yd to the headwaters of Haystack Brook and then begins climbing steeply to the former site of Sno-Bird Lean-to at 2.4 mi, now a designated campsite. Just past the former lean-to site, the trail crosses a small stream to a jct. with the red-marked Haystack Brook Trail (trail 59) to Upper Ausable Lake.

The Range Trail now begins a very rough and eroded climb to a trail jct. at 2.9 mi. (Trail L with yellow markers, trail 10, leads 0.6 mi to the summit of Mt. Haystack.) Turning R, the Range Trail climbs steeply to the top of a ridge at 3 mi, with a bare spot offering views just beyond on the R. Now the trail starts down at a moderate grade, getting progressively steeper until at 3.3 mi it descends a near-vertical pitch to the pass at the head of Panther Gorge, where the Phelps Trail (trail 1) comes in from the R at 3.4 mi. Turning L with red markers, the route from here to the summit of Mt. Marcy is the same as the Phelps Trail.

🐾 Distances: DEC Interior Outpost at Johns Brook to Gothics Col, 3.1 mi; to summit of Saddleback Mt., 3.6 mi; to summit of Basin Mt., 4.5 mi; to jct. with Shorey Short Cut, 5.2 mi; to Sno-Bird campsite, 5.3 mi; to jct. with trail to Mt. Haystack, 5.8 mi; to Phelps Trail, 6.3 mi; to Van Hoevenberg Trail, 7 mi; to summit of Mt. Marcy, 7.6 mi (12.3 km). Total ascent from Johns Brook via Range Trail, about 4890 ft (1490 m).

10 Mt. Haystack from the State Range Trail

ADK High Peaks Map: E10 | Trails Illustrated Map 742: X24

This third highest peak in the Adirondacks was named by Old Mountain Phelps in August 1849 when he made the first recorded ascent with Almeron Oliver and George Estey. Phelps remarked to his companions that the mountain was a great stack of rock but that he would call it Haystack; and Haystack it has been ever since.

▶ Locator: Mt. Haystack is approached from the State Range Trail (trail 9) either over Saddleback and Basin Mts. or more directly via the Phelps Trail (trail 1) to the head of Panther Gorge. The distance to the jct. with the Haystack Trail is 5.8 mi from the DEC Interior Outpost via Saddleback and Basin Mts., or 5.2 mi (and a lot less climbing) via the Phelps Trail and Slant Rock. ◀

Although reasonably well marked above timberline, care is still needed to follow it in fog or rain.

From the jct. with the State Range Trail (trail 9) (0.0 mi), the trail follows yellow markers to the first ledge, after which it is marked by cairns and yellow paint blazes. (The jct. is the beginning of the arctic-alpine zone. One must walk only on the trail or bare rock to protect this unique resource.) After a few sharp zigzags through the ledges, the trail reaches the summit of Little Haystack at 0.2 mi. Then bearing slightly L, the trail descends a diagonal ledge for 150 yd before turning sharp R and down to the few trees in the col at 0.3 mi. Ascending at an easier grade from the col, the trail sticks fairly close to the crest of the ridge, bears slightly R as it approaches the summit to avoid the sharpest part of the ridge, and reaches the totally bald summit at 0.6 mi. The view from the summit is considered one of the finest in the mountains, with the yawning abyss of Panther Gorge and the steep cliffs on Mt. Marcy dominating. The trail from the S is the Bartlett Ridge Trail (trail 58), giving access to Upper Ausable Lake and Panther Gorge.

🐾 Distances: State Range Trail to summit of Mt. Haystack, 0.6 mi (1 km). From the Johns Brook DEC Interior Outpost via Saddleback and Basin Mts., 6.4 mi

ALPINE ALERT
See page 14

(10.2 km); total ascent, 4170 ft (1271 m). From Johns Brook DEC Interior Outpost via Phelps Trail and Slant Rock, 5.8 mi (9.4 km); total ascent, 2790 ft (851 m). Elevation, 4960 ft (1512 m). Order of height, 3.

11 Shorey Short Cut from State Range Trail to Phelps Trail

ADK High Peaks Map: E10 | Trails Illustrated Map 742: Y24

This trail was cut in the 1940s by A. T. Shorey, former chair of the ADK Guidebook Committee, when he was with the Conservation Department. It has been much maligned by hikers over the years because it climbs well above the height of land needed to gain access to Johns Brook Valley, and it is rough going throughout. It does, however, lead past a viewpoint that offers a perfectly framed "portrait" of Mt. Haystack and Little Haystack.

▶ Locator: This trail connects the State Range Trail (trail 9) at the base of Basin Mt. with the Phelps Trail (trail 1) near Slant Rock and offers a shorter return from the State Range Trail to the Johns Brook valley. ◀

Leaving the Range Trail (0.0 mi), the trail with yellow DEC disks climbs a moderate to steep grade to a lookout on the L at 0.2 mi, after which the grade eases a bit up past a large boulder, and finally to a height of land on the shoulder of Haystack at 0.3 mi. Now descending steep to moderate grades, the trail passes several other glimpses of the Johns Brook Valley through the trees. The descent continues to the R bank of Johns Brook with the jct. with the Phelps Trail on the other side of the brook at 1.1 mi. This point is 0.1 mi above Slant Rock.

🚶 Distances: Range Trail to Phelps Trail, 1.1 mi (1.8 km).

MT. MARCY FROM KEENE VALLEY VIA THE COMPLETE GREAT RANGE

For over 100 years, a traverse of the Great Range has been considered a premier challenge for Adirondack hikers. The views along this spectacularly rugged route are some of the best in the Adirondacks; but as the distance and vertical ascent figures indicate, nearly every foot of this route is on steep terrain with very rough trail for most of the distance. This trip can be done as either a very long, strenuous day hike or as a backpacking trip.

Backpackers should not only allow several days but must also be aware that there are no lean-tos and only one designated campsite along this route. Unless camping at this one designated campsite (the site of the former Sno-Bird Lean-to), one must camp at least 150 ft away from any trail or water supply. Furthermore, camping is prohibited anywhere above 3500 ft in elevation except at the one designated campsite.

The following table of information is included for those who wish to traverse the entire Great Range from Keene Valley to Mt. Marcy. A list of applicable trail descriptions in the Keene Valley section is also included. One can return by either the Phelps or Hopkins trail (trails 1 and 2, respectively)

Great Range Trail Descriptions in Keene Valley Section	Trail Number
Rooster Comb from NY 73 in Keene Valley	18
Hedgehog Mt. from Rooster Comb Trail	19
W. A. White Trail to Lower Wolf Jaw Mt.	32
Lower Wolf Jaw Mt.	5
ADK Range Trail to Upper Wolf Jaw Mt., Armstrong Mt., and Gothics	4
State Range Trail to Saddleback Mt., Basin Mt., Mt. Haystack, and Mt. Marcy	9

SUMMARY OF GREAT RANGE TRAIL DISTANCES

Point	Distance Miles	(Km)	Approx. Total Ascent Feet	(Meters)
Rooster Comb trailhead (S of Keene Valley)	0.0	(0.0)		
Rooster Comb*	2.5	(4.0)	1640	(500)
Hedgehog	4.1	(6.6)	2530	(771)
W. A. White Trail	4.5	(7.3)		
Lower Wolf Jaw	6.0	(9.7)	3670	(1119)
Wolf Jaws Notch	6.4	(10.3)		
Upper Wolf Jaw	7.4	(11.9)	4510	(1375)
Armstrong	8.2	(13.2)	5030	(1534)
Beaver Meadow Trail	8.7	(14.0)		
Gothics	9.1	(14.7)	5530	(1686)
Gothics Col	9.8	(15.9)		
Saddleback	10.4	(16.8)	6130	(1869)
Basin	11.3	(18.2)	6800	(2073)
Shorey Short Cut	12.1	(19.5)		
Site of former Sno-Bird Lean-to	12.2	(19.7)		
Haystack Trail	12.7	(20.5)	7630	(2326)
Phelps Trail	13.2	(21.3)		
Van Hoevenberg Trail	13.7	(22.1)	8440	(2573)
Mt. Marcy	14.5	(23.4)	9000	(2744)

* The summit of Rooster Comb is a 0.5 mi side trip from the direct trail to Hedgehog and Lower Wolf Jaw Mt. The cumulative distances assume a side trip to the summit of Rooster Comb. Otherwise, subtract 1 mi.

12 Klondike Notch Trail to South Meadow

ADK High Peaks Map: E9–D8 | Trails Illustrated Map 742: Y25 and Z23

Klondike Notch between Howard and Yard Mts. has also been called Railroad Notch at times, but this name rightfully belongs to the lower notch between Porter and Big Slide Mts. that once was actually surveyed for a railroad.

Contrary to legends printed in various Adirondack histories and further immortalized in a best-selling novel, this route was not part of the Underground Railroad for escaped slaves to reach John Brown's farm. His farm was for freed slaves and was off the direct line to Canada, the only safe haven for an escaped slave.

▶ Locator: This route leads generally NW from Johns Brook Lodge and the Phelps Trail (trail 1) through Klondike Notch to South Meadow, where it meets a road coming in from Adirondack Loj Rd. providing access to Adirondak Loj. (See Heart Lake section, p. 95.) ◀

Leaving the JBL signpost (0.0 mi), the trail with red DEC disks heads across the backyard of JBL, crosses Black Brook, and climbs along the L bank of the brook at a moderate grade with occasional steep pitches to a jct. at 1.3 mi with the ADK-maintained blue-marked trail to Big Slide Mt. via Yard Mt. (trail 14). Continuing at a moderate grade, the trail soon descends slightly to cross a swampy area and then resumes the climb to the height of land at Klondike Notch at 1.7 mi, having gained 866 ft (264 m) in elevation from JBL.

Descending now at easy to moderate grades, the trail crosses Klondike Brook at 2.7 mi. The Klondike Lean-to is just beyond and up to the L. The trail swings R, follows a tote road up a short climb, and then continues mostly on the level to 3.7 mi where it starts down a moderate grade. Occasionally swinging away from the original tote road to avoid eroded sections, the trail reaches the level shortly before a jct. with the Mr. Van Ski Trail (trail 80), which enters from R at 4.6 mi.

At 4.8 mi the Mr. Van Ski Trail diverges to the L (distance to Adirondak Loj, 1.9 mi, but sections of this portion of the trail can be very wet. Continuing on, the Klondike Trail reaches South Meadow Brook at 5.1 mi, turns upstream, and reaches the end of the Meadow Ln. at 5.3 mi. Continuing W on this road, it is slightly over a mile to the Adirondack Loj Rd., and another mile to Adirondak Loj.

❄ Trail in winter: Although steep in spots, the Klondike Trail and the Phelps Trail make a good 10 mi traverse. The JBL side of the pass has the most difficult pieces of trail to ski, so many skiers choose to ascend this side and enjoy the easier ski down the N side, even though the reverse direction produces a net loss of altitude.

🏃 Distances: JBL to ADK Big Slide Trail, 1.3 mi; to Klondike Lean-to, 2.7 mi; to Meadow Ln., 5.3 mi (8.5 km); to Adirondak Loj, 7.3 mi (11.8). ◀

13 Big Slide Mt. via Slide Mt. Brook Trail

ADK High Peaks Map: E9 | Trails Illustrated Map 742: Z25

▶ Locator: This trail starts from the Phelps Trail (trail 1), 0.1 mi above the DEC Interior Outpost and 0.3 mi below JBL. ◀

Leaving the Phelps Trail (0.0 mi) and marked with red DEC markers, the trail starts at an easy grade and crosses Slide Mt. Brook at 0.2 mi, and then twice more before it comes to the base of an old slide. The trail climbs away from the brook on this slide, at the top of which, at 0.5 mi, is a good view of Gothics and some of the rest of the Great Range. The trail returns to the brook and follows close to it with more crossings, finally ending up on the R bank and leaving the brook at 1 mi.

The climbing is now moderate through open hardwoods with some glimpses of the Great Range back through the trees. Gradually becoming steeper, at 1.8 mi the trail comes to a good view of the bare rock slide that occurred in 1830 and from which the mountain takes its name. The climbing is now quite steep to a jct. at 2.1 mi. (Trail R with ADK markers leads over The Brothers to the Garden in 3.6 mi; see trail 15.) The climbing becomes very steep with some ladders before the trail reaches a side trail L to a truly spectacular view of the slide at 2.2 mi. As the main trail swings sharp R just above this side trail, the grade eases a bit. The trail works onto the N side of the peak, swings L, and climbs on past another view on the L to the summit at 2.4 mi.

There are magnificent views of the Great Range, Giant Mt., and Algonquin Peak, with only the view to the N blocked by trees. Trail 14, with ADK markers, continues over the summit and down over Yard Mt. to the Klondike Notch Trail (trail 12) and JBL in another 4 mi.

🏃 Distances: Phelps Trail to divergence from Slide Mt. Brook, 1 mi; to trail over The Brothers, 2.1 mi; to summit of Big Slide Mt., 2.4 mi (3.9 km). Ascent from Phelps Trail, 2000 ft (610 m). Elevation, 4240 ft (1293 m). Order of height, 27.

14 Big Slide Mt. via Yard Mt.

ADK High Peaks Map: E8 | Trails Illustrated Map 742: Z24

▶ Locator: This trail starts from the Klondike Notch Trail (trail 12), 1.3 mi from JBL or 0.4 mi below the height of land if one is coming from South Meadow. Combined with the Slide Mt. Brook Trail (trail 13), it makes an interesting loop of 6.3 mi from JBL. ◀

Leaving the Klondike Notch Trail (trail 12) (0.0 mi) with blue DEC markers, the trail is nearly flat for 0.2 mi before climbing moderately and then steeply along the base of a cliff. At 0.4 mi the trail swings L on a long and nearly flat traverse that ends with a descent of a few yards, after which the trail turns sharp R. (On the descent, this turn is easy to miss.) At 0.6 mi the trail again climbs steeply along the W ridge of Yard Mt. to a short side trail leading R to a view at 1.2 mi.

This view is relatively new and has been created by a fir die-back "wave" that has reached the crest of the ridge. (Fir die-back waves result when an even-aged stand of mature balsam firs is hit by an extraordinary wind. The trees not blown down in this first blast of wind are particularly susceptible to later winds because up until this point these trees had been protected by the other trees in the stand. The result is a domino effect that successively knocks down every tree until the wave reaches the crest of the ridge. Natural regrowth will, in time, block this view.) Just beyond this view at 1.3 mi is a side trail R to the viewless summit of Yard Mt. Yard's elevation is 4018 ft, but it is not one of the 46 High Peaks because it is too close to Big Slide Mt.

From the summit of Yard Mt., the trail drops slightly to a col at 1.6 mi and then begins a generally easy climb along the ridge toward Big Slide Mt., reaching its summit at 2.7 mi (See trail 13 for description of the view.)

🥾 Distances: JBL to jct. with Big Slide trail, 1.3 mi; to summit of Yard Mt., 2.6 mi; to summit of Big Slide Mt., 4 mi (6.5 km). Ascent from JBL, 1924 ft (587 m). Elevation, 4240 ft (1293 m). Order of height, 27.

15 Big Slide via The Brothers

ADK High Peaks Map: F8 | Trails Illustrated Map 742: Z25

This trail offers a spectacular approach to Big Slide Mt. from the Garden parking lot over the three Brothers, all of which offer excellent views. Combined with the Slide Mt. Brook Trail (trail 13) and the Phelps Trail (trail 1), an interesting loop of 9.5 mi from the Garden is possible. The First and Second Brother at 1.5 mi and 1.8 mi are good objectives for shorter hikes. This trail is currently maintained by the Long Island Chapter of ADK.

▶ Trailhead: See Phelps Trail (trail 1) for trailhead description. ◀

From the trail register at the end of the Garden (0.0 mi), the Big Slide trail with blue DEC markers goes sharp R and climbs moderately to a jct. with the new trail to Porter Mt. at 0.2 mi. At 0.4 mi the trail swings L and drops down to cross Juliet Brook before beginning a steady, moderate climb to the base of a steeper pitch at 0.7 mi. Here the trail traverses to the R to avoid the steepest climbing and then switchbacks L and up to the first steep open rock, which is now bypassed on the R, to reach the first ledge at 0.8 mi. Here there are good views of Keene Valley and the Great Range.

From this first ledge, the trail soon reenters the woods and then at 1 mi goes R and slightly down to avoid a steep cliff before reaching another good view at 1.1 mi. The climbing is now mostly steep to a broad, flat ledge with expansive views at 1.2 mi. Turning R at the end of this ledge, the trail enters the woods and climbs a few steep, rocky pitches to a preliminary summit, which the trail skirts to the L (W) side on steep slabs. Turning R just past this first summit, the trail passes a natural rock shelter and soon climbs to the bare summit of the First Brother at 1.5 mi (2.4 km). Elevation, 2940 ft (896 m). Ascent from the Garden, 1437 ft (438 m). There is a spectacular view of Big Slide Mt.

Dipping slightly, the trail soon climbs steeply up open rocks to the apparent summit of Second Brother at 1.7 mi, where there are good views to the E, S, and W. Turning L, the trail is mostly level for another 200 yd before descending at an easy grade over more open ledges to the col between the Second Brother and Third Brother at 2 mi. The trail now climbs moderately with a few short dips to the summit of the Third Brother at 2.7 mi (4.4 km). Elevation, 3681 ft (1122 m). Ascent from the Garden, 2160 ft (659 m). There is a spectacular view of Big Slide Mt.

From the summit of the Third Brother, avoid the trail R to an informal campsite and continue straight as the trail descends gradually, passes a rock shelter on the L at 2.8 mi, and soon flattens out in a mature spruce forest. The trail continues flat or gently down to a small stream where it swings L and up gradually and soon comes to a larger stream at 3.2 mi. Crossing the stream, the trail is wet for a few yards, and then climbs moderately to steeply to a jct. at 3.8 mi with the Slide Mt. Brook Trail (trail 13), which it follows to the Big Slide Mt. summit at 4 mi.

⚐ Distances: The Garden to First Brother, 1.5 mi; to view on Second Brother, 1.7 mi; to Third Brother, 2.7 mi; to jct. with Slide Mt. Brook Trail, 3.8 mi; to summit of Big Slide Mt., 4 mi (6.5 km). Total ascent from the Garden, 2800 ft (854 m). Elevation (Big Slide Mt.), 4240 ft (1292 m). Order of height, 27.

16   Porter Mt. from the Garden Parking Lot

ADK High Peaks Map: F8–E7 | Trails Illustrated Map 742: Z25

Once called West Mt., Porter Mt. is named for Noah Porter, PhD, president of Yale University from 1871 to 1886. A summer resident of Keene Valley, Porter made the first recorded ascent of the peak in 1875 with guide Ed Phelps. Although Porter Mt. does not have a bald summit, it offers nearly 360° views. In 2000 and 2001, ADK relocated much of the trail as far as Little Porter to avoid private driveways and houses, both at the start and on the ridge near the summit.

▶ Trailhead: The trail starts at the Garden. See Phelps Trail (trail 1) for directions to the Garden. ◀

Leaving the Garden (0.0 mi), the new route to Porter Mt. follows the Big Slide Mt. via The Brothers Trail (trail 15) for 0.2 mi to a jct. Turning R, the trail, now with red markers, climbs over a low ridge and descends gently to a bridge over Slide Brook at 0.4 mi. Turning sharp L at the far end of the bridge, the trail climbs gently and joins an old road at 0.5 mi. Now ascending at easy to moderate grades, the trail crosses onto private property at the site of an old sugar camp at 1 mi. Here the trail crosses a private dirt road and climbs more steeply to a L turn onto a newer trail at 1.1 mi.

The trail now proceeds moderately up two switchbacks and then across a steep slope beneath some small cliffs. Here there is a sign recognizing Jim Goodwin, who cut the original Little Porter trail in 1924 and in whose honor funds were contributed to construct this present trail, which avoids the roads and houses that have been built along the original route.

Reentering state land at 1.4 mi, the trail continues across the steep slope to somewhat rougher going at 1.5 mi. Soon after, it turns R and climbs via numerous rock staircases to a jct. at the top of the ridge at 1.8 mi. The open summit of Little Porter Mt., with its excellent views, is 30 yd to the R. Much of the rest of the trail to the summit of Porter Mt. is through open woods and fern-filled glades that are a legacy of the intense fire that burned this area in 1903.

Turning L at this jct., the trail to Porter Mt. is level through open woods to a crossing of the headwaters of Porter Brook at 2.1 mi. Following up the L bank, the trail begins climbing again at a moderate grade. After going through a thicket of spruce, the trail dips to cross a small brook at 2.3 mi. More climbing through open, grassy glades leads to another brook crossing at 2.9 mi. The trail now begins to slab across the side of Porter with alternating moderate grades, short descents, and small brook crossings before finally climbing to a jct. with the Ridge Trail from Marcy Airfield (trail 17) at 3.4 mi. Turning L, the trail continues at easy to moderate grades to the E summit and then is mostly flat to the summit of Porter at 3.8 mi. Trail 91, marked with yellow DEC disks, continues over the summit and on to Cascade Mt. and NY 73 in Cascade Pass (trail 90).

𝄞 Distances: The Garden to Little Porter Mt., 1.8 mi; to jct. with Ridge Trail, 3.4 mi; to summit of Porter Mt., 3.8 mi (6.1 km). Ascent from road, 2700 ft (823 m). Elevation, 4059 ft (1238 m). Order of height, 38.

17   Porter Mt. from Marcy Airfield via Ridge Trail

ADK High Peaks Map: F7 | Trails Illustrated Map 742: AA26

This trail is the longest route to Porter Mt. and there is some steep climbing in its lower sections, but the variety of views makes it worthwhile. The trail includes the summit of Blueberry Mt. This trail is marked with yellow DEC markers.

▶ Trailhead: From the High Peaks sign in the center of Keene Valley, proceed N on NY 73 for 2 mi to the second jct. with Airport Rd. which is also the access to the overflow lot and shuttle bus stop for the Garden parking lot. A new marked route known as the Town Trail also starts here. This trail makes an approximate 0.5 mi loop on a low hill W of the airfield. ◀

Leaving the end of the parking lot (0.0 mi), the trail follows a dirt road until the trail turns sharp L off the road at 0.1 mi (avoid Town Trail straight ahead) and climbs across a sidehill to the lower edge of a lumbered area at 0.2 mi. Soon after entering the lumbered area, the trail crosses a small height of land, descends slightly, and proceeds on the flat to a brook crossing at 0.5 mi. The trail now follows an eroded logging road up the R bank of the brook reaching state land and the end of the lumbering at 1 mi.

Above the lumbered area, the trail follows an old tote road until it turns sharp R and crosses the brook at 1.1 mi. The trail now traverses to the R on a moderate grade, crosses a brook bed at 1.3 mi, and begins a steep climb. Reaching a view of Hurricane Mt. at 1.4 mi, the trail continues to a better view at a ledge at 1.6 mi. Now marked with both trail markers and red paint blazes, it climbs steeply to a lookout at the E end of a ridge at 1.7 mi, where there are good views of Keene Valley. Now mostly on the flat, the trail comes to an open ledge on the S side of the ridge at 1.8 mi and then drops slightly to a sag before climbing to a large boulder at the summit of Blueberry Mt. at 2.3 mi, having ascended 1900 ft (579 m) from the trailhead.

After descending to a col at 2.5 mi, the trail winds through a spruce forest and then climbs steeply up a ravine. Passing the base of a cliff at 2.8 mi, the trail reaches a summit at 3 mi where there is a view from a rock up to the L. This is the end of the steep climbing, and the trail now continues along a beautiful ridge at easy grades. The trail passes over two fine lookouts at 3.4 mi and 3.9 mi before joining the trail from the Garden (trail 16) at 4 mi. Continuing straight ahead along the ridge, the trail climbs at easy to moderate grades to the E summit and then is mostly flat to the summit of Porter Mt. at 4.4 mi. Trail 91, with yellow DEC disks, continues over the summit and on to Cascade Mt. and NY 73 in Cascade Pass (trail 90).

🚶 Distances: Marcy Airfield to Blueberry Mt., 2.3 mi; to ADK trail from the Garden, 4 mi; to summit of Porter Mt., 4.4 mi (7.2 km). Ascent from Marcy Airfield, 3275 ft (999 m). Elevation, 4059 ft (1238 m). Order of height, 38.

18   Rooster Comb from NY 73 in Keene Valley

ADK High Peaks Map: F8 | Trails Illustrated Map 742: Z26

This trail, constructed in 1998 by the Adirondack Trail Improvement Society (ATIS), offers mostly moderate grades and generally good footing to the summit of this popular summit.

▶ Trailhead: A parking lot on NY 73 just S of Keene Valley (0.4 mi S of High Peaks sign in the center of the village). ◀

From the parking lot (0.0 mi) the trail crosses a boardwalk and reaches a small pond at 0.1 mi. Bearing L along the S shore of the pond, at 0.2 mi the trail passes a boardwalk on the R (part of a nature trail that circles the pond), swings L, and crosses another boardwalk to reach state land at 0.3 mi. The trail now climbs an elaborate series of steps and continues climbing moderately until easing off just before a jct., at 0.7 mi, with the Sachs Trail (trail 18A), which provides access to Snow Mt. as well as a slightly longer route to Rooster Comb.

Turning R at this jct., the Rooster Comb trail resumes a moderate climb and enters a section of private land. At 0.9 mi the grade eases as the trail follows an old logging road for about 300 yd and then swings L and up to state land again at 1.3 mi. Continuing at a steady grade, the trail crosses a small brook at 1.5 mi and reaches a four-way jct. at 2 mi. The trail on the L is the upper end of the Sachs Trail (trail 18A). Straight ahead leads to Hedgehog and Lower Wolf Jaw Mts. (trail 19).

Turning R at this jct., the Rooster Comb Trail passes under a mammoth boulder and turns R again to begin a sidehill traverse that leads to a jct. at the crest of a ridge at 2.2 mi. (Trail R at this jct. leads gently down for 0.1 mi to Valley View Ledge with good views to the N and E.) Turning L, the trail to the summit proceeds over a small bump after which the climbing becomes much steeper and rougher for about 200 yd over some ledges before easing back and reaching the broad summit ledge at 2.5 mi.

🏃 Distances: NY 73 to jct. with Sachs Trail, 0.7 mi; to jct. of Hedgehog Mt. trail, 2 mi; to summit of Rooster Comb, 2.5 mi (4 km). Ascent from NY 73, 1750 ft (534 m). Elevation, 2788 ft (850 m).

18A Sachs (Flume Brook) Trail to Rooster Comb and Snow Mt.

ADK High Peaks Map: F8 | Trails Illustrated Map 742: Z26

▶ Locator: This trail starts at the junction at 0.7 mi on trail 18. ◀

Bearing L at the jct. and marked with red markers, the Sachs Trail proceeds mostly on the level. After crossing a small brook at 1.1 mi. from the parking lot, the trail swings R and climbs moderately to steeply to a jct. at 1.8 mi with a trail L to Snow Mt. (trail 53). Soon after this jct., the grade moderates with the trail reaching a four-way jct. at 2.3 mi. Trail R and straight ahead is the main Rooster Comb Trail (trail 18). Trail L leads to Hedgehog and Lower Wolf Jaw Mts. (trail 19).

🏃 Distances: NY 73 to start of Sachs Trail, 0.7 mi; to jct. with trail to Snow Mt., 1.8 mi; to jct. with main Rooster Comb trail, 2.3 mi; to summit of Rooster Comb, 2.8 mi (4.5 km). Ascent from NY 73, 1750 ft (534 m). Elevation, 2788 ft (850 m).

19 Hedgehog Mt. from the Rooster Comb Trail

ADK High Peaks Map: F9 | Trails Illustrated Map 742: Z26

▶ Locator: This trail traverses the two wooded summits of Hedgehog Mt. and provides a direct connection to the W. A. White Trail (trail 32) and ultimately the ADK Range Trail (trail 4). The start is at a jct. at 2 mi on the Rooster Comb Trail (trail 18). ◀

From this jct. (0.0 mi) the yellow-marked trail climbs at moderate to steep grades with glimpses through the trees of the cliffs on Rooster Comb. The trail dips slightly at 0.4 mi, but soon resumes the climb to the N summit of Hedgehog at 0.7 mi. The trail now descends, crosses a brook at 1 mi, and then climbs to the main summit of Hedgehog Mt. at 1.1 mi. (Total distance from NY 73, 3.1 mi or 5 km; total ascent from NY. 73, 2340 ft or 713 m; elevation 3369 ft or 1027 m).

From the summit, the trail descends moderately to the W and SW to a brook. Just beyond the brook is a jct. with the red-marked W. A. White Trail (trail 32) at 1.5 mi. Turning R at this jct. it is another 1.5 mi to the summit of Lower Wolf Jaw Mt.

🚶 Distances: NY 73 to jct. with Hedgehog Mt. trail, 2 mi; to summit of Hedgehog Mt., 3.1 mi (5 km); to jct. with W. A. White Trail, 3.5 mi.

20   Baxter Mt. from NY9N on Spruce Hill

ADK High Peaks Map: F7–G7 | Trails Illustrated Map 742: AA26, 27

There are three trails to this popular summit, of which this approach is the easiest. The many ledges on Baxter offer both good blueberrying and outstanding views of Keene Valley, the Great Range, and Mt. Marcy at the head of the Johns Brook valley. This trail is currently maintained by the Algonquin Chapter of ADK and is now marked with red DEC markers.

▶ Trailhead: Start on NY 9N, at the top of a long climb, 2 mi from the intersection of NY 9N and NY 73 between Keene and Keene Valley. The trail begins 20 yd to the E of the jct. of Hurricane Rd. and NY 9N. ◀

From the road (0.0 mi), the trail heads SW through some pines, crosses under a power line, and begins an easy to moderate climb to the beginning of a series of new (2008) switchbacks at 0.4 mi. that lead to a height of land at 0.9 mi, after which it is level to a jct. 40 yd later with the trail from Beede Farm (trail 21). Turning R, another new switchback avoids a steep climb. Above the

Baxter Mountain. Richard J. Nowicki

switchback there are a few short, steep pitches and many side trails leading L to numerous views and blueberry patches. The trail continues with alternating steep pitches and flat areas to the SE summit at 1.2 mi. The trail now descends into a col and climbs to the NW summit at 1.3 mi, where there are more views. The trail continues over this summit and down to Beede Rd. near Keene Valley (trail 21).

🚶 Distances: NY 9N to jct. with Beede Farm Trail, 1 mi; to NW summit, 1.3 mi (2.2 km). Ascent from NY 9N, 770 ft (235 m). Elevation, 2440 ft (744 m).

21 Baxter Mt. from Beede Farm

ADK High Peaks Map: F8 | Trails Illustrated Map 742: AA26

This slightly longer approach to Baxter can be combined with a descent via the Upham Trail to make a nice loop. Because most hikers making this circuit do so in this direction, the Upham Trail is described going down. The Upham Trail is not well used, however, and it requires considerable care to follow.

▶ Trailhead: From the High Peaks sign in the center of Keene Valley go N 0.6 mi and turn E on Beede Ln. After crossing the Ausable River, bear L across a small bridge, and then bear L again at the jct. with Phelps Brook Rd., 0.4 mi from NY 73. The third driveway on the L from Phelps Brook Rd. is the approach for the Upham Trail, but no cars may be driven up this driveway. Beyond this driveway, Beede Rd. turns to gravel and reaches a jct. at 0.9 mi from NY 73, just below Beede Farm. Cars should be parked here and not at the farm. ◀

From the jct. (0.0 mi), the trail goes L up a driveway past the Beede Farm and continues up across an old pasture. There are few blue markers on this section, but in general the trail takes every L after the top of the pasture. At the top of the old pasture, the trail follows a grassy road and bears L at 0.3 mi. Continuing to bear L onto an older road, the trail becomes a footpath and is marked with occasional yellow paint blazes along with a few trail markers. At 1.1 mi the trail comes to a jct. with a trail from NY 9N (trail 20). Turning L, the trail quickly switchbacks to the R and back L to avoid a steep climb. Above the switchback there are a few short, steep pitches and many side trails leading L to numerous views and blueberry patches. The trail continues with alternating steep pitches and flat areas to the SE summit at 1.4 mi. It now descends into a col and climbs to the NW summit at 1.5 mi (2.5 km) where there are more views. Ascent from Beede Farm, 1150 ft (351 m). Elevation, 2440 ft (744 m).

The Upham Trail continues over the summit and descends to the W shoulder where there are good views to the W. Descending steeply off this shoulder, it flattens out at 1.8 mi and comes to some more views at 2 mi. Swinging L off the end of the ridge, the trail descends steeply through an open forest of red pines and then into thicker trees and down to a small brook at 2.3 mi. After climbing over a small hogback on the far side of the brook, the trail swings R on an old tote road and descends gradually along a shelf above the brook valley. Bearing L where another old road diverges R, the trail takes a sharp L off the tote road at 3 mi and goes over a low ridge and down to a driveway at 3.1 mi, just below a house. (Hikers ascending via this route should watch for this sharp R just before the house at the end of a switchback on the driveway.) The trail now descends the driveway to Beede Rd. at 3.3 mi.

🏃 Distances: Beede Farm to jct. with trail from NY 9N, 1.1 mi; to summit of Baxter Mt., 1.6 mi; to Beede Rd. via Upham Trail, 3.3 mi (5.3 km).

22 Spread Eagle and Hopkins Mts. from Beede Farm

ADK High Peaks Map: F8 | Trails Illustrated Map 742: Z26

The parking area and first 0.6 mi of trail as described in previous editions have been closed at the request of a private landowner. To date (2015) the Keene Valley Chapter of ADK has been unable to reach an agreement with an adjoining developer regarding either hiker parking or marking of a new route through the road system of the real estate development. Foot travel is, however, still permitted on the roads leading from the end of Beede Rd. (67see trail 21), but no formal marking exists to guide hikers through the road system.

From the upper end of the road system, both the Direct Trail to Hopkins Mt. (trail 23) and the trail over Spread Eagle Mt. are intact and marked. Thus, hikers confident of their ability to navigate through this road system may continue to climb and descend these peaks via this route. The only changes are that the old start is closed altogether and public vehicular traffic is not permitted beyond Beede Rd., making the distance to Hopkins and Spread Eagle Mts. 0.5 mi longer than the old route—2.9 mi for Spread Eagle and Hopkins and 2.7 mi for Hopkins via Direct Trail.

23 Hopkins Mt. via Direct Trail

ADK High Peaks Map: F8 | Trails Illustrated Map 742: Z26
See description for trail 22.

24 Hopkins Mt. via Ranney Trail

ADK High Peaks Map: F8 | Trails Illustrated Map 742: Z26

This trail to Hopkins Mt. is rarely used, but it has moderate grades throughout and generally good footing. The trail joins the Mossy Cascade Trail (trail 51) to Hopkins 0.9 mi below the summit of Hopkins.

▶ Trailhead: Start at an iron bridge over the Ausable River, 0.5 mi S of the High Peaks sign in the center of Keene Valley on NY 73. Because this is a private drive, cars should be parked on NY 73. At the landowner's request, there is no sign for this trail at the highway. ◀

From the highway (0.0 mi), follow the driveway on the flat to the far end of the clearing at 0.3 mi, where a sign pointing R marks the start of the trail. The trail, now with blue DEC markers, enters the woods on a lumber road following along the R bank of a stream on easy to moderate grades. Crossing the brook at 0.7 mi, it climbs steeply along an old lumber road and then turns sharp L at 0.9 mi. Now climbing moderately along the L bank of the brook, it continues at a moderate grade with a few steeper pitches to the jct. with the Mossy Cascade Trail (trail 51) coming in from the R at 1.8 mi.

🚶 Distances: NY. 73 to Mossy Cascade Trail, 1.8 mi; to summit of Hopkins Mt., 2.7 mi (4.4 km). Ascent from NY 73, 2140 ft (652 m). Elevation, 3183 ft (970 m). 🍂

Lower Ausable Lake from Indian Head. James Appleyard

St. Huberts Section

St. Huberts is located on NY 73, 2.5 mi S of Keene Valley. There are over 90 mi of trails in this area, offering a wide variety of hikes, from woodland walks along beautiful streams to ascents of Giant Mt., Gothics, and other peaks. Note, however, that many of the hikes in this section are on the land of the Adirondack Mountain Reserve (AMR)/Ausable Club, a private preserve stretching over 10 mi to the SW and incorporating both the Upper and Lower Ausable Lakes. Hikers should consult ADK's Trails of the Adirondack High Peaks map or Trails Illustrated Map 742 for the exact boundaries of the AMR and should follow carefully all special regulations regarding parking and use of AMR land (see sidebar, p. 61).

The approaches to trails 26–42 are from the Lake Road Trail (trail 25). Read the Lake Road Trail description carefully and be aware that NO DOGS are allowed on the Lake Road Trail or trails 26-42. Additionally, drop-offs and pickups are not permitted along the road in front of the clubhouse or at the Lake Road gate. All hikers must therefore start and finish at the designated parking area. An Ausable Club bus traverses the Lake Rd. in summer, but is not available to the public.

Except for the Dix Mt. trail from NY 73, all trails described in this section are maintained by the Adirondack Trail Improvement Society. Trails that are part of the public easement are marked with special DEC/AMR/ATIS markers in the standard colors. DEC Foot Trail markers in the same color continue when the trail reaches state land.

▶ Trailheads: Hikers approaching Round and Noonmark Mts. or any of the climbs off the Lake Rd. Trail (trail 25) are required to park at the designated hikers' parking lot just off NY 73 opposite the parking lot for the Roaring Brook Trail to Giant Mt. (trail 47). This location is on Ausable Rd. at the more southerly of its two jcts. with NY 73. This southerly jct. is 3 mi S of the High Peaks sign in Keene Valley and 0.5 mi S of the northerly jct. of Ausable Rd. and NY 73. From the S, the designated parking is 5.9 mi N of the jct. of NY 9 and NY 73, N of Exit 30 on the Adirondack Northway, I-87. From this parking lot, it is 0.5 mi W along the at-first gravel-surfaced and then paved Ausable Rd. along the golf course to the start of the Lake Rd. Trail (trail 25), which goes left and down between two tennis courts to the gate house 0.6 mi. from the parking area. ◀

The designated parking accommodates 35–40 cars, but on busy weekends this parking lot may be full. Parking is not permitted along the gravel road leading up to the golf course and clubhouse. Hikers must therefore find parking across NY 73 or at other designated parking areas.

❋ Trails in winter: With the exception of the Lake Rd. Trail, none of the trails in this section are suitable for skiing. In addition to snowshoes, crampons may be required to ascend any of the peaks, with an ice ax possibly required.

The Lake Rd. Trail is a classic ski tour and is often skiable early in the season. Note, however, that this is a private road and is used to haul supplies to Upper Ausable Lake when the lake ice makes this possible. Vehicles of all types may be encountered, even on weekends, and as a result the snow surface may be less than ideal for skiing.

Below are listed a few suggested hikes to help first-time visitors to the area choose among the many possibilities.

SHORT HIKES

Snow Mt.: 3.4 mi (5.5 km) round-trip. An easy trail along a pretty brook with a waterfall leads to an open summit with good views and plenty of blueberries. See trail 53.

Giants Nubble via the Washbowl: 3 mi (4.8 km) round-trip. This rocky summit offers a spectacular view of the slides on Giant Mt. and of Chapel Pond Pass with a unique mountainside pond on the way. See trails 48 and 49.

MODERATE HIKES

Hopkins Mt. via Mossy Cascade: 6.3 mi (10.2 km) round-trip. A generally moderate approach to a rocky summit, passing by a beautiful 50 ft high waterfall and several interesting lookouts. Seetrail 51.

East and West River trails: 7.4 mi (11.9 km) round-trip. A relatively flat walk through some beautiful forests along the banks of the Ausable River and past several waterfalls to make a loop trip to Lower Ausable Lake and back. See trails 25, 26, and 28.

HARDER HIKES

Giant Mt. via Ridge (Zander Scott) Trail with return over Green and Hopkins Mts.: 9.6 mi (15.5 km) point to point. An ascent of Giant Mt. along the open rocks of the ridge trail with a descent through some lovely virgin forests and a variety of additional views enroute. See trails 48, 51, and 52.

Gothics with return via Sawteeth Scenic Trail: 13.5 mi (21.8 km) round-trip. A rugged loop but one offering unforgettable views from the summits of Gothics,

Chapel Pond. **Mark Bowie**

Pyramid, and Sawteeth, plus five more lookouts on the way down Sawteeth. See trails 25, 34, 35, and 36.

25 Lake Rd. Trail to Lower Ausable Lake

ADK High Peaks Map: F9 | Trails Illustrated Map 742: Y26

This private road runs SW from the main club building to the boathouse at the foot of Lower Ausable Lake, gaining about 700 vertical ft in 3.5 mi. A quarter mile from the club is a locked gate, beyond which private vehicles (except those of members in the off-season) are not allowed. Foot traffic is permitted, but DOGS ARE PROHIBITED in this game reserve, as are bicycles. Note also that both the main clubhouse and the boathouse area at the Lower Ausable Lake end of the road are off limits to members of the public.

All hikers must sign in and sign out at the trail register located at the gatehouse at the start of the Lake Road Trail.

▶ Trailhead: From the public parking area at NY 73 (see Trailheads, p. 57), follow the gravel road up past the golf course for 0.5 mi to a jct. just before the main clubhouse. Here the approach to the Lake Road Trail turns L and down between two tennis courts, the golf house, and some private cottages to the AMR Gatehouse and register. Here the W. A. White Trail to Lower Wolf Jaw Mt. (trail 32) and the West River Trail (trail 28) diverge R. Continuing straight ahead, the Lake Road Trail reaches the gate in another 90 yd. Constructed as part of the AMR's centennial observances in 1986, the present gate is a replica of the original gate on the Lake Road.◀

From the gate (0.0 mi), the Ladies Mile (trail 27) branches R at both 45 yd and 0.3 mi. Just beyond this second jct. the East River Trail (trail 26) also branches R. At 0.7 mi the Henry Goddard Leach Trail to Dial and Nippletop (trail 42) branches L, and at 0.9 mi a bridge leads across Gill Brook to connect with the East and West River trails. Continuing on, the road crosses Gill Brook at 1.1 mi with a side trail L leading past a small flume on Gill Brook. At 1.8 mi a trail leads R to Beaver Meadow Falls and Gothics (trail 34), with the Gill Brook trail to Colvin and Nippletop (trail 40) diverging L a few yards beyond. The Gill Brook Cut-Off, a shorter trail to Mt. Colvin and Nippletop diverges L at 2.5 mi, and at 3.3 mi the road reaches a height of land where the Indian Head Trail (trail 38) diverges L. Just beyond the Indian Head Trail, the trails to Rainbow Falls, Gothics, and Sawteeth (trails 31, 35, and 36) diverge R down a side road, past a shed, and down to the Lower Ausable Lake dam. (The road continues to the lake, but members of the public are not permitted beyond this point.)

🏃 Distances: Gate to Lower Ausable Lake dam, 3.3 mi (5.3 km). Ascent, 700 ft (213 m).

26 East River Trail

ADK High Peaks Map: F9 | Trails Illustrated Map 742: Y26

This trail offers some very pleasant walking and some lovely views of various falls

ADIRONDACK MOUNTAIN RESERVE EASEMENTS

As part of the sale of higher land by the Adirondack Mountain Reserve (AMR) to the State of New York in 1978, the state acquired permanent public easements for foot travel over all of the hiking trails on AMR land with the exception of certain trails near the shores of Upper Ausable Lake. (See p. 86.) These easements guarantee public access to the summits of Mt. Colvin, Blake Peak, Dial Mt., Nippletop, Sawteeth, and the Great Range, but while on AMR land, hikers must obey the following rules:

- No camping, fishing, or hunting
- NO DOGS OR OTHER PETS are permitted in this game reserve
- No off-trail travel, including rock climbing or bushwhacking
- No boating or swimming, including portable boats brought by the public; there are no boats for rent by the public

These restrictions do not apply to approaches to Snow, Hopkins, Giant, Round, Noonmark, Dix, or Lower Wolf Jaw Mts. (the latter if approached via Deer Brook); and once past the private land boundaries one may camp and fish.

Hikers departing from St. Huberts on backpacking trips must, however, plan an early enough start so they can reach state land in time to set up camp. The AMR warden may turn backpackers away if it's clear they cannot reach a legal campsite by nightfall.

and pools in the river as well as of a few of the surrounding peaks.

▶ Locator: This red-marked trail follows the R bank of the Ausable River to the dam at Lower Ausable Lake. It diverges R from the Lake Rd. Trail 0.3 mi from the gate (see trail 25 for restrictions). ◀

From the Lake Rd. Trail (trail 25) (0.0 mi) the trail is flat to the Ausable River at 0.2 mi. (A bridge to the West River Trail is 50 yd downstream.) Bearing L, it follows along the riverbank, climbs the bank of the river, and quickly descends to cross Gill Brook on a bridge at 0.5 mi. The trail then follows up Gill Brook's L bank for a few yards before bearing R and reaching a gravel road at 0.7 mi. (Road R leads to Canyon Bridge across the Ausable River and connection to West River Trail, trail 28, in 0.3 mi. Road L leads 0.1 mi to Lake Rd. Trail.)

Crossing the gravel road, the East River Trail climbs to the top of a bank high above the river and levels out at 0.9 mi. At 1.6 mi the trail heads R and down across a steep sidehill and soon comes to a lookout over the gorge at 1.7 mi. The trail now draws slowly closer to the river, passing some other views of falls before coming to a crossing of a large plastic water line which transfers water from the Ausable River to Gill Brook to supplement the Ausable Club's water supply. At 2.2 mi the trail reaches a jct. with the Beaver Meadow Trail to Gothics (trail 34). The two trails are together until 2.3 mi, where the Gothics Trail goes sharp R and down to a bridge. Continuing straight ahead, there is a view of Sawteeth across Beaver Meadow at 2.4 mi, and the trail continues mostly on the flat to the bridge below the Lower Ausable Lake dam at 3.3 mi.

ᚸ Distances: Lake Rd. Trail to Beaver Meadow Trail to Gothics, 2.2 mi; to bridge and dam at Lower Ausable Lake, 3.3 mi (5.3 km). Total distance from parking area, 4.2 mi (6.8 km.).

27 Ladies Mile

ADK High Peaks Map: F9 | Trails Illustrated Map 742: Y26

The name for this trail probably comes from a 20-block section of lower Fifth Avenue in Manhattan that at the turn of the twentieth century was a nearly solid collection of shops selling women's clothing and home furnishings. This "proto-mall" was dubbed "the Ladies Mile."

▶ Locator: This is a short jaunt through the woods to the bank of the Ausable River and back, making about a 1 mi round-trip from the clubhouse. It leaves the Lake Rd. Trail (trail 25) 45 yd past the gate. ◀

Leaving the Lake Rd. (0.0 mi), the trail descends a short flight of steps, crosses a bridge over the usually dry bed of Leach Brook, and reaches a large woodshed at 0.1 mi. Bearing R at the woodshed, the trail soon crosses a small brook and swings sharp L and back to the L bank of Leach Brook with a jct shortly after. Trail R is the relocated "Mile" leading to the bank of the Ausable river. The trail L is the shorter "Half-Mile" going to the upper bridge and leading back to the Lake Rd.

Trail R reaches the bank of the Ausable River and follows this up to a jct. at 0.4 mi. at a bridge across the river. Turning L at this jct., the trail returns to the Lake Rd. at 0.6 mi.

28 West River Trail

ADK High Peaks Map: F9 | Trails Illustrated Map 742: Y26

This trail offers pleasant walking through some virgin stands of timber, as well as views of the pools and falls in the river and some of the surrounding peaks. The trail follows the L bank of the Ausable River to the dam at Lower Ausable Lake. Combined with either the East River Trail (trail 26) or the Lake Rd. Trail (trail 25), this provides a lovely woodland walk of about 7 mi with relatively little climbing.

▶ Locator: The start is on the Lake Rd. Trail (see trail 25 for restrictions) at the AMR gatehouse. ◀

From the gatehouse (0.0 mi), the trail, with yellow markers starts on a private driveway and descends slightly to the Ausable River, which it crosses on a bridge. A jct. with the W. A. White Trail (trail 32) is on the far side at 0.2 mi.

Turning L, the trail proceeds along the river to another jct. at a bridge at 0.6 mi with Cathedral Rocks and Bear Run (trail 29). (Bridge L leads to East River Trail, trail 26, and Ladies Mile, trail 27.) Continuing straight ahead, the West River Trail crosses Pyramid Brook on a bridge at 1.1 mi and then climbs to a jct. with the upper end of the Cathedral Rocks Trail (trail 29) at 1.3 mi. About 60 yd beyond the Cathedral Rocks jct. is another jct. with a trail L leading to Canyon Bridge and access to the East River Trail (trail 26) and the Lake Rd. Trail (trail 25).

Continuing straight ahead, alternating steep and easy grades lead to lookouts both into the gorge below and the Noonmark burn area above. The trail crosses Wedge Brook on a bridge and reaches a jct. with the Wedge Brook Trail (trail 33) just beyond at 2 mi. (A beautiful series of cascades can be seen less than 200 yd up this trail.) Turning L and down, the trail descends to the level of the river, and continues to a bridge below Beaver Meadow Falls at 2.7 mi. These falls of bridal veil–like appearance are well worth the trip alone.

Across the brook, the trail soon comes to a jct. with the Beaver Meadow Falls Trail (trail 34) that leads R to Gothics and the Lost Lookout. Trail L leads to the East River and Lake Rd. trails. Continuing straight ahead, the West River Trail crosses the flat open area known as Beaver Meadow. Following along the base of a steep cliff at 3.2 mi, the trail continues to a jct. with the S end of the Lost Lookout Trail at 3.7 mi and reaches the bridge and dam at the Lower Ausable Lake at 3.8 mi.

The trail R leads to Rainbow Falls, Sawteeth, and Gothics. Bridge L leads to the East River Trail and Lake Rd. Trail.

🚶 Distances: Lake Rd. Trail to trail to Cathedral Rocks, 0.6 mi; to Wedge Brook Trail to Lower Wolf Jaw, 2 mi; to Beaver Meadow Falls and Gothics trail, 2.7 mi; to Lower Lake bridge and dam, 3.8 mi. Total distance from parking area, 4.4 mi (7.1 km).

29   Cathedral Rocks and Bear Run

ADK High Peaks Map: F9 | Trails Illustrated Map 742: Y26

The full Bear Run loop trail offers a short round-trip with some interesting rock formations, two views, and a pretty little waterfall. A bypass trail that shortens the loop goes past the rock formation now identified as Cathedral Rocks, but misses the two higher views.

▶ Locator: The start is on the West River Trail (trail 28) at the bridge at 0.6 mi. ◀

Leaving the West River Trail (0.0 mi) and marked with red markers, the trail climbs moderately along the L bank of a small brook heading first W and then NW. The climbing steepens as the trail approaches the first rock face at 0.5 mi. Then swinging L, the trail continues along under a series of cliffs to a larger one on the R at 0.7 mi. (Earlier editions of this guide have identified this cliff as Cathedral Rocks, but the true Cathedral Rocks are on the trail that goes L at the jct. just past this cliff at 0.8 mi. This bypass trail continues past Cathedral Rocks to the main loop trail at 0.3 mi)

Bearing R and up at this jct. at 0.8 mi, the Bear Run trail crosses the property line of the AMR, with the base of a large cliff reached soon after at 1 mi. A side trail R leads 300 yd along the base of the cliff to a narrow slot in the cliff, which can be followed up to a panoramic view ranging from Giant on the L to Sawteeth on the R. As the sign at the jct. says, "don't miss."

Turning L at the base of the cliff, the trail climbs to a height of land and then descends to another lookout at 1.3 mi. Just beyond this lookout, the trail swings sharp L and descends a narrow shelf through the ledges. Now descending very steeply, it reaches the other end of the bypass trail at 1.4 mi, after which it continues descending steeply along the L bank of Pyramid Brook, past Pyramid Falls, to flatter terrain at 1.5 mi. After crossing to the R bank of the brook, the trail continues on a gentle downhill grade to the West River Trail at 1.7 mi.

🚶🚶 Distances: West River Trail to trail to Cathedral Rocks, 0.8 mi; to base of cliff at Bear Run, 1 mi; to West River Trail, 1.7 mi (2.7 km).

30 Lost Lookout

ADK High Peaks Map: F10 | Trails Illustrated Map 742: Y25

This trail climbs about 500 ft onto the side of Armstrong Mt. above Beaver Meadow to two exceptional viewpoints of Lower Ausable Lake and the surrounding mountains.

▶ Locator: The start is at Beaver Meadow Falls, which can be reached by either the East or West River Trail (trails 26 and 28) or directly from the Lake Rd. Trail (trail 25) by the Beaver Meadow Trail to Gothics (trail 34). ◀

Leaving Beaver Meadow Falls (0.0 mi), the trail coincides with the Gothics trail, climbing a ladder and ascending steeply to a jct. at 0.3 mi. Here the Lost Lookout trail branches L with red markers and climbs steadily to the first lookout at 0.6 mi. Leveling off, the trail descends slightly to the second lookout at 0.7 mi and then begins to descend. There is a lookout to Rainbow Falls on the R at 1.5 mi, after which the trail descends to the West River Trail at 1.7 mi and, turning R, reaches the bridge and dam at Lower Ausable Lake at 1.8 mi.

🚶🚶 Distances: Beaver Meadow Falls to first lookout, 0.6 mi; to bridge and dam at Lower Ausable Lake, 1.8 mi (2.9 km).

31 Rainbow Falls

ADK High Peaks Map: F10 | Trails Illustrated Map 742: Y25

This nearly 150 ft high waterfall is a sight that should not be missed, whether one makes a trip up the Lake Rd. Trail (trail 25) just to see the falls or as a side trip while on a longer hike in the area.

▶ Locator: This trail is found 3.3 mi S on the Lake Rd. Trail after a brief start on the Gothics trail (trail 35). ◀

From the W end of the bridge at the Lower Ausable Lake Dam, follow the Gothics Trail (trail 35) for 0.1 mi and diverge R for another 0.1 mi along, and sometimes in, the brook to the base of the falls at 0.2 mi.

🚶 Distances: From Lake Rd. Trail, 0.3 mi (0.5 km); total distance from parking area, 4.2 mi (6.8 km).

32 W. A. White Trail to Lower Wolf Jaw Mt.

ADK High Peaks Map: F9 | Trails Illustrated Map 742: Y26

This trail is named after one of the founders of ATIS and the designer of the Range Trail from Gothics to Mt. Haystack. It is a slightly longer route to Lower Wolf Jaw Mt. than the Wedge Brook Trail, but it does offer some views on the way up and the grades are generally easier.

▶ Trailhead: Start on Lake Rd. Trail (see trail 25 for directions and restrictions) at the AMR gatehouse. An alternate start via Deer Brook (trail 53) is shorter (when the walk from the parking area is counted) and avoids the short stretch on AMR lands where dogs are prohibited. ◀

From the gatehouse (0.0 mi), the trail starts down a private driveway and descends slightly to the Ausable River, where it crosses a bridge to reach a jct. on the far side at 0.2 mi with the West River Trail to Lower Ausable Lake (trail 28). Bearing R with red markers, the White Trail climbs at an easy grade along a sidehill to a jct. with a lumber road at 0.6 mi. Turning L, the trail follows this road through a lumbered area and up to a jct. at 1 mi. (Trail R leads along lumber road past link trail to Deer Brook Trail, trail 53, and on to a jct. with the Deer Brook Trail to Snow Mt., 0.7 mi from W. A. White Trail. Total distance to the summit of Snow Mt. is 2.2 mi from the gatehouse.)

The W. A. White Trail bears L at this jct. and climbs steeply at first and then moderately to some switchbacks up through a cliff band and gains the top of the ridge and an upper lumbered area at 1.4 mi. Climbing the ridge at a moderate grade, the trail reaches a side trail leading 25 yd to a lookout at 1.6 mi, just beyond the end of the lumbered area.

Past this jct., the trail again switchbacks to the R and continues at a moderate grade to another ledge at 1.9 mi, where there are good views of the Ausable Valley as well as of the surrounding peaks. After making a short descent, the trail climbs to a higher ledge at 2 mi. From here, it descends slightly and then begins an easy climb interspersed with level stretches to the jct. with the Hedgehog trail (trail 19) at 3 mi. Trail R with yellow markers leads over Hedgehog Mt. to Rooster Comb and Keene Valley.

Continuing straight ahead and now with yellow markers, the W. A. White Trail reaches the crest of a ridge and climbs at moderate to easy grades to a slight sag, after which the climbing increases to the top of the Wolf's "chin" at 4 mi. The trail then descends steeply to a col and soon begins a very steep scramble up a gully to the summit of Lower Wolf Jaw Mt. at 4.5 mi. There are good views from the summit lookout to the N and W.

Trail 5 continues over the summit, leading in 0.3 mi to the jct. with the Wedge Brook Trail (trail 33) and further to the jct. with the trail up from Johns Brook at the col between the two Wolf Jaws in 0.5 mi (trail 4).

🚶 Distances: Lake Rd. Trail to jct. with trail to Snow Mt., 1 mi; to jct. with Hedgehog trail, 3 mi; to summit of Lower Wolf Jaw Mt., 4.5 mi (7.3 km). Total distance from parking area, 5.1 mi (8.2 km). Ascent from Lake Rd., 2825 ft (861 m). Elevation, 4175 ft (1273 m). Order of height, 30.

33 Wedge Brook Trail to the Wolf Jaws

ADK High Peaks Map: F9 | Trails Illustrated Map 742: Y26

Alexander Wyant, a well-known artist who first came to Keene Valley in 1869, is credited with conferring the name Wolf Jaws, as suggested by the deep col between the two peaks. The spot on Noonmark Mt. from which Wyant painted a view of these peaks is said to offer the best representation of a wolf's jaw. The Wedge Brook Trail is the shortest route to either Wolf Jaw summit (upper and lower) from the Ausable Club. Combined with the W. A. White Trail, it makes a nice round-trip.

▶ Locator: This blue-marked trail branches off the West River Trail (trail 29) at the crossing of Wedge Brook, 2 mi from the Lake Rd. Trail. ◀

Leaving the West River Trail (0.0 mi), Wedge Brook Trail climbs fairly steeply for 200 yd to a view of Wedge Brook Cascades. After a few more yards of steep climbing along the bank of Wedge Brook, the trail leaves the brook on an easier grade and reaches a possible campsite on the R at 1.2 mi. Shortly after, the grade again becomes steep as the trail climbs the headwall of the ravine with the bare rock slides of Lower Wolf Jaw Mt. visible on the R. At 1.6 mi the cut-off trail to Wolf Jaws Notch branches L, leading 0.3 mi to the ADK Range Trail (trail 4) at the Notch.

Bearing R at this jct., the Wedge Brook Trail continues climbing to its jct. with the ADK Lower Wolf Jaw Trail (trail 5) at 1.9 mi. Turning R the trail climbs steeply to the summit of Lower Wolf Jaw at 2.2 mi, where there are good views to the N and W. Trail straight ahead is the W. A. White Trail (trail 32) leading to St. Huberts and connecting with trails to Hedgehog Mt., Rooster Comb, and Keene Valley.

🚶 Distances: Lake Rd. Trail to start of Wedge Brook Trail, 2 mi; to jct. with cut-off trail to Wolf Jaws Notch, 3.6 mi; to summit of Lower Wolf Jaw Mt., 4.2 mi (6.8 km). Total distance from parking area, 4.8 mi (7.7 km). Ascent from Lake Rd., 2825 ft (861 m). Elevation, 4175 ft (1273 m). Order of height, 30.

34 Gothics via Beaver Meadow Trail

ADK High Peaks Map: F9 | Trails Illustrated Map 742: Y25,26

For the naming of this peak, see description for Gothics via Orebed Brook Trail (trail 8). Cut in 1886, this was the first trail to Gothics and remains a popular route today. The upper section of this trail has become somewhat unattractive owing to erosion and blowdown, but is still worth incorporating into a loop trip.

▶ Locator: The trail starts on the Lake Rd. Trail (see trail 25 for directions and restrictions) just past the reservoir 1.8 mi from the gate. ◀

Turning R (W) from the road (0.0 mi), the blue-marked trail climbs at an easy grade to join the East River Trail (trail 26) at 0.5 mi. Swinging L on the East River Trail for 200 yd, the Beaver Meadow Trail turns sharp R and down to cross a bridge to a jct. with the West River Trail (trail 28) near the foot of Beaver Meadow Falls at 0.6 mi. Continuing straight across the West River Trail, the Gothics Trail climbs steeply up a ladder and then on at an easier grade to the jct. with the trail leading L to Lost Lookout at 0.8 mi (trail 30).

From this jct., the trail climbs at an easy grade, crosses the AMR boundary line at 1 mi and continues at an easy to moderate grade past two small streams to a crossing of a new (2011) slide at 1.8 mi. Past the slide, the trail swings L and begins a steep climb that does not moderate until just before a large balanced rock on the R at 2.5 mi. After this balanced rock, the trail again climbs steeply up past the base of a rock wall to the crest of the ridge at 2.8 mi. From here, the trail begins to work its way across the steep W slope of a shoulder of Armstrong Mt. with several good views of Gothics. Four ladders aid passage across the steep rocks. Beyond this section, the trail comes to a jct. with the ADK Range Trail (trail 4) at 3 mi. Turning L, the trail crosses a short, flat section and then begins a steep climb that eases as the trail passes the E peak. (This is the beginning of the arctic-alpine zone. One must walk only on the trail or bare rock to protect this unique resource.) Easier climbing leads to the summit of Gothics at 3.4 mi.

The view is unobstructed with about 30 major peaks discernible. The boathouse at Lower Ausable Lake can be seen, but to see any of Upper Ausable Lake one must proceed past the summit 0.1 mi to the ATIS trail over Pyramid (trail 35) and go L on this trail a few yards to a wide ledge with views to the S and W. (The ADK Range Trail continues over the summit and on to the upper Great Range with connecting trails to Johns Brook Lodge and Keene Valley; see Keene Valley section, p. 29.)

🚶🚶 Distances: Lake Rd. Trail to Beaver Meadow Falls, 0.6 mi; to ADK Range Trail, 3 mi; to summit of Gothics, 3.4 mi (5.5 km). Total distance from parking area, 5.8 mi (9.4 km). Ascent from Lake Rd. Trail, 3050 ft (930 m). Elevation, 4736 ft (1444 m). Order of height, 10.

35 Gothics from Lower Ausable Lake via Pyramid

ADK High Peaks Map: F10–E10 | Trails Illustrated Map 742: Y25

Known as the Alfred W. Weld Trail, this approach to Gothics was laid out and cut by Jim Goodwin in 1966. Extensive recent trail work has improved the footing for most of its length. Before reaching the summit, this trail passes over Pyramid Peak, which offers what many consider to be the single most spectacular view in the Adirondacks.

▶ Locator: The trail starts at the W end of the bridge below the dam at Lower Ausable Lake. (See trail 25 for description and restrictions.) ◀

From the bridge (0.0 mi), the blue-marked Gothics trail coincides with the Saw-teeth and Rainbow Falls trails (trails 36 and 31) at first, but the Sawteeth Trail diverges L in 100 yd and the Rainbow Falls trail goes R at 0.1 mi. Now the Gothics trail begins a steady ascent to a lookout over Rainbow Falls at 0.3 mi. Swinging L, the trail climbs for a few yards further before easing off, crossing a brook, and then continuing at a generally easy grade. A few more steep pitches are encountered before reaching state land at 0.7 mi at the beginning of a long, easy section that leads to a crossing of an old, grown-in slide coming down from Sawteeth at 0.9 mi.

Past this slide, the trail resumes moderate climbing and crosses a good-sized brook at 1.3 mi. A possible campsite is up to the L just before the brook. After the brook, the trail becomes steeper and rougher as it ascends to the col between Pyramid and Sawteeth at 1.7 mi. Here there is a jct. with the trail L leading 0.5 mi to Sawteeth (trail 37). Turning R, the Gothics trail starts at an easy grade, but soon begins climbing steeply.

At 2 mi the trail ascends along the L edge of a slide for 100 yd, after which there is a rough 200 yd reroute around the base of another slide. There is a good view at the top of this slide, after which the steady climbing continues until just short of the summit of Pyramid. Skirting the summit block to the R, the trail reaches the peak of Pyramid at 2.3 mi. The views encompass Gothics and all of the Great Range, seen at such an angle that nearly all of the considerable bare rock on the S side of these peaks is visible and serves as a spectacular foreground for the more distant view.

Turning R at the summit of Pyramid, the trail descends steeply to the bottom of the col at 2.5 mi and then climbs equally steeply to a ledge on the S side of Gothics at 2.6 mi. (This is the beginning of the arctic-alpine zone. One must walk only on the trail or bare rock to protect this unique resource.) A few yards on the level beyond, the trail meets the ADK Range Trail (trail 4). Turning R, the trail reaches the summit of Gothics at 2.7 mi.

👣 Distances: Bridge at Lower Ausable Lake to col between Sawteeth and Pyramid, 1.7 mi; to summit of Pyramid, 2.3 mi; to jct. with ADK Range Trail, 2.6 mi; to summit of Gothics, 2.7 mi (4.4 km). Total distance from parking area, 6.6 mi (10.6 km). Ascent from Lower Lake, 2870 ft (875 M). Elevation, 4736 ft (1444 m). Order of height, 10.

36 Sawteeth from Lower Ausable Lake via Scenic Trail

ADK High Peaks Map: F10–E10 | Trails Illustrated Map 742: Y25

The striking serrated profile of this mountain as seen from the Ausable Club suggested the obvious name of Sawteeth to the early inhabitants of the area. It was erroneously labeled "Sawtooth" on the 1953 USGS topographic maps, an error that was corrected on the 1979 maps.

There are two trails to the summit from Lower Ausable Lake. The older one, now known as the Scenic Trail, follows a wandering course up among the "teeth" and passes many interesting views. The newer trail follows the Gothics trail (trail 35) to the col between Pyramid and Sawteeth and then ascends directly up the N side. Most hikers make this a loop trip, with the descent of the Scenic Trail considered to be the easier direction.

▶ Locator: This trail leaves the W end of the bridge below the Lower Ausable Lake Dam (see trail 25 for description and restrictions) and proceeds on an indirect course roughly W to the summit of Sawteeth. ◀

Leaving the bridge (0.0 mi), the trail diverges L from the Gothics trail (trail 35) in 100 yd and, now with yellow markers, follows near the shore of the lake before beginning to climb away from the lake at 0.6 mi. At 1 mi the trail reaches Outlook 1, a spectacular ledge with a boulder 250 ft above the lake. A side trail to Outlook 2 goes L at 1.1 mi, after which the trail begins to climb steeply to the third lookout at 1.4 mi. After some easy going, the trail swings R up a gully with a ladder at the top. The steep climbing continues to Lookout Rock, which offers a precipitous view of Lower Ausable Lake 1300 ft below, at 1.8 mi. Leaving Lookout Rock, the trail is rough as it makes a mostly moderate climb to a jct. at 2.1 mi. (Side trail L leads 0.3 mi to a spectacular view at Marble Point, with an equally spectacular view of Lower Ausable Lake.) Continuing past this jct. at 2.2 mi the trail reaches a col that also marks the state land boundary.

From the col, the trail now swings sharp R (avoid painted boundary line straight ahead) and the climbing is very steep in spots as it ascends through some ledges and climbs two ladders to reach Outlook 5 on the L at 2.5 mi. From here the grade moderates, and after another short steep pitch becomes easy to the SE summit at 2.6 mi. Now descending to a col called Rifle Notch, the trail again climbs steeply out of the notch and then on easier grades to a jct. at 3 mi with trail L to Upper Ausable Lake (trail 57). Just beyond this jct. a boulder beside the trail indicates the NW summit with a lookout 20 yd beyond where there are good views of most of the Great Range.

🥾 Distances: Bridge at Lower Lake to Lookout Rock, 1.8 mi; to NW summit, 3 mi (4.8 km). Total distance from parking area, 6.9 mi (11.1 km). Ascent from Lower Lake, 2275 ft (694 m). Elevation, 4100 ft (1250 m). Order of height, 35.

37 Sawteeth via Pyramid-Gothics Trail

ADK High Peaks Map: E10 | Trails Illustrated Map 742: Y25

▶ Locator: This trail leads to Sawteeth from the jct. with the Pyramid-Gothics Trail at the Sawteeth-Pyramid col. ◀

The Pyramid-Gothics trail (trail 35) is followed from the bridge to the col at 1.7 mi. Turning L here with yellow markers, the Sawteeth trail proceeds nearly on the level before beginning to climb at 1.8 mi. Immediately it ascends a steep cleft in the rock face with poor footing and continues steep before leveling out at 2.1 mi and reaching the summit of Sawteeth at 2.2 mi.

38 Indian Head

ADK High Peaks Map: F10 | Trails Illustrated Map 742: Y25

▶ Locator: This rocky peak rises 750 ft directly above Lower Ausable Lake and offers excellent views of both Ausable lakes, Nippletop, Mt. Colvin, Sawteeth, and much of the Great Range. This trail is also the approach for Fish Hawk Cliffs (trail 39), and is a possible, though more difficult, start for Mt. Colvin and Nippletop (trails 40 and 41). There are two approaches to this peak, which can be combined to make a nice loop trip including some very pretty walking along Gill Brook. ◀

1. From the top of the hill on the Lake Rd. Trail (see trail 25 for directions and restrictions) just before Lower Ausable Lake (0.0 mi), the yellow-marked Indian Head Trail goes L on the flat to a jct. with a private trail leading R to the boathouse. Continuing straight through this jct., the trail soon begins climbing a series of switchbacks to a side trail R at 0.3 mi to a view of Gothics called "Gothic Window." Continuing up several more switchbacks, the trail ascends a ladder at 0.6 mi and proceeds under a beautiful mossy cliff for a few yards before climbing steeply to a jct. at the crest of the ridge at 0.8 mi. Trail L leads to Gill Brook (alternate route 2, below). Trail straight ahead leads to Fish Hawk Cliffs (trail 39).

Turning R at this jct., the trail emerges on the bare ledges in another 200 yd. Some broader ledges just below offer an even better view and some careful exploration to the R should find a view back down to the boathouse. One can also detour 0.3 mi along the trail from Gill Brook for a view of Giant Mt.

2. To approach Indian Head from Gill Brook, follow the longer approach to Mt. Colvin (trail 40) which leaves the Lake Rd. Trail (trail 25) 1.8 mi from the gate. From the Lake Rd. Trail (0.0 mi), follow the Gill Brook trail past its jct. with the shorter link from the Lake Rd. to a jct. at 1.3 mi. Here the blue-marked route to Indian Head goes R, crosses a small brook, and begins climbing steadily to a jct. at 1.7 mi with a spur trail R to a view. Bearing L, the trail is mostly level to the jct. with the trail from the Lower Lake at 2 mi

🚶 Distances: Lake Rd. Trail to Indian Head, 0.8 mi (1.3 km). Indian Head via Gill Brook trail and Colvin Trail from Lake Rd. Trail, 2 mi (3.2 km). Total distance from parking area, 4.7 mi (7.6 km). Ascent from Lake Rd. Trail, 730 ft (223 m). Elevation, 2700 ft (823 m).

39 Fish Hawk Cliffs

ADK High Peaks Map: F10 | Trails Illustrated Map 742: X25

▶ Locator: This slightly lower lookout just beyond Indian Head offers a spectacular view of the cliffs on Indian Head. A trail runs from Indian Head to Fish Hawk Cliffs and then on to the Mt. Colvin trail. ◀

Starting from the trail jct. near the top of Indian Head (trail 38) (0.0 mi), the yellow-marked trail descends very steeply to a col at 0.1 mi and then climbs gradually to the ledges on Fish Hawk Cliffs at 0.2 mi. Continuing L, the trail is pretty much on the level as it enters state land at 0.4 mi and continues to the jct. with the Mt. Colvin trail (trail 40) at 0.7 mi. This jct. is 0.6 mi above the jct. of the two trails from the Lake Rd. and 0.7 mi below the jct. with Elk Pass Trail to Nippletop (trail 41).

🚶 Distances: Indian Head to Fish Hawk Cliffs, 0.2 mi; to Mt. Colvin trail, 0.7 mi (1.1 km).

40 Mt. Colvin from Lake Rd. Trail

ADK High Peaks Map: F9–10 | Trails Illustrated Map 742: Y26

This mountain was named for Verplanck Colvin in 1873 by Rev. T. L. Cuyler, a member of Colvin's survey party, who thought the peak was nameless. A few years earlier, however, "Old Mountain" Phelps had named it "Sabele" for the Indian credited by some to have discovered the ore at the MacIntyre Iron Works. Colvin was superintendent of the Adirondack Survey and arguably the single most prominent character in Adirondack Mountain history. Besides making the first exact measurement of the height of Mt. Marcy in 1875 with level and rod, he was also largely responsible for the inauguration of the Adirondack Park and State Forest Preserve. It is therefore highly fitting that his name attached to this peak has endured.

▶ Locator: There are two approaches to Mt. Colvin from the Lake Rd. Trail (see trail 25 for description and restrictions), both of which branch L as you head SW. ◀

The longer approach turns L from the Lake Rd. Trail at 1.8 mi, just past the Gothics trail. This red-marked trail follows up the L bank of picturesque Gill Brook with its many waterfalls and small flumes to a jct. with the shorter route at 1.2 mi from the road. Though scenic, this trail is quite rough in spots and requires more time than its distance would indicate. It is, however, worth using this trail in at least one direction when climbing Mt. Colvin, Nippletop, or Indian Head.

The shorter route with yellow markers branches L from the Lake Rd. Trail 2.5 mi past the gate. Leaving the road (0.0 mi), the trail climbs at an easy grade to the jct. with the Gill Brook trail at 0.5 mi. Turning R, the trail reaches a jct. at 0.6 mi with the trail R to Indian Head (trail 38). Continuing past this jct., the trail reaches state land at 0.7 mi. Just beyond, a trail goes L across Gill Brook to a designated campsite, followed by trails R to designated campsites at 0.8 mi and 1 mi. Now climbing high above Gill Brook, the trail comes to a jct. at 1.1 mi with trail R to Fish Hawk Cliffs and Indian Head (trail 39).

Continuing on, the Colvin trail passes a view of Nippletop at 1.5 mi and shortly descends a bit before climbing with a few steep pitches to a jct. at 1.8 mi with trail L to Elk Pass and Nippletop (trail 41). Turning R and continuing with red markers, the Colvin Trail climbs in a series of alternating steep and flat sections to the top of the ridge and then down to a small sag on the ridge at 2.7 mi. Climbing steeply again, the trail drops into a second sag and then up very steeply to the summit at 2.9 mi. There is a lookout just to the R with splendid views of Lower Ausable Lake, Sawteeth, and the Great Range. About 100 yd S on the trail to Blake Peak there is another ledge offering views of Upper Ausable Lake, Allen Mt., and other peaks. (See trails 56 and 60, pp. 106 and 110, respectively, for description of trail leading to Blake Peak and on to the Elk Lake–Marcy Trail.)

🚶 Distances: Lake Rd. Trail via shorter route to Gill Brook trail, 0.5 mi (longer route: Lake Rd. Trail to jct. with shorter route, 1.2 mi); to Indian Head trail, 0.7 mi; to Fish Hawk Cliffs trail, 1.1 mi; to Nippletop trail, 1.8 mi; to summit of Mt. Colvin, 2.9 mi (4.7 km). Total distance from parking area, 6 mi (9.7 km). Ascent from Lake Rd. Trail, 2330 ft (710 m). Elevation, 4057 ft (1237 m). Order of height, 39.

41   Nippletop via Elk Pass

ADK High Peaks Map: F10 | Trails Illustrated Map 742: Y25

This peak is named for its characteristic profile when seen from Elk Lake. At one time more fastidious tourists and writers tried to eliminate the anatomical appellation used by the locals by substituting "Dial," a name probably given in 1837 by chemistry professor and geologist Ebenezer Emmons or one of his companions during their approach to Mt. Marcy. With the assistance of Old Mountain Phelps, however, the current name has survived and the name "Dial" has been transferred to a lower peak to the N. The trail described here is the shortest route to the summit, but one can also ascend Nippletop via Dial Mt. (trail 42), which makes a good loop trip.

▶ Locator: The Elk Pass approach begins on the Mt. Colvin Trail (trail 40), which departs from the Lake Rd. Trail (see trail 25 for directions and restrictions.). ◀

Proceed on trail 40 to the jct. at 1.8 mi. Bearing L here with blue markers, the climbing is generally moderate with two short steep sections before leveling off and then descending to a small pond on the L at 2.3 mi. Now crossing first the outlet to a second pond and then the combined outlet of both ponds on a bridge, the trail passes a trail L leading to a small designated campsite before swinging R and starting up. The grade is moderate at first, but soon steepens as the trail continues up the ridge which, in the aftermath of Hurricane Floyd in 1999, offers several good views. The best is from a rock at 2.9 mi. Otherwise, alternating steep and easier sections lead to a jct. with the trail from Bear Den and Dial Mts. at the crest of the ridge at 3.2 mi.

Turning R, the trail goes over a small knob and reaches the summit at 3.5 mi. The view of Dix Mt. and its slides is most impressive, with other good views of Mt. Colvin and the Great Range. The view of Elk Lake to the S is partially blocked by scrub growth. Although not a perfect 360° view, the impression from the summit is one of solid and all-encompassing wilderness, which prompted the Marshall brothers to rate this as having the third best view of all the High Peaks.

🏃 Distances: Lake Rd. Trail to departure from Mt. Colvin trail, 1.8 mi; to Elk Pass, 2.3 mi; to jct. with Bear Den–Dial Trail, 3.3 mi; to summit of Nippletop, 3.5 mi (5.6 km). Total distance from parking area, 6.6 mi (10.6 km). Ascent from Lake Rd. Trail, 2760 ft (842 m). Elevation, 4620 ft (1409 m). Order of height, 13.

42 Henry Goddard Leach Trail to Bear Den Mt., Dial Mt., and Nippletop

ADK High Peaks Map: F9 | Trails Illustrated Map 742: Y26

▶ Locator: This trail leaves the Lake Rd. Trail 0.7 mi from the AMR gate and is the shortest route to Dial Mt. The route includes spectacular views on the W shoulder of Noonmark Mt. created by a 1999 forest fire. ◀

Leaving the Lake Rd. Trail (see trail 25 for description and restrictions) (0.0 mi), the yellow-marked trail climbs moderately to steeply to the state land boundary and fire line at the edge of the burned area at 0.9 mi. Swinging L, the trail leaves the fire line and climbs steeply to a view of Noonmark Mt. at 1.1 mi. After a slight descent, the trail rejoins the fire line and continues at moderate to easy grades to the summit of the W shoulder of Noonmark Mt. at 1.6 mi. The view now ranges from Pharaoh Mt. on the SE to Whiteface Mt. on the N, plus a foreground that includes a large portion of the 90 acres burned by the fire.

Now swinging L, the trail descends at a moderate grade on the original pre-fire route to the col between Noonmark and Bear Den Mts. at 2 mi, having lost about 320 ft (98 m) in altitude from the shoulder of Noonmark.

The trail now climbs out of the col at a mostly moderate grade, with occasional small views back at Noonmark, to the wooded summit of Bear Den at 2.5 mi. Total ascent from road, 2280 ft (695 m). Elevation, 3423 ft (1044 m).

Leaving Bear Den, the trail descends to a col, ascends slightly, and then drops to the main col between Bear Den and Dial Mts. at 3 mi, having lost 220 ft (67 m) in altitude. The trail now climbs over one more small bump before beginning the final long climb to the summit of Dial Mt. at 3.8 mi. A large rock on the R offers good views to the N and W. Total ascent, 3060 ft (933 m). Elevation, 4020 ft (1226 m).

Leaving Dial, the trail descends to a col at 4 mi, and then climbs at easy to moderate grades to a summit at 4.3 mi. Leaving this summit, the trail descends to a col at 4.4 mi and climbs again at easy to moderate grades up a fern-covered ridge, reaching a summit with a bare spot at 5.4 mi. Continuing fairly level, the trail dips slightly to the jct. with the Elk Pass Trail (trail 41) coming in from the R at 5.6 mi. Continuing straight ahead, the trail climbs over one last bump and reaches the summit of Nippletop at 5.9 mi.

🕅 Distances: Lake Rd. Trail to W shoulder of Noonmark Mt., 1.7 mi; to Bear Den Mt., 2.5 mi; to Dial Mt., 3.8 mi (6.1 km); to trail from Elk Pass, 5.6 mi; to summit of Nippletop, 5.9 mi; (9.5 km). Total distance from parking area, 7.2 mi (11.6 km). Total ascent from Lake Rd. Trail, 4000 ft (1220 m). Elevation, 4620 ft (1409 m). Order of height, 13.

43 Noonmark Mt. via Stimson Trail

ADK High Peaks Map: F9 | Trails Illustrated Map 742: Y26

This prominent, pointed peak lies almost directly S of Keene Valley and therefore "marks noon" when the sun is directly over the summit. This trail was scouted by and named for Henry L. Stimson, secretary of commerce in President Coolidge's cabinet, secretary of state in President Hoover's cabinet and secretary of war under President Roosevelt. Combining this trail with the Felix Adler Trail (trail 44) and the Old Dix Trail (trail 43A) makes a pleasant 5.4 mi round-trip.

▶ Trailhead: See p. 57 for information on parking. From the hiker parking lot it is 0.4 mi up to the E edge of the golf course where the Noonmark Mt. trail leaves Ausable Rd. No parking is permitted on the road near the golf course or on any of the private driveways. ◀

Leaving the road at the golf course (0.0 mi), the trail, with yellow DEC markers, follows up a private driveway. Avoiding a side road R at 0.1 mi, the trail goes straight ahead before bearing R at 0.2 mi, where the driveway goes L to a barn. Now a footpath, the trail continues mostly on the level and crosses a small ravine at 0.4 mi. Now climbing moderately, the trail reaches a jct. at 0.6 mi. (Trail L is the Old Dix Trail, trail 43A, which leads to the pass between Noonmark and Round Mts. at 1.7 mi and on to the current Dix Mt. trail at 2.3 mi.)

Bearing R at this jct. and now with red DEC markers, the Stimson Trail climbs moderately to steeply with only a few breathers to the base of some ledges at 1.1 mi. Swinging sharp L and up very steeply, the trail emerges on the open ledges at 1.2 mi, where there are views of Keene Valley and the Ausable Club. The climbing is now easier along a ridge to a lookout on the R at 1.5 mi offering views of the Great Range. From this point, the grade increases with a small ladder at 1.7 mi and a longer ladder at 1.8 mi. Now the trail crosses an open section up to a sharp L turn at 1.9 mi. Here the trail enters the woods to avoid some steeper rocks ahead and, after dropping down a few feet, turns sharp R and ascends steeply back to the open rocks and then on to the summit at 2.1 mi. Trail 44 continues on over the summit and down the SE side to the Dix trail (trail 46) in 1 mi.

From the summit there is an unobstructed view in all directions, dominated by the Great Range to the W, the Dix Range to the S, and Giant Mt. to the NE. Both Rainbow Falls and Beaver Meadow Falls may be seen when the leaves are off the trees. To the W a small piece of the burn area from a forest fire in 1999 is also visible.

🚶🚶 Distances: Ausable Club Rd. at golf course to jct. with Dix Mt. trail, 0.6 mi; to first ledge, 1.2 mi; to summit of Noonmark Mt., 2.1 mi (3.4 km). Total distance from parking area, 2.5 mi (4 km). Ascent from road, 2175 ft (663 m). Elevation, 3556 ft (1084 m).

43A Old Dix Trail

ADK High Peaks Map: F9 | Trails Illustrated Map 742: Y26

Originally the main route to Dix Mt., this trail is now used mostly as an approach to Round Mt. or as part of a loop trip on Noonmark Mt. One may still use it to climb Dix, but the trail from Round Pond is shorter with a saving of over 400 vertical feet of ascent.

▶ Locator: The start is the same as the Stimson Trail (trail 43). ◀

From the golf course on Ausable Rd. (0.0 mi), follow the Stimson Trail for 0.6 mi to a jct. Bearing L and continuing with yellow DEC markers, the Old Dix Trail is at first nearly flat, but soon begins a moderate and occasionally rocky ascent as it follows the route of an old tote road. A few short detours avoid the most eroded sections. After crossing several small tributaries, the trail swings L, crosses the headwaters of Icy Brook at 1.3 mi, and continues to climb to a jct. at the height of land between Noonmark and Round Mts. at 1.6 mi. (Trail L, trail 45, leads 0.7 mi to the summit of Round Mt.)

From the jct., the trail descends gradually to a brook crossing at 1.9 mi, after which the trail becomes rougher as it proceeds to the R of a large beaver meadow and arrives at the jct. with the Dix and Felix Adler trails (trails 46 and 44, respectively) at 2.2 mi.

🚶🚶 Distances: Ausable Rd. at golf course to jct. with Stimson Trail, 0.6 mi; to jct. with trail to Round Mt., 1.6 mi; to jct. with Dix and Felix Adler trails, 2.2 mi.

44 Noonmark Mt. from the SE via Felix Adler Trail

ADK High Peaks Map: F9 | Trails Illustrated Map 742: Y26

This trail is named for Dr. Felix Adler, a philosopher and founder of the Ethical Culture Society, which sought to combine the common elements of the Christian and Jewish faiths. He spent many summers at his home at the start of the Noonmark Mt. trail and was an enthusiastic climber.

▶ Locator: This trail starts at the jct. of the Dix Mt. trail from Round Pond (trail 46) and the Old Dix Trail (trail 43A). It offers an alternate route to Noonmark Mt. from Round Pond, or it can be part of a round-trip from the Ausable Club side. ◀

From the jct. (0.0 mi), the trail, with red DEC markers, begins at a moderate grade, but steepens at 0.2 mi and remains generally steep until easing as it crests the partially open SE ridge of Noonmark at 0.5 mi. From here occasional views are available as the trail climbs moderately to the summit of Noonmark at 1 mi.

🏃 Distances: Dix trail jct. to summit of Noonmark Mt., 1 mi (1.6 km). Total distance from NY 73 via Round Pond, 3.3 mi (5.3 km). (Total distance from the Old Dix Trail approach, 3.3 mi.) Total ascent from NY 73, 1900 ft (579 m). Elevation, 3556 ft (1084 m).

45 Round Mt.

ADK High Peaks Map: F9 | Trails Illustrated Map 742: Y26

As distinctively round when seen from Keene Valley as its neighbor Noonmark Mt. is pointed, this little peak offers some marvelous views of the cliffs and slides on Giant Mt. One can also find solitude because this summit is often ignored in favor of its larger neighbors. The S. Burns Weston Trail ascends the NE side of the peak and continues down the W side to join the Old Dix Trail (trail 43A), which makes possible an easy round-trip.

▶ Trailhead: See p. 57, for information on parking and driving directions. ◀

Leaving the road (0.0 mi) and marked with red DEC markers, the trail soon becomes steep before leveling off at 0.1 mi and proceeding along the edge of a high bank with views out through openings in the beautiful hemlock forest high above NY 73. At 0.4 mi there is a good view on the L of Giant Mt. and Chapel Pond Pass, after which the trail swings R and away from the edge of the steep bank. The grades are now mostly easy with a few short dips as the trail traverses a sidehill.

Crossing a brook and old mossy slide at 1.3 mi, the trail now swings R and up more steeply and comes to an open ledge at 1.4 mi, where there is a good view of Giant Mt. The trail now climbs at a moderate to steep grade to a large ledge with good views at 1.9 mi. The trail enters thicker woods on the flat, and after one more short, steep pitch, emerges onto open rocks at 2.1 mi. Marked with cairns, the trail is now nearly flat along open rocks to the jct. with the descent route to the Old Dix Trail branching R at 2.2 mi. The summit is just beyond at 2.3 mi, with views in all directions. Ascent from Ausable Club Rd., 1820 ft (555 m). Elevation, 3100 ft (945 m).

The descent to the Old Dix Trail (trail 43A) heads W from the jct. near the summit. The trail descends over a series of open ledges and is marked with small cairns. In general the trail heads directly for the summit of Noonmark Mt., bearing R when there seems to be any choice. At the base of this series of ledges, the trail drops steeply into a small valley with a large cliff to the R. Bearing L at the bottom of the valley, the trail crosses a small brook at 2.8 mi, swings R to climb over one last bare spot, and descends to the jct. with the Old Dix Trail at 3 mi. Turning R on trail 43A, one reaches the Ausable Club Rd. at the golf course in another 1.6 mi, making a loop trip of 4.6 mi.

🥾 Distances: Ausable Club Rd. to summit of Round Mt., 2.3 mi (3.7 km); to Old Dix Trail, 3 mi; to Ausable Club Rd. at golf course via Old Dix Trail, 4.6 mi (7.4 km).

46 Dix Mt. from NY 73

ADK High Peaks Map: G9–F10 | Trails Illustrated Map 742: Y27

Dix Mt. was named by Ebenezer Emmons in 1837 for John A. Dix, then secretary of state for Governor Marcy and later governor himself. He also served as U.S. senator, secretary of the treasury, and a major general in the Civil War. The first ascent was in 1807, by a surveyor named Rykert, who had the task of running a line that now forms the southern boundary of the town of Keene and passes directly over the summit.

▶ Trailhead: Start on NY 73, 1.1 mi S of the parking area at Chapel Pond and 3.1 mi N of the jct. of NY. 9 and NY 73 N of Exit 30 on the Adirondack Northway, I-87. The start is marked with a small DEC sign, and there is a small parking area just N of the trailhead. This trail is maintained by the Adirondack Forty-Sixers. ◀

From the road (0.0 mi) and marked with blue DEC disks, the trail climbs moderately on a traverse across a steep hillside. The grade soon eases, and the trail crosses a height of land and descends to Round Pond just beyond at 0.6 mi. There is a designated campsite on the R at the top of the hill before the pond and another very attractive designated campsite 200 yd to the L near the outlet. Elsewhere, camping is not permitted unless one is at least 150 ft back from any trail or body of water.

Turning R, the trail follows around the N shore of the pond and begins climbing moderately at 1 mi. Crossing a brook at 1.2 mi, the trail climbs steadily to a notch at 1.6 mi. Now level or slightly downhill, it crosses a brook at 1.8 mi and continues across several wet areas to the jct. with the Old Dix and the Felix Adler Trails at 2.3 mi. Trail R (trail 43A) with yellow markers leads 2.2 mi to Ausable Club Rd. Trail straight ahead with red markers (trail 44) leads 1 mi to summit of Noonmark Mt.

Turning L, the trail is practically flat to the bank of the north fork of the Boquet River at 2.7 mi. The trail now follows near the L bank of the river on the flat, but soon swings away from the river through thicker woods and crosses a small brook and then Gravestone Brook at 3.7 mi. After the brook, the trail climbs briefly to drier ground and descends to the bank of the Boquet River at 4 mi, where the outlet to Dial Pond comes in from the R. The trail continues to the Boquet River Lean-to at 4.2 mi, having gained only 100 ft since the jct. with the Old Dix Trail.

Crossing the river on stones, the trail swings R and climbs away from the river on a steadily increasing grade. Reaching a fair-sized tributary at 5.1 mi, the trail follows up the R bank of this brook on a steady, moderate grade and crosses it at 5.2 mi. The trail now crosses and recrosses several other brooks and arrives at the base of a large slide at 5.8 mi. Crossing the base of the slide, the trail swings L and begins an unrelenting steep climb, with rough footing in spots, to a jct. at the top of the ridge at 6.4 mi with the Hunters Pass Trail from Elk Lake (trail 119).

Turning L, the climbing continues steady but not quite as steep along the ridge to the summit crest at 6.7 mi. (This is the beginning of the arctic-alpine zone where one must walk only on the trail or bare rock to protect this unique resource.) The going is now nearly level, past one rock on the L with a U.S. Coast and Geodetic Survey marker, and on to the summit with an older survey bolt at 6.8 mi. Verplanck Colvin placed this bolt in 1873 as part of his Adirondack Survey. The view is unobstructed in all directions with Elk Lake to the SW, Lake Champlain and the Green Mts. of Vermont to the E, and the Great Range to the NW. Trail 120 marked with yellow DEC disks continues over the summit to the Beckhorn and then on to Elk Lake.

🚶 Distances: NY 73 to Round Pond, 0.6 mi; to jct. with Old Dix Trail, 2.3 mi; to Boquet River Lean-to, 4.2 mi; to Hunters Pass trail from Elk Lake, 6.4 mi; to summit of Dix Mt., 6.8 mi (11 km). Ascent from NY 73, 3200 ft (976 m). Elevation, 4857 ft (1481 m). Order of height, 6.

47   Giant Mt. via Roaring Brook Trail

ADK High Peaks Map: F9–G9 | Trails Illustrated Map 742: Y26

The full name for Giant Mt., Giant of the Valley, is the name given this peak by early residents in Pleasant Valley on the E side of the mountain. From the low valley of the Boquet River, Giant does appear as a massive mountain with many ridges and subsidiary peaks towering 4000 ft above the valley. The first ascent of Giant Mt. (and the first of any 4000 ft peak) was in 1797, by Charles Brodhead. A surveyor, he had the task of surveying the boundaries of the Old Military Tract, which was to be divided up as compensation for soldiers who had fought in the Revolutionary War. Brodhead had to fight his way up the E face and directly down the W face—a route that has probably never been repeated.

The first trail was cut in 1866 via Hopkins Mt., with the Roaring Brook Trail cut soon after in 1873 and later improved enough to be passable by horses to within

300 ft of the summit. This early use accounts for the somewhat more moderate grades and the series of steep and sometimes washed away switchbacks as the trail approaches the crest of the ridge. Trail work by ADK and later by ATIS has greatly improved the footing on much of the trail.

▶ Trailhead: Begin at a small parking area on NY 73, 3.3 mi S of the High Peaks sign in Keene Valley and 5.6 mi N of the jct. of NY 9 and NY. 73 N of Exit 30 on the Adirondack Northway, I-87. ◀

From the end of the parking lot (0.0 mi), the red-marked trail begins on the level to a jct. at 0.1 mi with a trail leading R another 0.2 mi to the base of Roaring Brook Falls. Bearing L, the trail begins a moderate climb to a crest at 0.3 mi, after which it dips and continues at an easier grade to a jct. at 0.5 mi. Trail R leads 80 yd to the top of Roaring Brook Falls, where there are views of Noonmark Mt. and the lower Great Range. *Caution:* Approach this view with extreme care; there have been several serious accidents at this spot.

Bearing L, the grade soon moderates and reaches a jct. with an unmarked spur trail leading L at 1 mi, just short of the R bank of Roaring Brook. (Trail L leads 40 yd to a campsite.) In 1963 there were massive slides on all sides of Giant, and the rush of water down the W side widened the bed of Roaring Brook to nearly 200 yd in spots. All the trees near the brook have grown up since then.)

Continuing past this jct., the trail crosses Roaring Brook, and comes to a jct. on the far side at 1.1 mi with a trail leading R to the Giants Nubble and Giants Washbowl (trails 49 and 50). Turning L, the trail ascends an easy to moderate grade, crosses two brooks, and comes to a short side trail leading L to some open rocks in the brook at 1.4 mi. Now the trail begins to pull away from the brook at a mostly steady, moderate grade and soon steepens along the crest of a broad ridge. At 2.3 mi a side trail R leads to a good view and a welcome chance for a breather. Continuing to climb via some steep switchbacks, the trail reaches a badly eroded section at 2.6 mi. with a ladder assisting passage at the upper end. At 2.7mi, a reroute (2009) goes R for 150 yds and reaches a jct. with the Ridge (Zander Scott) Trail (trail 48) at a point 0.1 mi below the old jct. of these two trails.

Turning L, a short steep pitch is followed by more moderate grades to a small summit and a now somewhat obscured view of the slides at 3 mi. Now flat for a short way, the trail begins climbing again at 3.2 mi and after another short flat stretch climbs steeply to some open rock at 3.4 mi and the jct. with East Trail from New Russia and Rocky Peak (trail 112). From here, easy grades lead to the open summit at 3.6 mi. The views range from the Dix Range to Whiteface Mt. The Ausable Club is directly below to the W with the Great Range beyond. The view of Lake Champlain is becoming obscured, but the Green Mts. are still visible to the E. In all, 39 major peaks can be seen.

🏃 Distances: NY 73 to top of Roaring Brook Falls, 0.5 mi; to jct. with trail to Nubble and Washbowl, 1.1 mi; to jct. with Ridge Trail, 2 mi; to jct. with East Trail, 3.4 mi; to summit of Giant Mt., 3.6 mi (5.8 km). Ascent from NY 73, 3375 ft (1029 m). Elevation, 4627 ft (1411 m). Order of height, 12.

48 Giant Mt. via Ridge (Zander Scott) Trail

ADK High Peaks Map: F9–G9 | Trails Illustrated Map 742: Y27

This slightly shorter route to Giant Mt. was completed in 1954 and offers the easiest access to the Giants Washbowl and Nubble, as well as a route to the summit with many views from the long, open ridge. Known for most of the time as the "Ridge Trail," this trail was briefly renamed in memory of Zander Scott in 1992. A summer resident of Keene Valley, Zander had been an active member of the ATIS hiking program and trail crew before dying in a light plane crash shortly after graduating from Princeton University. Trailhead signs again identify this as the Ridge Trail with additional signage recognizing that gifts contributed in memory of Zander and later his mother, Sandy, funded a complete rebuilding of the switchbacks below the Washbowl along with additional switchbacks and other trail stabilization work above the Washbowl.

▶ Trailhead: Start on NY 73, 4.8 mi S of the High Peaks sign in Keene Valley and 4.1 mi N of the jct. of NY 9 and NY 73 N of Exit 30 on the Adirondack Northway, I-87. Parking is available for several cars at the trailhead with more available 0.2 mi to the N at Chapel Pond. Given the busy nature of this road, all cars should be parked well off the road. The trail is marked with blue DEC markers. ◀

From the road (0.0 mi), the trail crosses a small brook to the trail register and soon begins climbing. Taking a sharp L across a small stream in 150 yd, the trail recrosses the stream in another 150 yd and climbs steeply to a short, flat section. Soon after the end of this flat area, the trail turns sharp L at 0.3 mi in the first of several switchbacks leading up a steep slope. (Stay on marked trail; cutting switchbacks causes erosion and defeats the purpose of creating them.) The grade eases at 0.5 mi, but there are a few more steep sections as the trail crosses a usually dry streambed and climbs to an open lookout at 0.7 mi directly above Chapel Pond. The trail now makes a slight descent to a jct. at the S end of the Giants Washbowl. Trail L (trail 50) skirts the SW side of the pond and leads 1 mi to the Roaring Brook Trail. The many dead trees along the shore of the Washbowl are the result of the underground outlet of the Washbowl becoming plugged in 1988, remaining so until 1992, and again becoming plugged in 2009. This has raised the water level by nearly 5 ft and created an above-ground outlet.

The Ridge Trail bears R at this jct. and crosses the outlet of the Washbowl on a bridge. Just past the end of the bridge a side trail leads L to a designated campsite. The trail then swings sharp R with a designated campsite on the R just beyond. Past the campsite the trail climbs moderately to a jct. at 1 mi with the trail to the Giants Nubble (trail 49).

Bearing R, the Ridge Trail climbs steadily through conifers to a line of demarcation between the large conifers and smaller poplars and birches at 1.1 mi. This marks the farthest extent of the 1913 forest fire, which burned off much of the ridge above and created the views that make this trail so attractive. The trail now switchbacks to the R, followed by a steep, rough section up to the beginning of a series of seven switchbacks that have eased much of the climb up to the first ledge at 1.5 mi. There are good views of both the Washbowl and Chapel Pond. Turning sharp L at two cairns, the trail leaves this ledge and continues to some higher ledges with a view up the ridge.

Dipping to a small col at 1.6 mi, the trail climbs a few steep pitches and emerges at the base of a long climb across a large, open face. At 1.9 mi, near the top of this open area, is a jct. (Trail R goes up and over the top of a small bump with more views and is 100 yd longer than the trail L.) Bearing L, the trail slabs across the N side of the ridge and in 110 yd reaches the jct. with the longer trail over the bump. After a short, flat section in a col, the trail climbs again through another smaller bare section to easier climbing at 2.2 mi, after which the climbing is mostly easy to the jct. with the Roaring Brook Trail (trail 47) at 2.4 mi. From here the description to the summit is the same as that for the Roaring Brook Trail.

🚶 Distances: NY 73 to Giants Washbowl, 0.7 mi; to side trail to Giants Nubble, 1 mi; to Roaring Brook Trail, 2.4 mi; to East Trail, 3 mi; to summit of Giant Mt., 3.2 mi (4.8 km). Ascent from NY 73, 3050 ft (930 m). Elevation, 4627 ft (1411 m). Order of height, 12.

Giant Mt. viewed from Giants Nubble. David Hough

49 Giants Nubble

ADK High Peaks Map: F9–G9 | Trails Illustrated Map 742: Y27

This small, rocky knob at the end of the SW ridge of Giant Mt. offers some interesting views of St. Huberts and the slides on Giant's W face.

▶ Locator: There are two approaches to Giants Nubble, with the one branching from the Ridge (Zander Scott) Trail (trail 48) being the easiest. Approaching via the Roaring Brook trail (trail 47), however, one can make an interesting loop of 4.7 mi taking in Roaring Brook Falls, the Giants Washbowl, and the Giants Nubble. ◄

1. From the jct. 1 mi up the Ridge Trail (0.0 mi), the trail, with yellow DEC markers goes straight ahead before swinging L, crossing a small brook and climbing at mostly moderate grades to a view of the Giants Washbowl at 0.1 mi. Dipping across a small sag, the trail comes to better views to the S at 0.3 mi, after which the trail is flat and then climbs steeply up to a jct. at 0.4 mi. (Trail R leads to Roaring Brook Trail; see second approach below.) Bearing L, the trail now proceeds along a nearly flat, open ridge to the summit of the Nubble at 0.5 mi.

🏃 Distances: From Chapel Pond via Ridge Trail to jct. with Giants Nubble trail, 1 mi; to summit of Giants Nubble, 1.5 mi (2.4 km). Ascent from Chapel Pond, 1150 ft (351 m).

2. From the jct. (0.0 mi) on the Roaring Brook Trail (trail 47) at 1.1 mi the trail, with yellow DEC markers, starts on the flat but soon begins climbing after crossing a small stream and reaches a jct. at 0.2 mi with a trail R to Washbowl (trail 50). Turning L, the Nubble trail climbs moderately to steeply, crossing a stream at 0.3 mi, and another at 0.5 mi, before reaching a jct. at 0.8 mi. (Trail L leads to Ridge (Zander Scott) Trail and Giants Washbowl, trail 48.) Turning R, the trail swings R and onto a nearly flat open ridge to the summit of the Nubble at 0.9 mi.

🏃 Distances: From NY 73 via Roaring Brook Trail to jct. with Giants Nubble and Giants Washbowl trail, 1.1 mi; to summit of Giants Nubble, 2 mi (3.2 km). Ascent from road, 1480 ft (451 m). Elevation, 2760 ft (842 m).

50 Giants Washbowl from Roaring Brook Trail

ADK High Peaks Map: F9–G9 | Trails Illustrated Map 742: Y26–27

▶ Locator: This alternate approach to Giants Washbowl leaves the Roaring Brook Trail (trail 47) 1.1 mi from the parking lot on NY 73. ◄

Turning R at the jct. (0.0 mi), the trail soon crosses a small stream and then climbs to a jct. at 0.2 mi with trail L to Giants Nubble (trail 49). Bearing R, the trail, now with red DEC markers, continues to climb at a moderate grade until it eases at 0.5 mi and soon reaches a height of land below the Nubble. Now descending at an easy grade, it reaches the NW shore of the Giants Washbowl at 0.8 mi. Continuing along the shore of the pond, the trail reaches a jct. with the Ridge Trail (trail 48) at 1 mi. This point is 0.7 mi above NY 73 at Chapel Pond and 0.3 mi below the turnoff for the Nubble Trail.

🏃 Distances: Parking lot on NY 73 to turnoff from Roaring Brook Trail, 1.1 mi; to jct. with Ridge Trail at Giants Washbowl, 2.1 mi (3.4 km).

51 Mossy Cascade Trail to Hopkins Mt.

ADK High Peaks Map: F8–F9 | Trails Illustrated Map 742: Z26

Because the direct approach to Hopkins Mt. from Keene Valley was closed in 1992, the Mossy Cascade Trail is the best approach to this rocky little peak. Hopkins Mt. was named for Rev. Erastus Hopkins of Troy, New York, who later served several terms in the Massachusetts legislature while a resident of Northampton. It was he who suggested to Old Mountain Phelps the name "Resagone," meaning the "king's great saw," for the mountain we now call Sawteeth.

▶ Trailhead: Start on NY 73 just S of the steel-sided bridge over the East Branch Ausable River 2 mi S of Keene Valley. ◀

From the road (0.0 mi) and marked with red markers, the trail follows along above the R bank of the river to a house on the L at 0.4 mi. Swinging R onto a tote road at the house, the trail immediately swings L onto an older road and then in another 100 yd bears R at another jct. The trail now veers around from NE to SE while remaining mostly on flat going. At 0.5 mi the trail leaves the tote road, going L to the L bank of Mossy Cascade Brook, which is followed to a jct. at 0.7 mi. (Side trail L leads to the base of Mossy Cascade in 200 yd of sometimes rough going.) Bearing R, the trail now switchbacks away from the brook and climbs at a moderate grade to the edge of a clearing for a private camp on the R at 1 mi. Just past this camp the trail crosses the brook and climbs away from the brook with several steep pitches. It enters state land at a yellow-blazed property line at 1.1 mi and comes to a lookout on the L at 1.5 mi.

Past this lookout, the trail descends to a col, then climbs to another ledge with a view at 1.7 mi, and continues to climb through an open forest along an interesting monolithic ridge of granite. The grade moderates at 2.2 mi and the trail comes to a jct. at 2.3 mi with the Ranney Trail from Keene Valley (trail 24). The trail R continues up into a ravine between Hopkins and Green Mts. and arrives at a jct. in a col at 3 mi with trail R leading 3 mi over a shoulder of Green Mt. to the summit of Giant Mt. (trail 52). Turning L, the trail climbs very steeply for a few yards, and then eases off along bare slabs to the summit of Hopkins at 3.2 mi.

There are many blueberries and the views are unobstructed in all directions except NE, with 22 major peaks discernible. (Trail with ADK markers continues over the summit to Spread Eagle and Keene Valley; but owing to landowner problems the trail is no longer marked all the way to Keene Valley. See trail 22 description for more information.)

🚶 Distances: NY 73 to Mossy Cascade, 0.8 mi; to jct. with Ranney Trail, 2.3 mi; to jct. with trail to Giant Mt., 3 mi; to summit of Hopkins Mt., 3.2 mi (5.2 km). Ascent from NY 73, 2120 ft (646 m). Elevation, 3183 ft (970 m).

52 Giant Mt. from Hopkins Mt. via Green Mt.

ADK High Peaks Map: G8 | Trails Illustrated Map 742: Z27

Owing to its length and the lack of any views along the way, this is not as popular a route to the summit of Giant Mt., but it does offer pleasant walking through some virgin forests and makes for an interesting way to return from Giant Mt. to St. Huberts or Keene Valley.

▶ Locator: This trail departs from the jct. with the Mossy Cascade Trail (trail 51) in the Hopkins-Green col. ◀

Leaving the jct. (0.0 mi), the trail climbs a short steep pitch and then continues at moderate grades to the crest of a shoulder of Green Mt. at 0.4 mi. The trail now descends to a col at 0.5 mi, after which it slabs along a sidehill on the level and enters a swampy area with lush moss at 0.7 mi. After some more flat going, the trail descends and crosses a tributary to Putnam Brook (also called Beede Brook) at 1.1 mi. After climbing out of this small valley, the trail continues the easy to moderate descent and crosses the main branch of Putnam Brook at 1.7 mi before and coming to a jct. in the col between Green Mt. and Giant Mt. shortly after. The trail coming in from the L is the North Trail to Giant Mt. (trail 111), which leads 6.1 mi to NY 9N. From here, the route is marked with red DEC disks.

Turning R at the jct., trail 111 begins climbing steeply out of the col and at 1.9 mi there is a sharp switchback to the L to negotiate a small cliff band. From here the grade continues steep for a few yards, but slowly eases until it levels off at 2.5 mi. Descending slightly, the trail resumes its climb and arrives at a ledge on the R at 2.8 mi, soon after which it levels out and crosses other ledges to the summit at 3 mi. Trails 47 and 48 continue over the summit and down to NY 73 at Chapel Pond or St. Huberts.

🥾 Distances: NY 73 via Mossy Cascade Trail to Hopkins-Green col, 3 mi; to jct. with North Trail, 4.7 mi; to summit of Giant Mt., 6 mi (9.7 km). Ascent from NY 73, 3500 ft (1067 m). Elevation, 4627 ft (1411 m). Order of height, 12.

53 Snow Mt.

ADK High Peaks Map: F8–F9 | Trails Illustrated Map 742: Z26

This 2360 ft (720 m) peak NW of St. Huberts offers some splendid views of the surrounding peaks as well as acres of good blueberries. There are three possible approaches, but the most popular is via Deer Brook, as described here. In addition to being the shortest, the Deer Brook approach offers a short side trip to a waterfall. The downside of the Deer Brook approach is that the first 0.6 mi is on a private gravel driveway if high water prevents use of the trail through the attractive but rougher flume.

The W. A. White Trail approach is over a mile longer if one counts the walk from the Ausable Club parking area to the start of the trail, and it is described only as a spur trail from the W. A. White Trail (see trail 32). The approach from the N via the Rooster Comb trails (trails 18 and 18A) is 0.8 mi longer than Deer Brook. With all these trails there are a multitude of loop trips possible, combining Snow Mt., Rooster Comb, and any of these approaches. The Deer Brook Trail is also a good alternate approach to the W. A. White Trail to Lower Wolf Jaw and Hedgehog Mts. because it avoids travel on any AMR land and permits one to bring a dog.

▶ Deer Brook Trailhead: Start on NY 73, 0.1 mi N of the steel-sided bridge over the Ausable River, 1.9 mi S of the High Peaks sign in the center of Keene Valley. The start is marked with green signs and blue DEC markers. ◀

Leaving the highway (0.0 mi), the trail heads up the R bank of Deer Brook to a jct. at a private driveway at 0.1 mi. (Trail L, with yellow markers and signed as the high-water route, follows a private driveway—no public vehicular traffic or parking—for 0.6 mi where the high-water route enters the woods and joins the flume trail in another 120 yds.) Continuing straight ahead at the junction, the trail enters the flume and soon reaches the first of four crossings of Deer Brook. A steep scramble just beyond is the most challenging section as trail work to restore this route (2013) has made the going overall much easier. After the fourth crossing, the trail switchbacks up to join the high-water route. Turning R, in a few yards the trail reaches a junction at 0.7 mi. from the highway.

(Trail L at this jct., with red DEC markers is the connection to the W. A. White Trail, trail 32. It ascends a very steep bank and then goes up and R to a jct. at a wide logging road 0.2 mi after leaving the Deer Brook Trail, where it turns L, reaching the W. A. White Trail at 0.3 mi.)

Straight ahead at this three-way jct., the Deer Brook Trail continues with yellow DEC markers and comes to another jct. at the R bank of Deer Brook at 0.8 mi. (Trail L leads 90 yd to the base of a pretty little falls.) Turning R, the trail crosses Deer Brook on a bridge and follows a tote road at a moderate grade, which eases off just before a jct. at 1.3 mi. (Trail L is the approach from the Ausable Club via W. A. White Trail, trail 32.) Turning R, and now with blue DEC markers, the trail continues on the flat to a jct. at 1.4 mi.

(Trail straight ahead is the approach from the N. It leads mostly on the level for 0.4 mi to a jct. with the Sachs Trail, trail 18A, which leads down to Keene Valley or up to Rooster Comb.)

Turning R with yellow DEC markers, the Snow trail proceeds across a sidehill for a little over 100 yd and then turns R and ascends steeply to the first ledge at 1.6 mi with a spectacular view of the cliffs on Rooster Comb. The trail now reenters the woods and climbs to a second ledge. The summit is just beyond at 1.7 mi. The best views are on ledges down the SE side.

🚶🚶 Distances: NY 73 to connector to W. A. White Trail, 0.7 mi; to jct. with trail from Ausable Club, 1.3 mi; to jct. with trail to Sachs trail to Rooster Comb, 1.4 mi; to summit of Snow Mt., 1.7 mi (2.8 km). Ascent from NY 73, 1360 ft (414 m). Elevation, 2360 ft (720 m).

UPPER AUSABLE LAKE AREA

ADK High Peaks Map: E11 | Trails Illustrated Map 742: X24

Following the sale of the higher land by the Adirondack Mountain Reserve (AMR) to the State of New York in 1978, most of the trails approaching the shores and along the shores of Upper Ausable Lake have been closed to the public. Camping, fishing, and hunting on any of the private lands near this lake are prohibited, but several through trails still open to the public offer some interesting and rugged hiking. All access to the Upper Ausable Lake area is by foot over the summits of 4000 ft peaks because there is no trail along the shores of Lower Ausable Lake, bushwhacking is prohibited, no boats are available for rent by the public, and portable boats brought in by the public are not permitted on Lower Ausable Lake. Hiking in this area is therefore a serious undertaking, requiring careful planning to ensure that one can complete one's planned trip or arrive before nightfall at a campsite above the private-land boundary.

These restrictions are designed to protect the private camp owners on the lake, who in the past have complained of illegal camping on their land, break-ins, and even some instances of burglary. Their wishes and privacy should obviously be respected. There is a warden's camp at the N end of Upper Ausable Lake, from which the area is patrolled. During the summer months, the warden's camp has radio communication with the Ausable Club in St. Huberts.

There are many interesting trips available to the public in this region, provided one is willing to do a lot of climbing and descending. Camping is allowed on state land, generally above the 2500 ft level (see Trails Illustrated Map 742 for exact state and private land boundaries), although there are very few designated campsites on state land in this area. One must therefore be careful when establishing new campsites that the regulations regarding distances from streams and trails are obeyed and that exceptional care is taken in building fires. Much of the forest floor in this area is covered with a deep layer of duff, which can burn as easily as wood. (See information on camping in the introduction.)

Approaches to Upper Ausable Lake

ADK High Peaks Map: E11 | Trails Illustrated Map 742: X24

The "easiest" approach to this area is from St. Huberts over the summit of either Sawteeth or Mt. Colvin. A loop trip over both these summits makes an interesting but rugged day trip totaling 19 mi (30.6 km) and 4500 ft (1372 m) of climb

Loons. Mark Bowie

and descent. (See descriptions for: Sawteeth via Pyramid-Gothics Trail, trail 37; Sawteeth from Warden's Camp, trail 57; Carry Trail, trail 54; Mt. Colvin from the Carry, trail 55; Mt. Colvin from Lake Rd. Trail, trail 40.)

A considerably more difficult approach for backpackers is a possible loop trip from Keene Valley over Mt. Marcy, down the Elk Lake–Marcy Trail, and returning to St. Huberts along Pinnacle Ridge to Mt. Colvin and back to St. Huberts. Total distance for this loop is 27.1 mi (43.7 km). Total ascent and descent is approximately 7200 ft (2195 m). See descriptions for Mt. Marcy via Phelps Trail (trail 1), Elk Lake–Marcy Trail (trail 118), Blake Peak and Mt. Colvin via Pinnacle Ridge (trails 60 and 56), and Mt. Colvin from Lake Rd. Trail (trail 40).

Other approaches and loop trips are possible using these and other trails described in full below.

54 Carry Trail

ADK High Peaks Map: E10 | Trails Illustrated Map 742: X25

▶ Locator: This trail runs 1 mi from the boat sheds at the S end of Lower Ausable Lake to the warden's camp at the N end of Upper Ausable Lake. ◀

The trail follows close to the bank of the Ausable River on the flat. It is paralleled by a tractor trail farther up the slope away from the river. There is a small spring beside the trail at approximately the halfway point. A few yards from the boat sheds on Lower Ausable Lake is a jct. with the trail to Mt. Colvin and Blake Peak. At the warden's camp is a jct. with the trails leading to Sawteeth and Mts. Haystack and Marcy via Bartlett Ridge.

55 Mt. Colvin from Carry Trail

ADK High Peaks Map: E10 | Trails Illustrated Map 742: X25

For the history of the naming of Mt. Colvin, see description for Colvin from Lake Rd. Trail and Gill Brook (trail 40).

▶ Locator: This trail climbs steeply up the valley between Mt. Colvin and Blake Peak to the top of the ridge, where it connects with the trail to Blake, Pinnacle, and the Elk Lake–Marcy trail. ◀

From the jct. with the Carry Trail (trail 54) (0.0 mi), the trail, with yellow DEC markers, heads E on the flat on a road, but in a few yards bears R off the road and crosses the Ausable River on a bridge at 0.1 mi. The climbing starts almost immediately at the far side of the bridge, with the trail following the R bank of a small brook and then crossing it at 0.3 mi and beginning a very steep climb. The climbing soon eases a bit but remains steady, crossing onto state land at 0.4 mi. The trail climbs high above the brook and then back to brook level at 0.5 mi, where the brook forks. This area offers some very small but possible campsites.

The trail briefly follows and soon crosses the L fork of this stream and then continues at a steady grade with a few steeper pitches until the grade finally moderates shortly before the jct. in the col between Mt. Colvin and Blake Peak at 1.1 mi. Trail R leads 0.6 mi to summit of Blake Peak, 3.2 mi to Pinnacle, and 4.6 mi to Elk Lake–Marcy Trail (trails 56 and 60). Turning L, the Colvin Trail climbs very steeply with the aid of two ladders until the grade finally moderates at 1.3 mi. Now the trail crosses a ridge and dips slightly before continuing at relatively easy grades up the S ridge of the mountain. There is a lookout on the L, a few yards before the summit, with views of Upper Ausable Lake, Allen Mt., and other peaks. The actual summit is reached at 1.9 mi, where there are good views. (Trail 40 continues over the summit and down to St. Huberts.)

🏃 Distances: Carry Trail to jct. with Blake Trail, 1.1 mi; to summit of Mt. Colvin, 1.9 mi (3.1 km). Ascent from Carry Trail, 2100 ft (640 m). Elevation, 4057 ft (1237 m). Order of height, 39.

56 Blake Peak

ADK High Peaks Map: E10 | Trails Illustrated Map 742: X25

Blake Peak (Blake Mt. on map) was named for Mills Blake, who was Verplanck Colvin's chief assistant during the Adirondack Survey and his closest personal friend. The two worked and lived together for 48 years until Colvin died in 1920, so it is fitting that the peak adjacent to Mt. Colvin bears Blake's name.

▶ Locator: Blake Peak can be approached from St. Huberts over Mt. Colvin via the Lake Rd. Trail and Gill Brook to Colvin's summit (trail 40) and then trail 55 to the col between Colvin and Blake. ◀

Leaving the jct. in the col (0.0 mi), the trail climbs a short, steep pitch, moderates, and then begins a very steep pitch at 0.2 mi. Reaching the crest of a ridge at 0.5 mi, the trail climbs mostly easily to the summit at 0.6 mi, where there are views through the trees to Elk Lake. (Those who still have any ambition left and desire a better view can proceed 0.4 mi farther S to Lookout Rock. See trail 60.)

🚶 Distances: From Lake Rd. to jct. at Colvin-Blake col, 3.7 mi; to summit of Blake Peak, 4.2 mi (6.8 km). Total ascent from Lake Rd. Trail, 2800 ft (854 m). Elevation, 3960 ft (1207 m). Order of height among the original 46 peaks, 43.

57 Sawteeth from the Warden's Camp

ADK High Peaks Map: E10 | Trails Illustrated Map 742: X25

▶ Locator: This trail departs from the warden's camp at the N end of Upper Ausable Lake. ◀

From the warden's camp (see trail 54) (0.0 mi), this trail heads NW on the flat to a jct. at 0.2 mi. Trail straight ahead leads to Mts. Haystack and Marcy via Bartlett Ridge (trail 58). Turning R, the Sawteeth Trail, with red DEC markers, crosses Shanty Brook on rocks and briefly follows up the L bank before swinging away from the brook on easy grades alternating with moderate sections to a brook at 0.9 mi. From this brook, the climbing steepens to a jct. at 1.5 mi with a recently (2009) abandoned side trail that lead R to Stowe Ledges.

Continuing past the jct. with the side trail, the grades again moderate as the trail traverses a sidehill and then dips to cross a brook at 1.7 mi just after entering state land. (The crossing area offers a possible campsite and is the first brook encountered on the descent from Sawteeth.) After one more short climb and a dip past this brook, the trail begins to climb very

Camping. David Hough

steeply up the crest of the S ridge of Sawteeth. On the ridge crest, after several steep pitches alternating with more moderate sections, the trail reaches a small summit at 2.7 mi, and in 20 yd joins the trail from Lower Ausable Lake (trail 36). Turning L, the trail comes to the summit of Sawteeth at 2.8 mi. Trail 37 continues over the summit and on to Gothics or down to Lower Ausable Lake (trail 35).

👫 Distances: Warden's camp to jct. with Mts. Haystack and Marcy trail, 0.2 mi; to jct. with side trail to Stowe Ledges, 1.5 mi; to summit of Sawteeth, 2.8 mi (4.5 km). Ascent from warden's camp, 2110 ft (643 m). Elevation, 4100 ft (1250 m). Order of height, 35.

58 Mts. Haystack and Marcy via Bartlett Ridge from the Warden's Camp

ADK High Peaks Map: E10–D10 | Trails Illustrated Map 742: X25

▶ Locator: This trail leads from Upper Ausable Lake to the top of Bartlett Ridge, from which one may climb Mt. Haystack or descend into Panther Gorge and ascend Mt. Marcy from there via the Elk Lake–Marcy Trail. ◀

From the warden's camp (see trail 54) (0.0 mi), the trail goes NW on the flat to a jct. at 0.2 mi (Trail R leads to Sawteeth, trail 57). Continuing straight ahead with blue DEC markers, the trail climbs at an easy to moderate grade. After crossing several small brooks, the trail reaches a jct. with the Sages Folly Trail L (closed to the public) at 1.1 mi. Past this jct., the moderate grade continues to another jct. at 1.5 mi, with trail R leading via Haystack Brook to the Range Trail between Mt. Haystack and Basin Mt. (trail 59).

Turning L, the trail proceeds mostly on the flat around the end of a ridge to a jct. with the Crystal Brook Trail L (closed to the public) at 1.8 mi. Bearing R, the trail crosses Crystal Brook and enters state land just after the crossing at 1.9 mi. Now the trail begins a steep, rough climb to the crest of Bartlett Ridge at 2.5 mi, after which the grade eases and the trail crosses two brooks and several wet areas before reaching the jct. with the trail to Panther Gorge and Mt. Marcy at 2.8 mi.

[Trail L, with yellow DEC markers, leads steeply down the W side of Bartlett Ridge to the Elk Lake–Marcy Trail at the Panther Gorge Lean-to, 3.5 mi from the warden's camp, having lost 600 vertical ft from the top of Bartlett Ridge. From here it is another 1.8 mi to the summit of Mt. Marcy, making it 5.3 mi (8.5 km) and a total of approximately 4000 ft (1220 m) of climbing from the warden's camp to the summit of Mt. Marcy.]

Turning R with yellow DEC markers, the Haystack Trail begins one of the steepest climbs in the mountains up the S side of the peak. It is strongly recommended that backpackers not attempt this trail even though it is part of a seemingly attractive loop trip taking in the lean-to and campsites at Panther Gorge. It is unremittingly steep with numerous small ledges posing the danger of a serious fall—especially for less experienced backpackers. The trail is quite eroded in spots, with almost no respite to timberline at 3.2 mi. (This is the beginning of the arctic-alpine zone. One must walk only on the trail or bare rock to protect this unique resource.)

From here, the trail is marked with cairns and care is needed to follow it as it winds up through several ledges and finally to the R (E) side of the summit ridge to surmount the final large ledge. The summit is reached at 3.5 mi. Trail 10 continues 0.6 mi to the Range Trail and on to the Johns Brook Valley and Keene Valley (trail 9).

👥 Distances: Warden's camp to jct. with Haystack Brook Trail, 1.5 mi; to Bartlett Ridge and jct. with Mt. Marcy trail, 2.7 mi; to summit of Mt. Haystack, 3.5 mi (5.6 km). Ascent from warden's camp, 3070 ft (936 m). Elevation, 4960 ft (1512 m). Order of height, 3.

59 Mt. Haystack and the Great Range via Haystack Brook Trail

ADK High Peaks Map: E10 | Trails Illustrated Map 742: X24

▶ Locator: This trail leads to the State Range Trail at the former site of Sno-Bird Lean-to between Mt. Haystack and Basin Mt. ◀

The grade is easy for much of the way, but it finishes with some very steep climbing and several ladders that can be quite difficult when backpacking. There are several possible campsites along this trail, as it is on state land from just past the jct. with the Bartlett Ridge Trail.

From the warden's camp (see trail 54) (0.0 mi), follow the Bartlett Ridge Trail (trail 58) to the jct. at 1.5 mi. Turning R here, the red-marked trail is mostly flat, entering state land at 1.6 mi. Easy grades continue to a crossing of an old slide track and brook at 2.1 mi. Continuing at an easy grade along the lower slopes of Mt. Haystack, the trail comes near the R bank of Haystack Brook at 2.7 mi. From here the trail gets progressively steeper to the first ladder at 2.9 mi. There are several more ladders with short breathers in between before the Haystack Brook Trail reaches a jct. with the State Range Trail (trail 9) at 3.4 mi. (Trail R leads to Johns Brook Lodge via Shorey Short Cut and Slant Rock, 4.7 mi, or to JBL via Basin and Saddleback Mts., 5.1 mi. Trail L leads to Mt. Haystack, 1 mi.)

👥 Distances: Warden's camp to jct. with Bartlett Ridge Trail, 1.5 mi; to jct. with State Range Trail, 3.4 mi; to summit of Mt. Haystack, 4.4 mi (7.1 km). Ascent from warden's camp, 3070 ft (936 m). Elevation, 4960 ft (1512 m). Order of height, 3.

Mt. Marcy in winter. James Appleyard

60 Blake Peak and Mt. Colvin via Pinnacle Ridge from Elk Lake–Marcy Trail

ADK High Peaks Map: E11 | Trails Illustrated Map 742: W24

The Pinnacle Ridge leading to Blake Peak (Blake Mt. on map) and Mt. Colvin does not offer any striking 360° views, but it is a beautiful series of seldom-visited peaks. Virgin forests of spruce and balsam underlain with moss-covered rocks alternate with areas of severe damage caused by Hurricane Floyd in 1999. The best views before reaching Mt. Colvin are at Pinnacle, an unnamed 3717 ft peak, and Lookout Rock, but there are other narrower views, including many caused by the hurricane.

Since 1978, when the AMR sold its higher lands to the State of New York, this entire ridge has been public land. To facilitate public access, ATIS constructed a short connection between the existing trails on the ridge and the Elk Lake–Marcy Trail. There is no water on this ridge, but there are possible campsites on the access trail from the Elk Lake–Marcy Trail, and one could find a possible campsite by descending about 0.3 mi from the col between Mt. Colvin and Blake Peak. This trail is described from S to N since that is the direction in which it is hiked in the suggested loop trip in the introduction to the Upper Ausable Lake Area (p. 86).

▶ Locator: This approach to Blake Peak and Mt. Colvin begins on the Elk Lake–Marcy Trail (trail 118) 6 mi from the summit of Mt. Marcy and 5 mi from Elk Lake. This jct. is also 0.2 mi E of the log bridge over the inlet to Upper Ausable Lake. ◀

From the jct. (0.0 mi), the trail, with red DEC markers, heads NW on the flat, crossing two brooks and following a series of shelves. After climbing a short bit, the trail winds among rocks with a view of Mt. Haystack at 0.4 mi and continues on to a brook with a small waterfall at 0.7 mi, where there are some possible campsites. Crossing the brook, the trail climbs moderately with a few steep pitches to a jct. at 1 mi. (Trail L is the original Pinnacle trail, now closed to the public.)

Turning R, the trail climbs moderately to steeply to the beginning of a long traverse L at 1.2 mi. Crossing a stream at 1.3 mi, the trail climbs moderately to a jct. just below the summit of the Pinnacle at 1.6 mi.

(Spur trail going straight ahead ascends steeply with the aid of a ladder for 100 yd to a ledge on the R with views of the Great Range. From this ledge the trail continues to the summit of Pinnacle in 0.2 mi, where there is a spectacular view of Elk Lake and the Dix Range.)

Turning L at the jct., the trail descends briefly to a col before climbing and passing just W of another summit and down to another col at 2.2 mi. Shortly above this col the trail comes to a jct. with a now-abandoned trail. Climbing at first very steeply past this jct., the trail goes over another summit and drops steeply to another col at 2.5 mi. Now the trail climbs quite steeply, but eases off at 2.7 mi and soon comes to a side trail R leading to a good view of Elk Lake near the summit of the unnamed 3717 ft peak. Dropping steeply from this summit, the trail comes to a jct. at a col at 2.9 mi with a barely visible jct. with another abandoned trail.

Continuing on the level for a short stretch, the trail soon begins to climb, steeply at times, to a lookout on the R at 3.2 mi. The climbing is now easier and the trail passes between two large boulders just before reaching a summit at 3.6 mi. Shortly beyond this summit, the trail passes Lookout Rock on the L, from which there are good views, including one seemingly straight down to Upper Ausable Lake. The trail now descends gradually to a col and begins to climb Blake Peak, crossing a minor summit at 4 mi and reaching the true summit less than 100 yd later. Total ascent from Elk Lake–Marcy Trail, approximately 2800 ft (854 m). Elevation, 3960 ft (1207 m).

See trail 56 for history of the naming of Blake Peak as well as complete description of trail from the summit down to the col between Blake Peak and Mt. Colvin and then up the S side of Colvin to the summit at 5.4 mi. Trail from the summit leads down to St. Huberts.

🚶 Distances: Elk Lake–Marcy Trail to Pinnacle, 1.8 mi; to summit of Blake Peak, 4 mi; to summit of Mt. Colvin, 5.4 mi (8.7 km). Total ascent, approximately 3400 ft (1037 m). Elevation, 4057 ft (1237 m). Order of height, 39. 🦌

Heart Lake. Richard J. Nowicki

Heart Lake Section

This popular hiking center offers the shortest approaches to the state's two highest peaks, Mt. Marcy and Algonquin Peak, as well as numerous other hikes. Heart Lake and the surrounding property, known as the Heart Lake Program Center, are owned by the Adirondack Mountain Club and maintained for the benefit of the hiking public as well as members of the club. Facilities for hikers include Adirondak Loj* which offers overnight accommodations and meals; a campground, including lean-tos; and the High Peaks Information Center (HPIC). There is also parking for approximately 200 cars. The daily parking fee, $10 (as of 2012) and $5 for ADK members, helps to maintain this public facility and to support ADK's trails, conservation, and education programs.

Note: Parking is not permitted on the final mile of the entrance road. In recent years the parking lot has reached capacity on most long holiday weekends.

▶ Trailhead: Heart Lake is reached by turning S from NY 73, 4 mi SE of Lake Placid Village. There is a sign for the Adirondak Loj as well as a large DEC sign, "Trails to the High Peaks." The first mile of the road is open, offering views of many of the peaks that can be reached from Heart Lake. At 3.8 mi a gravel road, Meadow Ln., also marked with DEC signs, goes L to South Meadow, and at 4.8 mi one reaches a small entrance booth. Past the entrance booth, turn L for the parking lot and the High Peaks Information Center (HPIC). (Road R leads to the Loj.) At the HPIC, maps, guidebooks, and information are available as well as snacks, limited outdoor supplies, showers, and a dry area for packing up. ◀

❋ Trails in winter: The Heart Lake section has more trails suitable for skiing than either the St. Huberts or Keene Valley sections; nonetheless, a majority is suitable only for snowshoe travel unless specifically noted as ski routes. Crampons are likely to be needed either for the open summits or on any steep trail after a thaw-freeze cycle. Additional precautions and equipment such as a face mask may be needed above timberline.

Trying to select the best trails or loop trips in this region is difficult because almost every destination is both attractive and popular, but the following are some of the better possibilities this area offers.

SHORT HIKES

Mt. Jo: 2.3 mi (3.7 km) round-trip. Superior views of the High Peaks and Heart Lake for very little overall effort. See trail 77.

Rocky Falls: 4.8 mi (7.7 km) round-trip. An easy walk along the start of the Indian Pass trail to an attractive series of waterfalls and a large pool for swimming. See trail 75.

---

*Adirondak Loj is spelled as it is because its builder was Melvil Dewey, champion of "simplified spelling." Dewey was founder of the Lake Placid Club, which acquired the Loj property around 1900. The original Adirondack Lodge, built by Henry Van Hoevenberg, was destroyed in a forest fire in 1903. The Adirondack Mountain Club now owns the property and its facilities.

MODERATE HIKES

Phelps Mt.: 8.8 mi (14.2 km) round-trip. A wonderful close-up view of Mt. Marcy and other peaks without too much steep climbing. See trails 61 and 62.

Avalanche Lake: 10 mi (16.1 km) round-trip. A relatively flat hike through Avalanche Pass and on to the S end of the lake with spectacular cliffs on both sides. See trails 61 and 68.

HARDER HIKES

Mt. Colden with return via Avalanche Pass: 13.8 mi (22.3 km) round-trip. This loop takes in the summit of Mt. Colden with its view of Mt. Marcy, Algonquin Peak, Avalanche Lake, and Lake Colden, with a return through the spectacular Avalanche Pass. See trails 61, 68, 70, 73, and 74.

Algonquin and Iroquois peaks with return via Avalanche Pass: 13.5 mi (21.8 km) round-trip. This loop takes in the state's second highest peak with the option of a side trip to more remote Iroquois plus a return through the spectacular Avalanche Pass. See trails 64, 66, 68, 69, 70.

Mt. Colden from Flowed Lands. Henning Vahlenkamp

61 Mt. Marcy via Van Hoevenberg Trail

ADK High Peaks Map: D8–D10 | Trails Illustrated Map 742: Z23

This is one of the oldest and by far the most popular route to Mt. Marcy because it is the shortest route by over 1.5 mi. It was laid out by Henry Van Hoevenberg, builder of the original Adirondack Lodge, in the 1880s. The trail has been rerouted several times over the years as heavy use caused erosion, but the reroutes generally follow the original line that manages to ascend to the summit at a relatively easy grade. Mt. Marcy is the only major peak (save Whiteface Mt. via the highway) that can readily be skied by advanced skiers, and sections of the Van Hoevenberg Trail were widened in the 1930s to make skiing easier.

In the past few years, ADK and DEC trail crews have done extensive work on this trail and have stemmed the steady deterioration caused by erosion. The trail is now in better overall shape than it was 30 years ago, and it is a fine example of how modern trail work can both improve the hiking experience and protect the surrounding resource.

▶ Trailhead: The trail begins at the end of the parking lot near the Adirondack Mountain Club's HPIC. (See p. 95 for further directions.) ◀

Leaving the trail register (0.0 mi), it proceeds on the level, and then descends to a bridge over Algonquin Brook at 0.4 mi. At the far side of the bridge, the trail continues across a swampy area on a boardwalk and then turns R and up, while a ski route continues straight ahead. The trail now climbs away from the brook, passes several other ski trail jcts. and reaches a jct. at 1 mi, where the Algonquin Peak trail (trail 64) with yellow markers goes straight ahead. The original route of the Van Hoevenberg Trail comes in from the R.

Turning L, the trail proceeds mostly on the flat, with a few short climbs, to the L bank of Marcy Brook at 1.9 mi. Swinging R, it climbs two short pitches, levels off, and then drops slightly to the now-breached dam that once held back Marcy Dam Pond at 2.3 mi. The trail swings sharp L and down to the new (2012) bridge over Marcy Brook, which is located approximately 75 yd downstream from the breached dam. After crossing the brook, the Van Hoevenberg Trail comes to a jct. with the South Meadow Truck Trail (trail 78), turns R, and reaches the E side of the breached dam where there are views of Mt. Colden, Avalanche Mt., and Wright Peak. A trail register is located to the L with the DEC Interior Outpost at Marcy Dam located 50 yd due E from the trail register. (The yellow-marked truck trail is an alternate approach to Marcy Dam. It is 2.7 mi from Meadow Ln. or 3.6 mi from Adirondack Loj Rd. when Meadow Ln. is closed during the winter.)

There are four lean-tos and numerous designated campsites at this popular camping area. One lean-to is located on the E side of the former pond and three more are on the W side. A trail circles the pond and gives access to these lean-tos and campsites. Note that under current High Peaks regulations no campfires are permitted at any campsites here or in the rest of the Eastern High Peaks. (See introduction, p. 23, for complete information on current use regulations.)

Turning R at the trail register, the Van Hoevenberg Trail comes, in just over 100 yd, to a jct. with the Avalanche Pass Trail (trail 68), which leads R with yellow markers. Bearing L at this jct., the trail, still with blue markers, climbs gradually to the L bank of Phelps Brook at 2.5 mi. (Bridge on L crossing the brook is the high-water route and also the approach to a designated campsite. Turn R at far end of bridge to rejoin main trail in 125 yd.) Bearing R, the trail continues up the L bank of Phelps Brook to a crossing at 2.6 mi, with the high-water route rejoining the trail at the far side. Now climbing at a steady, easy to moderate grade along the R bank of the brook, the trail comes to a designated campsite on the L at 2.9

mi and then a jct. at 3.2 mi with red trail L leading 1.2 mi to summit of Phelps Mt. (trail 62).

Bearing R, the trail continues at the same easy grade to a bridge over Phelps Brook at 3.5 mi, after which it climbs steeply to a four-way jct. at 3.6 mi. The trails going straight ahead and L at this point are two variations of the ski route that take a slightly longer course from here to Indian Falls. (These trails are intended for winter use only.) The Van Hoevenberg Trail turns sharp R and climbs at a steady, moderate grade with some steeper pitches until finally easing off at 4.1 mi. Now crossing several wet areas, the trail climbs again at an easy grade to the jct. at the upper end of the ski route at 4.4 mi, (unmarked path to Table Top L), where it turns R and quickly arrives at a height of land just before Indian Falls. From here there is a view of Mt. Marcy straight ahead. (Owing to excessive deterioration, camping is currently prohibited in the vicinity of Indian Falls.)

Just past this height of land, the trail comes to the R bank of Marcy Brook, which it crosses (no bridge) at 4.4 mi. About 50 yd to the R and down from this point is the top of Indian Falls, with a spectacular view of the MacIntyre Range from the flat, open rocks. Just beyond the brook crossing, the trail comes to a jct. with the yellow trail leading R in 0.8 mi to the Lake Arnold trail (trail 63). Turning L at this jct., the trail climbs at an easy to moderate grade to a level spot at 5 mi, drops down slightly, and then begins climbing steeply at 5.2 mi. At 5.4 mi, the grade begins to ease off as the trail approaches the top of a ridge where there are views of Mt. Marcy. Continuing along the ridge with only a few short rises, the trail comes to a jct. at 6.2 mi. Yellow trail L is the Hopkins Trail to Keene Valley (trail 2).

Bearing R and slightly down, the trail passes the former site of the Hopkins Lean-to in 200 yd and then climbs to the former site of Plateau Lean-to at 6.5 mi, with the summit dome of Marcy in full view. Dipping briefly across a small stream, the trail then climbs through thick scrub to the jct. with the red-marked Phelps Trail (trail 1), which comes in from the L at 6.8 mi.

Swinging R, the trail makes a short climb to some bare rocks where there is the first close view of the summit. (This point marks the beginning of the arctic-alpine zone where hikers must walk only on the marked trail or bare rock to preserve the fragile vegetation.) The trail then dips, climbs a bit, and crosses a large high-altitude sphagnum bog on a boardwalk before climbing up to the first rocky shoulder of Marcy at 7 mi. Briefly leveling off, the trail now climbs over mostly bare rock and is marked with cairns and yellow paint blazes. Use care when following the trail, especially in poor weather. Proceeding up the bare rocks, the trail reaches the smaller E summit and flattens out for a few yd before coming to the true summit at 7.4 mi. From the summit, the yellow trail leading to Lake Colden (trail 121) and Elk Lake (trail 118) continues down the SW slope.

❈ Trail in winter: This trail can be skied to Marcy Dam with six inches of cover, but heavy foot traffic often makes the surface less than ideal. Beyond Marcy Dam the trail becomes steeper and is definitely for experienced skiers only, although for those capable of handling the descent, Marcy is one of the classic ski mountaineering trips in the East.

👥 Distances: Adirondak Loj to Marcy Dam, 2.3 mi; to Indian Falls, 4.4 mi; to Hopkins Trail, 6.2 mi; to Phelps Trail, 6.8 mi; to summit of Mt. Marcy, 7.4 mi (11.9 km). Ascent, 3166 ft (965 m). Elevation, 5344 ft (1629 m). Order of height, 1.

62 Phelps Mt.

ADK High Peaks Map: D9 | Trails Illustrated Map 742: Y24

Phelps Mt. is named for Orson Schofield Phelps, better known as "Old Mountain" Phelps, who cut the first trail up Mt. Marcy and over the years guided many parties to its summit. It is thus fitting that this peak whose view is so dominated by Mt. Marcy is named after Phelps, even though he probably never climbed the peak himself. Phelps Mt. is the easiest high peak to climb from the Marcy Dam area, and is thus a good alternative for Marcy-bound parties who find themselves short of time.

▶ Locator: This red-marked trail turns L from the Van Hoevenberg Trail to Mt. Marcy (trail 61) at a point 1 mi from Marcy Dam or 3.2 mi from Adirondak Loj. ◀

From the jct. (0.0 mi), the trail immediately climbs away from the Van Hoevenberg Trail on a moderate grade and continues with occasional steeper pitches to the first open rock at 1.1 mi. The red markers are now supplemented by yellow paint blazes as the trail soon comes to a second rocky outcrop with views of Marcy Dam. From here, the trail is mostly flat to large open ledges at the summit at 1.2 mi.

👥 Distances: Adirondak Loj to start of Phelps Trail, 3.2 mi; to summit of Phelps Mt., 4.4 mi (7.1 km). Ascent from Adirondak Loj, 1982 ft (604 m). Elevation, 4161 ft (1269 m). Order of height, 32.

Phelps Mountain. James Appleyard

Table Top Mt. *(Unmarked path; see introduction, p. 19.)*

ADK High Peaks Map: D9 | Trails Illustrated Map 742: Y24

In 1997, this route became the first "herd path" to be officially designated, or defined, to keep hikers on the most durable terrain. The path branches L from the Van Hoevenberg Trail (trail 61) just below Indian Falls at the jct. with the ski route, 4.4 mi from Adirondak Loj. Heading generally SE and marked with a few red markers at the start, the path gains the summit plateau in just over 0.5 mi, after which a few hundred yards of up and down lead to the summit at the S end of the plateau. The summit canister has been removed and replaced with a wooden sign to mark the summit. A few yards past the summit, a small open area provides a limited view of Mt. Marcy and neighboring peaks.

63 Indian Falls–Lake Arnold Crossover

ADK High Peaks Map: D9 | Trails Illustrated Map 742: Y24

▶ Locator: From the Van Hoevenberg Trail to Mt. Marcy (trail 61) at Indian Falls, 4.5 mi from Adirondak Loj, a trail with yellow markers branches R and connects with the blue trail to Lake Arnold and Feldspar Brook from Avalanche Camp (trail 73). It provides a connection between Indian Falls and Lake Colden without a traverse of Mt. Marcy or a descent to Marcy Dam. ◀

Leaving the jct. (0.0 mi) just above the brook crossing at Indian Falls, the trail descends for 75 yd to a good view of Indian Falls from below. In another few yards, the trail swings L and away from the original route of the Van Hoevenberg Trail, climbs briefly, and then begins a descent to a sharp L turn at 0.6 mi. From here, the trail climbs gradually, crosses an extensive wet area, and reaches the R bank of a stream. Following the R bank for a few yards, the trail crosses on the rocks to the jct. with the Lake Arnold trail at 0.8 mi. (Turn R for Avalanche Camp, 1 mi; L for Lake Arnold, 0.5 mi.)

🚶 Distance: Indian Falls to Lake Arnold trail, 0.8 mi (1.3 km).

THE MACINTYRE RANGE*

ADK High PeaksMap: C10–D9 | Trails Illustrated Map 742: Y22-23

The series of peaks known as the MacIntyre Mts., or the MacIntyre Range, rises loftily against the sky S of Heart Lake. Named in honor of Archibald McIntyre, the dominating figure in the Tahawus iron works enterprise that bore his name, this is one of the noblest groups of peaks in the Adirondacks. Standing apart from all surrounding peaks, the range extends for about 8 mi, running NE and SW. Its steep SW slopes form one side of Indian Pass and the NE spur forms the spectacular cliffs of Avalanche Pass.

The most northerly major peak is Wright Peak, 4580 ft, named after Governor Silas Wright. A lesser peak NE of Wright is called Whales Tail because of its shape when viewed from Marcy Dam. The NE shoulder of Wright, adjacent to Whales Tail, is sometimes referred to as "the Whale" and offers some interesting views for those willing to make the short bushwhack up to this point from the ski trail in Whales Tail Notch (trail 67).

To the SW of Wright is Algonquin Peak, 5114 ft, the highest peak in the range and second highest in the Adirondacks. Algonquin has also been called Mt. MacIntyre and is still referred to as such on a few DEC trail signs. SW of Algonquin Peak stands Boundary Peak, so named because it is supposed to have marked the boundary between the Algonquin and Iroquois Indian tribes. In reality, it stands

---

*The spelling of *MacIntyre* conforms to the USGS topographic map, which has been approved by the U. S. Board of Geographic Names. It is used throughout this guidebook for consistency, but the man for whom the range is named spelled his name *McIntyre*.

on the southern boundary of the Old Military Tract that was originally surveyed in 1797 by Charles Brodhead, who thus lays claim to the first ascent in the MacIntyre Range—40 years before Ebenezer Emmons first climbed Algonquin Peak in 1837. Although high enough to count as one of the 46 high peaks, Boundary Peak is considered merely a prominence on the ridge to Iroquois Peak.

At 4840 ft, Iroquois is the second highest peak in the range and the eighth highest in the Adirondacks. Its rocky summit offers many fine views, particularly of the cliffs of Wallface Mt. in Indian Pass.

Farther to the SW and separated from Iroquois Peak by a deep valley is Mt. Marshall. Verplanck Colvin first named this peak in honor of Governor DeWitt Clinton of Erie Canal fame. Colvin at first attached the name to the peak we now call Iroquois, but later transferred it to this southernmost peak of the MacIntyre Range. For some time this peak was also called Herbert in honor of Herbert Clark, the Marshall family's guide and one of the three original 46ers. After Robert Marshall's death in 1939, the Adirondack Forty-Sixers successfully petitioned the New York State Board of Geographic Names to officially name this peak Mt. Marshall. Even though the Board accepted this name, it was labeled Clinton on the 1954 USGS maps. The 1978 USGS Ampersand Lake 15' x 7½' metric series sheet, however, does show this peak as Mt. Marshall.

Robert (Bob) Marshall, with his brother George, drew up the original list of the 46 peaks and with Herb Clark became the first to climb them all. Bob Marshall was a noted forester, explorer, author, and conservationist. The naming of the 1,000,000-acre Bob Marshall Wilderness Area in western Montana is another tribute to his accomplishments.

64 Algonquin Peak from Heart Lake

ADK High Peaks Map: D9 | Trails Illustrated Map 742: Z23

Algonquin Peak is a spectacular and popular peak. Becoming progressively steeper as it approaches the summit, this trail will seem far longer than its actual length, and some recent reroutes have actually added a few tenths of a mile to it.

▶ Locator: This trail leads generally SW from its jct. with the Van Hoevenberg Trail (trail 61), 1 mi S of Adirondak Loj. (See p. 95 for further directions.) ◀

From the Adirondack Mountain Club's HPIC (0.0 mi), take the Van Hoevenberg Trail (trail 61) to a jct. at 1 mi. Here the trail to Algonquin Peak continues straight ahead. (Trail L leads to Marcy Dam.) Continuing at a generally easy grade with a few steeper pitches, the trail reaches the jct. with the Whales Tail Notch Ski Trail (trail 67) at 1.5 mi. Bearing R and up at this jct., the generally rough and rocky trail climbs moderately to steeply along the lower portion of what was originally cut as the Wright Peak Ski Trail. Crossing a brook at 2 mi, the trail veers R on a switchback and then continues its rocky ascent to the base of a small cliff at 2.5 mi. (Trail going L above this cliff is a ski trail that does not reach a summit and should not be used in the summer.) Here the trail to Algonquin and Wright turns R and is briefly narrow and flat as it crosses over to the old hiking trail. A rock scramble now leads to a side trail L to a designated campsite with the base of a waterfall 100 yd beyond at 2.6 mi.

After this waterfall, the trail climbs a short, steep pitch, levels out for a bit, and then climbs again steeply to a flat area at 3.1 mi with a small rock cobble on the R. Turning L and up, the trail climbs over one steep rock step, after which the grade eases a bit across a sidehill before reaching the jct. with the spur trail to Wright Peak (trail 65) at 3.4 mi.

Bearing R at this jct., the Algonquin trail begins to climb steeply, going up over several sections of smooth rock and leveling out just before reaching timberline at 3.9 mi. (This point marks the start of the arctic-alpine zone where hikers must remain on the marked trail or bare rock to protect the fragile vegetation.) From timberline the trail is marked with cairns and yellow paint blazes. A large expanse of grass L just before the summit is the best example to date of the successful restoration efforts developed by the late Prof. E. H. Ketchledge, PhD, of the SUNY College of Environmental Science and Forestry, and now proving successful on other summits as well.

Reaching the actual summit at 4.3 mi, the trail meets the Lake Colden trail (trail 71) coming up the SW slope and similarly marked with cairns and yellow paint blazes. The view from the summit is spectacular and expansive, highlighted by the view of Mt. Colden with its many slides and famous dike, or cleft, as well as by the view of Lake Colden and Flowed Lands at the foot of the mountain. The distant view encompasses most of the high peaks to the E and S, with many lakes visible to the W and N.

On the descent, hikers should pay close attention to the markers, especially in poor weather. The route down generally traverses slightly to the R across the fall line to reach the trail at timberline.

🚶 Distances: Adirondak Loj via blue trail to jct. with yellow trail for Algonquin Peak, 1 mi; to blue trail to Wright Peak, 3.4 mi; to summit of Algonquin Peak, 4.3 mi (6.9 km). Ascent, 2936 ft (895 m). Elevation, 5114 ft (1559 m). Order of height, 2.

65 Wright Peak

ADK High Peaks Map: D9 | Trails Illustrated Map 742: Y23

▶ Locator: The blue-marked trail to Wright Peak diverges L from the yellow trail to Algonquin Peak (trail 64) 3.4 mi from Adirondak Loj. ◀

Leaving the trail jct. (0.0 mi), the trail climbs steadily to timberline at 0.2 mi, after which the route is marked with cairns up the bare rock ridge. Soon after timberline the grade eases, with the summit reached at 0.4 mi.

A bronze plaque on a large vertical rock face just N (350° magnetic) of the summit memorializes four airmen who lost their lives in the crash of a U.S. Air Force B-47 bomber at that spot in 1962. Some parts of the ill-fated aircraft are still scattered around the area close to the top of the mountain.

🏃 Distances: Adirondak Loj to blue trail for Wright Peak, 3.4 mi; to summit of Wright Peak, 3.8 mi (6.1 km). Ascent from Adirondak Loj, 2400 ft (732 m). Elevation, 4580 ft (1396 m). Order of height, 16.

66   Boundary and Iroquois Peaks

(Minimum maintenance and marking; see introduction, p. 19.)

ADK High Peaks Map: D9 | Trails Illustrated Map 742: Y23

Although not an official trail, there is a reasonably well-defined route from the col between Algonquin and Boundary peaks along the mostly open ridge to Iroquois Peak. The trail is marked with cairns in the open areas, but there are no other signs or markers. In 1975, the Adirondack Forty-Sixers improved this trail somewhat, mainly to establish a route around a unique alpine bog on Boundary Peak, to prevent the bog from being trampled. More recently (2013) some major bog bridging has been added to further protect the unique vegetation. The route has remained reasonably well defined.

▶ Locator: The trail leaves the Lake Colden trail to Algonquin Peak (trail 71) 0.4 mi below the Algonquin summit, at a large cairn at timberline. The "herd path" for Iroquois goes straight ahead; the marked trail for Lake Colden swings L and down. ◀

Leaving the col (0.0 mi), the route climbs quickly to the first summit of Boundary Peak, dips down and bypasses the above-mentioned bog on the R, and comes to the summit of Boundary Peak at 0.2 mi. The route now descends over open rock, enters the woods for a few hundred yards, and finally climbs steeply up and slightly L to the summit of Iroquois Peak at 0.7 mi from the Algonquin trail.

🏃 Distances: Algonquin Peak summit to start of "herd path," 0.4 mi; to summit of Iroquois Peak, 1.1 mi (1.8 km). Elevation, 4840 ft (1476 m). Order of height, 8.

67   Whales Tail Notch Ski Trail

ADK High Peaks Map: D9 | Trails Illustrated Map 742: Y23

▶ Locator: This trail leads from Marcy Dam over a notch NE of Wright Peak to a point on the Algonquin trail. The trail is quite rough and is not maintained for summer travel. It does offer a 0.5 mi shorter approach to the Algonquin trail for those camped at Marcy Dam, but this saving in distance is not great when compared to the rough footing and 380 ft vertical climb through Whales Tail Notch.

The start of the Whales Tail Notch Ski Trail, which has no sign, is at the top of a slight rise a few yards from the W end of Marcy Dam on the Van Hoevenberg Trail (trail 61). ◀

Leaving the jct. (0.0 mi), proceed past the first lean-to to a trail R approximately 100 yd from the Van Hoevenberg Trail. (Trail straight ahead leads around Marcy Dam to other lean-tos and campsites.) Turning R, the trail proceeds mostly on the level through open forest before starting to climb at 0.3 mi. The climb is steady and becomes steeper near the height of land. Easing off at 0.6 mi, the trail reaches the actual top of the pass at 0.8 mi, having gained approximately 380 ft from Marcy Dam. Now starting down a slightly easier grade than that just ascended, and going in and out of a small brook, the trail reaches the Algonquin trail (trail 64) at 1.3 mi.

❄ Trail in winter: As the name implies, this was cut as a ski trail and is therefore a bit wider than most hiking trails. The Marcy Dam side is steeper and more of a challenge to ski down, while the other side has been badly eroded over the years and requires at least a foot of snow to be skiable. Skied in either direction, it is recommended only for advanced skiers.

🚶 Distance: Marcy Dam to Algonquin trail, 1.3 mi (2.1 km).

68 Avalanche Pass to Lake Colden

ADK High Peaks Map: D9 | Trails Illustrated Map 742: Y23

The trail through Avalanche Pass is probably the most spectacular route in the Adirondacks. Sheer rock walls rise directly out of the water on both sides of Avalanche Lake, and the trail is forced to wind among large boulders and even cross two catwalks set into the rock face in order to negotiate this impressive piece of terrain. At the actual top of the pass, a spectacular 1999 slide reaches the trail, adding to the expanses of steep rock viewed along this route. This is the most popular approach to Lake Colden and is much used. Backpackers should be aware, however, that this is a very rough trail in spots. Allow plenty of time so as not to have to rush. Many parties, for instance, find that it takes an hour to cover the 1 mi section from the top of the pass to the lower end of Avalanche Lake.

▶ Locator: The Avalanche Pass trail diverges R from the Van Hoevenberg Trail to Mt. Marcy (trail 61) at Marcy Dam just over 100 yd past the trail register. ◀

Leaving Marcy Dam (0.0 mi) and marked with yellow DEC disks, the trail proceeds along the flat for 200 yd where a trail leads R and over a bridge to additional lean-tos and campsites. Bearing L and still on the flat, the trail soon comes to the R bank of Marcy Brook, which it now follows. At 0.4 mi the trail swings away from the brook and soon crosses two small bridges. At the second bridge, an obscure trail leads R to Kagel Lean-to. Continuing up a gradual climb, the trail passes Marcy Brook Lean-to on the R at 0.8 mi and then crosses Marcy Brook on a bridge before reaching a jct. with the blue trail L to Lake Arnold (trail 73) at 1.1 mi. This jct. is also the former site of the Avalanche Camp lean-to. The lean-to is now approx. 200 yd uphill to the R of the former lean-to site.

Continuing R, the Avalanche Pass trail crosses a wet area and begins to climb steeply with several log stairs. At 1.2 mi the trail swings sharp L, and continues climbing as it comes to a jct. where the ski trail crosses at 1.3 mi. (This ski trail follows a slightly longer route down from the top of the pass and eventually joins the Lake Arnold trail just above Avalanche Camp. It is extremely rough and not suited for summer travel.) Continuing straight ahead, the trail swings R at 1.4 mi, where the ski trail again crosses, and then continues on to the top of the pass at 1.6 mi. A large slide in September 1999 deposited much debris here—raising the top of the pass by 25–30 vertical feet.

The trail now descends toward Avalanche Lake, which it reaches at 2.1 mi. The precipitous slopes of Mt. Colden rise on the left, while the even steeper slopes of Avalanche Mt. rise on the R. The trail proceeds along the R side and is quite rugged, but interesting—passing over ledges, around huge boulders, and across crevices aided by ladders and bridges. At two places the cliffs rise directly out of the water, and only bridges bolted into the cliff make the passage possible. These structures

are known as "Hitch-up Matildas" after a lady of that name who was carried across this section on the back of her guide. As the water became deeper, her husband stood on the shore exhorting her to "hitch up, Matilda!" The scene was recorded by an artist for *Harper's* magazine, whose drawing made this location famous.

Avalanche Lake. James Bullard

From the second such bridge at 2.5 mi, there is an impressive view directly up the slide of Mt. Colden, with the Trap Dike just to the left. The largest slides date from 1869, 1942, and 2011. The deep cleft of the Trap Dike was caused by the differential erosion of the gabbro dike intruded into the native anorthosite granite.

The trail reaches the foot of the lake at 2.6 mi, crosses the outlet, and follows down the L bank. There is a trail L 200 yd past the outlet, which leads in 125 yd to a designated campsite. Continuing down, the trail reaches a jct. and register box at 2.9 mi. The blue trail R leads around the NW shore of Lake Colden to the DEC Interior Outpost and then on to the dam at the outlet (see trail 69). (Unmarked trail straight ahead is the winter route to the north shore of Lake Colden.) Bearing L, the yellow trail leads to the E shore of Lake Colden and then along the shore to the jct. with the red trail leading L to Mt. Colden (trail 70) at 3.4 mi. Continuing on, the trail reaches the register at the jct. with the red trail to Marcy (trail 121) at 3.8 mi. Trail R leads 200 yd to a bridge and dam at the outlet, from which the red trail continues on to Flowed Lands and Lake Sanford. The far side of the dam is also the end of the blue trail around the NW shore of Lake Colden.

There are now just five lean-tos at Lake Colden where there were once as many as 13. This reduction in numbers is an attempt to reduce the physical deterioration of this popular camping area by offering fewer attractions for campers. One of the remaining lean-tos is located on the L (E) bank of the Opalescent River below the Lake Colden outlet and are reached by crossing the river (in high water, use the suspension bridge just upstream on the Mt. Marcy trail) and following the trail down the L bank. Two other lean-tos are located on a point on the S shore of Lake Colden and are reached by crossing the dam and turning R for 175 yd. The other two lean-tos are located a short distance down the trail to Flowed Lands and are reached by turning L after crossing the dam. There are designated campsites at many spots along both banks of the Opalescent River set back behind the trails that run along the river. No campfires may be built here or in any other part of the Eastern High Peaks. (See introduction, pp. 22–24, for complete information on current use regulations.)

❄ Trail in winter: The ski through Avalanche Pass and across the lakes is a classic tour and available to any strong intermediate skier. It is not uncommon to see more than 100 skiers on this trail when conditions are good. To be skiable, Avalanche Pass needs at least one foot, and preferably more, of snow. Crossing Avalanche Lake when it is windy can present problems similar to being above timberline; goggles and a face mask may be necessary.

Caution: At the top of Avalanche Pass, the DEC has placed signs alerting winter users to the potential danger of an avalanche from the new slide above the pass. Prudence dictates not lingering in this area. To reduce the chance of a human-caused avalanche, the DEC also prohibits skiing or climbing on the slide during snow season.

🥾 Distances: Marcy Dam to Avalanche Camp, 1.1 mi; to Avalanche Lake, 2.1 mi; to trail around NW shore of Lake Colden, 2.9 mi; to jct. with Mt. Marcy trail at Lake Colden, 3.8 mi (6.1 km). From Heart Lake, 6.1 mi (9.8 km).

69 Lake Colden Northwest Shore Trail

ADK High Peaks Map: D10 | Trails Illustrated Map 742: Y23

▶ Locator: Starting at the trail jct. 0.3 mi from the foot of Avalanche Lake or 2.9 mi from Marcy Dam, this trail connects with the Algonquin trail (trail 71), the DEC Interior Outpost on Lake Colden, and the Cold Brook Pass Trail to Indian Pass (trail 72). ◀

Leaving the jct. (0.0 mi), follow blue markers across a brook and continues on the level to the L bank of a stream at 0.4 mi and the jct. with the yellow trail leading R 2.1 mi to the summit of Algonquin Peak (trail 71). Continuing L across the bridge, the trail reaches a trail register at 0.6 mi. (Side trail L leads 150 yd to the DEC Interior Outpost on Lake Colden.) Continuing R, the trail immediately comes to the jct. with the yellow trail leading straight ahead 3.3 mi to Cold Brook Pass and the Indian Pass trail (trail 72). The blue trail turns sharp L, crosses Cold Brook, and swings L and back to Lake Colden. Near the S end of the lake there are now three designated campsites (marked with yellow campsite disks) up and to the R of the trail. Rounding the S end of the lake, the trail passes Beaver Point Lean-to on the L at 0.9 mi and West Lean-to 50 yd later. (The latter is named in honor of Clinton West, a ranger at Lake Colden for many years. This lean-to has also been called Cedar Point.) The trail swings R and comes to the dam at the outlet and the jct. with the Calamity Brook Trail (trail 121) at 1 mi, ending the blue markers. Red trail straight ahead leads to two additional lean-tos, Flowed Lands, and Upper Works. Trail L crosses the dam and leads to Mt. Marcy and the other lean-to and campsites described above.

🚶 Distances: Jct. with yellow trail to DEC Interior Outpost, 0.6 mi; to dam at outlet, 1 mi (1.6 km). From Heart Lake, 6.3 mi (10.2 km).

70 Mt. Colden from Lake Colden

ADK High Peaks Map: D10 | Trails Illustrated Map 742: Y23

Though seemingly dwarfed by its neighbors Mt. Marcy and Algonquin Peak, Mt. Colden is perhaps even more interesting with the extensive slides and unique large dike on its W side. Forming the SE rampart of Avalanche Pass, Mt. Colden offers an unforgettable view practically straight down from its summit to the inky depths of Avalanche Lake. Mt. Colden was named for David C. Colden, one of the proprietors of the McIntyre Iron Works.

Professor Ebenezer Emmons later tried to name it Mt. McMartin in honor of another leader in the McIntyre Iron Works, but the first name has endured. The trail from Lake Colden is very rough and steep, with the approach from Lake Arnold generally preferred. Ascending from Lake Arnold with a descent via this trail and a return via Avalanche Pass, however, makes for one of the most spectacular and interesting circuits in the mountains.

▶ Locator: The trail starts on the E side of Lake Colden, 0.4 mi NE from Lake Colden Outlet and 5.8 mi from Adirondak Loj (trail 68). ◀

Leaving the yellow-marked trail (0.0 mi), the red-marked trail immediately climbs several steep log steps but then eases off as it continues at a steady grade through a thick spruce forest. At 0.6 mi the trail swings L and up a ladder and begins a nearly unrelenting steep climb—much of it over trail washed right down to bare rock.

Finally moderating at 1.3 mi, the trail passes under two huge boulders and soon comes to a ladder leading up a small cliff to a flat area above. (This point marks the start of the arctic-alpine zone where hikers must remain on the marked trail or bare rock to protect the fragile vegetation.) Veering L, the trail emerges onto open rock and then veers back R and up a bare rock step to the top of the ridge just below the summit. When descending this section, follow the markers very carefully; it is easy to lose the trail and there is only one route to the ladder that makes it possible to get past the cliffs.

After a short, level stretch on the ridge, the trail climbs a final rock step and arrives at a large open area just S of the actual summit. Extensive reseeding has been done on the "lawn" just S of the balanced boulder. Step or sit only on the bare rock to avoid undoing this restoration. Here is the best view of Lake Colden and Flowed Lands, but just beyond at a large balanced boulder on the L is a view of

Avalanche Lake and the "Hitch-up Matildas" (see trail 68, p. 105) with the actual summit just beyond at 1.6 mi. Here the Lake Colden trail (trail 70) meets the L. Morgan Porter Trail (trail 74), which leads 1.4 mi to Lake Arnold.

👫 Distances: Lake Colden to summit of Mt. Colden, 1.6 mi (2.6 km). Ascent from Lake Colden, 1950 ft (595 m). Elevation, 4714 ft (1437 m). Order of height, 11.

71   Algonquin Peak from Lake Colden

ADK High Peaks Map: D10 | Trails Illustrated Map 742: Y23

This trail leads 2.1 mi from the trail on the NW shore of Lake Colden to the summit of Algonquin Peak. (For additional information on Algonquin Peak and the MacIntyre Range, see trail 64 and p. 101, respectively.) The trail climbs 2350 ft from Lake Colden to the summit, which makes this one of the most continuously steep climbs in the mountains. As a route between Lake Colden and Heart Lake, this trail up and over Algonquin Peak is only slightly longer than the Avalanche Pass Trail, but it will require at least an additional hour for day hikers and several additional hours for backpackers. Extensive trail work in recent years has stabilized and improved the footing on this trail, but it is still a serious undertaking for backpackers.

▶ Locator: The trail begins 0.2 mi NE of the Lake Colden DEC Interior Outpost at a bridge on the trail around the NW shore of Lake Colden (trail 69), 0.4 mi from its jct. with the Avalanche Pass trail (trail 68). ◀

Leaving this jct. (0.0 mi), the yellow-marked trail climbs moderately at first along the L bank of the stream. Reaching the top of a cataract at 0.2 mi, the grade soon eases and the trail comes to its first stream crossing at 0.3 mi. The trail crosses and recrosses the brook several times, finally returning to the L bank at 0.5 mi. Shortly after, the grade

Algonquin summit. Todd Martin

again steepens, and the trail reaches the foot of a waterfall at 0.6 mi. Jogging R to get around the falls, the trail then enters the stream bed and climbs the sloping ledges next to the stream, where there are some fine views of the slides of Mt. Colden.

The trail leaves the brook at 0.7 mi and continues steeply up the L bank, with only occasional slight breathers. At 0.9 mi the trail again crosses the brook and winds among the boulders on the R bank, returning to the L bank just before it reaches a big pool at 1 mi. The trail now climbs away from the brook on a steady, steep grade, returns a few hundred yards later, and again leaves the stream before finally crossing to the R bank for the last time. There is a very steep pitch up the bank of the brook before the trail settles down to being merely steep to timberline, just above the col between Boundary and Algonquin peaks, which is reached at 1.7 mi. (This point marks the start of the arctic-alpine zone where hikers must remain on the marked trail or bare rock to protect the fragile vegetation.) An unmarked trail leads L to Boundary and Iroquois peaks (trail 66). Following cairns and yellow paint blazes, the trail reaches the summit of Algonquin Peak at 2.1 mi, where it meets the trail from Heart Lake (trail 64).

🐾 Distances: Jct. with blue trail around NW shore of Lake Colden to waterfall, 0.6 mi; to trail to Boundary and Iroquois peaks, 1.7 mi; to summit of Algonquin Peak, 2.1 mi (3.4 km). Ascent from Lake Colden, 2350 ft (717 m). Elevation, 5114 ft (1559 m). Order of height, 2.

72 Cold Brook Pass Trail from Lake Colden to Indian Pass Trail

ADK High Peaks Map: D10 | Trails Illustrated Map 742: Y23

Cut in 1965, this trail leads from the trail on the NW shore of Lake Colden (trail 69), near the Interior Outpost, through Cold Brook Pass between Iroquois Peak and Mt. Marshall. This pass has previously been called Algonquin Pass or Iroquois Pass, but the DEC now refers to it as Cold Brook Pass to eliminate any confusion with the trails leading to the summits of Algonquin or Iroquois peaks. This trail is quite steep and rough in spots, which makes for slow going—especially with backpacks—but it is a useful connection for those wishing to combine a trip through Indian Pass with a stay at Lake Colden. The trail has not seen much use recently. As of 2011 the DEC ceased maintenance on this trail, although it will remain followable for some time to come.

▶ Locator: Marked with yellow markers, this trail starts just NE of the bridge over Cold Brook on the blue trail around the NW shore of Lake Colden (trail 69). This point is 0.6 mi from the Avalanche Pass Trail jct. and 0.4 mi from Lake Colden's outlet. ◀

Leaving the jct. (0.0 mi), the trail begins at an easy grade along the L bank of Cold Brook. Crossing two small tributaries as it begins to climb, the trail then crosses

Cold Brook at 0.3 mi, just below the jct. of the two branches of Cold Brook. The trail now climbs steeply along the banks of, and sometimes in, the S branch of Cold Brook until crossing it for the last time at 0.7 mi and climbing away from the brook onto a shoulder of Iroquois Peak. Several more steep pitches lead to easier grades if not smoother footing at 1 mi as the trail begins to slab across the shoulder of Iroquois. At 1.4 mi the trail drops slightly and then climbs to the top of Cold Brook Pass at 1.5 mi, having climbed approximately 1100 ft (335 m.) from Lake Colden.

The trail is now level through the grassy col. At the W end of the flat area, a cairn on the L marks the start of the unmarked path to Mt. Marshall. The trail then begins to descend easy to moderate grades, becoming steeper at 2.2 mi. After crossing two branches of a large brook coming from the L, the trail veers away from the brook into an adjacent valley, and descends to the R bank of another large brook at 2.5 mi. The trail then joins an old tote road, veers away from the brook, and then returns to cross it at 2.7 mi.

Passing a very steep falls in the brook, the trail crosses to the R bank at 2.8 mi, recrosses at 3 mi, and climbs briefly before dropping down to a jct. with the red-marked Indian Pass trail (trail 75) at 3.3 mi. Trail L leads 1.1 mi to Summit Rock in Indian Pass. Trail R leads 1.1 mi to Scott Clearing Lean-to.

🐾 Distances: Start of trail at Lake Colden to Cold Brook Pass, 1.5 mi; to Indian Pass trail, 3.3 mi (5.3 km).

Mt. Marshall *(Unmarked paths; see introduction, p. 19.)*

ADK High Peaks Map: C10–D10 | Trails Illustrated Map 742: Y23

For the history and naming of this peak, see the introduction to the MacIntyre Range, p. 101. The more popular route leaves the Cold Brook Pass Trail (trail 72) at the W end of the flat area at the height of land between Mt. Marshall and Iroquois Peak. The jct. is marked with a cairn. Very rough for its entire length, the path climbs approximately 0.3 mi over one intermediate peak, drops down across the head of Herbert Brook, and then goes on to the summit at 0.7 mi.

A slightly less used but far prettier approach is from Flowed Lands via Herbert Brook, a very appropriate name that recognizes Herbert Clark, the Marshalls' friend and guide. This brook crosses the red-marked trail 0.7 mi NE of the Calamity lean-tos and 0.3 mi from the Lake Colden dam. The Forty-Sixers have worked to designate both these routes.

The path starts along the E bank of Herbert Brook through the blowdown. Avoid following a tributary entering from the R (going up) about 0.5 mi up the brook. Open rock slides make the ascent attractive for part of the way. As it approaches the head of the brook at just over 1 mi, the path heads L and up to the E ridge, which it follows to the summit at approximately 1.5 mi from the marked trail near Flowed Lands. A yellow plastic disk marks the summit.

73 Avalanche Camp to Lake Arnold and Feldspar Brook

ADK High Peaks Map: D9 | Trails Illustrated Map 742: Y23

Once characterized by a very rough ascent from Avalanche Camp to Lake Arnold, followed by an equally undesirable swampy finish to Feldspar Brook, this trail has received a good deal of attention from both ADK and DEC trail crews in recent years. Their efforts have made this direct route to the upper Opalescent River valley more appealing although intermittent beaver activity may make the final stretch to Feldspar Lean-to quite wet.

▶ Locator: The Lake Arnold trail begins at Avalanche Camp, 1.1 mi from Marcy Dam on the yellow-marked Avalanche Pass trail (trail 68). ◀

Marked with blue markers, the Lake Arnold trail diverges L at a signpost (0.0 mi). Beginning on a gradual grade, in 250 yd the Lake Arnold Trail turns sharp L and crosses a small brook on a bridge. (Trail straight ahead is the ski route through Avalanche Pass.) The Lake Arnold trail now begins climbing along an old tote road high above Marcy Brook. At 1.1 mi the trail reaches a jct. with a yellow-marked trail L leading 0.8 mi to Indian Falls (trail 63).

From this jct., the trail bears R and crosses a brook in 75 yd. Swinging R after this crossing, the trail continues to climb along the R bank of the brook. At 1.4 mi the trail again crosses the brook, but stays practically in the brook bed to a jct. at 1.5 mi. Yellow trail R is the L. Morgan Porter Trail (trail 74) leading 1.4 mi to Mt. Colden. Lake Arnold and the former lean-to site are a few yards to the R. Although the lean-to has been removed, this remains a designated campsite.

Continuing straight through this jct., the trail resumes its climb to Lake Arnold Pass, which it reaches at 1.8 mi, having gained 1200 ft (366 m) from Avalanche Camp. The trail now descends steeply along a small brook before easing off at 2.1 mi. Continuing a moderate descent, the trail passes the bottom of a large slide on Mt. Colden just before reaching the R bank of the Opalescent River at 2.8 mi. Crossing the river on stones, the trail veers away from the L bank, crosses some wet areas on board bridges, and at 3.1 mi returns to the bank of the Opalescent River at a bridge leading to Feldspar Lean-to. In another 60 yd the trail crosses Feldspar Brook and comes to a jct. with the yellow-marked Mt. Marcy trail from Lake Colden (trail 121) at 3.2 mi. (Turn L for Mt. Marcy, 2.4 mi; R for Lake Colden Dam, 2.2 mi.)

🚶 Distances: Avalanche Camp to Indian Falls Crossover Trail, 1.1 mi; to Lake Arnold 1.5 mi; to jct. with Mt. Marcy trail, 3.2 mi (5.2 km).

74 Mt. Colden from Lake Arnold via L. Morgan Porter Trail

ADK High Peaks Map: D10 | Trails Illustrated Map 742: Y23

This approach to Mt. Colden from Lake Arnold was laid out by Rudy Strobel in 1966 and was cut by ADK with the approval of DEC, which now maintains it. It is named in memory of the man who produced the sixth and seventh editions of this guidebook.

▶ Locator: The trail starts from the Lake Arnold trail (trail 73) near the former lean-to site by Lake Arnold. ◀

Leaving the former lean-to site (0.0 mi), the trail, marked with yellow markers, is nearly flat for a few yards along the N shore of Lake Arnold, but soon begins ascending. The climbing is not steady, with steep pitches alternating with nearly flat areas. At 0.7 mi, the climbing becomes steeper, and at 1 mi the trail emerges onto the bare N summit of Mt. Colden, from which there are some interesting views. The trail veers L and quickly descends back into the timber. (This spot is not well marked. Hikers should note that the trail does not go over this summit, a fact that has caused considerable confusion over the years. Be sure to note this spot when descending the trail.) Dropping into a small sag, the trail climbs over another small bump and then drops to the col at the base of the main peak at 1.1 mi. From here the trail climbs steadily to the end of the summit ridge at 1.3 mi. (This marks the beginning of the arctic-alpine zone where hikers must walk only on the marked trail or bare rock to preserve the fragile vegetation.) The trail then proceeds on the level to the summit at 1.4 mi where it meets the route from Lake Colden. (See trail 70 for trail description and notes on the view.)

🥾 Distances: Lake Arnold to summit of Mt. Colden, 1.4 mi (2.3 km); from Heart Lake, 6.3 mi (10.2 km). Ascent from Heart Lake, 2535 ft (773 m). Elevation, 4714 ft (1437 m). Order of height, 11.

75 Indian Pass from Heart Lake

ADK High Peaks Map: D8–C9 | Trails Illustrated Map 742: Z23

Indian Pass is a stupendous gorge between Wallface Mt. and the MacIntyre Range. The pass is over a mile in length, and its sheer NW wall rises nearly 1000 ft, which makes it one of the highest cliffs in the East, rivaled only by Cannon Cliff in Franconia Notch in the White Mountains. At places, the bottom of the gorge is an almost impassable tangle of boulders that have fallen off the cliff over the ages. There are several places where ice and snow remain throughout the year deep in caves that never see the light of day. The trail passes above this rock jumble on the

SE side of the pass; nevertheless, the going is often difficult.

▶ Trailhead: The trail begins on the W side of Adirondack Loj Rd. at the far corner of the turnaround next to the entrance station. Because parking on the road is prohibited, hikers must park in the HPIC parking lot, and return to the entrance station to get to the start. (See p. 95 for further directions.) ◀

Leaving the road (0.0 mi) and marked by red markers, the trail proceeds gently down for 300 yd to a jct. with a trail (an old road) next to Heart Lake. The trail then turns sharp R, passing the trail R to Mt. Jo (trail 77) 60 yd later. Continuing straight ahead along the lake, the trail comes to a register box at 0.4 mi. At 0.5 mi the Old Nye Ski Trail diverges R, but the Indian Pass trail bears L and down past the end of Heart Lake and then up to the property line and West Side Speedway (ski) Trail at 0.6 mi. The trail now goes gently up and down through a mature open forest, crossing a brook on a bridge at 1.6 mi and then a second larger brook without a bridge at 2.1 mi. Just beyond this second brook is a jct. with the first of two trails leading to Rocky Falls. (Trail R leads 100 yd to the bank of Indian Pass Brook and one possible crossing point to a designated campsite below the lean-to. The side trail then goes up the R bank to a crossing to a lean-to above the upper part of Rocky Falls at approximately 300 yd from the Indian Pass trail. The falls are not high, but there is a good swimming hole below the lower falls. The side trail then continues steeply up to rejoin the Indian Pass trail in another 150 yd.)

Bearing L at this jct., the Indian Pass trail soon begins a steep climb of 150 yd, easing off just before the second jct. of the side trail to Rocky Falls at 2.4 mi. Now mostly on the flat with some extensive wet areas recently bridged, the trail crosses

Stream near Rocky Falls. **James Bullard**

a large stream at 2.6 mi, climbs for a few yd, and then continues with short rises and falls to another stream at 3.6 mi. Crossing this stream and another one shortly after, the trail comes to Scott Clearing Lean-to at 3.8 mi. From the lean-to bear R, cross another small stream, and climb gradually to Scotts Dam and several designated campsites at 4.1 mi and the jct. with the Wallface Ponds Trail (trail 76) leading R to Scott and Wallface ponds. Scott Clearing is the site of a former lumber camp, and the high rock dam was used to control the flow of water in Indian Pass Brook for driving logs. (The marked trail goes sharp L but the old low-water route that runs up the gravel bars next to Indian Pass Brook, though increasingly vague, is still followable and saves quite a bit of climbing compared to the high-water route.) Continuing on the marked trail (high-water route), follow up the L bank of a large brook before veering up and R to a height of land and on to rejoin the low-water route at 4.5 mi.

Turning L and crossing two brooks, the trail comes to a jct. with the trail through Cold Brook Pass (trail 72) at 4.9 mi. (Trail L leads 3.3 mi to Lake Colden.) At 5 mi the trail crosses Indian Pass Brook diagonally and shortly after recrosses it to the R bank. Now beginning a very steep, rough climb, the trail ascends into the pass. There is a short level stretch at 5.5 mi, where the first views of the cliff on Wallface are possible. The actual height of land is marked by a sign at 5.5 mi, but most hikers continue on to Summit Rock at 6 mi, where there is the most spectacular view of the cliff. From Summit Rock it is 4.4 mi to the Upper Works via trail 125.

❄ Trail in winter: With at least a foot of snow, this trail is skiable as far as the start of the steep climbing at just over 5 mi.

🏃 Distances: Adirondak Loj to Rocky Falls, 2.1 mi; to Scott Clearing Lean-to, 3.8 mi; to trail to Scott and Wallface ponds, 4.1 mi; to trail to Lake Colden, 4.9 mi; to Summit Rock, 6 mi (9.7 km).

Street and Nye Mts. *(Unmarked paths; see introduction, p. 19.)*

ADK High Peaks Map: D8–C8 | Trails Illustrated Map 742: Z22–23

Adirondack Survey Superintendent Verplanck Colvin named the first peak in honor of Alfred Billings Street, New York State law librarian and author of the book *The Indian Pass*. The latter peak bears the name of William B. Nye, the North Elba guide best known for having carried Matilda across the Hitch-Up-Matilda ford on Avalanche Lake (see p. 106). In 1998, these "herd paths" were designated, or defined, to keep hikers as much as possible on durable terrain.

The route to Street and Nye Mts. goes R from the Indian Pass trail (trail 75) 0.1 mi beyond the register box. The jct. is marked with signs for the Old Nye Ski Trail and Mt. Jo via Rock Garden Trail. From this jct. (0.0 mi) the route follows the marked trail for 250 yd to another jct. Here the marked trail goes sharp R to Mt. Jo while the route to Street and Nye Mts. continues straight ahead and follows the remains of the Old Nye Ski Trail due W and down to Indian Pass Brook at 0.9 mi. The path continues down the R bank of Indian Pass Brook to a sharp turn where the brook turns from W to N. Crossing Indian Pass Brook below this sharp turn, the path leads over a low ridge to the S side of a smaller brook that flows down from Street and Nye at 1.2 mi.

Soon the established path crosses the brook and cuts across to a brook flowing from a basin on the E side of Nye Mt. Crossing this second brook at the site of an old lumber camp at 1.7 mi, the path follows the R bank (looking downstream) for over 0.5 mi before bearing L and up to a col on the ridge S of this basin at 2.8 mi. The path then turns W and climbs steeply to a jct. marked by a cairn at 3.4 mi at the S end of the summit ridge of Nye. Turn R (N) and proceed another 0.2 mi over two intermediate bumps to the summit of Nye Mt., which is marked with a small plastic disk. Turn L for Street and follow the one defined path that has replaced the former maze down to the col between Street and Nye and then up to Street Mt. at 0.6 mi from the jct. on the Nye ridge, or 4 mi from Adirondak Loj. Vague paths lead to views from both a rock located 75 yd down the NE side and an open area 150 yd to the SW of the summit.

A beautiful but longer approach to Street and Nye Mts. lies up the valley above Wanika Falls, reached from Lake Placid via the Northville-Placid Trail (trail 99). From Wanika Falls, follow the larger, more easterly branch of Wanika Falls Brook (the headwaters of the Chubb River) and stick to the flanks of Nye in the brook's upper reaches.

76   Scott and Wallface Ponds

ADK High Peaks Map: C9 | Trails Illustrated Map 742: Y22

This trail climbs W from Scotts Dam on the Indian Pass trail to a series of remote and seldom-visited ponds. There are campsites at both Scott and Wallface Ponds as well as a spectacularly framed view of the MacIntyre Range from one of the upper Scott ponds. The area offers unexcelled opportunities for solitude in a very pretty setting, and is thus highly recommended as a place to camp for a night or more. The only thing lacking from these ponds is fish. Because of the ponds' altitude, they appear to have been among the first affected by acid precipitation. The only drawback is that this trail is quite wet in spots—particularly the final stretch to Wallface Pond.

▶ Locator: The trail leads W from Scotts Dam on the Indian Pass trail (trail 75) at a point 4.1 mi SW of Adirondack Loj Rd. (the Indian Pass trailhead). ◀

Leaving the Indian Pass trail at the stone dam (0.0 mi), the trail goes R (W) and crosses Indian Pass Brook just below the old spillway. Climbing the steep bank on the far side, the trail joins an old tote road and begins a steady, moderate climb to a flat area at 0.5 mi. Dropping slightly, the trail crosses a small stream and climbs again to a height of land at 1.1 mi. The trail now drops slightly, flattens out, and then drops more steeply to a trail sign at 1.5 mi with Scott Pond visible beyond. Just past this sign, a vague side trail goes R and steeply down 30 yd to a possible campsite at the inlet. The trail now drops down to the old dam at the outlet. At most water levels one can cross on the old dam, otherwise follow the markers downstream a few yards to an alternate crossing. An unmarked trail at the far side of the dam leads L to a designated campsite.

The trail now skirts the shore but quickly veers away to the L. Climbing to an open area, the trail crosses it, skirts a second open swampy area on the L, and then climbs, steeply at times, to a ridge at 2.2 mi. Dropping now, the trail passes a small pond on the L at 2.3 mi, and then swings R and down to a large open area with a small pond at one end at 2.4 mi. Here is an outstanding view of the MacIntyre

Range perfectly framed by the valley at the end of the pond. Bearing L, the trail enters the woods and climbs to an extremely wet area and finally to Wallface Pond and a campsite at 2.8 mi. From the shore of this attractive, large pond there are views of MacNaughton Mt. A vague trail leads L 150 yd to an attractive point and is also the start of the herd path to MacNaughton Mt.

🏃 Distances: Scotts Dam to Scott Pond, 1.5 mi; to Wallface Pond, 2.8 mi (4.5 km). Total distance from Heart Lake, 6.9 mi (11.1 km).

77 Mt. Jo

ADK High Peaks Map: D8 | P. 118 | Trails Illustrated Map 742: Z23

On the N shore of Heart Lake is Mt. Jo, a small but steep and rocky peak rising 710 ft above the lake. It was named in 1877 by Henry Van Hoevenberg in honor of his fiancée, Josephine Schofield. There are two main routes to its summit, both of which begin on the Indian Pass trail (trail 75). These trails have been used for training sessions by ADK trail crews for many years and now offer many examples of high-quality trail work.

▶ Trailhead: From the parking lot at the High Peaks Information Center (HPIC) at the end of Adirondack Loj Rd., return to the entrance station. The Mt. Jo and Indian Pass trails start at the far corner of the turnaround. *Note:* Parking is not permitted on this section of the road. (See p. 95 for further directions.) ◀

Leaving the road (0.0 mi), the trail proceeds gently down for 300 yd to a jct. with a trail (an old road) next to Heart Lake. In another 60 yd the Mt. Jo trail goes R, passes a register box, and climbs moderately up to a jct. at 0.4 mi. Here the Long Trail and Short Trail split. The Long Trail goes L and is 0.2 mi longer, but less strenuous. Bearing L, the Long Trail proceeds along a sidehill practically on the level before turning R and up at 0.7 mi. The Long Trail reaches a jct. with the Rock Garden Trail (trail 77A) at the base of a cliff at 0.9 mi. The Long Trail bears R and climbs to a jct. with the Short Trail, which enters on the R at 1.2 mi. (Just after this jct., a side trail leads L and up a rock step to the W summit, which offers only an obscured view.) Continuing on the flat to the base of the summit rocks, the trail reaches the summit at 1.3 mi. From the summit the views are impressive, reaching from Cascade Mt. to Mt. Marcy to Algonquin Peak to Indian Pass, making this one of the best views for the least effort in the Adirondacks.

The Short Trail, which diverges R at the jct. at 0.4 mi, climbs through some boulders and then up to the base of a large cliff on the L at 0.6 mi. Steeper climbing up some impressive rock staircases leads to a sharp L turn at 0.8 mi and the jct. with the Long Trail at 0.9 mi. Turn R to reach the summit at 1.1 mi.

🏃 Distances: Adirondack Loj Rd. to jct. of Short and Long trails, 0.4 mi; to summit via Long Trail, 1.3 mi (2.1 km); to summit via Short Trail, 1.1 mi (1.8 km). Ascent, 700 ft (213 m). Elevation, 2876 ft (877 m).

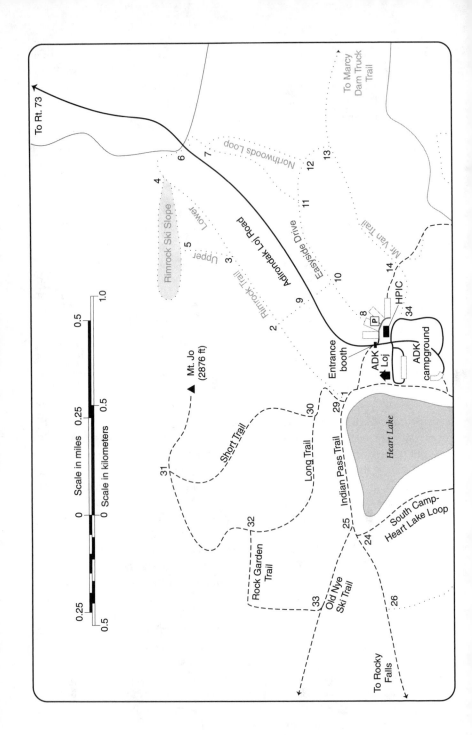

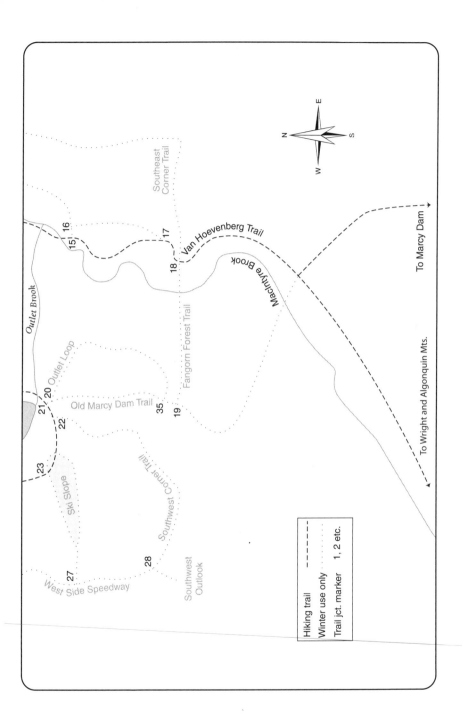

HEART LAKE PROPERTY TRAILS

ADK High Peaks Map: D8 | Pp. 118–119 | Trails Illustrated Map 742: Z23

The Adirondack Mt. Club has for many years maintained a network of ski and hiking trails on its property, in addition to its better known Mt. Jo trails. These trails are open to the public, and in recent years improved signs and markers have made them more accessible.

Following are brief descriptions of two hiking trails, one of which connects with the Mt. Jo trails while the other lies W of Heart Lake. Both offer some pleasant, easy summer hiking. Also described are two winter-use trails (77C) that combine to offer a pleasant ski or snowshoe loop. The ski trails connecting with the Mt. Marcy trail are not described.

Detailed property maps are available free at HPIC and Adirondak Loj.

Adirondak Loj. James Bullard

77A Rock Garden Trail

ADK High Peaks Map: D8 | P. 118

▶ Locator: This trail diverges from the Indian Pass trail (trail 75) 0.1 mi past the register box. It offers an alternative route to or from Mt. Jo. ◀

From the Indian Pass trail (0.0 mi), the Rock Garden Trail goes 250 yd to a jct. with the path to Street and Nye Mts. Here it turns sharp R and climbs gently through boulders (the "rock garden") before steepening at 0.3 mi and climbing to a sharp R turn off the boundary line at 0.4 mi. The trail now descends across a sidehill for 200 yd before climbing to a jct. with the Long Trail to Mt. Jo (see trail 77) at 0.6 mi.

77B   South Camp Trail

ADK High Peaks Map: D8 | Pp. 118–119

Combined with the Indian Pass trail, this trail permits a leisurely walk around Heart Lake.

▶ Locator: The trail leaves the Indian Pass trail (trail 75) at the W end of Heart Lake, 0.5 mi from its start and 50 yd beyond the jct. with the Rock Garden Trail (trail 77A). ◀

From the Indian Pass trail (0.0 mi), the South Camp Trail gradually pulls away from the lake and reaches the base of the ski slope at 0.4 mi. Turning L and gently down, the trail crosses a bridge at 0.5 mi with the jct. with the Southwest Corner Trail (trail 77C) just beyond. In another 20 yd the trail reaches the old trail to Marcy Dam. Turning L and down, the trail crosses the outlet to Heart Lake and climbs gently to reach the campground parking lot and road, which can be followed back to the High Peaks Information Center for a round-trip of 1.3 mi.

77C   Southwest Corner and
West Side Speedway Trails

ADK High Peaks Map: D8 | Pp. 118–119

▶ Locator: These winter-use trails lead from the Indian Pass trail along a ridge to a lookout at the SW corner of ADK's property, followed by a more direct return for a round-trip of just over 2 mi. The West Side Speedway starts at 0.6 mi along the Indian Pass trail. ◀

From the jct. (0.0 mi), the West Side Speedway climbs over a summit at 0.1 mi, descends briefly, and then climbs to a jct. with a trail L at 0.3 mi that leads to the ski slope. Continuing straight ahead, the trail now climbs steeply and reaches a jct. with the Southwest Corner Trail at 0.6 mi. The southwest lookout is reached in another 30 yd.

From the jct., the Southwest Corner Trail descends steadily before turning L at 1 mi and continuing at a more moderate grade to a jct. with the South Camp Trail (trail 77B) at 1.2 mi. From here, follow the route across the Heart Lake outlet and through the campground to the HPIC to complete the 2.1 mi round-trip.

SOUTH MEADOW

ADK High Peaks Map: D8 | Trails Illustrated Map 742: Z23

South Meadow is a clearing that can be reached by auto from Adirondack Loj Rd. The road is not plowed during winter months, and remains closed until the end of "mud season". There are many attractive primitive campsites along the road (look for camping markers) and at the end of the road, which is also the start for the Klondike Notch Trail (trail 12) and the South Meadow truck trail to Marcy Dam (trail 78). Marked with DEC signs and posted as Meadow Ln., the gravel road starts 3.8 mi S of NY 73 on Adirondack Loj Rd. and 1 mi N of Adirondak Loj. At 0.9 mi a gated road R is the start of the truck trail to Marcy Dam. The public road continues another 0.1 mi to the parking lot that is the start of the Klondike Notch Trail.

78 South Meadow to Marcy Dam

ADK High Peaks Map: D8 | Trails Illustrated Map 742: Z23

This fire truck trail is a graded gravel road offering an alternative route to Marcy Dam that is only about 0.4 mi longer than the approach from Heart Lake. The Civilian Conservation Corps constructed it in the 1930s. Because this area is now classified as wilderness, even DEC vehicles are prohibited from using this road except in the event of an emergency. This route can be especially recommended during the raspberry season.

▶ Trailhead: Parking is on Meadow Ln. at the jct. 0.9 mi from Adirondack Loj Rd. Do not block the gate. See South Meadow, above, for additional directions. ◀

From the gate (0.0 mi) bear R and down to the trail register at 0.1 mi. Past the register, the road crosses South Meadow Brook and proceeds along the flat to a jct. with the Mr. Van Ski Trail (trail 80) at 0.4 mi. The road now begins a short climb, and after several more ascents and descents crosses a large brook at 1.7 mi. At 2.1 mi the road dips down to the R, crosses another large brook, and climbs back before dropping down two pitches to the R bank of Marcy Brook at 2.4 mi. The road now continues straight up a gradual grade along the brook to the Van Hoevenberg Trail (trail 61) at Marcy Dam at 2.7 mi.

❄ Trail in winter: As a gravel road, this is a favorite ski tour from early in the season to late and is the preferred access for skiers to Mt. Marcy and Avalanche Pass. Because Meadow Ln. is no longer plowed, the winter distance is 0.9 mi longer.

🚶 Distance: Parking area at gate to Marcy Dam, 2.7 mi (4.3 km).

79 Mt. Van Hoevenberg from Meadow Ln.

ADK High Peaks Map: D8 | Trails Illustrated Map 742: Z23

Mt. Van Hoevenberg is a low mountain rising above South Meadow and offering a spectacular view of the High Peaks and Lake Placid for relatively little effort. Originally called South Mt., its name was changed in 1932 when the Olympic Bobsled Run was built on its north side. As of 2012, hikers may again descend the N side of the mountain to the top of the combined bobsled and luge track and then descend to the Mt. Van Hoevenberg cross-country trails via a new marked trail. This new connection to the cross-country trails makes the loop trip with the Mr. Van Trail much easier.

▶ Trailhead: The trail starts from Meadow Ln. 0.3 mi from Adirondack Loj Rd. and is marked with blue DEC disks. See South Meadow, p. 122, for additional directions. ◀

Starting on an old road blocked by a bar gate (0.0 mi), the trail proceeds on the level until it dips down and detours to the L to avoid a large beaver pond. After climbing a bit and dipping again to cross a small stream, the trail begins climbing steadily, first L across the slope and then R and under some small cliffs before arriving at a height of land at 1.6 mi.

From here, the trail climbs the W ridge of Mt. Van Hoevenberg to the first open ledges at 2.1 mi, where there are views of Mt. Marcy, Algonquin Peak, and Lake Placid. These first ledges offer perhaps the best views, but the trail continues on to the summit ledge at 2.2 mi, with a view farther to the E including Porter and Giant Mts.

Continuing down the N side, the trail goes L at the summit ledge and descends to the upper end of a road at 2.3 mi. Here signs announce "Entering OSC Trail System" and "Start of '32 Track." The original bobsled run constructed for the 1932 Olympics started here and was 1.5 mi long. The run was shortened to 1 mi in 1936 because greater speeds by technically superior sleds had made the longer run unsafe. The old run has now been cleared, and one may follow either the run or the old road down to the end of a drivable road at 2.8 mi. Both road and run have orange markers with arrows. At the drivable road, bear R and down across a parking area to a sign for a trail going R and down to the Cross-Country Lodge. This trail descends steeply to a wide cross-country ski trail at 3.1 mi. The orange markers continue across the ski trail and lead to the lodge and parking lot at 3.5 mi. To reach the Mr. Van Trail, turn R on the ski trail. After a short descent, climb, and second descent, bear R and up at the next three jcts. to reach Hi-Notch and the start of the Mr. Van Trail approx. 4 mi from the Meadow Ln. trailhead.

🚶 Distances: Meadow Ln. to summit of Mt. Van Hoevenberg, 2.2 mi (3.5 km). Ascent, 740 ft (226 m). Elevation, 2860 ft (872 m).

80 Mr. Van Ski Trail

ADK High Peaks Map: D8 | Trails Illustrated Map 742: Z23

The Mr. Van Ski Trail was named after Henry Van Hoevenberg, builder of the original Adirondack Lodge. It can provide a useful connection between the ski trails around Adirondak Loj and the cross-country center at Mt. Van Hoevenberg. Recent maintenance has made the section from the Loj to the South Meadow Truck Trail passable, although there is no bridge over Marcy Brook. The section from the Truck Trail to the Klondike Notch Trail has some beaver activity, which can be a problem for hikers, but usually not a problem for skiers. The remainder of the trail remains usable by both hikers and skiers and a loop trip incorporating the summit of Mt. Van Hoevenberg with a return via the Mr. Van Trail is again possible. (See above)

It is described from Adirondak Loj to Mt. Van Hoevenberg because that is the easiest direction in which to ski it.

▶ Locator: This trail starts at the parking lot at the Adirondack Mountain Club's HPIC, and after heading E and then NE it loops NW to connect to the cross-country ski trail complex at Mt. Van Hoevenberg. ◀

Leaving HPIC (0.0 mi), the Mr. Van Ski Trail proceeds along the Marcy trail (trail 61) for 175 yd to a jct. where the Mr. Van Ski Trail goes sharp L. (See p. 113 for further directions.) Proceeding through a thick spruce forest on the level, the trail passes a jct. with the Easyside ski trail and begins to descend gradually to Marcy Brook, which it reaches at 0.7 mi. Crossing the brook via a ford (difficult in high water), the trail at first traverses a generally open alder swamp, with views of Mt. Colden and Algonquin Peak. After crossing below two beaver dams the trail reaches the South Meadow truck trail (trail 78) at 1.3 mi.

Crossing the truck trail, the Mr. Van Ski Trail continues mostly on the flat but with additional beaver activity to the Klondike Trail (trail 12) at 2 mi and turns R for approximately 250 yd along the Klondike Trail. Diverging L at 2.1 mi, the trail soon crosses Klondike Brook and continues with short ups and downs along a sidehill to the Mr. Van Lean-to at 3.6 mi. Immediately crossing South Meadow Brook (no bridge), the trail crosses some flat, swampy ground before beginning a steady, moderate climb to Hi-Notch, which it reaches at 4.7 mi.

Hi-Notch is the edge of the Mt. Van Hoevenberg cross-country ski center, and the Mr. Van Ski Trail now follows wide, graded ski trails. Bearing L, the trail descends to a sharp L turn, passes straight through the first jct., continues to descend to a second jct., and then descends gradually to a jct. at 5.3 mi. Here skiers should follow the "Stadium" signs to the L to maintain one-way traffic, but hikers can save some distance by bearing R and down. Continue straight through the next jct. and finally arrive at the bottom of the descent at 5.6 mi at a small open area. From here, bear L on a very wide trail leading to the cross-country stadium. The parking lot is at the far end of the stadium at 6 mi. This parking lot is 200 yd from the entrance to the bobsled run and the end of the access road that leaves NY 73, 3 mi E of Adirondack Loj Rd.

Following this trail from the Mt. Van Hoevenberg end, in summer especially, is considerably more difficult, but by heading generally uphill and SE one should be able to arrive at Hi-Notch, where the Mr. Van Ski Trail leaves the developed cross-country ski trail system. The new trail connecting the top of the bobsled run with the ski trail system, however, allows one to find Hi-Notch relatively easily if doing the loop trip with the summit of Mt. Van Hoevenberg.

🚶 Distances: Adirondak Loj to South Meadow truck trail, 1.3 mi; to Mr. Van Lean-to, 3.6 mi; to Mt. Van Hoevenberg cross-country ski center, 6 mi (9.7 km). 🐦

Kids skiing in the High Peaks region. David Hough

Catamount Mt. Joanne Kennedy

Northern Section

 This section includes trails in the Saranac Lake and Lake Placid areas and a description of the Northville-Placid Trail from Averyville Rd. to Duck Hole. Both Saranac Lake and Lake Placid have been popular resort areas for many years, and little needs to be added here about Lake Placid's role in hosting the 1932 and 1980 Winter Olympics.

To provide hiking opportunities for early visitors to the Lake Placid area, the Adirondack Camp and Trail Club, initiated by Henry Van Hoevenberg in 1910, began to construct a system of formally marked and regularly maintained trails with shelters available along them. This system allowed far greater numbers of people to hike in the mountains, because getting lost was less of a problem and an overnight pack could be considerably lighter. Although no one can claim that Henry Van Hoevenberg "invented" such facilities for hikers, in this area at least he is the one who deserves the credit for starting the current system of trails and shelters (now maintained by the Department of Environmental Conservation, or DEC) that most hikers take for granted.

This northern region offers a great variety of hikes, particularly easy to moderate ones, and many of them should be more popular than they are. Below are a few recommended hikes.

SHORT HIKES
Owls Head: 1.1 mi (1.8 km) round-trip. A near-perfect little hike for children, with views starting almost immediately, plenty of blueberries, and a great view from the summit. See trail 93.

Baker Mt.: 1.7 mi (2.7 km) round-trip. The same could be said about Baker Mt. as about Owls Head, except that one must wait a little longer for the first view. See trail 101.

MODERATE HIKES
Pitchoff Mt.: 5.2 mi (8.4 km) point to point. A wonderful hike along a long, rocky ridge with two possible shorter destinations. See trail 92.

Ampersand Mt.: 5.4 mi (8.7 km) round-trip. The truly commanding view from this bald summit is good enough to make one forget the very steep spots on the way up. See map and description for trail 102.

HARDER HIKE
Whiteface via Whiteface Landing and Connery Pond Trail: 7 mi (11.3 km) round-trip hiking distance plus 6-mi (9.7 km) round-trip paddling. Surely the most civilized way to do this very civilized peak is to paddle from the state boat launch site at the S end of Lake Placid to Whiteface Landing and then ascend the peak. Great views from both the lake and summit. See general description of Whiteface, p. 129, for paddling information, and map and description of trail 81 for hiking information.

WHITEFACE MT.

Standing alone over 10 mi to the N of any other 4000 ft peak, Whiteface Mt. and its lower companion, Esther Mt., are an impressive sight from any viewpoint. Equally impressive are the views from the summit. Lake Placid and its heavily wooded islands are directly below, with the rest of the high peaks arrayed beyond, while to the N and E Lake Champlain and Mt. Royal (Mont Real) in Canada are visible. Even with the intrusions of the summit buildings and the accompanying throngs of tourists, there is still a magnificent wilderness view from this summit.

Geologically, Whiteface is unique in that its anorthosite granite welled up from the earth from a separate source from the rest of the high peaks. More recently, mountain glaciers clung to its higher slopes long enough in the aftermath of the last ice age to create the most distinct alpine features to be found on any Adirondack peak. On the N, W, and E faces of Whiteface are well-defined, bowl-shaped cirque valleys with sharp aretes separating the cirques. The walkway from the top of the highway ascends the sharpest of these aretes, while the Wilmington Trail ascends another.

Whiteface has also seen more development than any other High Peak; it has a paved two-lane highway, a major ski area, and a complete summit weather observatory. Beginning in Wilmington, the Whiteface Mt. Memorial Highway is a toll road leading to within 300 vertical feet of the summit. From here there is an elevator to the summit as well as an improved stone walkway up the spectacular NW arete. The summit observatory provides weather information for local and national forecasters as well as providing a base for atmospheric research on such phenomena as acid precipitation. Opened in 1958, the present Whiteface Mt. Ski Center replaced the original, smaller development on Marble Mt. Expanded several times since, the ski center was the site for the alpine events at the 1980 Winter Olympics.

There are two hiking trails to the summit of Whiteface Mt. One ascends steeply from Connery Pond and Lake Placid, with another coming from Wilmington. An only slightly harder and in many ways more scenic approach is via boat to Whiteface Landing on Lake Placid and then up the peak via the Connery Pond Trail. There is a boat launch site at the S end of Lake Placid on Mirror Lake Dr., 0.6 mi N of the jct. with Saranac Ave. at the N end of Main St. There are no canoes available for rent on Lake Placid, but several locations on Mirror Lake in downtown Lake Placid do rent canoes.

❈ Trails in winter: Unless otherwise noted, the trails in this section are too steep or rough to be suitable for anything but snowshoeing. Steeper trails may require crampons, and the exposed summits of Cascade and Whiteface Mts. may require a face mask and goggles in windy conditions. The Jackrabbit Ski Trail, begun in 1986, traverses this section. Mention is made when this trail follows any of the summer hiking routes. It is not, however, a continuous summer hiking trail as it crosses several golf courses and a number of wet areas along its 24-mi route between Keene and Saranac Lake.

81 Whiteface Mt. via Connery Pond and Whiteface Landing

ADK High Peaks Map: D5–E4 | Trails Illustrated Map 746: CC23, 24

▶ Trailhead: This trail starts on NY 86, 3.1 mi E from its jct. with NY 73 in Lake Placid and 0.2 mi W of the bridge over the West Branch Ausable River. From the small DEC sign on the highway, turn down a narrow dirt road marked with red DEC disks. Drive down the road and bear L at 0.5 mi to a parking area at a gate at 0.6 mi. ◀

From the parking lot (0.0 mi) continue on the road, bearing L after 130 yd to avoid a private residence. The trail skirts the NW shore of Connery Pond on an old road, before it bears away from the pond and reaches a bar gate at 0.4 mi. This is the start of an old truck trail used to salvage timber in the aftermath of the 1950 hurricane.

Great Blue Heron. Richard J. Nowicki

From the gate the road is at first on the level, but slowly begins climbing to a height of land at 1.4 mi, after which it gently descends to a jct. at 2.5 mi. (Trail L leads 110 yd to Whiteface Landing on Lake Placid. Trail straight ahead is a now-abandoned Shore Owners Association trail around the N side of Lake Placid; see p. 148.) Turning R, the trail climbs gently to a straight section of old road to the bank of Whiteface Brook at 3.1 mi. The trail now bears R on a section of trail constructed in 2010 that avoids any brook crossings to reach Whiteface Lean-to above the L bank of the brook at 3.6 mi.

Turning L here, the grade steepens as the trail climbs above the L bank, bearing away from the brook at about 4.5 mi. The grades are now easy to moderate for a short stretch, but soon the grade becomes mostly steep to a short breather where there is a view to the S at 5.6 mi. (This point marks the start of the arctic-alpine zone where hikers must stay on either the marked trail or bare rock to protect the fragile vegetation.) Reaching timberline at 5.8 mi, the trail is now marked with yellow paint blazes and climbs steeply over numerous ledges to the S summit. The actual summit is a few yards farther at 6 mi.

ALPINE ALERT
See page 14

❄ Trail in winter: Suitable for skiing for novices as far as Whiteface Landing. During the winter months, the road to the pond is closed by a gate. Park at one of the two turnouts 200 yd to the E and follow the trail parallel to the highway back to the road. This makes for a 6-mi round-trip to the landing.

🐾 Distances: Parking area at Connery Pond to jct. at Whiteface Landing, 2.5 mi; to Whiteface Lean-to, 3.6 mi; to summit of Whiteface, 6 mi (9.7 km). Ascent from Connery Pond, 3232 ft (985 m). Elevation, 4867 ft (1484 m). Order of height, 5.

82 Whiteface Mt. via Wilmington Trail

ADK High Peaks Map: E3 | Trails Illustrated Map 746: EE25

▶ Trailhead: This trail branches L from the Whiteface Mt. Memorial Highway 0.6 mi from NY 86 in Wilmington on a dirt road marked with a small DEC sign. At the Town of Wilmington reservoir, 0.2 mi up this road, there is a parking area on the L. ◀

From the parking area (0.0 mi), cross the brook below the dam on a good bridge and then turn R and up the R bank of the brook. The trail slowly veers away from the brook and comes to a jct. with a blue-marked snowmobile trail at 0.4 mi. (Trail R leads 0.8 mi up to the Marble Mt. Ski Area approach to the Wilmington Trail. Trail L leads down to NY 86 S of Wilmington.) Continuing straight, the trail soon heads S along a sidehill practically on the level through an open maple and oak forest to a jct at 1.3 mi. [Trail L (82A) leads 1.8 mi to the Flume trailhead on NY 86.] Finally reaching the S side of a ridge, the trail turns R at 1.4 mi and begins a steady, steep climb that continues to the summit of Marble Mt. at 2.2 mi. Here the unofficial route (trail 83) from the base of the old Marble Mt. Ski Area comes in from the R. The summit rocks on Marble Mt. can be reached by an overgrown trail that branches R a few ft from this jct. It is 150 yd to the top of the former T-bar lift, where there are views to the S and E.

Continuing on the level with a view of Esther Mt. straight ahead, the trail soon begins to climb and comes to a steep stretch of bare rock at 2.4 mi. The trail bears L a few feet up this rock, and climbs with alternating steep and level pitches to a flat area at an old toboggan shelter on the L at 3.3 mi. There is a good view of Whiteface straight ahead.

From this first view of Whiteface, the trail drops gently to the jct. at 3.5 mi with a sign pointing R to the unmarked trail leading right to Esther Mt. (see p. 132). The trail now continues generally down until it crosses a wet area at 4 mi, after which it is flat for a short ways before climbing moderately to a junction with a wide, rough trail at 4.3 mi. To the R is an old structure known as Porcupine Lodge, which was the warming hut when the ski tows were here. Past this rough trail is a new ski trail (the "Wilmington Trail") and the top of a new ski lift at 4.4 mi. (when descending, be careful not to end up on the wrong "Wilmington Trail"). Past the top of the lift, the trail goes steeply up an old ski towline before diverging L and coming to the base of the wall of Wilmington Turn, which is skirted on the L over large boulders to the Memorial Highway at 4.8 mi. The trail now climbs the steep ledge to the L and proceeds through small trees to timberline at 4.9 mi. (This point marks the start of the arctic-alpine zone where hikers must stay on either the marked trail or bare rock to protect the fragile vegetation.) The final climb along the arete is spectacular, with fresh slides visible down to the L and the top of the Whiteface Mt. Ski Center chairlift farther to the L. Veering L of the summit buildings, the trail arrives at the summit at 5.2 mi.

🏃 Distances: Parking area at Wilmington reservoir to summit of Marble Mt., 2.2 mi; to unmarked trail to Esther Mt., 3.4 mi; to summit of Whiteface Mt., 5.2 mi (8.4 km). Ascent from parking area, 3620 ft (1104 m). Elevation, 4867 ft (1484). Order of height, 5.

83   Old Marble Mt. Ski Area Approach to Wilmington Trail

ADK High Peaks Map: E3 | Trails Illustrated Map 746: EE25

An unofficial and unmarked variation to the Wilmington Trail starts at the Atmospheric Sciences Research Center 2.4 mi up the Whiteface Mt. Memorial Highway. Hikers should drive around the turnaround and park at the designated hiker parking, located on the R 0.6 mi from the highway. The route starts about one-third of the way along this parking lot and descends to a radio tower at the base of the old T-bar lift line. A new (2012) snowmobile trail goes L and down from the radio tower. Be sure to take the narrow lift line, which immediately starts climbing and which is followed almost to the top of Marble Mt. The route turns R just before the top and in a few yards joins the Wilmington Trail (trail 82). This route has no official signs or markers save a sign directing hikers where to park and another at the turnoff from the Wilmington Trail at the top of Marble Mt. On the return, be sure to avoid the new snowmobile trail by going L on the road leading back up from the radio tower to the parking area.

83A   Cobble Ledge

ADK High Peaks Map: E3 | Trails Illustrated Map 746 (not shown)

Constructed in 2014, this short and mostly flat trail leads to a spectacular view of Whiteface Mt., Giant Mt., and much of the Champlain Valley.

▶ Trailhead: On CR 72 at a turnout on the R, 0.3 mi from the Whiteface Highway toward Franklin Falls. ◀

From the road (0.0 mi.) the route, marked with blue DEC disks, follows an old road for 0.1 mi to an old quarry after which it becomes a trail. At 0.2 mi a short rock staircase begins a short moderate climb to a broad shelf, which is mostly flat, to a R turn and a gentle descent to an old lumber road at 0.9 mi. The trail soon crosses a small brook and reaches the ledge at 1.2 mi. An elaborate old stone fireplace indicates that this area was formerly quite popular. This new trail will likely make it so again.

🏃 Distance: Road to Cobble Ledge, 1.2 mi (1.9 km)

Esther Mt. *(Unmaintained trail; see introduction, p. 19.)*

ADK High Peaks Map: E3 | Trails Illustrated Map 746: DD24

This most northern of the major Adirondack peaks is named for Esther McComb. In 1839 at the age of 15, while trying to climb Whiteface Mt. from the N, she became lost and made the first recorded ascent of this mountain instead. The Adirondack Forty-Sixers placed a tablet to her memory on the summit in 1939. In 2002 they removed the original tablet for eventual transfer to the Adirondack Museum or the New York State Museum, replacing it with a replica.

This route follows a long-overgrown ski trail that was part of the network radiating from the former ski lodge on Lookout Mt.

Take the Whiteface Mt. via Wilmington trail (trail 82) to the jct., marked with a cairn, at 3.5 mi. Leaving the red-marked trail, the path climbs steeply for 100 yd before joining the old path and continuing at mostly moderate grades to the summit of Lookout Mt. at 0.3 mi where a ski lodge once stood. From here, the route to Esther Mt. descends into a col at 0.6 mi, crosses a bog on some good bridges, and continues N along the ridge to Esther's summit at 1.2 mi from the Whiteface Trail.

Whiteface Mt. from Connery Pond. James Bullard

WILMINGTON AREA TRAILS

As of 2012, the Town of Wilmington had essentially completed a network of mountain bike and hiking trails on the W side of the West Branch of the Ausable River between Whiteface Mt. Ski Center and the Flume trailhead. In addition to numerous loops for mountain bikers (not described), these trails provide an alternate approach to the Wilmington Trail to Whiteface Mt. as well as access to two unique views as described below. Additionally, not described but shown on ADK's High Peaks map and T.I. Map 746 is another system of mountain bike trails off Hardy Rd. to the E of Wilmington.

82A Flume Approach to Wilmington Trail to Whiteface Mt.

ADK High Peaks Map: E4 | Trails Illustrated Map 746: DD25

Longer by 0.5 mi and with some additional climbing as a start for Whiteface Mt., this route does offer better footing that the Wilmington Trail. Signs refer to this route as the Marble Mt. Trail.

▶ Trailhead: A parking area on NY 86 at the bridge over the West Branch of the Ausable River, 2 mi S of the four-way intersection in Wilmington or 1.2 mi N of the entrance to Whiteface Mt. Ski Center. ◀

From the trail register (0.0 mi), the trail goes R and up to a road-width trail on the flat. After several jcts. with narrower trails, at 0.2 mi. the Marble Mt. Trail (now with red markers) bears R and passes several more jcts. before reaching a jct. with the Ridge Trail at 0.9 mi. Again bearing R, the Marble Mt. Trail passes one more jct., crosses a brook and climbs to the jct. with the Wilmington Trail at 1.8 mi. This jct. is 1.3 mi. from the Wilmington reservoir start and 0.9 mi from the summit of Marble Mt.

🚶 Distances: Jct. with Ridge Trail, 0.9 mi (1.4 km); jct. with Wilmington Trail, 1.8 mi (2.9 km).

82B Flume Knob

ADK High Peaks Map: E4 | Trails Illustrated Map 746: DD25

This little rocky outcrop at the N end of a broad shelf offers unique views of Wilmington and the valley of the West Branch of the Ausable River. Although the trail has a few very steep pitches, they are relatively short, making Flume Knob considerably easier than the adjacent Bear Den. The numerous jcts. require one to be alert, but most jcts. have signs pointing to Flume Knob.

▶ Trailhead: Flume Knob can be approached either from the Flume trailhead (see above) or via the Bear Den trail. The latter approach is 0.3 mi. shorter, but the

Flume trailhead approach accesses numerous other trails that offer additional and mostly pleasant walking. [If approaching via the Bear Den trailhead (see below), turn R at the jct. at 0.5 mi. The trail descends to a brook crossing and then climbs to a jct. 0.9 mi. from the Flume trailhead.] ◀

From the register at the Flume trailhead parking lot (0.0 mi), bear R and up a short climb and then flat on a wide trail to a jct. at 0.2 mi. Bear L on the Corridor Trail and then bear R, now with blue markers, at 0.3 mi. After bearing L at 0.4 mi and still on a road-width trail, the route goes R at 0.5 mi and soon narrows. At 0.6 mi the trail swings sharp L, levels out , goes straight through the next jct. , and then swings R and up to a jct. with the Ridge Trail at 0.9 mi. Trail L at this jct. leads to Whiteface Mt. Ski Center and is the alternate approach from the Bear Den trailhead. Continuing straight ahead with blue markers, the trail becomes steep and narrow. At 1.3 mi the Flume Knob trail bears R and continues in alternating steep and moderate climbs to a flat shelf at 1.7 mi with the lookout at the far end of the shelf at 1.9 mi.

🚶 Distances: To Corridor Trail, 0.2 mi (0.3 km); to jct. with Ridge Trail, 0.9 mi (1.4 km); to lookout, 1.9 mi (3 km).

82C   Bear Den (Wilmington)

ADK High Peaks Map: E4 | Trails Illustrated Map 746: DD25

This rocky knob just north of the Whiteface Mt. Ski Center offers some unique views for a short but strenuous climb. This trail, new in 2011, replaces an informal trail that approached from the Flume trailhead.

▶ Trailhead: The trail starts (appropriately) at the Bear Den parking lot at Whiteface Mt. Ski Center, located on NY 86. Turn down the entrance road to the ski center. Cross the bridge over the West Branch of the Ausable River and turn R for 0.4 mi. The trailhead and register are on the R above the Bear Den parking lot just after the road swings L. ◀

From the register (0.0 mi) and marked with both red and yellow markers, the trail climbs in gradual stages to a jct. at 0.5 mi. (Trail R leads to the Flume trails and is an alternate approach to Flume Knob.) The Bear Den trail goes L with yellow markers and soon climbs steeply up and around to the top of a hogback at 0.7 mi. The grade briefly moderates as the trail follows a shelf high above a brook, but at 0.9 mi the trail bears L and up some steep switchbacks. With often rough footing, the trail then alternates between sidehill traverses and steep climbs to a saddle at 1.6 mi. Turning L, the trail ascends steeply to a summit at 1.7 mi. An informal trail continues to a higher summit 0.1 mi. beyond.

Both summits offer views of Algonquin, the Sentinel Range, and the ski center's trails. One can also venture past this second summit and down 200 yd to some sweeping views to the E. Additionally, an informal trail that goes R at the saddle gains some higher ledges with greater views.

🥾 Distances: Parking area to jct. with Flume system connection, 0.5 mi (0.8 km); to summit, 1.7 mi (2.7 km).

84 Cooper Kiln Pond

ADK High Peaks Map: E3–F2 | Trails Illustrated Map 746: EE24

This is an interesting walk through a notch between the Stephenson and Wilmington ranges to a seldom-visited pond with a lean-to. This pond has also been called Cooper "Kill" Pond on the USGS maps, but the name on the DEC signs is used here. The route is probably more often skied than hiked because it offers an exceptional downhill run of nearly 2000 ft and a net drop of over 1000 ft.

▶ Trailhead: Start on the Franklin Falls Rd., found by driving 2.8 mi up the Whiteface Mt. Memorial Highway from NY 86 in Wilmington and then bearing R just before the tollhouse. There is a DEC sign on the R 0.7 mi from the Memorial Highway. ◀

Leaving the road (0.0 mi), the trail climbs briefly, turns L, and proceeds on the flat on a good road. At 0.2 mi the trail bears R and begins a gentle climb to an open area at 0.3 mi. The climbing continues easy to moderate with some eroded sections past a jct. with a snowmobile trail going L at 0.6 mi and then to a bridge over a small brook at 1.6 mi. Here the climbing steepens a bit before easing off near a height of land at 1.8 mi.

Beginning to descend at 2.2 mi, the trail reaches the outlet to Cooper Kiln Pond at 2.7 mi, with the lean-to (incorrectly located on the 1978 USGS map) just beyond the outlet. The pond itself is approximately a quarter-mile long, with some large rocks that make nice picnic spots near the E shore. Swimming is possible but hardly ideal from these rocks, and it's likely there are few fish owing to the size and altitude of the pond; but this is a picturesque spot far from the populated trade routes, and solitude is just about guaranteed.

To continue past the pond, turn sharp R at the lean-to and descend to a crossing of the outlet at 2.8 mi. The trail ascends a short, steep bank and turns L onto an overgrown tote road that has been marked as a snowmobile trail. Following this old road, the trail crosses the outlet again at 3.3 mi and two additional times, ending up on the L bank at 3.7 mi, where it veers L away from the brook and comes to a good jeep trail at 3.9 mi. Joining another jeep trail coming in from the L at 4.2 mi, the route (still marked with snowmobile trail markers) turns R and down. Passing several other side roads, the grade slowly flattens as the trail crosses a large stream at 5.4 mi and levels out shortly thereafter. The trail reaches Bonnieview Rd. in Wilmington at 5.9 mi. This point is 3.2 mi N of NY 86 in the center of Wilmington and 2.9 mi S of the Silver Lake Rd. leading W from Au Sable Forks.

❄ Trail in winter: At least a foot of snow is desirable before trying to ski this route, and the terrain is suitable only for advanced-intermediate skiers or better.

🥾 Distances: Franklin Falls Rd. to Cooper Kiln Pond Lean-to, 2.7 mi (4.4 km);

to Bonnieview Rd., 5.9 mi (9.5 km).

85 Catamount Mt.

ADK High Peaks Map: E2 | Trails Illustrated Map 746: FF24

Catamount Mt. is one of the most spectacular small peaks in the Adirondacks. Much of the mountain's steep S side is bare as a result of first cutting for charcoal and later burning. As of 2013, this is an official DEC trail, but care may still be needed on the many open ledges—the old paint blazes are fading and the cairns are few.

▶ Trailhead: From NY 86 in the center of Wilmington, go up the Whiteface Mt. Memorial Highway for 2.8 mi and turn R on CR 72 toward Franklin Falls. At 3.3 mi from the Whiteface highway, turn R on Roseman Rd., and then in another 0.8 mi turn R onto Plank Rd., from which the mountain is soon visible. At 2.2 mi down Plank Rd., there is a gravel parking area on the L. (This point is also 6.2 mi S of the Silver Lake Rd. running W from Au Sable Forks.) ◀

Leaving the parking area and register box (0.0 mi), the trail is plain to a jct. at 0.4 mi where a new snowmobile trail (winter use only on private land) diverges L while the Catamont Mt. trail continues straight across an old field. At the far end of the old field, at 0.6 mi, do not follow the orange property line, but instead turn R and enter the woods at the far corner of the field. The trail soon begins to climb steeply before dipping briefly to cross a small brook at 0.8 mi. The trail now climbs at moderate to steep grades over several ledges to a balanced boulder at 1.3 mi. Soon thereafter, a steep rock scramble up the S summit begins, ending with a nearly vertical chimney in the rock. Reaching the S summit at 1.5 mi, the trail dips slightly through thick trees to the col and then climbs to the summit at 1.8 mi. The views from the summit are expansive and dominated by Whiteface Mt., Taylor Pond, and Silver Lake. In season, the blueberries are almost as good as the views.

🐾 Distance: Road to summit of Catamount Mt., 1.8 mi (2.9 km). Ascent from road, 1542 ft (470 m). Elevation, 3168 ft (966 m).

86 Silver Lake Mt.

Map: P. 138 | ADK High Peaks Map: E1a | Trails Illustrated Map 746: GG25

This peak is located about 10 mi N of Whiteface Mt. The attractions of this peak are the rocky ledges on the summit, which offer wonderful views of Whiteface Mt., Silver Lake, and Taylor Pond, as well as the many blueberries in season.

▶ Trailhead: The start is on Silver Lake Rd, which runs from Au Sable Forks to Silver Lake and Clayburg. It is 1 mi E of the road jct. in Silver Lake and 11 mi W of Au Sable Forks. There is a DEC sign at the entrance to a small parking area. ◀

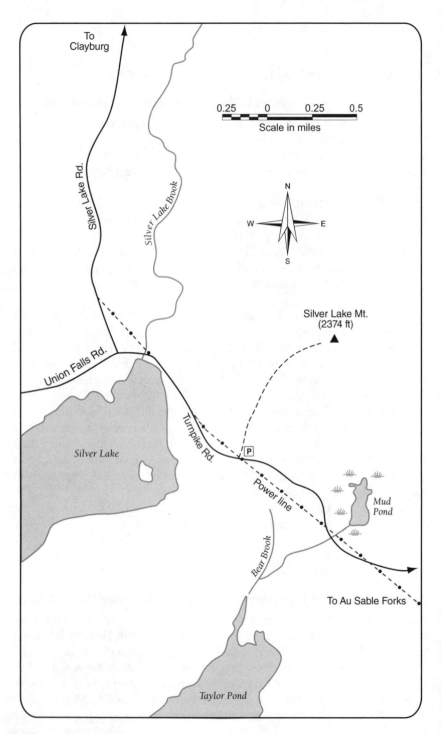

Leaving the road (0.0 mi), the trail is level for a few yards before climbing moderately to an open area at 0.3 mi, where the grade eases a bit. From here there are frequent red DEC markers. Soon after this open area, the grade again becomes moderate, with a lookout on the L at 0.5 mi and another at 0.7 mi where the trail turns sharp R just before reaching two angular boulders on the ledge. From here, the trail climbs steeply up a ridge with ever-expanding views to the summit at 0.9 mi. A vague trail continues over the summit, but fades out within 0.3 mi before reaching the first col on the ridge. For the adventurous, however, there are many more ledges on this more than 2 mi ridge.

🚶 Distance: Road to summit of Silver Lake Mt., 0.9 mi (1.5 km). Ascent from road, 900 ft (274 m). Elevation, 2374 ft (724 m).

87 Owen, Copperas, and Winch Ponds

ADK High Peaks Map: E5 | Trails Illustrated Map 746: CC24

This scenic trio of ponds offers some very pleasant walking with little climbing, good views, and ample opportunities for swimming, picnicking, and camping at the lean-to or the two designated campsites on Copperas Pond. Their easy accessibility makes these ponds some of the most popular destinations in the Lake Placid area.

▶ Trailheads: There are two starts from NY 86 in Wilmington Notch, approximately 1 mi apart. Both approaches are marked with small DEC signs. The easier approach is the southerly one, recently (2011) relocated 0.1 mi. N of the original trailhead or 5.1 mi from the jct. with NY 73 in Lake Placid and 3.8 mi S of the entrance to Whiteface Mt. Ski Center. ◀

Leaving the road (0.0 mi) at the southerly approach, the blue-marked trail is rough for 250 yd before joining the old trail that leads gradually up near the R bank of Owen Pond Brook and comes to the NW corner of Owen Pond at 0.6 mi. The trail follows the shore to the NE corner at 0.7 mi, where it veers away to the L as it climbs a few easy grades and then a steeper one at 1 mi. Swinging R at the top of this grade, the trail soon descends and reaches a designated campsite at the former lean-to site on the shore of Copperas Pond at 1.3 mi. From here there is an excellent view of Whiteface Mt.

The trail then immediately crosses the outlet and continues along the shore to a jct. at 1.4 mi, where the yellow-marked trail to Winch Pond turns R. (This trail climbs a short pitch, after which there are several gradual ups and downs to Winch Pond at 1.9 mi.) Continuing straight ahead, the blue trail follows the shore to an attractive designated campsite and then a jct. at 1.6 mi. (Trail straight ahead leads 0.1 mi along the shoreline to the Copperas Lean-to.) The blue trail now turns R, climbs to a height of land, and descends to a jct. at 1.8 mi. (Red trail R leads 0.5 mi to Winch Pond. Using this approach to Winch Pond from the N end of the blue trail, it is 0.7 mi from the highway to the pond.) The blue trail now continues down, becoming rocky and eroded in spots, and reaches the highway at 2 mi.

✴ Trail in winter: Although this trail is rough and needs a foot or more of snow to be skied, Copperas Pond is a worthwhile destination and makes an excellent beginning snowshoe hike.

🏃 Distances: Highway at S approach to Owen Pond, 0.6 mi; to Copperas Pond (S shore), 1.3 mi (2.1 km); to Winch Pond, 1.9 mi. Highway at N approach to Copperas Pond (N shore), 0.5 mi; to Winch Pond, 0.7 mi.

88 Moose Pond

ADK High Peaks Map: B4–C4 | Trails Illustrated Map 746: DD21

This short trail offers a very pleasant walk to the scenic, rocky SW shore of Moose Pond N of Saranac Lake. It follows an old road for most of the distance with virtually no climbing to the pond.

▶ Trailhead: On NY 3, 3.9 mi E of the intersection of NY 3 and NY 86 at the N end of Saranac Lake Village near the railroad station. This point is also 2.2 mi W of the four-way intersection in Bloomingdale. A narrow road leads 200 yd down to a small parking are at a footbridge across the Saranac River, which is clearly visible from the road. ◀

From the parking area (0.0 mi) the trail crosses the footbridge, swings R, and proceeds mostly on the flat along a wide road to a trail leading R at approximately 1.4 mi. This trail leads down to the rocky shore of the pond at 1.5 mi. with views of Moose and McKenzie Mts. An unmarked trail continues along the shore to a designated campsite. This designated campsite can also be reached by staying on the wide road for another 150 yd and turning R and down on a narrower road that passes an old chimney before reaching the shore.

✴ Trail in winter: Since the road down to the summer parking area is not plowed, parking can be a problem on busy NY 3. However, this nearly flat road is a perfect first ski tour for almost anyone. The road is smooth and can be skied with as little as six inches of snow. The second approach to the shore of the pond is much gentler and is the preferred approach for skiers.

🏃 Distance: NY 3 to Moose Pond, 1.5 mi (2.4 km).

SENTINEL RANGE

ADK High Peaks Map: E4–E5 | Trails Illustrated Map 742: AA24–26 to CC24–26

Running for nearly 10 mi NE and SW between the valleys of the east and west branches of the Ausable River, the Sentinel Range is the major feature of the 23,000-acre Sentinel Range Wilderness Area. The three major peaks, Stewart, Kilburn, and Sentinel Mts., lack significant views and thus have seen little hiker traffic over the years.

The best views are from 3893 ft Kilburn Mt., which can best be approached from the now-abandoned North Notch Trail. Sentinel Mt. also offers some views, although the approach from Bartlett Rd. is more difficult than the route to Kilburn. Stewart Mt. offers some views in the winter when the snow pack raises hikers above the level of the smaller balsams and permits some interesting views through the numerous blowdown areas. One can also find views from the 1995 slide on the W face of the lower NW peak of Kilburn. The approach to this slide starts S of Owen Pond and is somewhat difficult owing to damage from the 1998 ice storm. The only real rocky peak with a view is a 2080 ft eastern shoulder of Sentinel Mt. called Cobble Mt., which offers views of the valley of the East Branch Ausable River as well as of Cascade Mt. and other peaks. Cobble Mt. has no trail, but can be approached from Bartlett Rd. running between Keene and Upper Jay.

There were once ski trails through North Notch and South Notch that combined to form a long loop, parts of which were used for the 1932 Olympics. The E portions of these loops were abandoned long ago and no trace remains of them. The W approaches were maintained until the 1990s, but have now also been abandoned.

90   Cascade Mt. from Cascade Lakes

ADK High Peaks Map: E7 | Trails Illustrated Map 742: AA24

As the easiest of all the 4000 ft peaks to ascend, this bald summit attracts many hikers in all seasons to enjoy its marvelous views of the other peaks and the Champlain Valley. Once called Long Pond Mt., Cascade Mt. is named for the steep falls that tumbles down between the two Cascade lakes. The current trail follows a route laid out in 1974 by the Algonquin Chapter of ADK to replace the old trail, which was steep and badly eroded. It follows the SW ridge on generally moderate grades with only a few steeper pitches, making this a very enjoyable hike.

▶ Trailhead: The trail starts on NY 73, 6.8 mi from Keene and 4.5 mi from Adirondack Loj Rd., and is marked with red DEC disks. ◀

Parking can be a problem on popular weekends at this trailhead, especially given the heavy traffic on NY 73. Park as efficiently as possible and be prepared to use one of the wider turnouts either E or W of the trailhead, where one can get completely off the road. Parking on the road directly across from the Cascade trailhead is not recommended owing to the potential hazard created by cars parked on both sides of the road.

View from Cascade. Henning Vahlenkamp

Leaving the highway (0.0 mi), the trail descends for 30 yd to a register box and then begins an easy climb. Swinging R and leveling out, the trail crosses a small brook at 0.4 mi and resumes an easy climb until it steepens at 0.7 mi. It continues steep to moderate to the top of the ridge at 1.2 mi. Now on the crest of the ridge, several moderate climbs alternate with flatter sections until a short, steep climb brings the trail to a ledge with a good view at 1.8 mi. Now the grade eases, and the trail reaches a jct. with the trail to Porter Mt. (trail 91) at 2.1 mi. Bearing L, the trail soon reaches the base of the open rocks and ascends along the R side of the open rocks to the summit at 2.4 mi.

🚶 Distances: Highway to Porter Mt. trail jct., 2.1 mi; to summit of Cascade Mt., 2.4 mi (3.9 km). Ascent, 1940 ft (592 m). Elevation, 4098 ft (1249 m). Order of height, 36.

91 Porter Mt.

ADK High Peaks Map: E7 | Trails Illustrated Map 742: AA25

Once called West Mt., Porter Mt. is named for Noah Porter, PhD, president of Yale University from 1871 to 1886. A summer resident of Keene Valley, Porter made the first recorded ascent of the peak in 1875 with guide Ed Phelps. Although Porter Mt. does not have a bald summit, it offers nearly 360° views and is a worthwhile side trip from Cascade Mt. Two other trails (16 and 17) ascend the peak from the Keene Valley side.

▶ Locator: This trail runs from the Cascade Mt trail to the summit of Porter Mt., where it connects with the trails from Keene Valley. ◀

Leaving the jct. near the summit of Cascade Mt. (0.0 mi), the trail descends to a col at 0.2 mi and then climbs moderately to steeply to a large boulder at 0.6 mi with a side trail R to a view just beyond followed by easy grades along the ridge to the summit at 0.7 mi. (Trail 17 with yellow DEC markers continues straight ahead, leading to the Marcy Airfield at 4.5 mi, or trail 16 can be taken 3.8 mi to the Garden.)

🚶 Distances: Highway to Cascade summit trail jct., 2.1 mi; to summit of Porter Mt., 2.8 mi (4.5 km). Ascent from highway, 1960 ft (598 m). Elevation, 4059 ft (1238 m). Order of height, 38.

92 Pitchoff Mt.

ADK High Peaks Map: E6–E7 | Trails Illustrated Map 742: AA24

This bare ridge running SW to NE above the Cascade lakes offers exceptional views and, as described below, a nice traverse. Several worthwhile intermediate destinations make excellent up-and-back trips. In particular, the N summit is the most open of any on the ridge and is a 1.4 mi hike from the NE trailhead. The two

On Pitchoff Mt. viewing Giant Mt. Karen Fraser

ends of this trail are separated by 2.7 mi on NY 73. Two cars are advisable because the highway along the Cascade lakes is decidedly dangerous for pedestrians.

▶ Trailhead: The SW end of the trail starts just down and across the road from the Cascade trailhead (see trail 90 for trailhead description and parking considerations). ◀

Leaving the highway (0.0 mi) and marked with red DEC disks, it climbs some steps to the R of a retaining wall and enters the woods on a moderate climb. Soon swinging R, the trail levels off, and after some short ups and downs, comes to a lookout on the R at 0.8 mi. About 70 yd farther there is a better lookout with views of the Cascade lakes directly below, as well as of Mt. Marcy and other peaks.

Descending to a small saddle, the trail now climbs to the base of a slide created in 2001 when a large boulder slid across the trail. This boulder now sits 50 yd to the L of the trail.

After a 75-yd scramble up across the slide track, the trail again climbs steeply. At 1.1 mi, avoid the old trail going up steeply to R, instead angling L and then slightly down across a steep hillside below the base of some cliffs before swinging R and up to a jct. at the top of the ridge at 1.5 mi. (Trail R leads 0.1 mi on the level to the broad ledge with the balanced rocks. There is no sign at this jct., the side trail is not marked, and there are some potentially confusing splits on the way to the ledge, but all routes lead to the ledge and balanced rocks.) Turning L at this jct., the trail climbs at first easily and then encounters a few steep pitches before reaching the balanced boulder at the S summit of Pitchoff Mt. at 2 mi (3.2 km). Elevation, 3500 ft (1067 m). Ascent from highway, 1300 ft (396 m). There is no view from this highest summit, but a slightly lower summit at 2.2 mi offers a great view from a rock perch W of the trail.

From this view, the trail descends to a col at 2.5 mi and then climbs to a summit at 2.7 mi, where there are good views to the E. Continuing along the crest of the ridge, the trail reaches some broad, flat ledges with good views to the W at 2.8 mi followed by a gradual descent and climb to a 3480 ft summit at 3.2 mi. Descending easily at first, the trail soon descends a very steep gully, turns L for 30 yd, and then goes R and up very steeply for a few yards over a sharp little bump and then down to a col at 3.4 mi. Passing just W of another small summit, the trail drops to a lower col at the base of the N summit at 3.6 mi. From here, some scrambling over a minor summit and a few zigzags lead to the N summit at 3.8 mi where there are good views in all directions. As noted above, this 3323 ft summit is a good destination from the NE trailhead with an ascent of 1400 ft in 1.4 mi.

From the N summit, the trail at first heads N and begins to descend steeply to the woods, where it doubles back to the R under the summit rocks and soon begins a steep descent in an eroded gully. The grade eases as the trail begins to follow down the L bank of a brook, crosses a side stream, and then crosses the main brook at 4.8 mi. Recrossing the main brook 60 yards later, the trail continues an easy descent to the highway at 5.2 mi. This point is just below a small bridge 4.1 mi from Keene and 2.7 mi from the starting point.

🚶 Distances: Highway to balanced rocks, 1.6 mi; to summit of Pitchoff Mt., 2 mi; to N summit, 3.8 mi; to end of trail at highway, 5.2 mi (8.4 km).

93 Owls Head

ADK High Peaks Map: E7 | Trails Illustrated Map 742: AA–BB25

This little rocky peak has long been a popular climb and has probably been the first climb for many, many junior hikers. The start is now on a town road, but hikers must be aware that the surrounding land is private and subject to development, which could change the parking situation in the future.

▶ Trailhead: The start is on NY 73, 3.2 mi above Keene and 3.6 mi from the Cascade Mt. trailhead. Turn off NY 73 at Owls Head Ln. and follow the gravel road for 0.2 mi up to a turnout on the L, where the road makes a sharp R. There is a small green sign marking the start of the trail. There are no other markers on this trail. ◀

From the parking area (0.0 mi), the trail climbs moderately through open woods to the crest of a ridge. Turning L, the trail quickly reaches a ledge (mostly grown in)

Owls Head kids. Ann Hough

and continues on to a second and larger ledge at 0.3 mi. Flattening out above the second ledge, the trail soon resumes the climb and reaches a third ledge at 0.4 mi. Above this ledge, the trail flattens again before scrambling up the L side of the summit rocks and reaching the summit at 0.6 mi. There are views of Cascade, Pitchoff, Giant, and Hurricane Mts., with views to the N and E found by walking around the summit.

🚶 Distance: Parking area to summit of Owls Head, 0.6 mi (1 km). Ascent from parking area, 460 ft (140 m). Elevation, 2120 ft (646 m).

94 Old Mountain Rd. Section of the Jackrabbit Ski Trail

ADK High Peaks Map: E6–E7 | Trails Illustrated Map 742: AA24

This trail follows the route of the original road from Keene to Lake Placid through a wild, rugged notch with high cliffs rising to the E and many signs of beaver activity along the way. Recent research has determined that if the incident related in the famous poem "Allen's Bear Fight Up In Keene" actually happened, it would have happened on this road and not on the "Tight Nipping" road between Porter and Big Slide Mts. as suggested by Adirondack historian Alfred Donaldson. Hikers must still guess, however, which of the several large boulders is the one referred to by the lines, "Against the rock with giant strength / He held her out at his arm's length. / 'Oh God!' he cried in deep despair, / 'If you don't help me, don't help the bear.'"

Since 1986 this route has been part of the Jackrabbit Ski Trail and has received both regular maintenance and many improvements such as bridges and drainage to make for much easier walking than before. Because it is a ski trail, however, the beaver ponds are obstacles to summer travel as long as the beavers remain active. The route is marked with occasional yellow DEC ski trail disks. The trail is described from W to E, but up-and-back trips from either end are equally enjoyable.

▶ Trailheads: The Lake Placid trailhead is at the end of a dirt road that leaves NY 73 2.3 mi E of Adirondack Loj Rd. and 0.7 mi W of the entrance to the Mt. Van Hoevenberg recreation area. This road is passable for 1 mi, where there is parking for a few cars. ◀

The Keene trailhead is at the end of Alstead Hill Ln., which branches N off NY 73 0.9 mi W of the center of Keene. This road swings L at the Bark Eater Inn, after which it is straight uphill to the end of the road 3 mi from NY. 73.

*From the parking are*a at the Lake Placid trailhead (0.0 mi) the trail is mostly level, passing some large boulders on the L and then coming to a beaver meadow at 0.6 mi followed by a large sloping rock on the R at 0.7 mi. One can scramble to the top of this "summit in a valley" for a view of the cliffs and the notch ahead. About 150 yd beyond, the trail comes to a beaver dam and pond with a vague trail skirting the L shore until the original road is rejoined and the summit of the pass reached at 1 mi.

Now descending, the trail crosses a sidehill at 1.1 mi with a view through the trees down the valley and then past an old beaver pond on the L to a large beaver pond on the R. The trail descends a short, steep pitch to a beaver meadow at 1.4 mi. The trail continues to descend, crosses several small brooks, and reaches a final beaver pond with a large meadow on the R at 2.5 mi. crossing on or just below the dam, the descent is now easy to the end of Alstead Hill Rd. at 3.5 mi.

❄ Trail in winter: As part of the Jackrabbit Trail, this trail is frequently skied. The best approach is from the Keene end because the first mile of the Lake Placid end is plowed. The plowed section is not usually sanded, and parking at the end of the plowing is very limited. Until a bypass ski trail is constructed, winter parking and access will be a problem at the Lake Placid end of the trail. There is some parking just off NY 73.

🚶 Distance: Parking area to end of Alstead Hill Rd., 3.5 mi (5.6 km).

95 Cobble Hill

ADK High Peaks Map: D6 | Trails Illustrated Maps 742 and 746: CC23

This small, rocky knob rising directly above the village of Lake Placid offers interesting views of the village as well as of the high peaks farther away. The current trailhead (as of 2010) is the recommended start as it is much easier to find than the previous start on Cobble Hill Rd., although the Cobble Hill Rd. approach remains legal. One now has a choice of marked routes to the summit—one a short steep scramble, the other a longer, gentler approach.

▶ Trailhead: From the stoplight at the jct. of NY 73 and NY 86, proceed W on NY 86 (Main St.) through another stoplight to Mirror Lake Dr., which is the next R after the stoplight. Turn right, and from here it is 1.1 mi. to an entrance driveway to Northwood School, just past Northwood Rd. There is parking for a few cars on the left about 200 yds up this driveway. One can also park just beyond the Northwood School driveway at the entrance to (but not on) Mt. Whitney Way with access to the trail 100 yds up the road on the R. ◀

The trail from Mt. Whitney Way starts (0.0 mi) with a series of boardwalks to a currently unmaintained register box. From here, follow signs through a maze of trails next to the Northwood School driveway to the trailhead at 0.1 mi. and then to an old road at 0.4 mi. Proceeding straight across, as the sign now directs, it is another 0.4 mi of sometimes steep scrambling to the summit.

Turning L, the road leads past a cul-de-sac at the end of a new road to the E shore of Echo Pond. Bear R and follow along the E shore with a few red DEC disks to the N end of the pond. Bearing R at the next two jcts, now posted with old yellow signs, takes one to the summit. Total distance to the summit via Echo Pond is 1.6 mi, but the grades are much less than on the direct route.

🚶 Distance: Parking area to Cobble Hill summit via short route, 0.8 mi. (1.2 km), or longer route, 1.6 mi (2.4 km). Ascent, 460 ft (140 m). Elevation, 2343 ft (714 m).

PENINSULA NATURE TRAILS

ADK High Peaks Map: D5 | Trails Illustrated Map 746: CC23

This series of three loops offering a total of about 2 mi of trail is located on the Brewster Peninsula on the S shore of Lake Placid. There is a sign for these trails on Saranac Av. (NY 86) at the Howard Johnson's Restaurant, 0.5 mi W of Main St. Dr. 0.5 mi from Saranac Av. to a gate on the L. There are some interpretive panels along the central road and the Lakeshore Trail. A descriptive pamphlet on these trails is available from the Lake Placid–Essex County Visitors Bureau and is also posted (and usually available) at the register box at the gate at the start of the trails.

Henry's Woods

ADK High Peaks Map: D6 | Trails Illustrated Map 742: BB23

In 2008 the Uihlein Foundation completed a 2.5-mi. loop on a 212-acre parcel of land owned by the foundation. The loop is graded and constructed for all-season use by skiers, snowshoers, and hikers. Additional narrower hiking and snowshoe trails were added in 2010. The start is a parking lot on Bear Cub Ln. 200 yd S of Old Military Rd. Bear Cub Ln. is 0.8 mi. from the NY 73 end of Old Military Rd. at the ski jumps and 0.9 mi. east of the Northville-Placid Trail sign on Averyville Rd. From the parking lot, the trail climbs gradually to a junction at 0.3 mi. with the beginning of the loop. One could go either way, but bearing left the trail climbs moderately before leveling out at 0.8 mi. (Here one narrower trail, the Plateau Trail, goes R and makes possible a 1.5 mi. loop.) After some flat going next to the Cornell-Uihlein sugar bush, the trail begins a descent at 1.2 mi. and crosses a bridge at 1.4 mi. (Just beyond, the narrower Hilltop Trail diverges L and climbs to the summit of a small hill with some views, making a total loop of 3.5 mi.) The Main Loop crosses two more bridges and loops back to the junction with the outbound loop at 2.2 mi.

96 McKenzie Mt. from Whiteface Inn Ln.

ADK High Peaks Map: C5 | Trails Illustrated Map 746: CC22

This is the shortest approach to this 3861-ft peak that rises impressively above the W shore of Lake Placid. Though mostly wooded, the summit has two ledges that combine to offer a complete 360° view. As of 2012, one can no longer make this a loop trip by descending the old Shore Owners Association trail past Bartlett Pond to the W shore of Lake Placid because the landowners on the shore of Lake Placid have closed the Lakeshore Trail. At some point, the DEC intends to establish a new approach that stays on state land to restore this access.

▶ Trailhead: The start is on Whiteface Inn Ln. , which begins 1.3 mi W of the village of Lake Placid and just E of the Placid Outpost-Price Chopper shopping center on NY 86. Turn N on this road. The unmarked trailhead is a dirt road on the L, 1.4 mi from NY 86, just past the entrance for the Whiteface Club. The first 1.9 mi of this trail is the same as the Jackrabbit Ski Trail. ◀

Leaving Whiteface Inn Ln. (0.0 mi), the trail is road-width and is marked with yellow DEC disks plus occasional red Jackrabbit Trail markers. The trail passes a trail going L across a bridge after 20 yd; 40 yd beyond, a road goes R with a trail register just beyond. Past the trail register, the trail begins a steady climb. At 0.3 mi a road goes L and down to a small pond and dam. The steady climb continues until 0.7 mi before easing off just before a private road goes R and up. The McKenzie Mt. trail bears L and continues at an easy grade to Placid Lean-to on the R at 1.5 mi, with a brook crossing just beyond.

Past the lean-to, the trail descends gently to a four-way jct. at 1.9 mi, with the trail from NY 86 near Ray Brook (trail 97) coming in from the L and the Jackrabbit Trail (trail 98) continuing 3.6 mi straight ahead to McKenzie Pond Rd. near Saranac Lake. Turning sharp R at this jct., the trail is now marked with red DEC disks. The trail climbs moderately at first and even levels off for a brief stretch, but it soon begins a steep to very steep climb, gaining over 1000 ft in just over half a mile. The steep climbing ends at a side trail R to a view to the S at 2.6 mi.

Soon crossing the first summit, the trail descends and then climbs to pass just below the second summit at 2.8 mi. Dipping and climbing again, the trail arrives at the third summit at 3 mi, with views to the N and W from a ledge just L of the trail. The trail continues to the fourth summit at 3.2 mi, and then descends steeply before beginning the final climb to the true summit. Climbing over a ledge at 3.5 mi, the trail levels out near the summit with a trail L a few yards farther leading to a spectacular "balcony" over the NW Adirondacks, with views as far E as Mt. Marcy as well. This is the best and most unique view from McKenzie Mt., but just beyond at the true summit at 3.6 mi there is a good 180° view encompassing Whiteface Mt., Lake Placid, and many of the High Peaks. This is the end of the red DEC markers. The return via Bartlett Pond, as described in previous guides, is no longer legal owing to private property issues.

🚶 Distances: Whiteface Inn Rd. to jct. with trail from NY 86 near Ray Brook, 1.9 mi; to summit of McKenzie Mt., 3.6 mi (5.8 km). Ascent, 1940 ft (591 m). Elevation, 3861 ft (1177 m).

SHORE OWNERS ASSOCIATION TRAILS
(Minimum maintenance and marking; see introduction, p. 19.)

ADK High Peaks Map: C4–C5 | Trails Illustrated Map 746: CC22-23

Starting as far back as the end of the nineteenth century, the Lake Placid Shore Owners Association (SOA) cut and maintained a system of trails along the shores of Lake Placid and on to the mountains above. Maintenance continued long enough to clear away much of the damage left by the 1950 hurricane, but was largely given up in the 1970s. Since 1996, however, several individuals have taken on the task of reopening the system of trails along the west shore of Lake Placid to the summits of McKenzie Mt., Moose Mt., and Loch Bonnie. Although the trails are now marked with SOA disks and signs, the levels of maintenance and use are less than on other trail systems. For this reason, these trails should be regarded as unmarked paths similar to the formerly trailless 4000 ft peaks and the same cautions apply (see p. 19).

As of 2012, the Chipmunk Ln. access and the Lakeshore Trail have been closed to the public at the landowner's request. The Chipmunk Ln. approach has been replaced with legal access via Blodgett Rd., located on the L of Whiteface Inn Ln. 200 yd past the trailhead for trail 96. Park just in from Whiteface Inn Ln. and follow Blodgett Rd. to a gate where markers lead up to the L and then R in about 20 yds to stay off an ATV trail. The marked route then parallels the private road before turning R and down to a barrier at the end of the private road. The legal route then angles L and descends to the Lake Trail. Turn L on the Lake Trail and carefully follow the signs and markers for 0.3 mi. to a jct. with a trail L that leads to McKenzie Mt. via Bartlett Pond and the Two Brooks Trail to Moose Mt. The trail straight ahead is the Lake Trail, which is now closed to the public.

Wadsworth Trail from Moose Mt. to McKenzie Mt.

ADK High Peaks Map: C4 | Trails Illustrated Map 746: CC22

Originally cut in the 1950s, this trail never received much maintenance or use, so there is very little evidence of trail tread and great care is required to follow its twists and turns. The trail is marked with yellow SOA disks; but be aware that there are a few side trails, marked with solid yellow disks, that should not be confused with the through trail.

▶ Trailhead: See Undercliff Approach to Loch Bonnie and Moose Mt., below. ◀

From the summit of Moose Mt. (0.0 mi) the trail descends at a mostly moderate grade to a yellow-marked side route L at 0.9 mi. Continuing down, the trail reaches the low point between the two peaks at 1.4 mi, where it turns sharp L and up for 200 yd. At the top of this climb, another yellow-marked side trail goes L. (Markers, but no trail, lead three-tenths of a mile to the small pond shown on the map between the two peaks.) Bearing R and up gradually, the trail comes to a glade at 1.8 mi, where it again goes sharp L and up steeply to a summit at 1.9 mi. Yellow markers lead a few yards R to a view.

From this summit the trail descends to a col at 2.2 mi, followed by a zigzagging climb through a cliff band to an overgrown summit and then down again to a col at 2.5 mi. From here the trail climbs steeply to a side trail leading L at 2.7 mi. (Side trail leads 100 yd to a view of Moose Mt.)

Now at a gentle grade, the Wadsworth Trail reaches the jct. with the Bartlett Pond Trail to McKenzie Mt. at 3 mi. From here it is 0.1 mi to the summit of McKenzie Mt.

Undercliff Approach to Loch Bonnie and Moose Mt.

ADK High Peaks Map: D4 | Trails Illustrated Map 746: CC23

This trail starts on the only piece of state land that reaches the W shore of Lake Placid. It provides the opportunity for a paddle approach to Loch Bonnie and Moose Mt. The landing for canoes is somewhat difficult and parts of the lower section of this trail are obscure, but for the adventurous this is a unique and different experience.

The paddle starts at the state boat launch on George and Bliss Rds. at the N end of Mirror Lake Dr. The trailhead is on the piece of state land just S of Undercliff. There is no marker except for a green pedestal for the Lake Placid Village Electric on the shore. The trail, marked with a sign, starts just N of the pedestal.

From the lake shore, the trail (often with no visible tread) starts up a valley with cliffs on the R. At 0.2 mi there is a signed jct with a equally vague trail. (Trail L is the Lake Trail, which soon reaches private land that is closed to the public. Trail R climbs over a steep ridge to avoid private property and connects with the Eagle Eyrie trail at the N end of Lake Placid.) The trail to Loch Bonnie and Moose Mt. continues to a jct at 0.5 mi with the Minnow Brook trail. Still with yellow SOA disks, the trail goes R and climbs to the lean-to at Loch Bonnie at 1.3 mi. From the lean-to (which has no floor and is slowly sinking into the marsh), a few logs permit one to cross the inlet to Loch Bonnie to the W edge of the bog surrounding the pond. About 10 yd steeply up into the woods the trail reaches a jct. with a trail leading L (with white markers) that connects with the Two Brooks Trail in approximately 0.2 mi. From this jct. the trail climbs steeply with a few breaks to the base of a cliff at 2.1 mi. Here the trail goes L and down for a few yards before turning R and up to a jct. with the Two Brooks Trail at 2.2 mi, with the summit just beyond at 2.3 mi.

97   Haystack Mt. from NY 86 near Ray Brook

ADK High Peaks Map: C5 | Trails Illustrated Map 746: CC22

Haystack Mt. (not to be confused with the 4960 ft Mt. Haystack) offers a very rewarding view and has become a popular destination owing to its easy access from a good parking area between Lake Placid and Saranac Lake.

▶ Trailhead: The trail begins at a turnout on NY 86, 1.6 mi E of DEC Headquarters in Ray Brook and 1.4 mi W of the jct. with Old Military Rd. The trail is marked with a DEC sign and blue DEC markers. ◀

From the highway (0.0 mi), the trail crosses a small knoll and dips to cross a small wet area after 100 yd before swinging first R and then L and beginning a gradual climb to a crest at 0.3 mi in an open hardwood forest. Dipping slightly, the trail climbs gradually to a second crest and soon crosses a stream at 0.5 mi. Swinging L after crossing the stream, the trail slabs gently upward along the base of low ledges until it begins an equally gentle descent at 1.1 mi. Following down a small ridge, the trail comes to a small open area at 1.5 mi. After a short, moderate descent, the trail swings R and continues to descend gently to a small brook at 1.8 mi, where the old route (abandoned in 1984) comes in from the L.

Now following an old road, the trail is practically level for a few hundred yards before beginning a gradual to moderate climb along the L bank of Little Ray Brook. Passing some old foundations on the R at 2.2 mi, the trail reaches a jct. at 2.4 mi with a red-marked trail on the R to McKenzie Mt. (This trail continues at a moderate grade with some wet areas for 1.2 mi to a jct. with the trail from Whiteface Inn Rd., trail 96.)

Bearing L at this jct. and still with blue markers, the Haystack Mt. trail crosses a small brook in 25 yd and then Little Ray Brook just below a rebuilt dam in another 50 yd. From this dam the trail begins to climb a series of steep pitches interspersed with short stretches of easier going. At 3 mi the trail begins the final pitch, going up a steep gully to the L of some cliffs to emerge on the first ledge at 3.2 mi. After a slight dip, the trail continues to the summit at 3.3 mi, where there are good views from Whiteface Mt. to Mt. Marcy, Algonquin Peak, the Seward Range, and many of the larger lakes to the W.

🐾 Distances: NY 86 to jct. with trail to McKenzie Mt.; 2.4 mi; to summit of Haystack Mt., 3.3 mi (5.3 km). Ascent, 1240 ft (378 m). Elevation, 2878 ft (877 m).

98 Jackrabbit Ski Trail from McKenzie Pond Rd.

ADK High Peaks Map: B5–C5 | Trails Illustrated Map 746: CC21

Although built primarily as a ski trail, the Jackrabbit Trail is usable in all seasons. The trail offers the only public trail access to McKenzie Pond while also providing a pleasant, if longer, approach to McKenzie Mt. or an easy 5.5 mi walk through to Lake Placid.

▶ Trailhead: On McKenzie Pond Rd. 2.2 mi from NY 86 in Ray Brook and 2.1 mi from the bank on NY. 86 (Lake Flower Ave.) in Saranac Lake. A blue and red sign marks the start. ◀

From the road (0.0 mi), the trail is marked with red Jackrabbit Trail markers, later interspersed with yellow DEC ski trail markers. The trail climbs slightly and then is flat to a power line, which is followed for 100 yd before descending slightly to a small brook at 0.3 mi. Crossing the brook on a bridge, the trail ascends slightly to reach state land and a register box at 0.5 mi, after which some more short climbs and descents lead to a bridge across the outlet to McKenzie Pond at 0.9 mi.

Past the bridge, the trail ascends gently and at 1 mi joins an old road that is followed on the flat to a jct. at 1.9 mi. (Side trail L leads 0.2 mi to the dam at the outlet to McKenzie Pond.) Continuing straight ahead, the road-width trail soon begins a steady, moderate climb, while gaining 900 ft (274 m), to a height of land at 3.4 mi. Descending moderately from the height of land, the trail reaches the jct. with the trail to McKenzie Mt. from Whiteface Inn (trail 96) at 3.6 mi.

❄ Trail in winter: A popular ski route, this trail receives more use in winter than in summer. The ski to McKenzie Pond is suitable for novices, whereas the hill to the height of land requires strong-intermediate skills.

🐾 Distances: McKenzie Pond Rd. to jct. with side trail to McKenzie Pond, 1.9 mi; to jct. with Whiteface Inn Rd. trail to McKenzie Mt., 3.6 mi.

99 Northville–Placid Trail (N–P Trail) from Averyville Rd. to Duck Hole

ADK High Peaks Map: C6–C7 | Trails Illustrated Map 742: BB22

This is the most northerly section of the 132-mi N–P Trail. ADK has published a separate guidebook covering the entire trail for those interested in traversing this classic route. This partial description is included here for those interested in access to the remote areas at the headwaters of the Cold River. This guide also describes two more adjoining sections that cover Long Lake to Duck Hole via Shattuck Clearing (trail 133, pp. 209 and 211).

▶ Trailhead: The start is on Averyville Rd. near Lake Placid. From the jct. of NY 73 and NY 86 in Lake Placid, proceed 0.2 mi E on NY 73 and turn S on Station St. At Old Military Rd. at 1 mi there is a large DEC sign marking the official start/terminus of the N-P Trail. Continuing straight ahead and now on Averyville Rd., the trailhead is another 1.2 mi on the L, just before a bridge over the Chubb River. There is a small turnout on the L. ◀

Leaving the road (0.0 mi) and marked with blue DEC disks, the trail begins following an old road along the R bank of the Chubb River, but veers L away from the river at 0.1 mi and soon arrives at the trail register. From the register the trail climbs at a steady, gradual grade until 0.5 mi, where it levels out and continues with short ups and downs. An obscure angler's trail from Bear Cub Rd. to the Chubb River crosses the trail at 1.3 mi, and the trail begins crossing an extensive spruce swamp at 2.2 mi. At 2.4 mi, an unmarked trail diverges L, with the end of the spruce swamp coming at 2.5 mi. The trail crosses a large brook on a good bridge at 3.3 mi and continues on to join an old tote road at 3.7 mi, where it swings L and begins a gradual climb to a beaver pond on the R at 4.1 mi. From here there is a view of a slide on the W side of Nye Mt., the slide a result of the earthquake of October 7, 1983.

The trail, now on the flat, passes E of the beaver pond, with another unmarked trail diverging R at 4.4 mi. Bearing L, the trail crosses a large brook at 4.8 mi, and crosses two more brooks before descending slightly to a bridge over the Chubb River at 6.1 mi. On the far side of the bridge the trail joins the original route from Averyville. Turning L and proceeding up the L bank of the Chubb River, the trail reaches a jct. with a side trail leading L to the former site of Wanika Falls Lean-to at 6.7 mi. (This trail climbs steeply to a crossing of the Chubb River just above a small falls. The former lean-to site is on the far bank, 0.1 mi from the main trail, while the actual Wanika Falls are about 100 yd above this point.)

From the jct. with the side trail to Wanika Falls, the N-P Trail climbs steeply at first and then more easily to a height of land at 7 mi and begins descending. Crossing several brooks as it descends, the trail levels out past a brook at 7.6 mi and continues with easy ups and downs to Moose Pond Lean-to at 8.3 mi. This is a picturesque spot to camp, with wild and rugged views of the Sawtooth Range across the pond.

Past the lean-to, the trail descends to the L bank of Moose Creek at 8.5 mi, but soon leaves the brook and crosses a beaver dam at 8.8 mi. The trail now continues to parallel Moose Creek but remains some distance back from it. At 9.7 mi the trail begins to climb away from Moose Creek and reaches a small height of land at 10.2 mi, after which it descends into the valley of Roaring Brook. At 10.5 mi there is a short, steep pitch up, followed by a more moderate descent to the R bank of Roaring Brook at 10.6 mi. The trail now continues along the brook to a jct. at 11.7 mi with a trail L to Preston Ponds and Upper Works (trail 127). Continuing straight ahead at this jct. and now marked with both red and blue markers, the trail proceeds with several easy ups and downs to a large, open area leading down to the now-breached dam (2011) at Duck Hole at 12.2 mi.

Here there are two lean-tos and plenty of tent sites. One lean-to is just before the bridge and dam, and the other is in the woods on a point of land 100 yd E of the dam. A ranger station at the W edge of the clearing was removed in December 1977 in order to bring the area into compliance with wilderness use guidelines. Blue-marked trail 128 crosses below the breached dam and leads to Bradley Pond and the trailhead at Tahawus (trail 128). The N-P Trail heads W along an old truck trail that connects with a trail heading to Ward Brook and the trailhead at Coreys. See Southern Section, p. 179, for descriptions of all these trails.

🚶 Distances: Parking area on Averyville Rd. to Wanika Falls, 6.7 mi; to Moose Pond Lean-to, 8.3 mi; to jct. with trail 127 to Preston Ponds Trail, 11.7 mi; to Duck Hole, 12.2 mi (19.7 km).

99A Averyville to Pine Pond

ADK High Peaks Map: C7 | Trails Illustrated Map 742: AA21–BB20

Following an old road, this often muddy 6-mi route is more popular with mountain bikers and cross-country skiers than hikers. It is also used by snowmobiles and ATVs. Pine Pond is an attractive destination, although more often reached via the portage trail from Oseetah Lake.

▶ Trailhead: At the end of Averyville Rd., 3 mi. past the Northville–Placid Trail parking area (see trail 99) there is a small parking area down and to the L. ◀

From the parking area (0.0 mi.). the road-width trail climbs for 0.3 mi and then descends gently to a flat area at 1.4 mi. Now mostly flat or gradually downhill, the trail comes close to the R bank of Cold Brook at 4 mi before swinging R and gradually up to a broad ridge at 4.8 mi. After a brief descent, the trail is again mostly flat to a jct. at 6.3 mi. Trail L leads 0.3 mi. to Pine Pond. Trail R leads 0.2 mi. to Oseetah Lake.

❄ Trail in winter: Easy terrain makes this route suitable for even low-intermediate skiers, but weekend snowmobile traffic may reduce the overall experience. In some winters, one can make this a point-to-point trip by (ice conditions permitting) skiing across Oseetah Lake and down the Saranac River to a trail that reaches NY 86 just E of the village of Saranac Lake at the railroad crossing.

🚶 Distances: Parking area to Pine Pond, 6.6 mi (10.6 km)

100 Scarface Mt.

ADK High Peaks Map: B5–B6 | Trails Illustrated Map 742: CC21

The trail to this peak offers some pleasant, easy walking through some attractive forests before a climb to some unique but increasingly obscured views from several ledges on the way to Scarface's wooded summit.

▶ Trailhead: The trail starts 0.1 mi down Ray Brook Rd. from NY 86, directly across from the DEC Region 5 Headquarters. A large sign marks the start, and there is a small parking lot off the road. ◀

From the parking lot (0.0 mi), the trail goes through a pine forest, crosses a railroad track, and comes to an elaborate bridge over Ray Brook at 0.5 mi. Climbing the opposite bank on a series of steps, the trail continues on the flat to a clearing at 0.7 mi and then gradually ascends to a higher plateau and clearing with a large rock in its center. Just beyond this point, at 1.5 mi, the trail joins a road, which was the original route. Note this turn well for the return trip.

Turning L, the trail descends slightly along this road and then turns sharp L off the road at 1.7 mi. Continuing mostly on the level, the trail crosses a brook at 2.2 mi. After several alternating steep and easy pitches, the trail comes close to the top of a col on the ridge leading W from Scarface Mt., and then at 3 mi begins a steep climb to a ledge at 3.1 mi from which there are some views to the SW, W, and NW. From the first ledge, the marked trail bears R and up. Some 50 yd beyond the first ledge a 25 yd bushwhack to the R leads to a ledge with excellent views to the SE, S, and W. At 3.2 mi the trail comes to more open rock with the best views to the SE and S. The trail continues at easy grades to a western summit of Scarface Mt., which now offers only obscured views, at 3.4 mi. A marked trail now continues to the viewless summit of Scarface at approximately 3.8 mi.

🚶 Distances: Parking lot on Ray Brook Rd. to jct. with old route, 1.5 mi; to ledge near summit of Scarface Mt., 3.2 mi (5.2 km). Ascent from parking lot, 1480 ft (451 m). Elevation, 3088 ft (942 m).

101 Baker Mt.

ADK High Peaks Map: B5 | Trails Illustrated Map 746: CC21

This little mountain offers some of the best views of lakes and mountains for the amount of effort involved. From its partially wooded summit, lookouts provide views of Moose and McKenzie Mts. to the E, many of the high peaks to the SE and S, and many lakes to the SW and W.

▶ Trailhead: Start at the N end of Moody Pond just N of the village of Saranac Lake. Coming into Saranac Lake on NY 86 from Lake Placid, turn R onto Brandy Brook Rd. at the traffic islands with a bank on the R. After crossing the railroad track 200 yd from the bank, immediately turn L on Pine St., which recrosses the track in 0.5 mi. In another quarter mile, at the top of a hill, Forest Hill Av. goes R on a bridge over the railroad track and leads in 0.5 mi to the N end of Moody Pond. Forest Hill Av. can also be reached by turning off NY 3 just N of the village onto Pine St. The start is marked with a standard DEC sign and the trail is marked with red DEC markers. ◀

From the road (0.0 mi), the trail ascends an old road, crosses under a power line, and turns sharp R 120 yd from the start. In another 75 yd the trail bears L, climbs past an old quarry for 50 yd, and then bears R—avoiding the trail that continues along the upper edge of the quarry. At 0.2 mi a house is visible on the R, and now the trail ascends to a brief level area at 0.4 mi. Soon climbing again, the marked trail splits at 0.6 mi. The R branch is easier to follow and offers more views, but it is steeper and more exposed than the L branch. The two routes rejoin after 100 yd but then split before joining again at a large ledge at 0.8 mi just below the summit at 0.9 mi.

Note: Markers are scarce, especially on the descent. Be alert and carefully supervise any children or inexperienced members of the party when leaving the summit as there are several unmarked side trails leading away from it.

🚶 Distance: Moody Pond to summit of Baker Mt., 0.9 mi (1.5 km). Ascent, 900 ft (274 m). Elevation, 2452 ft (748 m).

102 Ampersand Mt.

ADK High Peaks Map: A7 | Trails Illustrated Map 742: AA19

The view from the totally bald summit of this former fire tower peak is one of the best in the Adirondacks. Sitting on the boundary between the mountains and the lake country, Ampersand Mt. offers the best of both views. The name for the peak apparently comes from Ampersand Creek, which was so named because it twisted and turned so much that it resembled the ampersand symbol, "&."

▶ Trailhead: The start is on NY 3, 8.1 mi W of Saranac Lake and 7.3 mi E of the jct. of NY3 and NY 30 E of Tupper Lake. There is a large turnout on the N side of the road which is also the parking area for the 0.6-mi trail leading down to Middle Saranac Lake and Ampersand Beach—a nice spot to swim after the climb. ◀

*Leaving the S side of the highwa*y (0.0 mi) at a small DEC sign, the trail, marked with red DEC disks and yellow paint blazes, proceeds past a locked gate on the level on an old jeep road. This section of the trail has been well maintained and is very easy walking as it gently rises and falls through a beautiful, mature forest. At 0.8 mi the trail crosses a long, wet section on an extensive series of bridges, and at 1.2 mi begins a steady climb to the site of the former observer's cabin, which is reached at 1.7 mi.

Turning sharp R, the trail follows up the L bank of a small brook at easy to moderate grades before becoming much steeper at 1.9 mi. The next half mile of trail has benefited greatly from some very intensive trail work that has turned this formerly rough and eroded section into an example of how even the worst trail can be stabilized to prevent further erosion and consequent resource deterioration. At 2.4 mi the grade eases just before the crest of the ridge, and the trail now swings L and climbs easily up to a large split boulder on the R at 2.5 mi. Just beyond, the trail reaches a height of land and descends slightly before turning sharp R and climbing onto the open rocks. From here, the trail is marked profusely with yellow paint blazes to the summit at 2.7 mi.

The site of the former fire tower is just beyond and slightly below the true summit. There is a tablet on a rock face near this spot dedicated to the memory of Walter Channing Rice, 1852–1924, the "Hermit of Ampersand, who kept Vigil from this peak, 1915–1923." The summit was once wooded, but Verplanck Colvin in his nineteenth-century survey had the trees removed from this essential survey station. Erosion set in and washed all the soil away, and now nothing remains but the bare rock.

🐾 Distances: NY 3 to site of observer's cabin, 1.7 mi; to summit of Ampersand Mt., 2.7 mi (4.4 km). Ascent from highway, 1775 ft (541 m). Elevation, 3352 ft (1022 m).

103 Taylor Pond Trail

ADK High Peaks Map: F1/1a–E1 | Trails Illustrated Map 746: GG25

As a hiking trail, the loop around the pond is not particularly scenic since it remains back from the shore for much of its length and provides direct access only to the lean-to on the SE shore. It does, however, offer a long, nearly flat walk through a variety of forested terrain where solitude is practically guaranteed. The trail is designated as a snowmobile trail with some of it part of a "corridor trail" leading W from AuSable Forks. Winter users use ice to cross the two inlets at the south end of the pond, which necessitates hikers making a short bushwhack upstream to cross these inlets.

There is a relatively undeveloped state campground at the start of the trail, offering primitive tent sites with well water and privies. When the campground is in operation, the two lean-tos and two designated campsites on the shore are subject to the same fee as the sites in the campground with camping restricted to those sites. There is a day-use parking fee, and canoes are available for rent.

▶ Trailhead: The entrance to Taylor Pond Campground is located on Silver Lake Rd. 2.8 mi E of its jct. with Union Falls Rd. at Silver Lake and 3.8 mi W of Bonnieview Rd. or approximately 10 mi W of Au Sable Forks. ◀

Starting at the caretaker's cabin (0.0 mi), the trail goes straight for 50 yd and then bears R to the end of the campground road in another 200 yd. Now on an old tote road with occasional snowmobile trail markers, the trail climbs over a low ridge and at 1.3 mi reaches a jct. with a trail L that leads to the two designated campsites on the NE shore. (This jct., like many others on this trail, is not marked, and hikers must remain alert and look for the trail markers at each jct.) Continuing on, the trail swings farther R with a bit of the NW bay visible. At 1.7 mi, another unmarked trail diverges L to the shore.

Now following a series of old roads, the trail swings sharp L at 1.8 mi and again at a jct. at 2 mi. The trail then crosses a beautiful, fern-filled swamp before swinging sharp R and up at 2.1 mi. (Trail straight ahead at this jct. also leads to the shore.) Soon crossing a stream, the trail begins a steady, gradual climb to a jct. at 2.8 mi (jct "CL 39" according to the snowmobile sign.) Turning L on a better road and now marked as "Corridor 8," the trail continues to climb in gentle stages until it swings L and away from the good road (on "Secondary 81A") at 3.3 mi. Now the trail descends to within 100 vertical ft of the pond at 5 mi, parallels the shore, and then pulls away again at 5.5 mi and becomes rougher as it begins to circle the SW end of the pond.

At 6 mi the trail crosses an inlet (bushwhack upstream to cross) and then swings sharp L and up onto a flat shelf. Reaching a second inlet at 6.5 mi, (also bushwhack upstream to cross) the trail continues to a road at 7 mi, after which the walking is easier to a lean-to at 8.1 mi. Beyond the lean-to the trail follows a wider road that gradually pulls away from the pond. Several other roads diverge R and the trail climbs gradually to a jct. at 9.5 mi. The snowmobile trail continues straight ahead, coming out on the Silver Lake Rd. E of the campground. The shortest return to the campground is to turn L and down to another jct. at 10.3 mi. Turning L, the trail goes up over a small knoll and down to the end of the dam at the NE corner of the pond. Crossing the dam, the trail reaches the caretaker's cabin at 10.5 mi.

❄ Trail in winter: Because most of this trail sees little snowmobile traffic, it makes a good ski trip. Ice conditions permitting, most skiers will choose to ski across the pond from the point at 5 mi. where the trail most closely approaches the shore.

🚶🚶 Distances: Caretaker's cabin to S end of pond, 6 mi; to E shore lean-to, 8.1 mi; complete loop around pond, 10.5 mi (16.9 km). 🍂

Cascade on the Boquet River. Richard J. Nowicki

Eastern Section

 This section includes hikes from Poke-O-Moonshine Mt. to trails around North Hudson. With the exception of the summits of Giant Mt. and Rocky Peak Ridge, this area is characterized by lower rocky peaks with young second-growth forests and many views from numerous ledges. Included here are the entire Jay Mountain and Hurricane Mountain Wilderness Areas as well as the Giant Mountain Wilderness Area.

With its proximity to the Champlain Valley, this area was the first to be visited by settlers, and the natural route along the Boquet and Schroon Rivers, now followed by NY 9, was important as early as the Revolutionary War. Many of the now seemingly remote areas were once the homes of productive farms that existed for many generations. The higher hillsides have nearly all been lumbered or burned, which means there is little virgin timber to appreciate, but the multitude of views makes this an interesting area to explore.

❋ Trails in winter: Unless noted otherwise, these trails are not suited for skiing. Ascents of Giant Mt. and Rocky Peak Ridge may require the use of crampons and an ice axe.

The following are some of the best hikes the area has to offer.

SHORT HIKES

Poke-O-Moonshine Mt.: 2.4 mi (3.9 km) round-trip. This popular fire tower peak offers tremendous views of lakes and mountains for just over 1 mi of ascent. See trail 110.

The Crows: 3.5 mi (5.6 km) round-trip. These two rocky peaks offer numerous views with a complete loop, finishing with a pleasant walk down a dirt road. Many shorter variations are also possible. See trail 108.

MODERATE HIKES

Hurricane Mt. from NY 9N: 5.3 mi (8.5 km) round-trip. Excellent views with not too much strenuous climbing. See trail 104.

Bald Peak: 7.7 mi (12.4 km) round-trip. A spectacular hike, finishing with a long, open ridge leading to an unparalleled view of the Champlain Valley. See trail 112.

HARDER HIKE

Giant Mt. from the East via Rocky Peak Ridge with descent via Ridge Trail: 11 mi (17.7 km) point to point. The outstanding hike in the Adirondacks, with more than 5 mi of open walking. Over 5300 vertical feet of climbing means this hike is for experienced hikers only, but the rewards are commensurate with the effort. See trails 48 and 112.

HURRICANE MT.

ADK High Peaks Map: G7 | Trails Illustrated Map 742: AA27

There are three approaches to this popular rocky summit. The trail from NY 9N is the most popular. Significant rerouting and improved bridging has added 0.8 mi. to the ascent, but footing is good throughout with now several new views before the summit. Hurricane Mt. offers one of the most commanding views of any of the lesser peaks, and because of this was an important survey station for Verplanck Colvin during his Adirondack survey. For many years there was an active fire tower on this peak, but the tower was abandoned in the late 1970s. As of 2015, the tower is unsafe to climb, but is no longer slated for removal and may be restored.

The view from the summit of Hurricane encompasses much of the length of Lake Champlain and the Green Mountains in Vermont as well as many of the high peaks. There are plenty of blueberries, starting in early August.

104 Hurricane Mt. from NY 9N

ADK High Peaks Map: G7 | Trails Illustrated Map 742: AA27

▶ Trailhead: This trail leaves the N side of NY 9N at the height of land 3.5 mi E of the jct. of NY 9N and NY 73 between Keene and Keene Valley, and 6.5 mi W of the jct. of NY 9N and NY 9 at the S end of the village of Elizabethtown. ◀

Marked with red DEC disks, the trail leaves the highway (0.0 mi) and immediately begins switchbacking up to a first view at 0.4 mi. Leveling off, the trail reaches the first set of bridges at 1 mi. Now mostly on the level, the trail reaches a longer series of bridges leading to an open vlei with a view of Tripod Mt. and Mt. Marcy at 1.1 mi.

The trail now crosses a brook and begins climbing through a hardwood forest on a new section of trail. Briefly rejoining the old trail at 1.5 mi. the trail again diverges L at 1.7 mi for the longest section of new trail that avoids all the steepest climbs and poor footing. Continuing at mostly moderate grades, a long traverse to the R leads to a small ledge at 2.6 mi followed by a larger ledge with a view of the tower and the High Peaks at 2.8 mi. After passing another open ledge, the trail reaches a jct. with the ADK trail from Keene (trail 106) at 3.2 mi. Turning R, the trail reaches the jct with the old trail at 3.3 mi just before the final climb up summit rocks to the summit at 3.4 mi.

🚶 Distance: NY 9N to summit of Hurricane Mt., 3.4 mi (5.5 km). Ascent from highway, 2000 ft (610 m). Elevation, 3694 ft (1126 m).

105   Hurricane Mt. from the East

ADK High Peaks Map: G7 | Trails Illustrated Map 742: AA28

This approach was once used by the fire tower observer and was the shortest route to the summit, but now one must hike from the end of the town road, 1.2 mi below the former observer's cabin—making this approach the same length as the trail from NY. 9N (trail 104).

▶ Trailhead: The start is at the end of a road that branches R off NY 9N 2.2 mi from the jct. of NY 9N and NY 9 at the S end of the village of Elizabethtown. The dirt road goes R just before a bridge and climbs steadily to a gate blocking further vehicular access at 2.7 mi, where there is a small parking area on the R. Parking is not permitted on the road. The road that continues past the gate is private and only provides access to a private inholding. Therefore, do not proceed even if the gate is open. ◀

From the gate (0.0 mi), the grade is gentle to a L turn away from a private driveway at 0.4 mi, after which the old road climbs to the site of the former observer's cabin at the end of the road at 1.2 mi. Past this point, the trail drops down a few yards to a stream with the former lean-to site on the R. From here the trail begins climbing moderately, but after crossing another stream at 1.4 mi, it climbs steeply with only a few breathers until it emerges on the rocks just before reaching the summit at 2.7 mi.

🚶 Distances: Gate at end of public road to observer's cabin site, 1.2 mi; to summit of Hurricane Mt., 2.7 mi (4.4 km). Ascent from gate, 1700 ft (518 m). Elevation, 3694 ft (1126 m).

106 Hurricane Mt. from Keene

ADK High Peaks Map: G6–G7 | Trails Illustrated Map 742: BB27

Commonly known as the North Trail to Hurricane Mt., this is the longest approach to Hurricane but the grades are mostly moderate. There also is an attractive and little-used lean-to just over a mile from the end of the road, which makes this approach a wonderful first camping trip for young families. The trail is marked with blue DEC markers and maintained by the Hurricane Chapter of ADK.

▶ Trailhead: The start is at the end of O'Toole Ln. off Hurricane Rd. above Keene. From just S of the center of the hamlet of Keene, proceed E 2.3 mi up a long hill. Bear L on O'Toole Ln. where Hurricane Rd. makes a sharp R turn. This point can also be reached by following Hurricane Rd. approximately 4 mi N from NY 9N. Proceed up the dirt road 1.2 mi to Crow Clearing, where cars may be parked. ◀

Leaving the R side of the clearing (0.0 mi), the Hurricane Trail crosses a bridge over a small brook, crosses another small stream at 0.4 mi, and continues mostly on the level to a jct. at 1.1 mi, where an ADK trail bears L to Lost Pond (trail 107). Gulf Brook Lean-to has been relocated 0.1 mi. up the trail to Lost Pond.

Turning sharp R at the former lean-to site, the Hurricane Trail crosses Gulf Brook (designated campsites to the L) and begins a gradual to moderate ascent on a new (2013) section of trail that avoids several brook crossings. Rejoining the old route at 1.7 mi, the trail now climbs next to a small brook before swinging R and up more steeply at 2.1 mi. The steeper climbing continues with a few breaks through a beautiful birch forest to the jct. with the trail from NY 9N (trail 104) at 2.7 mi. Continuing straight ahead, the trail soon reaches the summit rocks and then the summit at 3 mi.

🐾 Distances: Crow Clearing to Gulf Brook Lean-to, 1.1 mi; to summit of Hurricane Mt., 3 mi (4.8 km). Ascent from Crow Clearing, 1600 ft (488 m). Elevation, 3694 ft (1126 m).

107 Lost Pond and Weston Mt.

ADK High Peaks Map: G6 | Trails Illustrated Map 742: BB27

▶ Locator: The trail to this hidden little body of water branches L from the North Trail to Hurricane Mt. at Gulf Brook Lean-to, 1.1 mi from Crow Clearing (see trail 106). ◀

Bearing L at the jct. (0.0 mi), the trail, with yellow DEC markers, follows near the R bank of Gulf Brook, past Gulf Brook Lean-to on the L at 0.1 mi, until it turns sharp L and up at 0.3 mi. The trail climbs steadily with a few switchbacks until it levels off about 300 yd before reaching the end of Lost Pond at 0.7 mi. The trail continues around the W shore of the pond to the Walter Biesemeyer Memorial Lean-to at 1.1 mi.

A trail, now marked with red DEC markers, continues past the lean-to approximately 0.3 mi to the summit of Weston Mt. The view from this rocky summit ranges from Hurricane Mt. to Mt. Marcy to Whiteface Mt., with only the NE blocked by some low trees. The mostly unmarked trail now continues down the N side and along Nun-da-ga-o Ridge (trail 109).

🚶 Distances: Crow Clearing to Gulf Brook Lean-to, 1.1 mi; to Biesemeyer Lean-to on Lost Pond, 2.1 mi (3.4 km); to Weston Mt., 2.4 mi (3.9 km).

108 Big Crow and Little Crow Mts.

ADK High Peaks Map: G6 | Trails Illustrated Map 742: BB26

These two rocky pinnacles, which dominate the landscape at the top of East Hill, have long been favorites of local hikers. They offer a variety of views from their many ledges, including 28 major peaks from Big Crow. Some care is needed in following this trail both up and down because it makes many sharp turns winding through the many ledges. Big Crow can also be ascended separately in 0.7 mi if one drives to Crow Clearing (see trailhead information, trail 106, p. 162).

▶ Trailhead: The start is 2 mi above Keene on Hurricane Rd. or 0.2 mi W of the jct. of Hurricane Rd. and O'Toole Ln. There is a small sign with an ADK marker at the start. The first part of this trail is on private land. Hikers must be very careful to stay on the trail until reaching state land and, of course, not camp or build fires on the private land. ◀

Leaving the road (0.0 mi), the trail climbs at an easy grade past several houses. At 0.2 mi the trail passes a large boulder on the L, after which the grade steepens past an enormous oak tree followed by a traverse to the R. At 0.4 mi the trail takes a sharp R at the base of a 12 ft high cliff and reaches a jct. at 0.5 mi. Here an alternate route diverges L. (This route climbs the partially open W ridge of Little Crow and rejoins the older route at the W summit. It offers views to the W and N that begin almost immediately above the jct. The distance to the summit is approximately the same. If descending this route, watch carefully for the sharp L turn on open rock to return to this intersection.)

Bearing R at this intersection, the regular trail climbs steeply to very steeply to a ledge that offers excellent views of the High Peaks at 0.7 mi. Now mostly on bare rock, the trail continues to climb to a summit, with the jct. with the alternate trail just beyond at 0.9 mi. Elevation, 2450 ft (747 m).

The trail now passes over the E summit of Little Crow, goes sharp R, and descends gradually to the col between the two Crows at 1.1 mi. Climbing at first on a traverse, the trail soon swings R and climbs to the summit of Big Crow at 1.4 mi, elevation, 2800 ft (854 m). Continuing on the flat to an eastern summit, the trail then begins descending over rocks and reaches a jct. at 1.6 mi. Trail L (trail 109) leads to Nun-da-ga-o Ridge. Continuing to descend after this jct., the trail levels off at 1.8 mi and reaches Crow Clearing at 2.1 mi. From here it is 1.2 mi down the road to the Mountain House and another 0.2 mi to the starting point.

🚶 Distances: East Hill Rd. to Little Crow, 0.9 mi; to Big Crow, 1.4 mi; to Crow Clearing, 2.1 mi; round-trip, 3.5 mi (5.6 km).

109 Nun-da-ga-o Ridge
(Minimum maintenance and marking; see introduction, p. 19.)

ADK High Peaks Map: G6 | Trails Illustrated Map 742: BB27

Also called the Soda Range on USGS maps, this series of ledges stretching in a shallow arc between the Crows and Weston Mt. offers a variety of unique views. Though recently improved from its nearly lost condition, this trail is only lightly used and sparsely marked, so care is needed to follow it.

▶ Trailhead: The trail starts on the Crows trail (trail 108) 0.5 mi from Crow Clearing. (See trail 106 for driving directions.) ◀

Turning R from the Crows trail (0.0 mi) the Nun-da-ga-o Ridge trail slabs across a sidehill to the notch between Big Crow and the ridge at 0.2 mi. The trail then climbs over one bump and on to the first good ledge at 0.4 mi. From here, several more short ups and downs lead to a steep switchbacking ascent to the summit of Nun-da-ga-o Ridge at 1.4 mi.

This is the best view on the ridge, but more views follow as the trail works its way down over several other bumps to the notch at the base of Weston Mt. at 2.8 mi. From here it is a steady climb through a beautiful birch forest to the summit of Weston Mt. at 3.5 mi. (To descend via Lost Pond, follow description for Lost Pond, trail 107).

🚶 Distances: Crow Clearing to jct. with Nun-da-ga-o Ridge trail, 0.4 mi; to summit of ridge, 1.8 mi; to Weston Mt., 3.4 mi; to Lost Pond, 3.7 mi; complete circuit back to Crow Clearing, 6.2 mi (10 km).

109A Jay Mt.

See Trailless Peaks North of Hurricane Mt., p. 165.

Completed in 2012, this trail follows a totally different route than the former unmarked path to the summit with views at the W end of the Jay Mt. ridge. It remains an unmarked path to the summit of Jay Mt. Construction of the trail was a collaborative effort between the DEC, ADK trail crews, and Student Conservation Association Crews. Major funding for the project came from a generous bequest to the Hurricane Mt. Chapter of ADK.

▶ Trailhead: The trail starts at a new parking turnout on Jay Mt. Rd. just below its jct. with Upland Meadows Rd. From NY 9N in Upper Jay, follow Trumbulls Rd. for 2.5 mi to a jct. where it becomes Jay Mt. Rd. From here it is another 0.8 mi to

Upland Meadows Rd. ◀

From the road, the blue-marked trail climbs moderately with a few switchbacks to a crossing of the old route at 1.2 mi. After a gradual descent to a brook crossing, the climbing resumes with additional switchbacks to some views to the SW at 1.9 mi, after which some steeper climbing leads to a more expansive view at 2.5 mi. Soon after this view, the trail crests the ridge and reaches a jct. at 2.6 mi. Trail L leads 100 yd up over some rocks to the summit at the W end of the ridge. Trail R is the unmarked path that leads to more views and the summit of Jay Mt.

109B Clements Pond

ADK High Peaks Map: F5 | Trails Illustrated Map 746 (not shown)

Constructed in 2012, this trail offers a pleasant walk to a pretty bog-rimmed pond.
▶ Trailhead: On Styles Brook Rd. 1 mi from NY 9N between Keene and Upper Jay. There is parking on the R with the trail on the L. ◀

From the road (0.0 mi) and marked with blue DEC disks, the trail crosses a small bridge and is flat to a second brook crossing at 0.2 mi. The trail then climbs in several mostly moderate stages up a valley with cliffs on both sides to a height of land at 1 mi. After a short flat stretch, the trail angles left and down to a switchback R and then down to the S end of the pond at 1.4 mi. The trail continues along a narrow ridge with a bog and beaver swamp on the R and the pond on the L, ending at a grassy area at the N end of the pond at 1.5 mi.
🚶 Distance: Road to Clements Pond, 1.5 mi (2.4 km). Ascent to height of land, 550 ft (170 m).

TRAILLESS PEAKS
NORTH OF HURRICANE MT.

(Unmarked paths; see introduction, p. 19)

Stretching for nearly fifteen miles N of Hurricane Mt. through the Hurricane Mountain and Jay Mountain Wilderness Areas is an interesting series of peaks with some outstanding views. Except for Poke-O-Moonshine Mt., whose official trail is described separately below, and Jay Mt., which has an informal trail, also described below, none of these peaks have trails. There are numerous old roads into the area, and the forests are generally open second growth, making for generally easy traveling. What follows are some brief descriptions of what is available in this area, and some hints on how to approach these peaks. Beyond this, hikers must rely on map and compass to find their way. Many former approaches on private land have been posted in recent years. Mention is therefore made only of those peaks that can be approached via public land or lumber company land on which hikers are still permitted.

Peak   3373

ADK High Peaks Map: G6 | Trails Illustrated Map 742: BB28
See Trailless Peaks North of Hurricane Mt., above.

Also labeled "Ausable No. 4," this peak has some interesting wide ledges giving excellent views to the S and E. The best approach is from the Lost Pond Trail (trail 107) where that trail turns sharp L 0.3 mi above Gulf Brook Lean-to. Continue straight ahead through an old lumber clearing and slowly slab upwards to the top of this broad ridge, which can be followed to its N end. There are several other ledges to be found along the way as well.

Peaked Mt.

ADK High Peaks Map: G6 | Trails Illustrated Map 742: BB27
See Trailless Peaks North of Hurricane Mt., p. 165.

An easy bushwhack of less than 0.5 mi from the summit of Weston Mt. leads to a mostly open summit.

Jay Range

ADK High Peaks Map: G5–H5 | Trails Illustrated Map 742: CC27-28
See Trailless Peaks North of Hurricane Mt., p. 165.

Reaching a height of 3600 ft with many bald summits, these peaks, though officially trailless, are popular enough to have one well-defined path to the top of their bare ridge.

Saddleback Mt.

ADK High Peaks Map: H5 | Trails Illustrated Map 742: CC28
See Trailless Peaks North of Hurricane Mt., p. 165.

At 3615 ft, this mountain offers a variety of views from its summit. One can approach it from the height of land to the S on the road between Upper Jay and Lewis, along the ridge from Jay Mt., or from the same approach as for Slip Mt. (see below).

Slip Mt.

ADK High Peaks Map: H5 | Trails Illustrated Map 742: CC28
See Trailless Peaks North of Hurricane Mt., p. 165.

Slip Mt. can be reached from Jay Mt. or can be climbed via its long NE ridge from the end of Seventy Rd. Both Seventy Mt. and Bald Peak on this ridge offer views, and there are several other views along the ridge, including a spectacular view of Slip's steep E face.

Death Mt.

ADK High Peaks Map: H5 | Trails Illustrated Map 742: CC28
See Trailless Peaks North of Hurricane Mt., p. 165.

Farther to the N, this mountain has an open summit and can be approached from the end of Seventy Rd. One also can continue E on the summit of Jay Mt. along the obvious ridge.

Mt. Fay

Trails Illustrated Map 742: CC29
See Trailless Peaks North of Hurricane Mt., p. 165.

This prominent, rocky little bump to the E is a rewarding short climb with views of the Boquet River Valley. Approach Mt. Fay from the end of Seventy Rd.

Bluff Mt.

ADK High Peaks Map: H4 | Trails Illustrated Map 742: CC28
See Trailless Peaks North of Hurricane Mt., p. 165.

The summit and approaches are on private land that is now posted.

110 Poke-O-Moonshine Mt.

Trails Illustrated Map 742: EE30

This fire tower peak is extremely popular because of its tremendous view of Lake Champlain and of the High Peaks in the distance to the SW. Its unusual name appears to be a derivation of two Algonquin Indian words, "Pohqui" and "Moosie," which mean "broken" and "smooth," respectively. The name seems to refer to the smooth rocks of the summit or the prominent slab on the SE side, and the broken rocks of the impressive cliff on the E side. Friends of Poke-O-Moonshine, a private group operating under the auspices of Adirondack Architectural Heritage and in cooperation with the DEC, has restored the fire tower so that one may again climb it. The Friends have also prepared an interpretive pamphlet to this trail that is available at the trailhead register. On most days in season, an interpreter hired by Friends of Poke-O-Moonshine is on duty in the tower.

View from Poke-O-Moonshine. Mark Meschinelli

▶ Trailhead: The trail starts at the Poke-O-Moonshine state campground on NY 9, 9.3 mi N of the jct. of the road from Lewis to Exit 32 on I-87 and 3 mi S of Exit 33. Parking is permitted on the highway (NY 9). If the campground is open, there is also parking at the S end. ◀

Starting from the S end of the campground (0.0 mi), the red-marked trail enters the woods and immediately begins climbing, steeply at times, to the base of a cliff at 0.3 mi. Skirting the cliff on the L, the trail switchbacks R to a good lookout on the R at 0.4 mi. The grade now eases somewhat but remains steady to a saddle S of the summit at 0.8 mi. Here are the remains of the fire observer's cabin with a lean-to approximately 65 yd to the L.

From this saddle, the trail goes L and up past a lookout on the L and along a shelf before turning R and up to the summit plateau. Turning R again, the trail goes through open woods to the summit and tower at 1.2 mi.

🚶 Distance: Campground to summit of Poke-O-Moonshine Mt., 1.2 mi (1.9 km). Ascent, 1280 ft (390 m). Elevation, 2180 ft (665 m).

110A   Poke-O-Moonshine Observer Trail

Trails Illustrated Map 742: EE30

There is now also an alternate route to the summit that starts 1 mi S of the campground at a new (2014) parking area with a DEC sign on the W side of NY 9. From the parking area (0.0 mi), the trail descends to a brook crossing and then climbs moderately to join the jeep road once used to access the observer's cabin. Turning R, the road climbs moderately to a jct. at 0.7 mi, where the road turns R and climbs steadily and more steeply to the lean-to at 2 mi. This route is a good alternative for snowshoeing, but requires advanced skills for skiing.

111 Giant Mt. from NY 9N

ADK High Peaks Map: G7 | Trails Illustrated Map 742: AA28

This is one of the longer approaches to Giant Mt., but it has its attractions for those who don't like company while approaching a popular peak like Giant. (See trail 47, for history and naming of Giant Mt.) This trail from NY 9N, also referred to as the North Trail, offers generally easy grades, an interesting lookout, a unique geological formation, and a lean-to. Owl Head Lookout (not the plural form, to distinguish it from the peak above the Cascade Pass Rd., trail 93) is also popular as a short day trip, with its magnificent view of the E face of Giant Mt. as well as Rocky Peak, Lake Champlain, and the Green Mts.

▶ Trailhead: Start on NY 9N at a large DEC sign, 4.5 mi W of the jct. with NY 9 at the S end of the village of Elizabethtown or 5.5 mi E of the jct. of NY 9N and NY. 73 between Keene and Keene Valley. Off the highway, there is a small parking lot and trail register L of a private gravel road. Park here (0.0 mi.). ◀

Continue down the road on foot and cross a small bridge in 150 yd. Immediately after the bridge, the trail (now marked with red markers) turns sharp L off this road and begins a gradual climb as it joins and then leaves a lumber road. Entering state land at 0.4 mi, the trail continues its gradual climb before leveling out and then reaching Slide Brook at 1.1 mi. There are several possible campsites in this area.

Crossing Slide Brook on a good bridge, the trail climbs steeply up the bank of the brook, swings L and crosses a small tributary brook before beginning a steady easy to moderate climb above the R bank of the small brook. Returning to the brook, the trail crosses it several times as it works up through a small ravine. At the top of the ravine at 1.8 mi, the trail swings sharply R, crosses a few boggy areas, and continues to swing slowly to the R as it climbs at a moderate grade to the top of the ridge at 2.5 mi. Here there is a jct. with a side trail leading L and up 0.1 mi to the summit of Owl Head Lookout. (Climbers ending their trip here should go 0.1 mi L when returning to the main trail for a spectacular view of the cliffs on the Lookout.)

The trail to Giant Mt. soon begins to descend through a small open area to a small valley at 2.7 mi, after which it climbs briefly and then descends again before starting up through a very open grove of maples at 3.4 mi. Just beyond this point, there is a good view from rocks just off to the L of the trail. There is one more short descent before the climbing continues to the top of High Bank, a remarkable bank of glacial gravel with only a few birches growing on it, at 4.1 mi. Continuing on, the trail crosses a dry streambed at 4.4 mi. At 4.6 mi there is a view of the slides on Giant Mt. 50 ft on the L.

The grade continues steady and moderate, but begins to slacken at 5.7 mi, just before a jct. with a side trail leading 50 yd L to a lean-to. Past the lean-to the grade eases off as the trail approaches the jct. with the yellow-marked trail from Hopkins Mt. (trail 52) at 6.1 mi. Turning L, the trail begins climbing steeply out of the col. At 6.2 mi there is a sharp switchback to the L to negotiate a small cliff band. From here the grade continues steep for a few yards, but slowly eases until it levels off at 6.8 mi. Descending slightly, the trail resumes its climb and arrives at a ledge on the R at 7.2 mi, soon after which the trail levels out and crosses other ledges to the summit at 7.4 mi. Trails 47 and 48 continue over the summit to St. Huberts.)

🥾 Distances: NY 9N to Owl Head Lookout, 2.6 mi; to lean-to, 5.7 mi; to jct. with trail from Hopkins Mt., 6.1 mi; to summit of Giant Mt., 7.4 mi (11.9 km). Ascent from NY 9N, 3327 ft (1014 m). Elevation, 4427 ft (1350 m). Order of height, 12.

112   East Trail to Rocky Peak Ridge and Giant Mt.

ADK High Peaks Map: H9–G9 | Trails Illustrated Map 742: Y28–29

This route up the long E ridge of Rocky Peak Ridge and on to Giant Mt. is a very challenging but also very rewarding climb. Approximately half of the trail is in the open, and there are exceptional views at nearly every turn. Bring plenty of water along on any day and think twice before attempting this route on a particularly hot day; but on a cool day with fall colors at their height this trail is probably the best hike in all of the Adirondacks. For those with less ambition, two intermediate points, Blueberry Cobbles at 2 mi and Bald Peak at 3.9 mi, are also worthy objectives.

Except for a small stand of first-growth hemlock near the start of the trail, this entire route is through smaller second growth. This is the result of the great fire of 1913, which burned all of Rocky Peak and much of Giant Mt. Nearly all of the views along this route are a direct result of this last great fire in the Adirondacks.

▶ Trailhead: The trail begins at a parking lot on NY 9, 4.9 mi N of the jct. with NY 73 and 1.3 mi S of the U. S. Post Office in New Russia. ◀

From the parking lot (0.0 mi), the trail is flat through an open pine forest but soon begins to climb an old tote road, coming to the L bank of a small stream at 0.7 mi. Following up the L bank, the trail enters a flat notch, at the far end of which it swings L and climbs to the first view on the L at 1.6 mi. A second view is just off the trail to the R at 1.8 mi.

Continuing up, the trail comes to the first lookout on Blueberry Cobbles on the L at 1.9 mi, and then comes to a jct. at 2 mi with a red trail that bypasses the top of Blueberry Cobbles leading R. (In season there should be no doubt that Blueberry Cobbles is most appropriately named.) The yellow trail L leads past many other views of the Boquet River Valley and the Dix Range before turning sharp R and down at 2.3 mi to Mason Notch, where the red bypass trail rejoins it. The trail climbs over the lightly wooded summit of Mason Mt. (2330 ft) at 2.8 mi before descending to Hedgehog Notch at the base of Bald Peak. There is an interesting cleft in the rock just to the L of the trail. Now the trail begins to climb steeply over mostly bare rock to the summit of Bald Peak (3060 ft, 933 m) at 3.9 mi, where there are good views in all directions.

Turning L and following the ridge W, the trail passes a huge balanced glacial erratic at 4 mi and then begins to descend the R side of the ridge to Dickerson Notch at 4.2 mi. From the notch, the trail begins a long climb to the prominence at the E end of the summit ridge. There is a good ledge (and sometimes water) on the L at 4.8 mi with another good ledge on the R as the grade begins to ease off just before reaching the bald summit of Rocky Peak (4060 ft, 1237 m) at 5.4 mi.

The trail now crosses several minor rocky bumps before descending to the outlet to Mary Louise Pond (designated campsite on L just before the outlet) at 6.1 mi. Skirting the N side of the pond, the trail now climbs the beautiful open meadows to the summit of Rocky Peak Ridge at 6.7 mi. From the summit there are views in all directions, with the slides on Giant's E face dominating. Total ascent from the parking lot, 4700 ft (1433 m). Elevation, 4420 ft (1347 m). Order of height, 20.

Bearing NW, the trail descends steadily into the col between Giant Mt. and Rocky Peak Ridge at 7.4 mi and immediately begins to climb steeply, first through an open meadow and then into the woods. Angling R, the trail comes to a jct. with a side trail at 7.7 mi. (Trail R leads 60 yd to a spectacular view of some of the slides on the E face of Giant Mt.) Swinging back to the L after this jct., the trail soon gains the crest of a ridge and follows this up to its jct. with the blue-marked trail from St. Huberts at 7.9 mi (trail 47). Turning R, it is an easy hike to the summit of Giant Mt. at 8 mi.

🚶 Distances: Parking lot to Blueberry Cobbles, 1.9 mi; to Bald Peak, 3.9 mi; to summit of Rocky Peak Ridge, 6.7 mi; to summit of Giant Mt., 8 mi (12.9 km). Total ascent from parking lot, 5300 ft (1616 m). Elevation, 4627 ft (1410 m). Order of height, 12.

113   Sunrise Trail to Mt. Gilligan

ADK High Peaks Map: H9 | Trails Illustrated Map 742: Y28

Formerly known as Sunrise Mt., this little peak rises directly above the Boquet River and offers views of Pleasant Valley, Rocky Peak Ridge, and the Dix Range from the summit and several lookouts along the way.

▶ Trailhead: The trail starts on Scriver Rd. which branches from NY 9, 3.6 mi N of its jct. with NY 73 and 2.6 mi S of the U. S. Post Office in New Russia. There is a fishing access parking lot just before the bridge over the Boquet River. Park here (0.0 mi.), cross the bridge, and proceed 150 yd on the road before turning L off the road just before reaching a house on the L. ◀

Marked with ADK markers, the trail proceeds on the flat for a few hundred yards before climbing to a higher shelf up to the R and then, after some more flat going, climbs steeply up to the first lookout at 0.3 mi, with a good view of Dix Mt. Continuing on, the trail dips briefly and then climbs steadily to another lookout at 0.6 mi. Now the grade is easier along the top of the ridge before it dips down and crosses an old lumber road in a small col at 0.8 mi. Climbing past an interesting overhung rock, the trail reaches a broad, open area at 0.9 mi, with good views of Rocky Peak Ridge and the Dix Range. Just after this ledge, the trail joins and briefly follows an old lumber road before branching L and up to the final lookout at 1.1 mi at the end of the trail. The wooded summit of Mt. Gilligan is about 100 yd beyond.

🏃 Distance: Parking area near NY 9 to lookout below summit of Mt. Gilligan, 1.1 mi (1.8 km). Ascent, 670 ft (204 m). Elevation, 1420 ft (433 m).

114   Trail from Sharp Bridge Campground to Round Pond and East Mill Flow

ADK High Peaks Map: G12–H12 | Trails Illustrated Map 742: W28

This trail is a relatively flat and pleasant walk through some fine woods, giving access to picturesque Round Pond as well as the beautiful and unique open area known as East Mill Flow. This trail was cut about 1975 and has sometimes suffered from lack of maintenance, but as of 2012 the trail is again in relatively good shape.

▶ Trailhead: The start is at Sharp Bridge Campground on NY 9, 7.1 mi N of the village of North Hudson and 2.9 mi S of Exit 30 on I-87. Parking is at the gravel turnout just outside the gate. ◀

Round Pond. Henning Vahlenkamp

From the parking area (0.0 mi), the trail goes to the far end of the large, flat field near the Schroon River and then goes along the L bank of the river on an old road. Crossing several small brooks, the trail comes to an old bridge abutment at 0.8 mi. This appears to have been the original crossing point used as early as the 1830s both by the predecessor of NY. 9 and by a road leading W from Port Henry to Tahawus and beyond.

Turning sharp L at this point, the trail follows this old road for several miles. It climbs briefly, drops to cross a small brook, and then begins a steady climb to a height of land at 1.5 mi. Dropping down the other side in two short pitches, the trail continues mostly on the level through several magnificent stands of white pine to the R bank of East Mill Brook at 2.7 mi, at the S end of East Mill Flow. Swinging R, the trail drops down and makes a somewhat difficult crossing of the brook before scrambling up the far bank and continuing along the E side of this extensive open swamp. At 3.4 mi the trail crosses the outlet to Round Pond in a thick clump of alders, turns sharp R, and heads up a gentle grade. At 3.6 mi, just before coming within sight of Round Pond, the trail turns sharp R off the old road and proceeds to the outlet of Round Pond at 3.9 mi. (The old road leads straight ahead to the NW shore of Round Pond with a good campsite located across the pond on some low rocks.)

From the outlet, the trail climbs S away from the pond and skirts numerous small swampy areas as it crosses a low divide, proceeds down to the W shore of Trout Pond, and comes to Ensign Pond Rd. (CR 4) at 5.2 mi. This trailhead is approximately 6 mi E of NY 9, N of North Hudson, and is marked by a large DEC sign.

❄ Trail in winter: This is an excellent ski trip from Sharp Bridge to Round Pond.

🏃 Distances: Sharp Bridge Campground to East Mill Flow, 2.7 mi; to outlet to Round Pond, 3.9 mi; to Ensign Pond Rd., 5.2 mi (8.4 km).

Dix Range via North Fork Boquet River
(Unmarked path; see introduction, p. 19.)

ADK High Peaks Map: G10–G11 | Trails Illustrated Map 742: X–Y27

The trailless peaks of the Dix Range may be approached via this unmarked hunter's path. There are several interesting ponds in this area, as well as some nice camping spots. Although the trail is fairly plain, there are no signs or markers, and one should carry a map and compass in the event one loses one's way.

▶ Trailhead: The path begins on NY 73 on the S side of the North Fork Boquet River, at a stone bridge approximately 1.5 mi N of the jct. of NY 73 and NY 9. ◀

Leaving the highway (0.0 mi), the path goes up along the R bank of the stream to a crossing point at 0.4 mi. Now heading away from the Boquet River, the path crosses a small stream and returns to a bank high above the river 150 yd later at 0.7 mi. There is a good swimming hole and picnic spot at the small flume in the river, which can be seen through the trees. (This swimming hole may also be

Boquet River. James Bullard

reached by following a rougher trail that remains on the S side of the river. A continuation of this rougher trail pulls away from the river and continues up a steep hogback before reaching a dead end in approx. 0.5 mi at Rhododendron Pond.)

From this swimming hole, the main path climbs high above the river before turning L and down to a crossing of the North Fork at 1.2 mi. (Path R at the jct. leads approx. ¼ mi to a campsite.) Heading SW after crossing the North Fork, the path crosses another large tributary at 1.4 mi, passes some beaver activity on the L, and then climbs along a sidehill. At the top of this climb at 1.6 mi. a side trail leads L to a designated campsite on Lilypad Pond, which is just out of sight to the L of the path. Past this jct. the path descends briefly and then climbs easily before descending to the L bank of the South Fork Boquet River at 2.3 mi. Soon after reaching the South Fork, there is a designated campsite on the R and another one on the L 0.2 mi farther. The path continues up the L bank, much of the time high above it, passing the "Rock of Gibraltar" on the L at 3.1 mi and coming to the L bank of a tributary descending from Dix Mt. at 3.3 mi. From here there are easy approaches to almost all of the Dix Range, as well as another designated campsite ¼ mi past Dix Brook.

From the crossing of this tributary a herd path continues close to the South Fork, eventually reaching the base of the slide on East Dix. For the first half mile the herd path crosses and recrosses the South Fork, but then settles on the R (S) bank at the first major tributary coming in from the S. Although slightly widened, this is not the brook from the base of the slide. The latter is found about another half mile along the herd path that leads directly to the base of the slide and even provides an alternative to some of the lower sections of the slide that have become too overgrown with moss to provide easy going. At the top of the slide, bear R for the easiest access to the crest of the ridge, but watch the loose rock.

NORTHWAY ACCESS POINTS TO THE DIX WILDERNESS

ADK High Peaks Map: H11–G12 | Trails Illustrated Map 742: W28

With the construction of I-87, the Adirondack Northway, through this area in the mid-1960s came a need to provide access to the W side of this highway because parking is of course prohibited on the highway itself. There are now three points where one can easily cross I-87 along the 10-mi stretch from North Hudson to Exit 30. These access routes connect with the valleys of, West Mill Brook, and Walker Brook, plus Shingletree Pond, and are described briefly below.

Note that parking for the purpose of hiking or camping is not permitted at any I-87 rest area. The former approach to Lindsay Brook has been abandoned owing to beaver activity while a fifth approach 1 mi. N of North Hudson has become obscured.

115   Shingletree Pond Access

ADK High Peaks Map: G12 | Trails Illustrated Map 742: W28

This access starts 0.2 mi S of the Sharp Bridge Campground (see trail 114) at the N end of Courtney Pond. The access skirts the end of the pond and then turns L and proceeds S along a sidehill before joining an old road at approximately 0.7 mi from NY 9. From here the trail climbs for another 0.1 mi to a long culvert under both lanes of the Northway before ending at Shingletree Pond. No trail continues beyond this point.

116   West Mill Brook Access

ADK High Peaks Map: G12 | Trails Illustrated Map 742: W27–28

This route begins 1.6 mi S of Sharp Bridge Campground (see trail 114) or 5.5 mi N of the village of North Hudson. There is a large wooden signpost at the start of a narrow dirt road (high-clearance vehicles recommended) that leads down to West Mill Brook at 0.2 mi, where there is a good ford. (Park just before on R at times of high water.) From the ford, the road crosses an extensive, open sandy area and reaches a concrete culvert under I-87 at 0.8 mi. At 1.1 mi there is a parking area just before a gate that controls further access along the old road leading along the R bank of West Mill Brook. This road leads approximately 2 mi farther W before turning S and becoming obscure. Bear, Buck, and Saunders Mts. are all attractive trailless destinations that can be accessed from this route.

Note that parking for the purpose of hiking or camping is not permitted at any I-87 rest area.

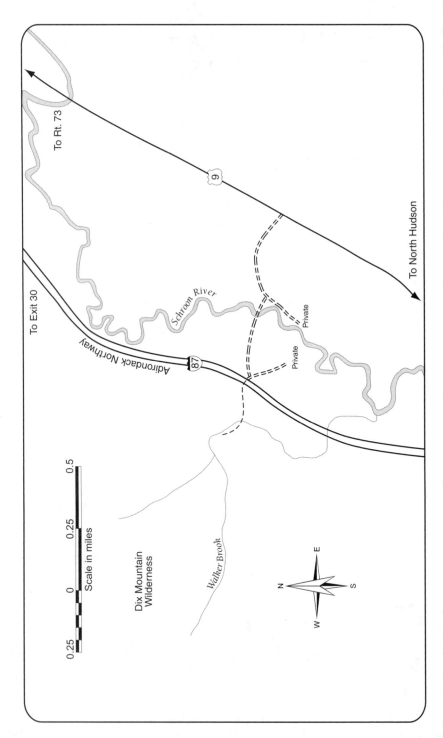

To Rt. 73

To North Hudson

9

Schroon River

Private

Private

To Exit 30

Adirondack Northway

87

Dix Mountain
Wilderness

Walker Brook

0.25   0   0.25   0.5

Scale in miles

N
W   E
S

117 Walker Brook Access

Map: P. 176 | Trails Illustrated Map 743: V27

This access, also described in *Eastern Trails*, is found on NY 9, 3.7 mi S of Sharp Bridge Campground (see trail 114) or 3.4 mi N of North Hudson, just south of two houses. Go down a dirt road for 0.3 mi and bear R on a poorer road that leads down to the L bank of the Schroon River. Bear in mind that this is private land and that the road going L at 0.3 mi is not for public use.

There is no bridge over the Schroon River, and fording could be difficult in high water. On the far side there is a good road that is followed uphill to a flat area 0.5 mi from NY 9. Bear R just beyond and cross under I-87 through a concrete culvert at 0.7 mi. Walker Brook is approximately 0.2 mi beyond, with an old road leading up its R (S) bank giving access to Camels Hump, Niagara, and Nippletop Mts. (The latter is not the 4620-ft High Peak, which is W of the Dix Range from here.)

From Elk Lake, looking toward Nippletop and Dix Mt. Robert Meyer

Snowshoer on Santanoni. **Joanne Kennedy**

Southern Section

This region stretches across the southern and western edges of the High Peaks Wilderness Area and includes a small portion of the Dix Mountain Wilderness Area. With the exception of the well-traveled trails leading to Mt. Marcy and Dix Mt., much of this area is remote and seldom visited. There are outstanding opportunities for solitude, and one must be willing to backpack to reach much of the terrain within the section's boundaries.

Except for Goodnow Mt., there are no short hikes in this area, and very few moderate hikes, but there are great possibilities for extended backpacking trips beyond the obvious traverse of the Northville-Placid Trail (N-P Trail). For the serious and experienced hiker, this area is the place to go to find new challenges.

❊ Trails in winter: More of the trails in this section are skiable than elsewhere in the High Peaks region, but unless specific details are given, one should assume that a trail is steep enough to require snowshoes and possibly crampons.

SHORT HIKES

Goodnow Mt.: 3-mi (4.8 km) round-trip. An easy ascent on a good trail leads to a fire tower with expansive views of the High Peaks and of the equally wild country to the S. See trail 139.

MODERATE HIKES

Summit Rock in Indian Pass: 8.7-mi (14 km) round-trip. Except for the final half mile, this is an easy hike to a close-up view of the largest (nearly 1000 ft high) cliff in the Adirondacks. See trail 125.

Camp Santanoni on Newcomb Lake: 9-mi (14.5 km) round-trip.

The road to Newcomb Lake has easy grades and leads to an authentic Great Camp on the shore of a beautiful lake. See trail 135.

HARDER HIKES

Dix Mt. via Hunters Pass with return via the Beckhorn: 13.9-mi (22.4 km) round-trip. An interesting loop trip on this impressively rugged peak, with outstanding summit views. See trails 119 and 120.

Newcomb Lake, Shattuck Clearing, Duck Hole, and Henderson Lake backpacking trip: 35.2 mi (56.8 km) point to point. This four- to five-day trip leads along little-used trails past three attractive lakes with good campsites and also parallels the ruggedly beautiful Cold River for several miles. It requires only a short shuttle between start and finish points. See trails 127, 133–136, and 138.

ELK LAKE AREA

ADK High Peaks Map E12–F12 | Trails Illustrated Map 742: W25

▶ Trailhead: To reach the trails starting from Elk Lake, leave I-87 (the Adirondack Northway) at Exit 29 in North Hudson. Then go W 4 mi on Blue Ridge Rd., following signs for Newcomb. Turn R off Blue Ridge Rd. onto a gravel road marked with a sign for Elk Lake Lodge. At 5.2 mi on this gravel road there is a parking lot on the R just before the road drops down to Elk Lake. The road beyond here is private and open only to guests at Elk Lake Lodge. In winter, this road is only plowed as far as Clear Pond, 3.3 mi from Blue Ridge Rd. ◄

All of the trails starting from this parking lot cross private land, and hikers should observe the normal courtesies when on private land. There is no camping permitted for 5 mi along the Elk Lake–Marcy Trail (trail 118) or for 1.9 mi along the Dix Trail (trail 119). Furthermore, both of these trail segments are closed to the public during the big-game hunting season (normally the next-to-last Saturday in October to the first Sunday in December). All privately maintained trails branching from the public trails are closed at all times. Refer to the maps referenced above for the exact location of private lands in this area.

118 Elk Lake–Marcy Trail

ADK High Peaks Map: F12 | Trails Illustrated Map 742: W25

This is one of the longer approaches to Mt. Marcy and involves an additional climb and descent of about 700 feet over the Boreas-Colvin Range before actually beginning the ascent of Mt. Marcy. Though long, this trail is an attractive alternative for those who prefer to avoid the crowds for as much of the ascent as possible. Given the length of this trail, most will choose to make this an overnight, and there is an attractive lean-to at Panther Gorge from which one can also ascend Haystack Mt. The trail as far as Four Corners is maintained by ATIS.

Because much of this trail is on private land, hikers should be aware that no camping is permitted until approximately 6.5 mi, with the exception of a small piece of state land at 5 mi that offers no attractive campsites unless one detours 0.2 mi N on the Colvin Range connection (trail 60). The trail is closed during the big-game hunting season; see Elk Lake Area (p. 180) for more information.

▶ Trailhead: See Elk Lake Area, p. 180. ◄

Leaving the register across the road from the parking lot (0.0 mi), the blue-marked trail crosses a private trail at 0.1 mi and descends to a suspension bridge over The Branch (outlet to Elk Lake) at 0.3 mi and then reaches a good road at 0.4 mi. Turning L on the road, the trail crosses Nellie Brook, takes an immediate R up a steep bank, and after a few zigzags on older roads reaches a newer road at 0.7 mi. Turning R on this road, it passes an active beaver pond on the L at 0.9 mi.

At 1.1 mi the trail bears R, crosses Nellie Brook, and climbs over a low ridge to a jct. with a private trail on the R at 1.4 mi. Continuing to descend gently, the trail reaches the jct. of the private Lightning Hill Trail on the L just before crossing Guide Board Brook at 1.7 mi. Avoid the yellow can-top markers on the private trail and bear slightly R to the end of an open area where the blue DEC markers resume. At 2 mi, another private trail diverges R. Bearing L, the blue-marked DEC trail climbs and then eases and comes to another private trail jct. at 2.7 mi.

Turning sharp L at this jct., the Mt. Marcy trail goes over a low ridge and down to a brook crossing at 2.9 mi just above a large beaver swamp. From here, the trail climbs to the top of the pass on the Boreas-Colvin ridge at 3.3 mi. Elevation 2650 ft (808 m). Ascent from Elk Lake, 600 ft (183 m).

From this pass, the trail descends moderately, crosses a small brook at 3.5 mi and continues along a sidehill with short ups and downs, followed by a moderate climb to another height of land at 4.3 mi. Elevation, 2590 ft (790 m). From here, the trail descends moderately and crosses several old lumber roads before turning sharp R and down at 4.9 mi and entering state land shortly before reaching a jct. at 5 mi. Trail R leads along Pinnacle Ridge over Blake Peak and Mt. Colvin to St. Huberts (trail 60).

The Elk Lake–Marcy Trail continues to descend to a jct. at 5.2 mi, where it again enters private land. (Trail R and L at this jct. is private and closed to the public.) Continuing straight ahead a few yards, the trail crosses the Upper Ausable Lake inlet on a log bridge. The trail is now on the flat in Marcy Swamp with many log bridges and at 5.5 mi enters an open area affording a view of Mt. Marcy. The trail then reenters the woods and at 5.7 mi begins to climb through an area heavily damaged by Hurricane Floyd in 1999.

At 6.1 mi the grade steepens and remains steady to a jct. at 6.5 mi. (Trail R is private and closed to the public.) Now on the level, the trail again enters state land at 6.6 mi and begins climbing the first of several pitches. At about 7 mi the trail levels off in a wet area, crosses a fair-sized brook at 7.7 mi, and then traverses a small bog, with Marcy Brook coming into view on the L. Shortly after, the trail turns sharp R away from an old tote road the trail had briefly followed. Soon swinging back L, the trail parallels Marcy Brook to a brook crossing at the confluence of two streams (PBM 3012 ft on large rock between two brooks) at 8.3 mi.

Continuing on, the trail enters thick woods at 8.7 mi and passes Panther Gorge Lean-to on the R (with several designated campsites on the L) just before a short descent to the jct. at 9 mi, with the yellow-marked trail leading R to Mt. Haystack (trail 58). Turning L and continuing with blue markers, the Elk Lake–Marcy Trail crosses Marcy Brook and bears R and up a steep climb. At 9.1 mi the trail crosses a small brook and resumes the steep climb. (The steepest pitch is made much easier thanks to the legendary 60-plus-step rock staircase constructed by the ADK trail crew in the 1980s.) After a few more steep pitches, the grade begins to ease off, but the trail remains very rough all the way to Four Corners and the jct. with the yellow trail from Lake Colden and Upper Works at 10.2 mi (trail 121). Red trail L leads 0.5 mi to the summit of Mt. Skylight (trail 122). This jct. is the former site of Four Corners Lean-to, and because it is above 4000 ft, no camping is permitted here now.

Turning R and now with yellow markers, the route climbs steadily up a rocky, eroded section of trail. At 10.4 mi a boulder on the L has split away from the mountain, forming a crevice. A few yards through this crevice there is a lookout at Gray Peak and Lake Tear.

Swinging R, the trail continues the ascent to a good lookout on the R at 10.6 mi. (This marks the beginning of the arctic-alpine zone where one must remain on the marked trail or bare rock to preserve the frag-

ALPINE ALERT

See page 14

ile vegetation.) Reaching timberline soon after, the trail climbs over bare rock to the top of Schofield Cobble at 10.7 mi. This little prominence is named for Peter Schofield, an early climber in the High Peaks whose favorite campsite was "Junction Camp," as Four Corners was then called. Schofield was also a member of the New York Board of Trade and Transportation and in his official capacity he played an important part in securing the adoption of the "forever wild" clause in the 1894 New York State Constitution. The name was suggested by Russell M. L. Carson in his classic book, *Peaks and People of the Adirondacks*.

After dipping slightly beyond Schofield Cobble, the trail, marked with cairns and yellow paint blazes, begins its final steep ascent to the summit of Marcy at 11 mi. At the summit the trail joins the trail from Heart Lake, which also connects with the trails to Johns Brook Lodge and Keene Valley (trails 1 and 61).

🏃 Distances: Elk Lake parking lot to pass over Boreas-Colvin Range, 3.3 mi; to Upper Ausable Lake Inlet, 5.2 mi; to Panther Gorge Lean-to, 9 mi; to jct. at Four Corners, 10.2 mi; to summit of Mt. Marcy, 11 mi (17.7 km). Total ascent from Elk Lake, 4200 ft (1281 m). Elevation, 5344 ft (1629 m). Order of height, 1.

119   Dix Mt. via Hunters Pass

ADK High Peaks Map: F12–F10 | Trails Illustrated Map 742: W25

Dix Mt. was named by Ebenezer Emmons in 1837 for John A. Dix, then secretary of state for Governor William Marcy and later governor himself. He was also a U.S. senator, secretary of the Treasury, and a major general in the Civil War. The first ascent was in 1807 by a surveyor named Rykert, who had the unenviable task of running a line that now forms the southern boundary of the town of Keene and passes directly over the summit.

There are two routes to Dix Mt. from Elk Lake, which coincide for the first 4.3 mi. The Hunters Pass Trail is 0.8 mi longer than the route via the Beckhorn (trail 120), but has a little less steep climbing and some interesting views from above Hunters Pass. The first few miles of this trail to Lillian Brook suffered some of the worst damage wrought by Hurricane Floyd in 1999. There are many new views of the surrounding peaks as a result. The trail is closed during the big-game hunting season; see Elk Lake Area, p. 180, for more information.

▶ Trailhead: See Lake Elk Lake Area, p. 180. ◀

Leaving the parking lot (0.0 mi) with red DEC markers, the trail proceeds mostly on the level through the first area of heavy blowdown. Soon crossing a private trail, the Dix Mt. trail reaches a wide gravel lumber road at 0.5 mi, where it turns L. (Hikers returning on this section of trail should watch very carefully for the sharp R turn off the lumber road.) Gentle rises and falls lead to Big Sally Brook at 1.6 mi, and the wide road ends shortly afterwards at another brook crossing. From here the trail is quite wet to the yellow-blazed state land boundary at 1.9 mi.

Continuing on the flat and crossing two small brooks, the trail crosses the first of several small brooks that are discolored by iron as a result of the great Macomb Mt. slide of 1947. At 2.3 mi the trail crosses Slide Brook, which is the favored approach to the Macomb slide (see p. 186). Just past this brook are some designated campsites on both sides of the trail, after which the trail crosses a smaller brook and comes to Slide Brook Lean-to on the L at the edge of a large clearing just over 100 yd past the first brook.

Swinging L and slightly down through the clearing, the trail crosses a brook at the far edge of the clearing and continues on at easy grades through an open hardwood forest before reaching another area of heavy hurricane damage at 3.2 mi. The Dix trail soon swings L and begins a steady descent toward Lillian Brook Lean-to. Soon after beginning this descent and at the crossing of a small water course, a cairn marks the start of the unmarked path to Hough and South Dix via Lillian Brook goes R. Lillian Brook Lean-to is now located on a short side trail that goes L at 3.6 mi just before the main trail reaches Lillian Brook at 3.7 mi. Swinging R and crossing the brook, the trail climbs to 3.8 mi and then descends moderately to steeply to some rough going along a sidehill above Dix Pond. Descending to the level of Dix Pond at 4.1 mi, the trail passes through two lumber clearings to a jct. at 4.3 mi with a yellow trail R to the Beckhorn (trail 120).

Continuing straight ahead, the trail crosses East Inlet and begins a steady climb along the R bank of the brook. Eventually pulling away from the brook, the trail crosses a large tributary at 5.6 mi and continues at a moderate grade, finishing with a steep pitch to Hunters Pass at 6.2 mi. Crossing to the far side of the boulder-strewn pass, the trail begins a steep to very steep climb up past some overhanging rocks to a short breather at 6.4 mi. The climbing soon resumes to another level stretch and view toward Nippletop at 6.5 mi. Just beyond, the trail reaches Balanced Rock Lookout, followed by slightly easier but still steady climbing to a jct. at 7 mi with the trail from Round Pond (trail 46).

Turning R, the climbing continues steady but not quite as steep along the ridge to the summit crest at 7.2 mi. (This marks the beginning of the arctic-alpine zone where one must remain on the marked trail or bare rock to preserve the fragile vegetation.) The going is now nearly level past one rock on the L with a U.S. Coast and Geodetic Survey marker and on to the summit with an old survey bolt at 7.4 mi. This bolt was placed by Verplanck Colvin in 1873 as part of his Adirondack Survey. The view is unobstructed in all directions, with Elk Lake to the SW, Lake Champlain and the Green Mts. to the E, and the Great Range to the NW. The trail with yellow DEC disks from the lumber clearing via the Beckhorn continues straight over the summit.

ALPINE ALERT
See page 14

 Distances: Elk Lake parking lot to Slide Brook Lean-to, 2.3 mi; to Lillian Brook Lean-to, 3.7 mi; to jct. with Beckhorn Trail, 4.3 mi; to Hunters Pass, 6.2 mi; to Round Pond Trail from NY. 73, 7 mi; to summit of Dix Mt., 7.4 mi (11.9 km). Ascent from Elk Lake, 2800 ft (854 m). Elevation, 4857 ft (1481 m). Order of height, 6.

120 Dix Mt. via the Beckhorn

ADK High Peaks Map: F11 | Trails Illustrated Map 742: X–W26

▶ Locator: This trail leads up the steep SW ridge of Dix Mt. to a small subsidiary peak known as the Beckhorn, a name conferred by Old Mountain Phelps because of its resemblance to the beak-iron at the end of a blacksmith's anvil. Take the red-marked Dix Trail (trail 119) to the lumber clearing at 4.3 mi. ◀

Leaving the jct. (0.0 mi) with yellow markers, the trail soon begins climbing steeply, with one short, easier stretch, before reaching a small brook at 0.5 mi. Climbing out of the brook, the trail gains the crest of a ridge with some more easy going until the climbing starts again at 0.9 mi. From here the trail climbs at a steady, steep grade, with a few views possible back to Elk Lake, to a slight sag at 1.5 mi, followed by more steep climbing to the open rocks just below the Beckhorn. (This marks the beginning of the arctic-alpine zone where one must remain on the marked trail or bare rock to preserve the fragile vegetation.) Now following cairns and paint blazes, the trail passes over the Beckhorn at 2.1 mi, down steeply, and on to the summit at 2.3 mi.

🏃 Distances: Elk Lake parking lot to jct. at lumber clearing, 4.3 mi; to summit of Dix Mt., 6.6 mi (10.6 km). Ascent from lumber clearing, 2600 ft (793 m). Elevation, 4857 ft (1480 m). Order of height, 6.

THE DIX RANGE: MACOMB MT., EAST DIX, SOUTH DIX, AND HOUGH PEAK

(Unmaintained trail; see introduction, p. 19.)

ADK High Peaks Map: F11 | Trails Illustrated Map 742: W26–X26 to W27–X27

Macomb Mt. honors the memory of Alexander Macomb, who defeated the British in the Battle of Plattsburgh on September 11, 1814. Like Dix Mt., East Dix and South Dix were named for John A. Dix, then Secretary of State for Governor Marcy and later governor himself. In 2014, East Dix was renamed Grace Peak to honor the late Grace Hudowalski, who served for many years as historian of the Adirondack Forty-Sixers. (Some have suggested that South Dix be renamed Carson Peak in honor of Russell M. L. Carson, author of *Peaks and People of the Adirondacks*.) Hough Mt. (pronounced "Huff") bears the name of one of the early Adirondack conservationists and American foresters, Franklin B. Hough, who was born and raised on the western edge of the Adirondacks.

The Elk Lake approach to all of these peaks (trail 119) is closed during the big-game hunting season; see Elk Lake Area, p. 180, for more information. All of the paths to the Dixes from the Elk Lake side and the path along the crest of the range are now officially designated and maintained by volunteer members of the Adirondack Forty-Sixers.

Macomb Mt.

ADK High Peaks Map: F11 | Trails Illustrated Map 742: W26

The designated path up Macomb Mt. follows Slide Brook to the base of a new slide that leads to a point close to the summit. The hurricane of September 1999 did extensive damage to this side of the Dix Range, but the Adirondack 46-Rs have now established a good approach to the base of the slide. This approach starts from the Elk Lake-Dix Trail (trail 119) on the N bank of Slide Brook, 2.3 mi from Elk Lake. The route at first follows closely to the brook, but soon pulls away, reaching a brook at the base of the slide about 1 mi. from the marked trail. When descending, be sure to cross the brook and look to the R to find the upper end of this unmarked path.

The first part of the slide is quite loose, but angling to the L puts one on firmer ground. From the top of the main part of the slide, one path goes R, but the more popular route continues up through some scrub to a higher (and somewhat steeper) section of slide that ends with a traverse under a huge boulder. A path continues above the boulder and, joining the lesser-used path, emerges on the top of the ridge just S of the summit.

Another possible route follows the valley of West Mill Brook up from NY 9 near North Hudson, beginning at the end of the West Mill Brook Access (trail 116).

Dix Range Crest Path

ADK High Peaks Map: F11 | Trails Illustrated Map 742: W26

From Macomb Mt. to South Dix, the going is easy, following the ridge down to the col between the two peaks and then up spectacular open rocks below South Dix's summit. From South Dix to East Dix is likewise an easy walk of about an hour on a good herd path running along the crest of the ridge.

Going from South Dix to Hough Peak, skirt the blowdown just N of the South Dix summit on its W side and then climb the hogback between South Dix and Hough. The path is steep but plain from the col to the summit of Hough with a few tricky moves around some cliffs near the summit. From Hough Peak to Dix Mt., continue along the ridge to the Beckhorn of Dix Mt.

Lillian Brook Path

ADK High Peaks Map F11 | Trails Illustrated Map 742: W26

Lillian Brook was restored as a route to peaks in the Dix Range in 2007, following major hurricane damage eight years before. This path goes R at about 3.4 mi. on the Hunter's Pass Trail to Dix (see trail 119) and reaches the L bank of Lillian Brook near the upper end of the blowdown area. Staying mostly on the L bank, the path comes to a jct. in a flat section near the jct of two large brooks. Path R leads to the Macomb/South Dix col, while the path L leads to the Hough/South Dix col.

SANFORD LAKE AREA

ADK High Peaks Map: C11–C9 | Trails Illustrated Map 742: Y21–W22

This area has a long and interesting history, beginning in 1826 when an Indian guide led a party through Indian Pass to show them a vein of iron ore. For the next thirty years or so this was a thriving operation, which employed up to 400 men. The last expansion during this early phase in 1854 included the building of the great stone furnace, the remains of which can still be seen next to the road. This operation was built up the river from the original development located near the present center of mining operations, hence the name "Upper Works." By 1858 operations had ceased only to start again during World War II, when this deposit became a major source for the important metal titanium. For various reasons, operations now have virtually ceased.

In 2003, the Open Space Institute acquired 10,000 acres from the mine owner with 6800 transferred to the state for inclusion in the Forest Preserve in 2008. These 6800 acres include Henderson Lake, Preston Ponds, and Mt. Adams, the first two miles of the trail to Bradley Pond, and Bradley Pond itself. As of 2010, this tract had not been officially classified as part of the High Peaks Wilderness Area. Therefore, its use is governed by the general Forest Preserve regulations. When finally classified, however, the High Peaks regulations will apply with the tract divided between the Eastern and Western zones of the High Peaks Wilderness Area.

(The 6,800 acres does not include the land E of the gate at 2.9 mi on the Flowed Lands via Hanging Spear Falls Trail. This former Finch, Pruyn property is now owned by the Nature Conservancy, but as of 2012 the lease holders still retain their rights. Thus, travel continues to be restricted to the marked trail and designated path to Allen Mt. even though this area is eventually slated to become part of the Forest Preserve as well.)

▶ Trailhead: The road to the Upper Works trailhead is reached from NY 28N, 7.3 mi N of Aiden Lair or about 5 mi E of the Town Hall in Newcomb. Turn N onto Blue Ridge Rd. (CR 84) for 1.6 mi. to the jct. with Tahawus Rd. (CR 25). An alternate approach to this jct. is to go 18 mi W from Exit 29 of I-87 (the Adirondack Northway) via Blue Ridge Rd. This junction is marked with a large DEC sign for Mt. Marcy and the High Peaks.

On Tahawus Rd, it is 6.3 mi from Blue Ridge Rd. to a L turn onto a narrower road marked with a sign for Mt. Marcy and the High Peaks. At 2 mi from this turn, there is a parking lot on the L for the Bradley Pond Trail to Duck Hole (trail 128). At 2.8 mi, one passes the large stone furnace on the R, and at 3 mi there is a parking lot on the R for the Hanging Spear Falls approach to Flowed Lands (trail 123) as well as the route to Allen Mt. Shortly beyond are some abandoned buildings, and the parking lot at Upper Works is reached at 3.5 mi. ◀

121 Mt. Marcy and Lake Colden via Calamity Brook Trail

ADK High Peaks Map: C10 | Trails Illustrated Map 742: X22

This is the shortest approach to Mt. Marcy from the S and it is an attractive route highlighted by the camping areas on Flowed Lands and Lake Colden and the pretty falls and flumes on the Opalescent River. In 1999, salvage lumbering activity on the first few miles of this trail and the Indian Pass trail created some large open areas.

▶ Trailhead: See Sanford Lake Area, p. 187, and Trailhead above. ◀

Starting at the Upper Works parking lot (0.0 mi) with red and yellow markers, the trail follows a wide road for 0.2 mi. to a bridge over the outlet of Henderson Lake. Just beyond, a road leads L 0.1 mi to the shore of the lake. The Calamity Brook Trail bears R, and after a short climb and descent comes to a jct. at 0.4 mi with a yellow-marked trail straight ahead for Indian Pass and Duck Hole (trails 125 and 127). Turning sharp R on a wide lumber road, the trail goes gently up to the edge of an extensive open area at 0.5 mi. Gentle ups and downs through this open area lead to the beginning of a recent (2011) reroute at 1.2 mi that remains on the R bank of Calamity Brook and avoids the previous two brook crossings. Going straight, the trail descends to brook level with a large beaver meadow on the L and a view of Marshall straight ahead. At 1.6 mi the trail becomes rougher and reaches a jct. with the blue-marked Indian Pass Crossover Trail in another 120 yd. Turning R across a bridge and now with blue markers, the trail reaches the jct. with the old trail at the "iron pipe" bridge crossing at 1.9 mi.

Continuing, the trail follows the R bank of the brook at a gentle grade, but then pulls away from the brook at 2.1 mi and begins a steady, moderate climb. Shortly above a switchback to the R at 2.3 mi, the grade begins to ease, and the trail reaches a sign at the former boundary of state land at 2.4 mi. The trail now continues a gradual climb with a designated campsite on the R at 2.5 mi. At 2.9 mi the trail swings sharp L away from the old tote road and soon descends a ladder to a bridge over the brook. (At low water one can save a few steps by crossing the brook on the stones.) Crossing the bridge, the trail quickly rejoins the tote road and climbs at a moderate grade until 3.3 mi, where it eases. The trail is now gently rolling, crossing numerous small streams and reaching an open area with many log bridges at 4.1 mi. After a short climb and descent, the trail reaches another open marsh that it skirts on the R side and reaches the N end of Calamity Pond at 4.3 mi.

A side trail leads 20 yd straight ahead to the Henderson Monument, erected in memory of David Henderson who was killed on this spot when his gun accidentally discharged (the "calamity"). He was scouting for additional water sources to power the blast furnaces at the iron works, and his efforts eventually led to the construction of Flowed Lands dam. This dam could at one time divert the entire flow of the Opalescent River down Calamity Brook.

Turning sharp R, the Calamity Brook Trail climbs gradually along a very rocky section of trail to a jct. at Flowed Lands at 4.7 mi, with the Calamity lean-to up to the R. The red trail R is the Hanging Spear Falls Trail (trail 123), which leads to several lean-tos on Flowed Lands and eventually back to the road below Upper Works. The dam at Flowed Lands was breached in 1984 because it was deemed unsafe, which accounts for the current low water level in the lake.

Turning sharp L and now with red markers again, the trail crosses the now dry channel by which the Opalescent River was once diverted to Calamity Brook. The trail follows around the NW shore of the lake and at 5 mi begins a climb up behind a rocky promontory before descending again to lake level and crossing Herbert Brook at 5.4 mi. (One approach to Mt. Marshall goes L here; see p. 133.) Just beyond Herbert Brook, a side trail goes R to an attractive lean-to located on the N end of Flowed Lands. Continuing on with a few short climbs and descents and another lean-to on the L, the trail reaches a jct. at the top of the ladder leading to the bridge over Lake Colden Dam at 5.7 mi. Blue trail straight ahead (trail 69) leads in 300 yd to two lean-tos on the S shore of Lake Colden, and in 0.5 mi to the DEC Interior Outpost on the NW shore of Lake Colden and then on to Heart Lake.

Turning R and down across the dam (still with red markers), the trail passes several designated camping areas and comes to a trail register and jct. at 5.8 mi. Yellow trail L (trail 68) leads along the E shore of Lake Colden to Avalanche Pass and Heart Lake. One lean-to is located on the L (E) bank of the Opalescent River below the Lake Colden outlet and is reached by crossing the river (in high water, use the suspension bridge described below) and following the trail down the L bank. There are also numerous designated campsites in the area. See Avalanche Pass Trail (trail 68, p. 105) for information on camping restrictions.

Bearing R from the trail register, the trail soon reaches a suspension bridge over the Opalescent and turns sharp L on the far side. Continuing up the L bank at easy grades, the trail passes a waterfall at 6.1 mi and ascends a ladder at 6.4 mi to some ledges above a beautiful flume in the Opalescent. The grade eases above the flume and, after crossing a small tributary, the trail joins an old tote road and climbs away from the river at easy to moderate grades. At 7.3 mi the trail reaches a height of land and descends a moderate grade to the jct. with the abandoned Twin Brook Trail at 7.4 mi. This is the end of the red markers, and the trail is now marked with yellow DEC disks, the color of the former Twin Brook Trail.

From here, the trail bears L and gently down 200 yd to Uphill Lean-to, located just down and to the L of the trail. (The unmarked paths to Mt. Redfield and Cliff Mt. go R here.) Past the lean-to, the trail continues down and crosses Uphill Brook on stones near its confluence with the Opalescent River. The trail now follows close to the L bank of the Opalescent at an easy grade to a jct. at 8 mi with the blue-marked Lake Arnold trail (trail 73). Feldspar Lean-to is located 100 yd up this trail and across the Opalescent River. Turning R, the Mt. Marcy trail soon begins climbing at a moderate grade, crosses a tributary at 8.1 mi, and begins a steady, steep climb high above the L bank of Feldspar Brook. This section of trail received extensive stabilization work in the early 1980s and now offers mostly good footing.

At about 8.8 mi the grade begins to moderate and finally becomes level just before reaching the outlet to Lake Tear of the Clouds, the highest pond source of the Hudson River (elevation, 4346 ft, 1325 m), at 9.2 mi. Across this little body of water, fringed with spruce and balsam, the rocky dome of Mt. Marcy rises in full view.

Bearing R, the trail ascends a few yards to the former site of Lake Tear Lean-to. (Camping is prohibited in this area as it is over 4000 ft in elevation) Continuing on, the trail drops back to the lake level and continues mostly on the level through some very wet terrain to Four Corners, where it joins the blue trail from Elk Lake (trail 118) at 9.5 mi. The red trail R (trail 122) leads 0.5 mi to the summit of Mt. Skylight. As at Lake Tear, no camping is permitted at this former lean-to site because it is above 4000 ft in elevation.

Turning L and still with yellow markers, the trail climbs steadily up a rocky, eroded section of trail. At 9.7 mi a boulder on the L has split away from the mountain, forming a crevice. A few yards through this crevice there is a lookout at Gray Peak and Lake Tear. Swinging R, the trail continues the ascent to a good lookout on the R at 10 mi. (This marks the beginning of the arctic-alpine zone where one must remain on the marked trail or bare rock to preserve the fragile vegetation.) Reaching timberline soon after, the trail climbs over bare rock to the top of Schofield Cobble at 10.1 mi. (See p. 183 for information about Peter Schofield, for whom the Cobble is named.)

After dipping slightly beyond Schofield Cobble, the trail, marked with cairns and yellow paint blazes, begins its final steep ascent to the summit of Mt. Marcy at 10.3 mi. At the summit the trail joins the trail from Heart Lake (trail 61), which also connects with the trails to Johns Brook Lodge and Keene Valley (trail 1).

❅ Trail in winter: This has long been a popular ski trip for advanced intermediate skiers as far as Lake Colden. At least one foot of snow is needed to cover the rocks. With luck, the stream crossings will be frozen. The 2011 reroute has eliminated two of the potentially tricky brook crossing as well as a steep climb and descent near the start. From Calamity Lean-to, ski across Flowed Lands and find the trail to Lake Colden on the L (E) bank of the Opalescent River.

🏃 Distances: Upper Works parking lot to Calamity lean-to at Flowed Lands, 4.7 mi; to jct. at Lake Colden dam, 5.7 mi; to Uphill Lean-to, 7.5 mi; to jct. with Lake Arnold Trail near Feldspar Lean-to, 8 mi; to Four Corners and jct. with Elk Lake–Marcy Trail, 9.5 mi; to summit of Mt. Marcy, 10.3 mi (16.6 km). Ascent from Upper Works, 3800 ft (1159 m). Elevation, 5344 ft (1629 m). Order of height, 1.

122 Mt. Skylight from Four Corners

ADK High Peaks Map: D10 | Trails Illustrated Map 742: X24

▶ Locator: From Four Corners, the jct. of the Elk Lake and Calamity Brook trails to Mt. Marcy (trails 118 and 121, respectively), a red-marked trail leads S and up to the open, rounded dome of Mt. Skylight. ◀

Leaving the jct. (0.0 mi), the trail makes a steady climb up a wet, rocky trail to timberline at 0.4 mi. (This marks the beginning of the arctic-alpine zone where one must remain on the marked trail or bare rock to preserve the fragile vegetation.) From here the grade is easier through an open alpine meadow with cairns to mark the way to the summit at 0.5 mi. There are outstanding views of the surrounding peaks, with 30 major peaks discernible. Legend states that if a climber fails to carry a rock from timberline to place on the summit cairn, it will surely rain.

🚶 Distance: Four Corners to summit of Mt. Skylight, 0.5 mi (0.8 km). Ascent from Four Corners, 578 ft (176 m). Elevation, 4926 ft (1502 m). Order of height, 4.

Gray Peak *(Unmaintained trail; see introduction, p. 19.)*

ADK High Peaks Map: D10 | Trails Illustrated Map 742: X24

This mountain, the highest of the trailless peaks, was named by Colvin for Professor Asa Gray, one of the most noted botanists of his day. Start at the outlet of Lake Tear of the Clouds (see trail 121) and climb over a ridge and across into a valley. (When descending, do not be misled down this valley; it is very rough going and joins Feldspar Brook well below Lake Tear.) The route then heads N to the summit ridge, striking it about 200 yards W of the summit.

The direct route between Mt. Marcy and Gray Peak has been closed by the DEC in order to help preserve fragile alpine vegetation.

Mt. Redfield *(Unmarked path; see introduction, p. 19)*

ADK High Peaks Map: D10 | Trails Illustrated Map 742: X23

This peak was named by Colvin for Professor William C. Redfield, meteorologist and organizer of the first expedition to Mt. Marcy. It was Redfield who first described Mt. Marcy as the "High Peak of Essex" after an 1836 reconnaissance up the Opalescent River above Lake Colden prior to the first ascent in 1837.

This designated herd path follows Uphill Brook from Uphill Lean-to (see trail 121). The start is marked with a cairn and is located near the side trail to the lean-to or about 120 yards W of the Uphill Brook crossing. This is also the start for the path to Cliff Mt., which diverges R about 200 yd from the start. The lower part of the path stays high on the L bank of the brook for approximately 0.3 mi before returning to the brook at a waterfall The path then follows close to Uphill Brook to a point about 0.3 mile above the waterfall where a tributary comes in from the R (S). The path now follows this tributary and then heads straight for the summit. Another route to Mt. Redfield leads from Lake Tear of the Clouds SW to the summit. Stay below the summit ridge until directly under the top of the mountain. There is no continuous herd path on this route.

Cliff Mt. *(Unmarked path; see introduction, p. 19)*

ADK High Peaks Map: D10 | Trails Illustrated Map 742: X23

This self-explanatory name was bestowed by the surveyor Verplanck Colvin.

The start is the same as for Mt. Redfield (see above). From the cairn, it is 200 yd to a jct. where the path to Cliff Mt. goes R. It soon joins the very muddy abandoned Twin Brook trail for another 300 yd, where the path diverges R. Head W, go L of the first band of cliffs encountered and then in general keep R of the higher cliffs. After reaching the NE summit, follow the broad ridge SW about 0.5 miles to the true summit, which rises steeply beyond the col. The extensive blowdown in 1999 now offers an excellent view of Mt. Colden from Cliff's formerly viewless summit.

123 Flowed Lands via Hanging Spear Falls

ADK High Peaks Map: C11 | Trails Illustrated Map 742: X22

This much longer approach to Flowed Lands leads past the beautiful Hanging Spear Falls, one of the highest falls in the Adirondacks. The trail also is the start of the most popular approach for Allen Mt. The most recent (2015) state acquisitions mean that all but a short section of this trail near Lake Sally is on public land. Hikers should take note, however, that the bridge over the Opalescent River is still out with no immediate plans to replace it. Crossing the river involves wading at most water levels and can be dangerous at high water levels.

This trail has changed significantly in the wake of the 1999 hurricane damage and subsequent salvage logging operations. The trail now passes through long sections of lumber clearings with great views of the peaks but also scenes of devastation in the foreground. Note, however, that most of the damage was caused by natural forces. Furthermore, to the loggers' credit, there is no evidence of litter or abandoned equipment along the trail—a sharp contrast to logging operations in earlier days.

▶ Trailhead: The trail starts at a parking lot on the R side of the road to Upper Works, 3 mi from the jct. with the road leading to the mining operations. (See Sanford Lake Area, Trailhead, p. 187, for complete driving directions.) ◀

From the trail register (0.0 mi), with yellow markers, the trail follows a road 0.1 mi to the R bank of the Hudson River, where it turns R a few yards to a suspension bridge. Crossing the bridge, the trail soon rejoins the road and continues on the level to a new (2014) trail L at 0.5 mi. This new trail avoids the long bridge over the N end of Lake Jimmy that had become impassable. The trail crosses the outlet to Lake Jimmy at 0.6 mi and then swings back to the R, rejoining the old road and reaching the observer's cabin at 1.1 mi where the trail swings R. (Watch for this sharp L on the return trip. Also, from this point on, markers are few and far between, so pay

Hanging Spear Falls. **James Appleyard**

attention at each jct.)

From the observer's cabin the trail follows a wide gravel road up over a cleared knoll where the trail to Mt. Adams goes L and then down and R to a brook crossing at 1.2 mi. A short climb leads to a large clearing at 1.3 mi followed by a sharp R turn at 1.4 mi. (This is another jct. to note on the return trip.) After this turn, the road descends and proceeds through another large clearing to a jct. at 1.7 mi. Here the trail turns sharp L (well signed) and enters private land on a narrower gravel road to a clearing on the shore of Lake Sally at 1.8 mi. Now dirt, in another 50 yd the trail turns R and then takes a sharp R to avoid a muddy area at 1 mi. Returning to a lumber road at 2.1 mi, there is a final view of Lake Sally at 2.2 mi, followed by a climb to a muddy clearing at 2.3 mi. At 2.4 mi the route swings sharp L onto a trail-width path for a short while before joining a wide gravel road at 2.6 mi.

Turning L on this road, there are ultimately views that range from North River Mt. to Mts. Redfield and Skylight. There are no markers as the road passes through an extensive clearing and then nears the bank of the Opalescent River at 2.9 mi. At 3.1 mi the trail reaches a gate that delineates what once was the boundary between Kronos (National Lead Company) and Finch, Pruyn & Co. land but now marks the end of private land. Beyond this gate, the road continues to a jct. with a road leading R across the river at 3.9 mi. In another 175 yd there is a sharp R to the ford across the Opalescent River.

After the ford, the trail is in the woods for only 200 yd before reaching another cleared area and turning L on a rough road. Now marked with a profusion of plastic flagging and an occasional marker, the trail reaches the jct. with the Allen Mt. herd path, marked with a large sign at 5.3 mi (see Allen Mt., p. 195).

The trail to Flowed Lands turns sharp L at this jct., crosses Upper Twin Brook, and climbs gradually to a jct. with a gravel road coming in from the R at 5.6 mi. Turning sharp L and now with red markers, the trail remains mostly level as it crosses several rough salvage roads. Continuing level and straight, the trail passes a designated campsite with a privy at 6.3 mi. At 6.8 mi the trail crosses a brook and begins to climb more steeply along a sidehill near the gorge in an area of heavy blowdown offering views of Calamity Mt. and Mt. Adams.

Continuing to climb, the trail crosses another small brook at 7.5 mi. Shortly after this stream crossing there is a side trail L (which rejoins the old road 70 yd farther on) leading to several views of Hanging Spear Falls. At a certain volume of water, the falls are divided by a rock that is said to give the appearance of a hanging spearhead.

The trail continues its steep climb, passing another lookout on the L at 7.8 mi and reaching easier going soon after. The trail now follows the L bank of the river at easy grades to the breached dam at Flowed Lands at 8.3 mi. See Calamity Brook Trail (trail 121) for history and current status of this dam. (From the dam, a yellow-marked side trail leads R 0.6 mi to Livingston Point Lean-to. With the current low water levels it is also relatively easy to continue along the open shore of Flowed Lands to the lean-tos at Lake Colden, but this route is not marked and will likely become more of a bushwhack in years to come as alders grow on the formerly flooded areas.)

Turning L at the dam, the trail crosses the river on stones and comes to a side trail that leads L and up 50 yd to Griffin Lean-to. It is usually possible to walk along the open area next to the water, but the trail climbs up away from the shore and after several ups and downs comes to a side trail R at 8.5 mi leading to Flowed Lands Lean-to, which has one of the prettiest locations of any lean-to in the Adirondacks. Continuing past this jct., the trail climbs over one more knoll and descends to a jct. at the shore of the lake near the Calamity Lean-to at 8.7 mi. Trail L and straight ahead is Calamity Brook Trail (trail 121) leading to Upper Works or Lake Colden and Mt. Marcy.

❄ Trail in winter: Although rarely skied, the trail is skiable all the way to the base of the climb to Hanging Spear Falls at 7.7 mi. If one is willing to struggle for 0.5 mi, this is a feasible, if long, route to Flowed Lands.

🥾 Distances: Parking lot to jct. with Allen Mt. path, 5.3 mi; to Hanging Spear Falls, 7.8 mi; to Flowed Lands Dam, 8.3 mi; to jct. with Calamity Brook Trail, 8.7 mi (14.0 km).

Allen Mt. *(Unmaintained Trail; see introduction, p. 19)*

(see introduction, p. 19)

ADK High Peaks Map: D11 | Trails Illustrated Map 742: X–W24

This mountain was named by Rev. Joseph Twichell for his close friend, Rev. Frederick B. Allen, who became superintendent of the Episcopal City Mission in Boston. The naming took place on a camping trip to Upper Ausable Lake with Charles Dudley Warner and Dr. Horace Bushnell when they were caught in the great cloudburst of August 20, 1869, that caused the great slide (or "avalanche," as in the lake) on Mt. Colden. The most used route follows a herd path from the jct. at 5.1 mi. on the trail to Flowed Lands via Hanging Spear Falls (trail 123).

From the jct., the path is at first marked with orange and green or black flagging as it heads generally SE. Crossing a rough skid road after 100 yd, the path turns more to the E and reaches a gravel road at 0.3 mi. Here the route to Allen Mt. turns L for 50 yd and then sharp R to the far end of a gravel pit.

Now marked with orange and yellow flagging, the path climbs away from the brook to a jct. at 0.7 mi, where it bears R onto a wider road. (On the return, be sure not to miss this turn off the wider road onto the narrower marked route.) The path follows this road past a view of a waterfall and up to a R turn onto a rough, wet road at 0.9 mi. This road ends at 1.1 mi at the bank of Lower Twin Brook.

Crossing the brook at 1.3 mi, the path goes through an area of blowdown and reaches a low pass at 1.8 mi. Reaching state land soon after this pass, the route descends past beaver ponds and crosses a sizable brook shortly before crossing Skylight Brook to join an old lumber road on the L bank of the brook. Continuing NE up the Skylight Brook valley for some 0.7 mi, the herd path turns SE again, following a tributary, the beautiful Allen Brook, past its source to the ridgetop a short distance S of the summit. Allow at least four hours from the marked trail to the summit.

Climbing Allen Mt. from either Mt. Skylight or the Elk Lake–Marcy Trail involves travel through blowdown and thick second growth without the aid of herd paths, and is not recommended.

124 Mt. Adams

ADK High Peaks Map: C11 | Trails Illustrated Map 742: X22

The fire tower on this peak was restored in 2005. With the tower, hikers are rewarded with a marvelous panorama, including close-up views of Wallface.

The DEC has resumed maintaining the trail, but it is still very steep and wet in places. Marked with red DEC markers, the Mt. Adams trail diverges L from the Hanging Spear Falls trail to Flowed Lands (trail 123) just past the old observer's cabin at a cairn. At first, the trail ascends at moderate grades, but becomes very steep before reaching the summit, 2.4 mi from the parking lot, having ascended 1800 ft.

125 Indian Pass from Upper Works

ADK High Peaks Map: C10 | Trails Illustrated Map 742: X22

This trail leads to Summit Rock in Indian Pass, where it connects with the trail from Heart Lake. The view of Wallface's huge cliff from Summit Rock is one of the most impressive in the Adirondacks, and is a good objective for a day hike or as a point to be included in a backpacking trip.

▶ Trailhead: The trail starts at the Upper Works parking lot (see Sanford Lake Area, Trailhead, p. 187, for driving directions) with yellow markers and initially coincides with the red-marked Calamity Brook Trail (trail 121). ◀

From the trail register (0.0 mi) the trail follows a wide gravel road for 0.2 mi. to a bridge over the outlet of Henderson Lake. Just beyond, a road leads L 0.1 mi to the shore of the lake. The Indian Pass Trail bears R, and after a short climb and descent comes to a jct. at 0.4 mi (Red trail R is the Calamity Brook Trail, trail 121). Continuing straight ahead on a wide road, the trail soon begins a gradual climb. Avoid road L at 0.7 mi. At a large clearing at 0.9 mi the trail bears L and down, and then goes straight across a final clearing at 1.1 mi at the end of recent lumbering before coming to the jct. at 1.5 mi with the red-marked trail L leading to Duck Hole (trail 127). Yellow markers end here.

Continuing straight ahead with red markers, at 1.7 mi the Indian Pass trail passes Henderson Lean-to on the L and reaches an old lumber clearing at 2 mi. At the N end of the clearing, the trail turns sharp R at a signpost, coming to the jct. with the Indian Pass-Calamity Brook Crossover (trail 126) in another 100 yd. Turning L, the Indian Pass trail crosses the brook on a bridge with a designated campsite on the R just past the bridge. The trail then proceeds at easy grades to Wallface Lean-to at 2.7 mi near the R bank of Indian Pass Brook.

Still pretty much on the level, the trail veers away from the brook just before reaching a large rock on the R at 2.9 mi where there is a view of Wallface ahead. After crossing three smaller brooks, the trail crosses the outlet to Wallface Ponds at 3.2 mi and recrosses Indian Pass Brook at 3.9 mi. The grade soon becomes steep as it winds among large boulders and ledges. After a short downgrade at 4.1 mi the trail again climbs steeply, with ladders necessary at two points, until it reaches a side trail leading L a few yards to Summit Rock at 4.4 mi. This is not the actual summit of the pass, but has by far the best view and is the usual destination coming from either direction. The actual height of land is another 0.5 mi beyond, and the trail continues 6 mi more to Heart Lake (trail 75).

❇ Trail in winter: Skiable for the first 3 mi or close enough to get some spectacular views of Wallface, but definitely not skiable to Summit Rock.

🐾 Distances: Upper Works to jct. with Duck Hole Trail, 1.5 mi; to Henderson Lean-to, 1.7 mi; to jct. with crossover to Calamity Brook Trail, 2 mi; to Wallface Lean-to, 2.7 mi; to Summit Rock, 4.4 mi (7.1 km). Ascent from Upper Works, 870 ft (265 m). Elevation, 2660 ft (811 m).

126 Indian Pass–Calamity Brook Crossover

ADK High Peaks Map: C10 | Trails Illustrated Map 742: X22

▶ Locator: This trail leads through a pass at the end of the MacIntyre Range to connect the Indian Pass and Calamity Brook trails (trails 125 and 121, respectively).

The trail's construction dates back to a time when the Tahawus Club controlled the area near Upper Works and would not permit hikers to pass through. An alternate route was thus needed to allow hikers to travel between Duck Hole and Lake Colden. With the current layout, however, this crossover trail saves no distance between these two points and involves some rough, wet walking—complicated by recent beaver activity—plus 500 ft of additional climbing. Hikers approaching from Indian Pass do save almost 1 mi, but the trail is now infrequently used. ◀

From the jct., 2 mi from Upper Works on the Indian Pass trail (trail 125) (0.0 mi), the grade is easy at first, but soon becomes steeper as the trail follows a brook, crossing and recrossing it several times before climbing more steeply to the top of the pass at 0.9 mi, having gained 500 ft from the Indian Pass trail. Descending, the trail skirts a meadow at 1 mi and follows a brook, crossing it several times and reaching a beaver swamp at 1.7 mi. After some tough going around the R side of the swamp, the trail crosses the swamp at 1.8 mi and 150 yd later veers R on a new lumber road, reaching the bank of Calamity Brook at 2 mi and then swinging L along the brook to the jct. with the Calamity Brook Trail (trail 121) at 2.1 mi.

🚶 Distance: Indian Pass Trail to Calamity Brook trail, 2.1 mi (3.4 km).

127 Duck Hole via Henderson Lake and Preston Ponds

ADK High Peaks Map: C10 | Trails Illustrated Map 742: X22

This is the easiest route to Duck Hole and involves relatively little climbing compared to the route via Bradley Pond (trail 128).

▶ Locator: The trail begins at Upper Works (see Sanford Lake Area, Trailhead, p. 187, for driving directions) and follows the Indian Pass Trail (trail 125) to the jct. at 1.5 mi. ◀

Leaving the jct. (0.0 mi), the trail immediately crosses Indian Pass Brook and turns L, but soon swings R and away from the brook and at 0.3 mi crosses a beaver flow. Past the beaver flow, the trail is mostly level to a jct. at 0.6 mi with a trail leading L and down to a lean-to on Henderson Lake. Swinging R, the trail crosses a long series of bridges over a wet area and reaches a brook, which it crosses at 0.7 mi. Recrossing the brook at 0.8 mi, the trail veers away and approaches the R bank of another brook, which it follows up past some interesting cascades at 0.9 mi. Just beyond, the trail skirts a beaver pond on its L side and continues on to a brook

Henderson Lake. Joanne Kennedy

crossing at 1.3 mi. Recrossing this brook twice more, the trail begins a moderate climb that levels off at 1.8 mi. Descending slightly, the trail is now mostly level through an almost imperceptible divide between the St. Lawrence and Hudson watersheds, having gained only 370 ft (113 m) from Henderson Lake.

Dropping slightly after the pass, the trail comes to a jct. in the middle of a series of bridges over some wet areas. (Trail straight ahead leads to a dock on the Preston Ponds.) Turning sharp R, the trail soon begins climbing along the outlet to Hunter Pond, crossing it at 2.4 mi. The trail continues up the L bank, reaches Hunter Pond at 2.7 mi, crosses the outlet, and skirts the pond to the N before climbing a short steep pitch to the top of a pass at 2.8 mi. Starting down, the trail skirts a beaver pond on its R side at 3 mi and joins an old lumber road just past the pond. The trail now descends a wet and eroded section of lumber road to the remains of Piche's lumber camp at 3.2 mi.

After the camp, the trail crosses to the R side of the brook and continues descending at easy grades before veering away from the brook and descending more steeply over old corduroys with Lower Preston Pond visible through trees to the L. Crossing a small swamp at 4 mi, the trail climbs easily to a boundary line at 4.2 mi that formerly marked the entry to state land. After another descent and climb to a height of land, the trail descends to the NE shore of Duck Hole at 4.4 mi. Turning N and after several more short, steep ups and downs, the trail reaches the L bank of Roaring Brook, which it crosses on a bridge to a jct. with the N–P Trail (trail 99) on the far bank at 4.9 mi.

Turning L and now with red and blue markers, the trail proceeds with several easy ups and downs to a large, open area leading down to the now-breached dam (2011) at Duck Hole at 5.3 mi. There are two lean-tos at Duck Hole and plenty of tent sites. One lean-to is just before the outlet; the other is in the woods on a point of land 100 yd E of the outlet. A ranger station at the W edge of the clearing was removed in December 1977 in order to bring the area into compliance with wilderness use guidelines. A blue trail crosses below the dam and leads to Bradley Pond (trail 128) and the trailhead at Tahawus. The N–P Trail heads W along an old truck trail that connects with a trail heading to Ward Brook and the trailhead at Coreys (trails 129 and 133).

❋ Trail in winter: Very skiable as far as the Preston Ponds. With favorable ice conditions, this is a very skiable route across the Preston Ponds to Duck Hole. The hiking trail is the recommended connection from the Lower Preston Pond to Duck Hole rather than the bushwhack from the outlet to Duck Hole.

🏃 Distances: Trail jct. S of Henderson Lean-to near bridge over Indian Pass trail to E end of Preston Ponds, 2.3 mi; to jct. with N–P Trail at Roaring Brook, 4.9 mi; to Duck Hole, 5.3 mi (8.5 km). (Distance from Upper Works, 6.9 mi or 11.1 km).

MacNaughton Mt. *(Unmaintained trail; see introduction, p. 19.)*

ADK High Peaks Map: C9 | Trails Illustrated Map 742: Y22

MacNaughton Mt. is named after James MacNaughton, grandson of Archibald McIntyre, who headed the original Adirondack Iron Works. Though not officially one of the 46 peaks, it is the one mountain to be raised to the 4000 ft status on the 1953 USGS map. The new series of metric maps, however, shows the highest contour elevation to be 1214 m or 3983 ft. The upper reaches of the mountain are almost completely covered with blowdown.

The most popular route is from the Wallface Ponds on a vague herd path that follows a compass line generally SW to a lower summit where the register once was placed. A continuation of the path leads SE for 300 yd to a slightly higher summit with a view. Another approach leaves the Duck Hole via Henderson Lake trail (trail 127) at the brook crossing beyond the beaver pond about 0.6 mi NW of Hunter Pond. It follows the SE side of the brook valley nearly to the summit ridge. Climb N over one summit to a second summit with a good view and shown on the metric map as the highest point.

128 Duck Hole via Bradley Pond

ADK High Peaks Map: C11 | Trails Illustrated Map 742: X22

This trail leads to Duck Hole through the pass between the Santanoni Range and Henderson Mt. and gives access to the paths up Santanoni, Panther, and Couchsachraga peaks (see pp. 201–202). With the recent acquisition, the R (N) side of the road is now Forest Preserve, and it is all Forest Preserve after 3 mi. The previously closed old trail to Santanoni Peak is again open.

▶ Trailhead: The trail begins at a parking lot on the L side of the road to Upper Works, 2 mi N of the bridge to the mining operations. (See Sanford Lake Area, Trailhead, p. 187, for complete driving directions.) There is a large parking lot 100 yd back from the road. ◀

From the trail register (0.0 mi), the trail follows a good gravel road with blue markers at gentle grades. At 1.1 mi it crosses the outlet to Harkness Lake, where there is a great view of Wallface Mt. The trail now climbs over a small rise, drops down, and begins a longer climb that eases just before a sharp R turn off the road at 1.8 mi.

The trail now descends along the R bank of a brook, crosses the brook on a good bridge, and continues on the flat through a grassy clearing with plenty of raspberries. At the far end of the clearing, the trail swings L and crosses Santanoni Brook at 2.1 mi on an elaborate bridge with a series of log steps up the far bank. At the top of the bank, the trail swings L onto an old tote road and begins ascending at easy to moderate grades up the valley to a series of beautiful cascades on the L at 3.4 mi. Approximately 200 yd past the cascades, the now legal path to Santanoni Peak goes L just after a sharp R turn at the end of a muddy area. The marked trail continues to a crest at 3.6 mi. After a short descent, the trail crosses a wet area on a series of good bridges, but beyond here it is almost unremittingly wet until well past Santanoni Lean-to. At 4.3 mi the path to Panther Peak and the other peaks in the Santanoni Range diverges L across a beaver dam.

The trail reaches a brook at 4.4 mi with the Santanoni Lean-to located on a knoll above and to the R of the former site. Designated campsites are so far quite limited in this area. This is the top of the pass, 2950 ft (900 m), 1110 ft (338 m) above the trailhead.

Past the lean-to the trail begins to descend, and maintenance of this section of the trail has often been spotty. It is often difficult to distinguish the trail and the brook for the first part of the descent until at 4.8 mi the trail crosses a larger stream, swings to the R and then back L to recross the stream, and then continues down to a crossing of the L fork of the main stream at 5.1 mi. Turning R on relatively flat ground, the trail crosses the main brook but returns to the L bank at 5.6 mi. Still mostly on the flat, the trail detours to the L to avoid some beaver and blowdown activity and crosses a beaver dam at 6 mi.

At 6.6 mi the trail returns to the L bank of the stream. From here it is mostly very enjoyable walking along the picturesque stream. At 7.1 mi the trail crosses again to the R bank and continues on the level to 7.8 mi, where it turns L and crosses the brook for the final time and climbs over a small ridge to the SW shore of Duck Hole at 7.9 mi. Skirting the pond, the trail crosses a rock crib dike at 8 mi and soon comes to the dam. The bridge has been removed and the dam is now breached (2011). Cross downstream (may be difficult with high water) to reach the lean-to and trail jct. just beyond at 8.2 mi. Here the trail meets the N–P Trail (trails 99 and 133), marked here with blue and red markers. It leads R to Averyville Rd. near Lake Placid with a connection to the trail from Upper Works (trail 127). To the L, the N–P Trail leads to Shattuck Clearing and Long Lake with a connection to the trail to Ward Brook and Coreys (trail 129).

❄ Trail in winter: Both the climb to Bradley Pond and the descent off the N side of the pass are for advanced skiers, but overall this is a skiable route. It is rarely done, but makes a beautiful though very rugged 14-mi loop when combined with trail 127, Duck Hole via Henderson Lake.

🏃 Distances: Parking lot to Santanoni Lean-to, 4.4 mi; to Duck Hole, 8.2 mi (13.2 km).

SANTANONI RANGE

ADK High Peaks Map: B10–B11 | Trails Illustrated Map 742: X20

Santanoni, Panther, and Couchsachraga peaks form the Santanoni Range.

Thanks to recent (2008) acquisitions, there are now two approaches to the Santanoni Range, making possible a loop that reduces the amount of backtracking required to visit all three peaks. The route in use since the early 1980s (at the time the only legal route) is now described as the approach to Panther Peak while the now-legal trail direct to Santanoni Peak is described directly below.

Santanoni Peak *(Unmarked paths; see introduction, p. 19)*

ADK High Peaks Map: B10 | Trails Illustrated Map 742: X20

The name of the highest peak W of the Hudson River and the dominating one in the range is derived from Saint Anthony. This name filtered down through the French Canadians to the Abenaki Indians, who adopted their own pronunciation of the words.

This path follows the route of a trail originally cut by the Tahawus Club. Formal maintenance ceased at least 70 years ago and only sporadic informal maintenance kept this trail passable through to 1980 when the private landowner closed it to public travel. Since the sale of this land to first the Open Space Institute and then to the state, a new round of informal maintenance has again made this a feasible route direct to or from Santanoni.

The path starts at 3.5 mi. on the Duck Hole via Bradley Pond trail (trail 128) at a cairn approximately 200 yd past the cascades in Santanoni Brook. The path immediately crosses the brook and then veers L to avoid beaver activity. It then follows the R bank of Santanoni Brook before pulling steeply away and up to a reroute to the R of the "Hillary Step" at just over a mile from the marked trail. Soon gaining the crest of a ridge running E from the peak, the path is briefly flat before climbing steeply through thick scrub to an open knob just N of the actual summit at about 2 mi from the marked trail. Here the path joins the path that follows the crest of the ridge between Panther Peak and Santanoni Peak. For those electing to descend this path, the open knob is the second bump N of the actual summit.

Ermine Brook Slide: A challenging route on Santanoni Peak follows a slide that came down Santanoni's W face in September 1985. The route leaves the Moose Pond Horse Trail (trail 138) where it crosses Ermine Brook, 1.4 mi past Moose Pond. Take the R fork (looking up) just over a half mile from the trail to stay in the main branch of Ermine Brook. The base of this long, narrow slide is reached about 2 mi from the trail. From the top of the slide, it is a few yards to the crest of the ridge and then nearly half a mile of very thick bushwhacking to the summit of Santanoni Peak.

Panther Peak *(Unmarked paths; see introduction, p. 19)*

ADK High Peaks Map: B:10 | Trails Illustrated Map 742: X20

The direct route leaves the Duck Hole to Bradley Pond trail (trail 128) 4.3 mi from the road and about 0.3 mi S of the Santanoni Lean-to at a beaver dam. Crossing the beaver dam and then following an old survey line past the northern end of Bradley Pond, the path climbs steeply over rough terrain and then contours westerly some 0.3 mi to Panther Brook, which descends from the Panther-Santanoni ridge.

A half mile of rock-hopping up the brook leads to a herd path that in another half mile reaches the crest of the ridge and a small beaten-down area at a four-way jct. (This jct. should perhaps be called "Herald Square" to differentiate it from nearby "Times Square.") The path R leads in about a half mile to the summit of Panther Peak. Both the path straight ahead and the one L lead in about 150 yd to a larger beaten-down area known informally as "Times Square." From this point, a herd path leads W down a ridge to Couchsachraga Peak. The route to Santanoni leads S along the ridge, a distance of more than 1 mi.

Couchsachraga Peak *(Unmarked paths; see introduction, p. 19)*

ADK High Peaks Map: B10 | Trails Illustrated Map 742: X20

Pronounced "Kook-sa-KRA-ga," this term is an ancient Algonquin name for the Adirondacks that means "dismal wilderness." Most people today reach Couchsachraga Peak by way of herd paths leading W down the long ridge from the point 0.5 mi S of Panther's summit where the route from the trail to Duck Hole via Bradley Pond strikes the ridge (see trail 128). Travel from the Panther-Santanoni ridge to Couchsachraga can take two hours or more. The easiest way back from Couchsachraga to the above-mentioned trail is to return by the same route.

Another approach is from the Cold River area up a stream crossed by the horse trail (trail 134) about 6 mi E of Shattuck Clearing and 4 mi W of the N–P Trail NW of Duck Hole. An abandoned trail from the Santanoni Preserve joins the horse trail at this point.

129　Duck Hole from Coreys via Ward Brook Truck Trail

ADK High Peaks Map: AA8–B9 | Trails Illustrated Map 742: Z18

This is the western access to Duck Hole and the High Peaks region and also offers the easiest access to the routes up the Seward Range (see p. 208).

▶ Trailhead: The start is on a road that leaves NY 3, 12.7 mi W of the traffic light in Saranac Lake and 2.7 mi E of the jct. of NY 3 and NY 30 E of Tupper Lake. This road is marked with a large DEC sign for "High Peaks via Duck Hole." It is paved through the little settlement of Coreys, but turns to gravel at about 1.5 mi (end of winter plowing) and crosses Stony Creek at 2.5 mi. At 0.9 mi past Stony Creek a short (0.5 mi) trail goes R to Rock Pond followed at 1.7 mi by another short (0.3 mi) trail on the R for Pickerel Pond. The road to the Seward trailhead continues to a parking area on the R, 5.8 mi from NY 3. As the signs indicate, the road enters a private preserve shortly beyond the parking lot, and this is as far as the public may travel. From this parking lot, both a foot trail and a horse trail depart for the Ward Brook Truck Trail and Duck Hole. The horse trail is not described here because it exactly parallels the hiking trail, is considerably wetter, and is generally unsuited for hiking. ◀

Leaving the trail register (0.0 mi), the foot trail and horse trail follow the same route with both horse trail and red DEC foot trail markers to a jct. at 0.5 mi. Here the foot trail goes L, after which it begins following the posted property line of the Ampersand Club and reaches the Calkins Brook trail at 1.2 mi. (Road L is blocked by a gate at the boundary of private land. Road R leads to Calkins Brook and Shattuck Clearing, trail 130).

Continuing past the road and still mostly level, the trail crosses several brooks, including a large brook at 3.5 mi, and at 4.5 mi comes to Blueberry Lean-to on the R. Just beyond the lean-to, the trail joins the Ward Brook Truck Trail coming in from the L from the private Ampersand Club. (Hikers heading W toward Coreys must be sure to make this sharp L turn off the truck trail.)

Turning R on the road, the trail passes the jct. with the horse trail at 4.7 mi and then crosses three fair-sized brooks before reaching Ward Brook Lean-to at 5.4 mi. The first of these brooks is the favored approach to Seward Mt. (see p. 208). The first brook beyond Ward Brook Lean-to is the favored approach to Seymour Mt.; after this brook the trail climbs easily to a crest before dipping down a bit to two lean-tos, Number Four 1 and 2, at 6.1 mi.

Climbing again at easy to moderate grades, the trail reaches its highest point at 7 mi and descends in several stages to an open swamp at 8.4 mi before climbing over another hill and dropping down to a jct. with the N–P Trail (trail 133) at 8.7 mi. Continuing on with red and blue markers, the trail comes to the two Cold River lean-tos (1 and 2) at 9.1 mi. Just past the lean-tos, the trail crosses Moose Creek just above its confluence with the Cold River, climbs the far bank, and then follows along the R bank of the Cold River to a jct. at 9.4 mi with Cold River Horse Trail R (trail 134), which fords the Cold River and continues down the E side of the river to Shattuck Clearing with a connection to the Santanoni Preserve and Newcomb.

Past this jct., the trail climbs over a low ridge and arrives at the trail jct. and the former ranger station site at 10.3 mi. Blue trail R crosses below the now-breached dam (2011) and leads to Bradley Pond and the road below Upper Works (trail 128). Trail bearing L with blue and red markers is the continuation of the N–P Trail leading to Lake Placid (trail 99) and with a connection to a trail leading to Henderson Lake and Upper Works (trail 127). There are two lean-tos and several good campsites at Duck Hole. One lean-to is located by the dam; the other is 100 yd E of the dam on a beautiful wooded point.

❄ Trail in winter: The road is not officially plowed beyond a point 1 mi short of the bridge over Stony Creek., add 4.3 mi to all distances for winter travel. This route is very skiable for as far as time permits. (Private plowing may permit vehicular travel beyond the designated parking area at the end of official plowing, but this travel is strictly at one's own risk.)

🏃 Distances: Parking area to Blueberry Lean-to, 4.5 mi; to Ward Brook Lean-to, 5.4 mi; to N–P Trail, 8.7 mi; to Cold River Lean-tos 1 and 2, 9.1 mi; to Duck Hole, 10.3 mi (16.6 km).

130 Shattuck Clearing from Coreys via Calkins Brook Truck Trail

ADK High Peaks Map: A8–AA10 | Trails Illustrated Map 742: Z19

This is the shortest access to Shattuck Clearing and the Cold River from the W. It follows valleys to the W of the Seward Range at generally easy grades. For much of its distance it parallels Calkins Brook, which is, however, frequently referred to as Calkins "Creek." Because all maps show this stream as "Brook," this designation is used throughout for consistency. Except for the first 1.2 mi, this entire route is on gravel roads that are also part of the Cold River horse trail system.

▶ Trailhead: The trail begins at the same parking lot, on the road from Coreys, where the Ward Brook approach to Duck Hole begins. (See trail 129, p. 202, for driving directions.) ◀

From the trail register at the parking lot (0.0 mi), this trail coincides with the trail to Duck Hole for 1.2 mi to the jct. with the Calkins Brook Truck Trail (trail 130). Turning R, the road climbs at an easy grade to a jct. with the horse trail at 1.4 mi. (Trail R leads back to the parking lot. Trail L leads to Ward Brook Truck Trail, trail 129.) Continuing straight ahead, the Calkins Brook Truck Trail continues climbing at easy grades to a height of land at 2.1 mi, after which the road dips, climbs again, and then begins a gradual, rolling descent to a brook crossing at 2.8 mi. Now mostly flat or gently down, the trail comes to a jct. with the herd path to Mt. Donaldson at 3.3 mi (see Seward Mt. and Mts. Donaldson and Emmons, p. 248). Just beyond, at 3.4 mi, the road comes to the R bank of Calkins Brook, soon crosses and then recrosses the brook at 3.7 mi, and continues the descent. At 4.2 mi the road climbs sharply and begins a series of slight ups and downs leading to a jct. at 4.9 mi with the Raquette River Horse Trail (trail 131), which leads 5.5 mi to the road to Raquette Falls and the parking lot near the bridge over Stony Creek.

Continuing straight ahead, the road makes a rolling descent to a clearing with the two Calkins Brook lean-tos at 6.1 mi. Swinging L, the road crosses Calkins Brook and begins to climb past a large sand pit. The grades are easy at first, but increase to moderate before reaching a height of land at 7 mi. The road now begins a long, gradual descent through occasional small clearings to a larger clearing at 8.1 mi, with a brief view back toward the Seward Range. At 8.8 mi the road skirts the R side of a large alder swamp with even better views before crossing Boulder Brook at 8.9 mi and climbing over a small knoll and down to a jct. at 9.6 mi. (Trail L leads 200 yd to Latham Pond, where there are some good campsites and a view of the Sewards.)

Turning R, the road gently descends through a beautiful grove of pines to a jct. on the R bank of the Cold River at 10.4 mi. (Road L leads up along the R bank of the Cold River to two lean-tos. Cold River Lean-to 3 is 0.4 mi from this jct. and Cold River Lean-to 4 is 0.6 mi, at the point where the N–P Trail crosses the Cold River on a suspension bridge.) Turning R at this jct. for 200 yd, the road comes to a reasonably easy ford, after which the road climbs the far bank to the site of the former Shattuck Clearing ranger station at 10.6 mi. Like the station at Duck Hole, this structure was removed in 1977 to bring this area into compliance with wilderness area guidelines.

At Shattuck Clearing is a jct. with the blue-marked N–P Trail (trail 133). Trail R leads 12.5 mi to NY 28N near Long Lake. Trail L leads 0.7 mi to the suspension bridge over the Cold River and then on to Duck Hole at 11.9 mi. Trail L also leads to the Cold River Horse Trail (trail 134), which follows the E bank of the Cold River to Duck Hole and connects with another horse trail leading to Newcomb.

Also to the R from Shattuck Clearing is the Pine Point Trail, which branches R from the N–P Trail 0.1 mi from the clearing. It is somewhat overgrown and difficult to follow as it leads 3 mi down the L bank of the Cold River to a point about 1 mi above the mouth of Calkins Brook. The end of this trail is at the upper limit for paddlers on the Cold River.

❋ Trail in winter: Same as for trail 129. The shorter winter approach to Calkins Brook is via Raquette Falls Horse Trail.

🏃 Distances: Parking lot on Coreys Rd. to jct. with Calkins Brook Truck Trail, 1.2 mi; to jct. with Raquette River Horse Trail, 4.9 mi; to Calkins Brook lean-tos, 6.1 mi; to Latham Pond jct., 9 mi; to Shattuck Clearing, 10.6 mi (17.1 km).

131 Shattuck Clearing and Calkins Brook via Raquette River Horse Trail

ADK High Peaks Map: AA8–9 | Trails Illustrated Map 742: Z17

This approach to the Calkins Brook Horse Trail is 0.6 mi longer than the one described above, but for those walking from the little settlement of Coreys or for winter travelers when the road is not plowed beyond Coreys, this route saves 2.8 mi.

▶ Trailhead: The trail begins at a parking area on the R side of Coreys Rd., which leaves NY 3, 12.7 mi W of the traffic light in Saranac Lake and 2.7 mi E of the jct. of NY3 and NY 30 E of Tupper Lake. This road is paved for about 1.5 mi (end of

Raquette River below Tupper Lake. Richard J. Nowicki

winter plowing) through the little settlement of Coreys and then turns to gravel, crosses Stony Creek at 2.5 mi, and comes to the parking lot 2.8 mi from NY 3. ◀

From the trail register (0.0 mi), the trail follows a gravel road, avoiding a road R 100 yd from the register, and continues with easy ups and downs, crossing several brooks. At 1.5 mi, where an obscure lumber road goes R toward the river, the trail goes L and climbs away from the river along a small brook. Crossing the brook at 1.7 mi, the trail levels off and at 2.1 mi comes to a trail leading R to Hemlock Hill Lean-to. Beyond this, the trail dips down to a jct. at 2.2 mi with a trail R to Raquette Falls (trail 132).

The horse trail bears L, follows Palmer Brook, and then bears away from the brook over a hill. Descending to a swamp, the trail crosses Palmer Brook at 2.7 mi, climbs over another hill, and descends to cross a brook at 3.4 mi. This marks the end of the gravel-based road and the beginning of a very muddy section.

Crossing another brook at 3.5 mi, the trail begins a long ascent. At 4.6 mi the trail crosses a small brook and climbs steeply for about 50 yd, after which the grade eases and the trail reaches the top of a pass at 5.1 mi. After a short, level stretch, the trail descends steeply to the jct. with the Calkins Brook Truck Trail (trail 130) at 5.5 mi. From here it is 1.2 mi to the Calkins Brook lean-tos and 5.7 mi to Shattuck Clearing.

❄ Trail in winter: Add 1.3 mi to all distances. Day skiers often push a fair distance along this trail, but don't count on broken track beyond the height of land before Calkins Brook. The mile of trail up and over the height of land requires at least two feet of snow to be skiable, but otherwise trail is very skiable to Shattuck Clearing and beyond.

🏃 Distances: Parking lot to jct. with Raquette Falls Trail, 2.2 mi; to jct. with Calkins Brook Truck Trail, 5.5 mi; to Calkins Brook lean-tos, 6.7 mi; to Shattuck Clearing, 11.2 mi (18.1 km).

132 Raquette Falls

ADK High Peaks Map: AA8–9 | Trails Illustrated Map 742: Z17

This spot on the Raquette River is more often visited by canoeists on the route from Long Lake down the Raquette River, but it is also a worthwhile and relatively easy hike. Besides the series of falls on the Raquette River, there are a DEC Interior Outpost, two lean-tos, and many good campsites at Raquette Falls.

▶ Locator: This trail diverges generally S and then SW after leaving trail 131 at approximately the 2-mi mark. ◀

The trail starts at the same parking lot as the Raquette River Horse Trail (trail 131) (0.0 mi) and follows the horse trail for the first 2.2 mi. Turning R at the jct. next to Palmer Brook, the trail crosses the brook, climbs over a knoll, and drops down to the edge of a slough of the Raquette River at 2.8 mi. After several more ups and downs, the trail begins a longer climb at 3.5 mi. and reaches the top of the hill at 3.8 mi. The trail now descends some steep switchbacks to the edge of an old clearing and then continues on the flat to a signpost at 4.2 mi at the jct. with the Raquette Falls canoe carry. Trail R leads a few yards to the river at the lower end of the carry. Trail L leads just over 1 mi to the upper end of the carry. The best view of the falls is found by going about 100 yd up the canoe carry and looking for a vague trail leading R to the bank of the river and up along the top of a small gorge. Just up and to the L of the signpost are the DEC Interior Outpost and a large field with the lean-tos located on the edge of the field.

❄ Trail in winter: This is one of the classic Adirondack ski tours. Count on broken track to the falls as well as good snow being likely here even if it is not plentiful elsewhere. Add 1.3 mi to all distances.

🏃 Distances: Parking lot to jct. at Palmer Brook, 2.2 mi; to Raquette Falls, 4.2 mi (6.8 km).

SEWARD RANGE

ADK High Peaks Map: A9 | Trails Illustrated Map 742: Y19

Seymour and Seward Mts. and Mts. Donaldson and Emmons form the Seward Range.

Seymour Mt. *(Unmarked path; see introduction, p. 19)*

ADK High Peaks Map: A9 | Trails Illustrated Map 742: Y19

This Seward Range peak was named for Horatio Seymour, several times governor of New York. The popular route ascends the first brook 0.1 mi SE of Ward Brook Lean-to. The most westerly branch leads to an old slide track which has become eroded and difficult. Above the slide, the going is easier to the top of the ridge. Follow the ridge SW to the summit. Ascent from the SW by way of Ouluska Brook is more difficult because of blowdown. The descent into Ouluska Pass, the col between Seymour and Seward Mts., is complicated because of blowdown and cliffs.

Seward Mt. and Mts. Donaldson and Emmons
(Unmarked paths; see introduction, p. 19)

ADK High Peaks Map: A9 | Trails Illustrated Map 742: Y19–20

Seward Mt. was named for William Henry Seward, who succeeded William L. Marcy as governor. He was one of the founders of the Republican Party and secretary of state in Lincoln's cabinet. Mt. Donaldson, the first Adirondack peak to be named during the twentieth century, stands as a monument to Alfred Lee Donaldson, who wrote the first and most complete history of the Adirondacks. The southernmost peak in the Seward Range honors the memory of Ebenezer Emmons, state geologist and leader of the 1837 expedition that made the first ascent of Mt. Marcy, and the man who gave the name "Adirondacks" to this mountain region.

One route to the Seward Range begins at the bridge 0.2 mi SE of the clearing where the red foot trail from Coreys (trail 129) joins the truck trail. This is also the third bridge NW of Ward Brook Lean-to. The route starts on the E side of the brook, but crosses after about 0.5 mi to follow traces of old tote roads on the W side to the end of the second growth, where blowdown and steep climbing begins. Now very rough and eroded, the route continues up to a cliff at the end of the NE ridge of Seward Mt. Bypass this cliff on the L and then follow the ridge SW to the summit. Herd paths descend to the S flanks of the western Seward ridge, reaching Mt. Donaldson more or less on a compass line from Seward's summit. The route to Mt. Emmons from Mt. Donaldson follows the ridge, detouring occasionally to the W to avoid areas of blowdown.

Today, most people reaching Mt. Emmons over Seward Mt. and Mt. Donaldson from the Ward Brook Lean-to area find it easier to return by retracing their steps over the latter two peaks.

An alternate route to the midpoint of the Seward Range and now the preferred route is from the W by way of Calkins Brook. The start of this route is reached from Coreys by way of the Ward Brook and Calkins Brook truck trails (trails 129 and 130, respectively) and is 3.3 mi from the parking lot. The route proceeds along the R bank of Calkins Brook for approximately 0.3 mi before crossing and proceeding on the flat for an additional 0.2 mi. Here the route climbs steeply to join an old lumber road that ascends at a moderate grade high above Calkins Brook. After crossing two streams coming in from the R, the route enters an area of recent blowdown. Angling generally L through this blowdown, the route becomes easier after approximately 0.5 mi, with the herd path on the summit ridge reached at approximately 3 mi from the marked trail. This point is approximately 0.2 mi N of the summit of Mt. Donaldson.

133 Shattuck Clearing from Long Lake via Northville–Placid Trail

ADK High Peaks Map: AA11–10 | Trails Illustrated Map 742: V16

This approach to Shattuck Clearing is a section of the 133 mi Northville–Placid Trail (N–P Trail), which runs from Northville, near the S boundary of the Adirondack Park, to Lake Placid. This trail is described in full in a separate guidebook, *Adirondack Mountain Club Northville–Placid Trail*, published by ADK, and on Trails Illustrated Map 736, published by National Geographic in partnership with ADK. The description below and the description of the section from Shattuck Clearing to Duck Hole (p. 211) are adapted from that guide.

The trail generally follows the E shore of Long Lake for the first 7.5 mi but is sometimes forced to detour away from the lake to avoid private property. There are several attractive lean-tos and many campsites on the lake in this section, but hikers should be aware that some of the land is private, in particular a large inholding from 5.6 mi to 7.5 mi.

▶ Trailhead: The trail begins at a parking lot on Tarbell Rd., which leads N from NY 28N, 1.5 mi E of the jct. of NY 28N and NY 30 in Long Lake Village. There is a large DEC sign on the highway. At 0.7 mi up Tarbell Rd. there is a parking area on the R at the top of a hill, and the trail starts just beyond on the R. ◀

Leaving the road (0.0 mi) the trail descends to a trail register and continues to descend to the outlet to Polliwog Pond at 0.6 mi. Crossing the brook on a wide board bridge, avoid a trail L at 0.9 mi and cross another brook at 1.1 mi. There are two lean-tos on Catlin Bay. The first is visible from the Northville–Placid Trail, and the second is reached by continuing to the shore of Long Lake and circling L and over a small rise to the lean-to sitting in a beautiful location above the lake.

Continuing straight through the jct., the N–P Trail proceeds over easy ups and downs and soon enters the High Peaks Wilderness Area. At 1.9 mi a side trail leads L 0.1 mi to Hidden Cove Lean-to. At 2 mi the trail bears L and then back R, coming near Long Lake and following the shore to a sandy beach and stream at 2.4 mi. Swinging away from the lake, the trail climbs, descends, and ascends again to a height of land 200 ft above the lake at 3.2 mi. Now descending, the trail crosses a brook at 4 mi and comes within view of a large clearing on the L at 4.1 mi, where there are two privies and several side trails. This is Kelly Point, and two lean-tos are visible on the lakeshore from the clearing. These are perhaps the most attractive lean-tos on this section of trail, but they are heavily used by both hikers and paddlers.

Passing behind the clearing, the N–P Trail reaches a jct. at 4.5 mi with the now unmaintained trail leading R to Kempshall Mt. Without the tower, which the DEC removed several years ago, there is virtually no view from the summit and this is no longer a worthwhile side trip. The trail L leads a short distance to the lake. Continuing on, the N–P Trail soon joins a wide tote road, crosses a brook at 5.2 mi, and reaches a jct. at 5.4 mi, with a side trail leading to the first of two lean-tos at Rodney Point. There is a spring on the L about halfway to the lean-to, and a nice sandy beach on the shore makes this a pleasant place to camp.

Just beyond this jct., the N–P Trail leaves state land and crosses several brooks as well as some private water pipes before coming to a muddy bog, which it skirts at 6.7 mi. After crossing a small brook at 7.4 mi, the trail comes to a jct. at 7.6 mi, with a side trail leading 0.1 mi L to the two lean-tos at Plumleys. The first lean-to sits on a grassy knoll with a commanding view of the lake, and the second one is 50 yd farther N along the shore. Both lean-tos are attractive camping spots and are worth the side trip even for a lunch break.

Leading out of Plumleys, there is a maze of side trails, and hikers must be careful to look for the blue markers. The N–P Trail joins a good tote road swinging away from the lake, crossing a small brook at 8 mi, and then climbing to a height of land at 8.5 mi. Gradually descending from this crest at 9.3 mi, the trail enters a fine stand of white pine developed after a forest fire and differing from the surrounding forest. Just past this stand of pines, the trail reaches a brook flowing out of an open marsh (or vlei) at 9.9 mi. Owing to beaver flooding, the trail detours L before rejoining the original trail 10.5 mi comes to Pine Brook, which is easily crossed on stones. The trail is now pleasant walking to some beaver activity at 11.3 mi, where it abruptly turns L off the tote road to circumvent the beaver pond. Once past this obstacle, the N–P Trail joins a gravel road at 11.7 mi and turns R and down.

Just after this point, the Pine Point Trail, also with blue markers, diverges L (see trail 130, last paragraph, p. 205), but the N–P Trail continues R and down to a jct. at Shattuck Clearing at 11.8 mi. The ranger station formerly on this site was removed by the DEC in 1977 to bring this area into compliance with wilderness area guidelines. The gravel road L from the jct. is the Calkins Brook Truck Trail, which leads to a ford of the Cold River and on to Coreys in 10.6 mi (See trail 130.) The gravel road R is the continuation of the N–P Trail to Duck Hole as well as the Cold River Horse Trail (trail 134). The Wolf Pond Truck Trail, which also leads R from Shattuck Clearing (and is followed for short distances by both the N–P Trail and the Cold River Horse Trail), leads to private lands and is not an access route to Shattuck Clearing.

❋ Trail in winter: The entire N–P Trail is skiable and has been skied in one continuous trip on several occasions. This section is very pleasant skiing even with an overnight pack, but a tour this long is not for novices. Depending on surface and wind conditions, it may be easier to ski on Long Lake as far as Plumleys.

🏃 Distances: Parking lot to Catlin Bay lean-tos, 1.1 mi; to Kelly Point lean-tos, 4.1 mi; to first Rodney Point lean-to, 5.4 mi; to trail to Plumleys (two lean-tos), 7.6 mi; to Shattuck Clearing, 11.8 mi (19 km).

133   Duck Hole from Shattuck Clearing via Northville–Placid Trail

ADK High Peaks Map: A10–B9 | Trails Illustrated Map 742: X18

▶ Locator: This section of the Northville–Placid Trail (N-P Trail) generally follows the NE bank of the Cold River to Duck Hole. This is the wildest section of the entire trail, with the trailless Seward and Santanoni ranges flanking the valley of the Cold River See also p. 209 for the southern section of trail 133. ◀

Leaving the jct. at Shattuck Clearing (0.0 mi), the N-P Trail bears slightly R on a gravel road to a somewhat obscure L turn off the road at 0.2 mi. The trail soon crosses a suspension bridge over Moose Creek, with a good view of the Santanoni Range from the bridge. Beyond this bridge, a pleasant trail leads to another suspension bridge over the Cold River at 0.7 mi, from which there is also a good view of the Santanoni Range. At the far side, the trail comes to a jct. with a trail leading L a few yards to Cold River Lean-to 4. Just beyond this jct., the N–P Trail joins a gravel lumber road. (Cold River Lean-to 3 is .02 mi to the L on this road, which continues on to connect with the Calkins Brook Truck Trail and is also an alternative route from Shattuck Clearing.) The N–P Trail turns R on this gravel lumber road, which was constructed in the early 1950s to allow lumbermen to clean up some of the terrific damage left by the 1950 hurricane. This area is now quite open and there are many views of the surrounding peaks for the next several miles.

After one short descent and climb, the trail descends to the Cold River at a large pool, known as Big Eddy, at 2 mi. An interesting falls drops into this pool and the water turns gracefully in its eddy. Beyond Big Eddy, the route climbs away from the river, crosses a brook on a bridge at 3.1 mi, and after a short, steep climb turns sharp R and leaves the gravel road at 3.6 mi. The trail descends steeply and crosses two steep gullies before reaching Seward Lean-to at 4 mi.

Just above the lean-to, a large outcrop of rock forms a natural dam called Millers Falls, where one can swim. Just below the falls, a dark gray dike cuts through the lighter-colored anorthosite granite, and several potholes have been carved in the bedrock. Past the lean-to, the trail again climbs a steep bank to an open area above the river at 4.2 mi and then descends to the river at 4.4 mi. Now following the river closely, the trail crosses a grassy, muddy stretch at 5.3 mi and at 5.7 mi a painted tree indicates a nearby benchmark (PBM 1876) located on a boulder 25 ft E of the trail. Crossing first a smaller brook, the trail crosses Ouluska Brook at 6.1 mi and reaches Ouluska Lean-to just beyond at 6.3 mi.

Beyond the lean-to, the trail follows the Cold River to a sharp bend in the river where the trail climbs away from the river and an old lumber road enters from the L at 6.8 mi. Almost immediately, however, the trail swings sharp R away from the road and climbs gradually to the top of a knoll that was the site of Noah John Rondeau's "Hermitage." It was on this high, open bluff that Rondeau lived off and on (mostly on) from 1915 to 1950. He built two diminutive cabins and developed a unique lifestyle that has been the subject of at least two books and numerous articles. He left the woods briefly in 1947 to appear at the New York Sportsmen's Show, where he became the feature attraction. Leaving the woods for good during the 1950 hurricane, he continued to appear at other sportsmen's shows, dying in Lake Placid in 1967 at the age of 84.

From Rondeau's, the trail turns sharp L and down across a small valley and then descends gradually to the old lumber road. The trail soon begins climbing, passing a yellow boundary post marking one's passage from Essex to Franklin County, and coming to a large brook which is crossed on stones at 7.5 mi. The trail continues to climb, and an old tote road enters from the L at 7.8 mi.

Just past this old road, the trail swings R, levels off, and begins to descend at 8 mi, with a pond visible to the L. With one short interruption, the descent continues to a large brook at 8.7 mi. Crossing this brook, the trail climbs briefly and then continues to descend to another large brook at 9.3 mi, with a small clearing on the far side. Heading across the clearing, the trail soon reaches the R bank of the outlet to Mountain Pond, climbs along the bank, and crosses the brook on a bridge at 9.6 mi. Just beyond, the pond is visible to the L and a series of small ups and downs leads to the jct. with the Ward Brook Truck Trail (trail 129) at 10.3 mi.

Turning R and now with red and blue markers, the trail comes to Cold River Lean-tos 1 and 2 at 10.8 mi. Just past the lean-tos, the trail crosses Moose Creek just above its confluence with the Cold River, climbs the far bank, and then follows along the R bank of the Cold River to a jct. with Cold River Horse Trail at 11 mi (trail 134). This trail fords the Cold River and continues down the E side of the river to Shattuck Clearing with a connection to the Santanoni Preserve and Newcomb.

Past this jct., the trail climbs over a low ridge and arrives at the trail jct. and the former ranger station site at 12 mi. The blue-marked trail crosses below the now-breached dam and leads to Bradley Pond and the road below Upper Works (see trail 128). Trail bearing L with blue and red markers is the continuation of the N-P Trail leading to Lake Placid (trail 99) and with a connection to a trail leading to Henderson Lake and Upper Works (trail 127). There are two lean-tos and several good campsites at Duck Hole. One lean-to is located by the dam; the other is 100 yd E of the dam on a beautiful wooded point.

Ledges on the Cold River. A. T. *Shorey*

❄ Trail in winter: Except for some rough going approximately 0.5 mi either side of Seward Lean-to, this section of trail is easily skiable, even with a backpack—a definite requirement on this remote section.

🐾 Distances: Shattuck Clearing to turnoff for Cold River Lean-tos 3 and 4, 0.7 mi; Seward Lean-to, 4 mi; Ouluska Lean-to, 6.2 mi; Rondeau's Hermitage, 6.7 mi; jct. with Ward Brook Truck Trail, 10.3 mi; Cold River Lean-tos 1 and 2, 10.7 mi; Duck Hole, 11.9 mi (19.2 km).

134 Cold River Horse Trail from Shattuck Clearing to Ward Brook Truck Trail

ADK High Peaks Map: A11–B9 | Trails Illustrated Map 742: X18

▶ Locator: This seldom-used section of the Cold River horse trail system travels through low, rolling terrain SE of the Cold River. ◀

For much of its length, this section of trail follows an old gravel lumber road and is delightfully easy walking through spectacularly remote country where solitude is practically guaranteed. The final mile leading to the Ward Brook Truck Trail, however, is unfortunately quite wet and rather unpleasant to walk, with the additional problem that there is no bridge over the Cold River at the N end of the trail, and crossing could be difficult in high water.

From the jct. at the former ranger station site at Shattuck Clearing (0.0 mi), the horse trail follows the gravel road SE for 0.8 mi, where it turns L onto another gravel road. (Road straight ahead is the Wolf Pond Truck Trail, which is closed to the public where it enters private land just over 1 mi beyond.) From this jct., the trail descends at a gentle grade to Moose Pond Stream at 1.8 mi, with two lean-tos on the far side.

Past the lean-tos, the trail climbs at easy to moderate grades to a jct. at 2.6 mi with a blue-marked horse trail to Moose Pond and Newcomb (trail 138). Turning sharp L, the Cold River Horse Trail descends in gradual rolls to an open area at an old gravel pit at 3.5 mi, passes a pond on the L at 4.7 mi, and continues with short ups and downs. There is a good view of the Seward Range at 5.3 mi and the crossing of a large stream at 6.9 mi before Northern lean-tos at 8.2 mi. Shortly beyond these lean-tos, the gravel-based road swings R while the horse trail continues straight ahead and becomes quite wet, remaining so nearly all the way to the crossing of the Cold River at 10.1 mi and the jct. with the Ward Brook Truck Trail (trail 129) just beyond. To the R it is 0.9 mi to Duck Hole and to the L 0.3 mi to the Cold River lean-tos.

❋ Trail in winter: Although the 1.5 mi section at the N end is more difficult to ski, the rest of this route is quite easy.

🐎 Distances: Shattuck Clearing to turnoff from Wolf Pond Truck Trail, 0.8 mi; to Moose Pond Stream lean-tos, 1.8 mi; to jct. with Moose Pond Horse Trail, 2.6 mi; to Northern Lean-tos, 8.2 mi; to Ward Brook Truck Trail, 10.2 mi (16.5 km).

SANTANONI PRESERVE

ADK High Peaks Map: A12–B12 | Trails Illustrated Map 742: U20

This tract of land was transferred from private ownership to the State of New York in 1972 through the efforts of the Adirondack Nature Conservancy. Most of this land is now part of the High Peaks Wilderness Area and provides a SE approach to the Cold River area. Except for skiers and mountain bikers going to Newcomb Lake, this area has received very little use even though it offers some outstanding opportunities for hiking, fishing, horseback riding, and skiing. The centerpiece of the area is 2-mile-long Newcomb Lake, which has two lean-tos and many campsites along its pristine shores.

Remaining from the days of private ownership are two roads leading to Newcomb Lake and Moose Pond, as well as a huge log structure known as Camp Santanoni on the NE shore of Newcomb Lake. This structure, the farm buildings, and the road are now included in a special "historic" land classification unit. The road to Newcomb Lake is still hard-packed and both legal and suitable for bicycles. Some people have also used various wheeled carriers to transport boats to Newcomb Lake via the road. There is also a commercial outfitter in Newcomb that offers wagon transport to Newcomb Lake. No special camping permits are required, although of course the normal restrictions that apply to camping on any state land still pertain.

▶ Trailhead: The trails described below all start from the gatehouse of the San-tanoni Preserve on a road that leaves NY 28N just W of the Town Hall in the village of Newcomb. A small sign for the Santanoni Preserve marks this road, which crosses a narrow iron bridge, passes the stone gatehouse on the R, and comes to a small parking area on the R at the top of the hill, 0.3 mi from NY 28N. ◀

135 Road to Newcomb Lake and Camp Santanoni

ADK High Peaks Map: B12 | Trails Illustrated Map 742: U20

▶ Trailhead: See above. This wide gravel road leads at easy grades from the gatehouse near Newcomb to Camp Santanoni, an abandoned Great Camp at the E end of Newcomb Lake. Just past the gate, a new trail goes L and reaches the Newcomb VIC in 1.5 mi. ◀

From the trail register (0.0 mi), the road is practically level to a jct. with a trail L to the Adirondack Interpretive Center at 0.3 mi followed by some buildings at the Farm Complex at 0.9 m. Past the farm complex the road swings L and up to an open field at 1.1 mi. Descending slightly, the road comes to a beautiful moss-covered stone bridge and begins a steady, gradual climb to a jct. at 2.2 mi with a road L to Moose Pond and the Cold River Horse Trail (trail 138).

Turning R, the grade soon eases and the road begins a gentle descent across a sidehill with more beautiful stonework and some glimpses of the Santanoni Range through the trees. At 3.6 mi the red-marked trail along the S side of Newcomb Lake (trail 136) branches L, after which the road drops down to a picnic area on the S shore of the lake at 3.9 mi. Swinging R, the road crosses a bridge and then swings back L along the NE side of a narrow channel and on to Camp Santanoni at the E end of Newcomb Lake at 4.5 mi. This immense, rambling log structure and its numerous outbuildings were built by the Pruyn family of Albany, using material cut on the site. Because this structure has been placed on the National Register of Historic Places, the land surrounding the camp has been classified as an "historic district," meaning that this four-walled structure will remain even though this is Forest Preserve. Yet to be determined is what exact use will be made of the structure.

❄ Trail in winter: Since 1972, when the area was opened to the public, this road has probably seen more skiers each year than hikers. Not only is it easy skiing all the way to Newcomb Lake, but the smooth gravel road coupled with Newcomb's propensity to accumulate snow has meant that many times this has been practically the only good cross-country skiing in the entire Northeast.

🚶 Distances: Trail register near gatehouse to jct. with Moose Pond Rd., 2.2 mi; to foot trail along S shore, 3.6 mi; to picnic area on S shore, 3.9 mi; to Camp Santanoni, 4.5 mi (7.3 km).

136 Moose Pond via Foot Trail from Newcomb Lake

ADK High Peaks Map: B12–A11 | Trails Illustrated Map 742: V20

▶ Locator: This trail leads from trail 135, the road to Newcomb Lake, along the S shore of Newcomb Lake, giving access to a lean-to on the shore. The trail then continues NW and joins the Moose Pond Horse Trail just E of Moose Pond. It provides a useful connection from the beautiful camping areas on Newcomb Lake to Moose Pond and the Cold River area. (See also Santanoni Preserve, p. 214).

The trail, with red markers, starts 3.6 mi up the road to Newcomb Lake (trail 135). ◀

From the road (0.0 mi), the trail drops down and soon joins an old road that follows a broad shelf above a swamp. After a steep descent at 0.7 mi the trail crosses one brook and begins a rolling descent to a second brook crossing at 1 mi, with a beaver dam to the L and a large open area to the R. At 1.2 mi a side trail with blue markers branches R and leads 300 yd to a lean-to on a beautiful rocky point on the S shore of Newcomb Lake. This is one of the nicest campsites anywhere.

Continuing on the flat, the trail comes to a small ladder leading down to a bridge over the main inlet to the lake at 1.8 mi. Some care is needed to follow the trail through the thick alders beyond the bridge. Beaver activity has also required frequent reroutes and may require some wading Climbing the far bank, the trail comes to a jct. at 1.9 mi with a yellow trail R leading along the N shore of the lake to a lean-to and the end of the road at Camp Santanoni (trail 137).

Beyond this jct., the trail is flat through a thicket of fir trees next to an extensive open swamp until it swings R and up at 2.6 mi. The trail now follows a series of old roads with several sharp turns which, though marked with a few disks, require close attention. At 2.8 mi the trail crosses a large beaver dam and meadow and joins an old grassy road that slowly swings L around a large swamp.

Taking a sharp R off this road at 3.5 mi, the trail joins another old road, which it follows up and down along a sidehill to the L bank of a large stream at 4.1 mi. The trail now swings sharp R without crossing the stream and follows another vague road. At 4.2 mi the trail joins a slightly better road and goes R and up some steep to moderate grades before descending to cross a small stream. Swinging L after this stream crossing, the trail joins the Moose Pond Horse Trail (trail 138) at approximately 4.7 mi. (To the L at this jct., it is approximately 6.2 mi to the Santanoni Preserve gatehouse.) Turning R at this jct. it is approximately 0.5 mi to Moose Pond.

🚶 Distances: Santanoni Preserve gatehouse to turnoff from road to Newcomb Lake, 3.6 mi; to turnoff to lean-to, 4.8 mi; to jct. with trail on N shore of Newcomb Lake, 5.5 mi; to jct. with Moose Pond Horse Trail, 8.3 mi (13.4 km).

137 Newcomb Lake North Shore Trail

ADK High Peaks Map: B12 | Trails Illustrated Map 742: V20

▶ Locator: This trail leads from Camp Santanoni past several campsites and on to the Ward Pond Brook Lean-to and a jct. with the S shore trail leading to Moose Pond. (See also Santanoni Preserve, p. 214.) ◀

Starting from Camp Santanoni (0.0 mi) at the end of the road to Newcomb Lake (trail 135), the trail goes past some outbuildings to the E shore of the lake. There are no signs or markers at the start, but the route is obvious next to the shore past a campsite, at an old bathhouse at a small beach, and on to some campsites near the mouth of Sucker Brook at 0.3 mi. From these campsites, the trail swings R and up to an old lumber road where it turns L, crosses Sucker Brook, and now with a few yellow markers climbs to a crest at 0.7 mi. Continuing to follow the lumber road, the trail descends, climbs over another hill and descends to Santanoni Brook at 1.5 mi. The road ends past this brook, but the trail continues on the flat to Ward Pond Brook Lean-to on the N shore of the lake at 1.6 mi. This little-used lean-to is in excellent condition and is nearly as nice a site as its companion lean-to on the S shore. Passing behind the lean-to, the trail continues on the flat to the jct. with the S shore trail at 2.3 mi.

🚶 Distances: Camp Santanoni to campsites on Sucker Brook, 0.3 mi; to Ward Pond Brook Lean-to, 1.6 mi; to jct. with S shore trail, 2.3 mi (3.7 km.).

138 Moose Pond Horse Trail

ADK High Peaks Map: B12–A11 | Trails Illustrated Map 742: V20

▶ Locator: This trail branches NW from the road to Newcomb Lake. Following good road for most of its distance, the trail provides access to some nice campsites on Moose Pond and then connects with the Cold River horse trail system. (See also Santanoni Preserve, p. 214.) ◀

From the Santanoni Preserve gatehouse (0.0 mi), follow the road to Newcomb Lake (trail 135) to the jct. at 2.2 mi. Turning L, the road is gently rolling until it begins a steady descent at 3.6 mi. Crossing a brook at the bottom of the descent, the road swings R and climbs gently to a large clearing at 4.7 mi. There are some good views as the road climbs up through this large open area. After some more gently rolling terrain, the road enters another clearing at 6 mi. Turning L, the road comes to the jct. with the foot trail from Newcomb Lake (trail 136) at approximately 6.2 mi just before climbing a steady, moderate grade to a height of land and then descends to a jct. near Moose Pond at 6.7 mi. (Road L leads 0.2 mi to two campsites on Moose Pond.) Bearing R, the road (now marked with blue horse trail disks) passes several large open swamps, crosses Ermine Brook at 8.1 mi, and swings L. The road now goes up and down along a sidehill above the outlet to Moose Pond before dropping steeply down to Calahan Brook at 10.4 mi. This is the end of the gravel road.

The trail now climbs moderately to an old lumber road at 10.7 mi, turns sharp R and continues climbing to a better road at 10.9 mi. Again turning sharp R, the trail follows this sometimes muddy road along a gently rolling profile to the jct. with the Cold River Horse Trail (trail 134) at 11.8 mi. (Trail straight ahead leads to Moose Pond Stream Lean-tos and Shattuck Clearing. Trail R leads to Northern lean-tos and Duck Hole.)

❆ Trail in winter: An old road, this is ideal for skiing with just a bit more terrain to make the actual skiing somewhat more interesting than the Newcomb Lake road. A few years ago one cross-country ski manufacturer had as its slogan, "As far as you want to go"—a slogan that perfectly sums up the possibilities not only for this trail but for the whole truck- and horse-trail system near the Cold River.

🚶 Distances: Santanoni Preserve gatehouse to turnoff from road to Newcomb Lake, 2.2 mi; to Moose Pond, 6.7 mi; to jct. with Cold River Horse Trail, 11.8 mi (19 km.).

139 Goodnow Mt.

Trails Illustrated Map 742: U19

This wonderful, easy hike to a summit with an intact fire tower offers a marvelous view of the High Peaks. The trail to the summit is also now a self-guided nature walk with interpretive pamphlets (available at the trailhead) that are keyed to marked posts along the trail. Although not directly related, this hike is a perfect complement to the displays at the Adirondack Interpretive Center at Newcomb.

This trail is entirely on the private land of the Archer and Anna Huntington Forest, owned by the College of Environmental Science and Forestry (ESF) in Syracuse. It is ESF students and faculty who, in 1993, produced the interpretive pamphlets and coordinated a grant that enabled the Town of Newcomb to hire a work crew. The latter built a new parking area and 0.9 mi of new trail, adding frequent benches along the trail for resting. ESF staff continues to maintain the fire tower. Because this is private land, no camping or fires are permitted, and the area is closed from sunset to sunrise. No hunting is permitted on this private preserve, so this is a good choice for hikers who are concerned about possible danger during the hunting season.

▶ Trailhead: The trail starts on NY 28N, 1.5 mi W of the entrance to the Adirondack Interpretive Center W of the hamlet of Newcomb. This point is also 11.4 mi E of Long Lake. A large white sign marks the turn to a new parking area and kiosk that contains a register and interpretive pamphlets. ◀

The trail is marked by red markers with small black arrows. From the parking area (0.0 mi), the trail climbs moderately for 200 yd before swinging R and continuing with small rises and falls along a shelf parallel to the highway. Reaching a bridge across a small brook at 0.5 mi, the trail swings L and at 0.7 mi begins to climb moderately. After a steady climb, the trail reaches the crest of a ridge and joins the old trail at 0.9 mi. Swinging sharply L, the trail descends slightly before climbing to a flat notch with a well and old horse barn at 1.5 mi. Climbing gradually to the crest of the ridge, the trail dips and then climbs easily to the tower on the summit at 1.9 mi. There are some views to the E and S without climbing the tower, but from the tower one can see 23 of the major peaks, with the Santanoni Range, Algonquin Peak, and Mt. Marcy particularly prominent.

❄ Trail in winter: The new start for this trail is narrower and steeper than the original route. It is no longer feasible as a ski trip, but its short distance and the absence of any really steep terrain make it an ideal introductory snowshoe trip.

🚶 Distance: NY 28N to summit of Goodnow Mt., 1.9 mi (3.1 km). Ascent from road, 1040 ft (317 m.) Elevation, 2690 ft (820 m).

140   Cheney Pond and Lester Flow

Trails Illustrated Map 742: U23

The walk to Lester Flow is along an almost level grassy woods road. It makes a pleasant day hike or a fine introductory backpacker route. The view of the Great Range up Lester Flow from the Lester Flow dam site is unusually good. There is also an attractive new lean-to on the SE shore of Cheney Pond most easily reached by boat. The dam at the S End of Lester Flow once made an extensive waterway connecting Lester Flow and Cheney Pond. With some difficulty, however, paddlers can still pass from Cheney Pond into Lester Flow and paddle to the dam. Except in periods of very low water levels, it is difficult to cross the outlet of Lester Flow below the dam site and thereby continue another 8.9 mi to Irishtown. This trail is not as pleasant hiking, and is mostly used as a ski or snowmobile trail.

▶ Trailhead: Access is from Blue Ridge Rd. (CR 84), 5.3 mi N and then E from the intersection NY 28N or 9.2 mi W of the Elk Lake Rd. A DEC signpost and parking area mark the location on the S side of Blue Ridge Rd. ◀

The trail descends S on a hardscrabble road (high-clearance vehicles recommended) to a jct. at 0.4 mi. (The hardscrabble road continues straight ahead 0.2 mi to Cheney Pond where there is a turnaround and picnic table at the water's edge.) Turning R at the jct. the trail to Lester Flow continues through a small clearing and soon reaches a barrier, prohibiting further vehicular travel. The road becomes a grassy lane and trends principally S. For the most part the way is level. A long gradual downgrade leads to an extensive beaver dam bordering the R edge of the trail at 2.4 mi. Turning L at a jct. at 2.5 mi, the trail reaches a campsite with a path leading 40 ft to the shore of Lester Flow at 2.6 mi, just above the dam site.

Beaver. Walter Schoonmaker

Up Lester Flow in the distant NNW, the Great Range in the High Peaks can be seen. The bare rock faces of Basin and Gothics are prominent. Downstream, the remains of the large crib-dam site are interesting.

❄ Trail in winter: This is an excellent ski trail in a region of dependable snow. Skiers often make a loop trip by skiing up the flow to the Cheney Pond turnaround point. Be sure to test ice thickness carefully before setting out on the flow.

🚶 Distances: To Cheney Pond jct., 0.4 mi; to beaver dam, 2.4 mi; to Lester Flow, 2.6 mi (4.2 km).

141 Roosevelt Truck Trail

Trails Illustrated Map 742: U22

This is an old state truck trail between Blue Ridge Rd. and NY 28N. It offers some pleasant walking through a variety of forest types where solitude will be practically guaranteed. The southern 2 mi have received some recent maintenance because this is one of the trails now designated for handicapped motor vehicle access, but there is little evidence of any actual vehicular use. Given the poor parking and difficulty of spotting the N trailhead, the S trailhead is recommended.

▶ Trailhead: Access to the S trailhead is off NY 28N, 0.3 mi S of the railroad tracks and 1.6 mi N of the Boreas River bridge. A narrow paved road runs SE off the E side of NY 28N. There is a barrier at the trailhead on the L side of this road 0.1 mi from the highway. (The road dead-ends a short distance past the trailhead at an open campsite. No water is at this location.) Access to the N trailhead is off the S side of Blue Ridge Rd. (CR 84) 4 mi N and then E of the intersection with NY 28N and 10.5 mi W of the Elk Lake Rd. Since the trailhead is on the outside bank of a curve, care must be taken to spot it. There is a barrier gate with low stone walls on each side at the trailhead. ◀

From the S trailhead, the road climbs gradually for 0.5 mi after which some gently rolling terrain leads to a downgrade to a barrier at a bridge at 2 mi. This is the end of the section designated for handicapped vehicular access. Past the bridge, the trail, which shows little evidence of either use or maintenance, climbs to the N trailhead at 2.5 mi.

❄ Trail in winter: This is an easy ski trail, but recommended only as an out and back trip from the S end owing to a lack of parking at the N end.

🚶 Distances: To tributary bridge, 2 mi; to N trailhead, 2.5 mi (4 km).

142 Interpretive Center Trail to the Newcomb Lake Rd.

Trails Illustrated Map 742: U20

This trail provides an alternative and 1.2 mi longer approach to Newcomb Lake and Camp Santanoni from the Adirondack Interpretive Center, formerly the Newcomb Visitors Interpretive Center. A branch of SUNY College of Environmental Science and Forestry now operates the Center.

▶ Trailhead: The Center is located on NY 28N, one mile W of the Newcomb Town Hall and the access to the Newcomb Lake road. ◀

From the parking area (0.0 mi), follow the Sucker Brook Trail for 0.4 mi to a jct. with the R.W. Sage Memorial Trail. Bear L and follow this trail to the jct. with the connector trail on the L at 0.9 mi. From the jct., the trail climbs to an old road at 1 mi and turns sharp R, climbs gradually across a sidehill to a crest at 1.3 mi, and then descends to the jct. with the road to Newcomb Lake at 1.5 mi. This jct. is 0.3 mi from the gate at the start of the road to Newcomb Lake.

❄ Trail in winter: A good addition to the AIC trails for both snowshoeing and skiing, although the skiing is a bit more difficult that on the road to Newcomb Lake.

🚶 Distances: To jct. with connector trail, 0.9 mi, to the Newcomb Lake road, 1.5 mi (2.4 km). 🚶

Northern Section *continued*

143 Deer Pond Loop

Trails Illustrated Map 742: AA17

This loop, marked as a ski trail by DEC, can be hiked or skied as described; but using the alternative access points provides shorter access to Deer Pond and its several attractive campsites.

▶ Trailhead: Access is from the N side of NY 3, 0.9 mi E of the Raquette River Boat Launch and 0.6 mi W of Wawbeek Corners, where NY 30 and NY 3 meet. This point is also 4.8 mi E of the NY 3/30 intersection in Tupper Lake. ◀

From the parking area (0.0 mi), follow yellow ski disks past a gate and R onto an old road (Old Wawbeek Rd.) that was the original highway between Tupper Lake and Saranac Lake. The old road is flat with some truly majestic white pines lining the route in places. At 1.2 mi, the old road reaches a jct. (The old road goes R and remains nearly flat for 0.7 mi to Bull Point on NY 30, 1.7 mi N of Wawbeek Corners. This is a shorter access for Deer Pond.)

Now a trail, the Deer Pond Loop goes L at the jct. and continues mostly level through flats on a series of bog bridges to a bridge over a stream at 1.6 mi. At 2.1 mi the trail begins to climb in easy to moderate stages to a crest at 2.8 mi. Glacial erratics are strewn liberally across the landscape with a steep cliff looming over the trail on the R. At 2.9 mi the trail comes to a jct. on a ridge top overlooking Deer Pond in the distance. (The trail R is the Lead Pond Trail, which as of 2012 has been abandoned. It is easily followable to attractive campsites at 0.1 and 0.5 mi. Though somewhat grown in and with a difficult crossing of the Deer Pond outlet, the trail reaches another campsite at the N end of the pond. The trail remains followable to Lead Pond, where it ends at a bog 200 yd from the actual pond.)

Continuing L at this jct., the Deer Pond Loop descends to cross an inlet to Deer Pond at a neck between the pond and an enlarged beaver flow to the L at 3 mi. Deer Pond is noted locally for its excellent smallmouth bass fishing. The trail then bears L and slowly surmounts another ridge clothed with mature specimens of sugar maple and yellow birch. At 3.9 mi, the trail descends to Mosquito Pond. This tiny glacial pond is encircled by a mat of sedges and heath plants that keep growing year by year. In a relatively short time a boreal wetland will occupy the spot where the pond is today.

The trail climbs again and then descends to cross the outlet of a beaver pond at 4.4 mi before crossing yet another ridge on a moderate gradient. The Norway spruce encountered on this low ridge were a part of the many plantations laid out in this area around 1900 by Bernhard Fernow, the father of American forestry. They persist today, slowly succumbing to the ravages of age and completely surrounded by a natural forest comprised solely of native species. Descending from the ridge, the trail reaches the Old Wawbeek Rd. at 4.8 mi. (Just to the R at this point is another access point at the end of the drivable portion of Old Wawbeek Rd E of Tupper Lake. At 1.8 mi, this is the shortest approach to Deer Pond.) The Deer Pond Loop now turns L on Old Wawbeek Rd and follows this nearly level grade back to the beginning point at 7.3 mi.

❄ Trail in winter: With good cover, this is a popular ski tour. Intermediate-level skiers will find a few pitches on the complete loop challenging. Novices can enjoy over 4 mi of nearly flat skiing on the Old Wawbeek Rd. portion of the loop.

🚶 Distances: To Bull Point spur

Raquette River cedars. Richard J. Nowicki

jct., 1.2 mi; to Lead Pond Trail jct., 2.9 mi; to Deer Pond, 3 mi; to Mosquito Pond, 3.9 mi; to Old Wawbeek Rd., 4.8 mi; to trailhead, 7.3 mi (11.7 km).

144   Trombley Landing

Trails Illustrated Map 742: AA17

A short, easy hike on an old road to a lean-to on the Raquette River. The trail is marked with yellow ski trail markers.

▶ Trailhead: On NY 30 at its jct. with NY 3 E of Tupper Lake. There is a small parking area just off the highway. ◀

From the gate (0.0 mi) the trail descends to a brook crossing before climbing gradually to a ridge at 0.5 mi. From here, the trail descends at a lesser grade to the flat and then to the lean-to on the L at 1.5 mi. The Raquette River is just beyond.

❄ Trail in winter: Easy skiing suitable for most any ability.

🚶 Distance: To Trombley Landing, 1.5 mi (2.4 km).

145   Fernow Plantation Trail

Trails Illustrated Map 742: BB17

This short loop trail goes through one of the earliest state plantations in New York. These early forest plantations, although a curious anomaly today, played a part in reforesting the Adirondacks after the disastrous forest fires early in the 20th Century. This plantation was started in 1900 under the direction of Bernhard Fernow, who many consider to be one of the fathers of modern forestry.

▶ Trailhead: Access is on the W side of NY 30 approximately 0.3 mi N of Wawbeek Corners, where NY 3 and NY 30 join. There is a small parking area here. ◀

From the parking area (0.0 mi), the trail, marked by red DEC disks, immediately enters the forest, arriving at a trail register at 0.1 mi. Large, almost mature planted white pine and Norway spruce dominate the canopy here. At 0.3 mi, a large glacial erratic signals a R turn. The trail continues on a mostly level grade, skirting the boundary of private land and continuing through the mature conifers, with little evidence of undergrowth except for a luxurious carpet of oxalis blanketing the forest floor in spring. At 0.8 mi, the trail completes a loop, and the route proceeds back to NY 30 at 1.1 mi.

❄ Trail in winter: Suitable for a short ski or snowshoe outing.

🏃 Distance: NY 30 trailhead to erratic, 0.3 mi; to end of loop, 0.8 mi; to trailhead, 1.1 mi (1.8 km).

146   Panther Mt. Trail

Trails Illustrated Map 742: AA17

This short, steep, red-marked trail climbs steadily to the top of an isolated, moderate-sized mountain between the villages of Tupper Lake and Saranac Lake.

▶ Trailhead: Access is from NY 3, 1.5 mi E of the jct. of NY 3 and NY 30 at Wawbeek Corners, E of Tupper Lake and 0.8 mi W of CR 45. Vehicles should be parked at the small lot across the road from the trailhead. ◀

From the sign marking the start of the trail (0.0 mi), the trail immediately begins to ascend through a mixed mature forest of beech and hemlock. At 0.3 mi hemlock becomes dominant with little undergrowth. This sparseness of low-growing vegetation and the high humidity are both typical of hemlock forests. Shortly afterward, sugar maple begins to appear, and with it a resultant lush understory of striped maple, thanks to increased sunlight. At 0.4 mi, scattered white birch begin to appear. This usually denotes the scene of a past fire. The trail continues to ascend more or less steadily.

At 0.6 mi, the trail reaches the exposed rock summit of Panther Mt. USGS markers are scattered among the blueberry bushes sprawling along the summit. Although beginning to grow in, the view includes Tupper Lake and County Line Island the W with Mt. Morris, the Seward Range and the High Peaks to the S and SE.

❄ Trail in winter: Suitable for snowshoeing.

🏃 Distance: NY 3 to summit, 0.6 mi (1 km). Ascent, 499 ft (152 m). Elevation: 2247 ft (685 m).

147 Loon Lake Mt.

Trails Illustrated Map 746: I120

The newly opened (2011) route to this fire tower peak is a great addition to hiking in this part of the Adirondacks. Summit ledges provide a good view without climbing the tower, officially closed but perhaps eligible for later rehabilitation.

▶ Trailhead: From NY 3 at Merrills Corners between Vermontville and Redford, turn N on CR 26 toward Loon Lake. There is a sharp R turn at 3.1 mi at the cluster of buildings at Loon Lake, followed by the concrete abutments of an old railroad overpass at 6.6 mi. At 7.6 mi there is a large sign for Grass Pond fishing access, followed by a parking area and trailhead sign on the L at 8.1 mi. ◀

The trail, with yellow DEC markers, starts at the L side of the parking area (0.0 mi) and heads for the far L corner of the clearing. There is a trail register just after entering the woods. At 0.1 mi the trail reaches a good gravel road, turns R, and follows the road to an arrow pointing L at 0.2 mi. Leaving the road, the trail is mostly flat before climbing to a little-used gravel lumber road at 0.5 mi where the route turns R. (Note this spot well for the return.) The lumber road proceeds through recent logging, and at 0.9 mi begins a steady gradual climb to a sign indicating a L turn off the road at 1.3 mi. Now on a narrower road, the trail climbs moderately to a R turn near the site of the observer's cabin at 1.7 mi. Beyond here, the route becomes a trail. Steepening at 2.2 mi, the trail swings L at 2.6 mi and heads straight up the slope. The grade eases shortly before reaching the tower at 2.9 mi.

❄ Trail in winter: Easy skiing for the first 1.7 mi, but definitely suitable only for snowshoes beyond that point.

🚶 Distances: To L turn, 1.3 mi; to summit, 2.9 mi (4.7 km). Ascent, 1640 ft (500 m). Elevation, 3320 ft (1012 m).

147A Debar Mt. Game Area and Beaver Valley Trail

Trails Illustrated Map 746: I119–20

This remote area offers some pleasant walking through a variety of forest habitats. There is currently no active game management, but the roads are a legacy of a 1930s effort to propagate many species of plants, trees, and wildlife, including elk. Along the way one will notice several pine plantations and remnants of wire fencing built to contain the nascent elk herd. One can either hike through to Meacham Lake in 8.7 mi or make a 5 mi loop trip using the Beaver Valley Trail.

▶ Trailhead: At the end of a side road off CR 26 at a bridge over Hatch Brook, 2.9 mi N of the trailhead for Loon Lake Mt. (see above) or 9 mi SE of NY 30 in

Duane. The gravel side road leads 1.5 mi to a clearing just past the state land boundary. Vehicles should be parked here before the edge of a large field as the road soon becomes less passable. ◄

From the clearing (0.0 mi), the road soon reaches the edge of a large cleared area and turns S. At 0.2 mi at the S end of the open area there is a jct. with three roads. Road L is the return via Beaver Valley as described. The middle road leads down to a gate at a beaver dam at 0.7 mi where the R hand road rejoins the route. From the gate, the road is gently rolling to a jct. at 2.5 mi. (Road L is the Beaver Valley Trail that crosses a wetland and then passes Skiff Pond before turning N and climbing and then descending gradually along the side of a ridge and back to the open area and the parking area at 5 mi.) Continuing straight ahead the road reaches a jct. at 4 mi with the somewhat vague Hays Brook Wetland Trail which leads L for 0.9 mi to an old cabin. Going R, the route to Meacham Lake climbs gently and then descends past Winnebago Pond to a jct. with the Debar Mt. Trail at 6.3 mi. From here it is another 1.1 mi to the Debar Mt. trailhead.

❄ Trail in winter: Easy terrain for cross-country skiing, although the trail must be shared with snowmobiles. In winter add 1.5 mi to the distances from the E end and 1.2 mi at the W end for a through traverse of 10.2 mi.)

🚶 Distances: Parking area to jct. with Beaver Valley Trail, 2.5 mi; to jct. with Debar Mt. Trail, 6.3 mi; to Debar Mt. summer trailhead, 7.4 mi. (11.8 km)

148   Silver Lake Bog

ADK High Peaks Map: E1a | Trails Illustrated Map 746: GG24

This Nature Conservancy Preserve offers a nearly half-mile of boardwalk through a spruce bog followed by a hike to a view of Whiteface Mt. from a bluff high over Silver Lake.

▶ Trailhead: Access is from Old Hawkeye Rd. which branches S off Union Falls Rd. 1.1 mi W of the jct. of Silver Lake Rd. (CR 13) and Union Falls Rd. or 1.8 mi E of the bridge over the Saranac River at Union Falls. ◄

From the register and kiosk (0.0 mi) the trail follows a boardwalk as it twists through the spruce bog past numerous benches ideal for resting or bird-watching. Leaving the bog at 0.4 mi, the trail climbs briefly, bears L and down, and then climbs at a mostly moderate grade to the bluff overlook at 1 mi.

❄ Trail in winter: An excellent snowshoe hike with many animal tracks to observe in the bog. Generally easy skiing except for the final few yards to the overlook.

149   Lyon Mt.

Trails Illustrated Map 746: LL25

This massive peak stands alone well north of any other high mountains. On a clear day, both the city of Montreal and the High Peaks are equally visible. Topped by a still serviceable fire tower, Lyon Mt. is reached by a new trail constructed by the Adirondack Mt. Club in 2009 and 2011. The original route, which followed the steep phone line, is badly eroded and will not be maintained.

▶ Trailhead: Access is via a dirt road off of Chazy Lake Rd. Marked by a DEC sign for Chazy Highlands, the turn is 1.7 mi S of NY 374 between Lyon Mt. and Dannemora. Alternatively, if coming from the S from the town of Saranac, the turn is 1.2 mi N of the Dannemora town line. It is 1 mi. up the dirt road to the parking area. ◀

From the parking area (0.0 mi), the trail is rocky for 0.2 mi to a sharp L turn to a bridge and the beginning of the new trail. After a steady climb across a sidehill, the trail reaches a crest at 0.5 mi, after which the grade eases to a small bridge at 1.1 mi. Climbing resumes after the bridge with another small bridge at 1.5 mi. The trail now switchbacks upwards at a steady gradual to moderate grade to a crossing of the old trail at 3.5 mi. After crossing the old trail, a few more switch backs lead to a junction with the old trail at 3.9 mi. From here the grade soon eases with the fire tower reached at 4.3 mi.

❈ Trail in winter: Excellent for snowshoeing, but too narrow for skiing.

🏃 Distance: Parking lot to crossing of old trail 3.5 mi; to summit, 4.3 mi. (6.9 km). Ascent, 1930 ft (588 m). Elevation, 3830 ft (1167 m).

149A   New Land Trust
Trails Illustrated Map 746: KK25

Located on Plumadore Rd. NW of Saranac and S of Lyon Mt., this popular and accessible 287-acre preserve offers 28 different trails suitable for walking, snow-shoeing, and skiing, but not mountain biking.

149B   Lewis Preserve Wildlife Management Area
Trails Illustrated Map 746: OO–NN27

A generally level red-marked trail runs 1.5 mi north-south through this 1300 acre area of abandoned orchards and farmland.

149C   Mud Pond
Trails Illustrated Map 746: II24

A mostly gentle 1.4 mi trail leads from Rt. 3 W of Clayburg to an attractive half-mile-long pond. 🦆

On Valcour Island. Carl Heilman II

Champlain Valley Section

Though very different in character from the rest of the trails in the High Peaks, the area lying generally between the Adirondack Northway and Lake Champlain offers many interesting destinations for shorter walks and hikes. Most significantly, in recent years the Champlain Area Trail System (CATS), a non-profit organization, has created many new trails that open up previously unknown vistas and natural areas. This section also includes several new nature preserves and wildlife management areas with attendant trail networks. The larger areas are described in some detail below, while others are just listed with a brief description and their Trails Illustrated map coordinates.

SHORT HIKES

Wildway Overlook Trail to South Bouquet Mt.: 2.2 mi. round trip. Mostly easy grades lead to a spectacular view of the Champlain Valley from the several outlooks near the summit of the mountain. See trail 174.

Cheney Mt.: 1.8 mi round trip. Located near the village of Port Henry, this newest addition to area trails leads to a summit with some unique views of Lake Champlain, its new bridge, historic mining operations, and some of the High Peaks. There are a few short steep pitches, but the grades are generally moderate. See trail 182.

MODERATE HIKES

Barn Rock Trail: 5 mi round trip. This up, down, back up, and down round trip leads to a unique viewpoint directly above the shore of Lake Champlain. See trail 159.

Perimeter of Valcour Island: 4.7 mi. loop hike plus 2 mi paddling to and from the island. This very different combination of paddling and hiking takes one around historic Valcour Island with several views from the higher points. See trail 150.

HARDER HIKE

Split Rock Mountain loop: 5.8 mi loop. This trail follows the highest crest of the Split Rock ridge with views of both Lake Champlain and the High Peaks. The additional vertical ascent can make this loop seem more challenging than the Valcour Island loop described above. See trails 156 and 157.

VALCOUR ISLAND

Trails Illustrated 742: JJ31–32

Valcour (which means "almost one rock" in French) Island is a jewel in Lake Champlain. The island itself is varied and fascinating, with coves that offer good anchorage for boaters and pleasant, easy trails that often give the hiker spectacular views of the Adirondacks and Vermont's Green Mountains. Rocky shelves provide excellent seats to watch crashing waves on the E side, as well as a lovely, quiet sandy beach on the W side. The island, which gave its name to an important battle in the Revolutionary War (see below), is about 980 acres.

All trails are marked with special Valcour Island yellow disks. The Perimeter Trail (trail 1) circles the island in 5.7 mi; two interior trails combine for a total of 7.8 mi of trails on the island. A loop using both interior trails is 3.5 mi. Campsites are well kept and in idyllic settings. The thorn among these roses is the profusion of poison ivy on the island.

▶ Trailhead: From the rotary on US 9 just S of downtown Plattsburgh, drive S 4.5 mi to the Peru Boat Launch. Coming from the S, from the jct. of US 9 and NY 22 in Keeseville, drive N on US 9 8.8 mi to the Peru Boat Launch. From Exit 35 (Peru–Valcour) on the Northway (I-87), take NY 422 (Bear Swamp Rd.) E 3 mi to US 9, and turn L (N) 3.3 mi to the Peru Boat Launch. ◀

There is a parking lot and public bathroom at the Peru Boat Launch site. A warning: Lake Champlain's deep waters are notorious for being cold. Huge waves can sweep across the lake on rough days. Do not use a canoe in cold weather or if the water is rough. Hypothermia can set in quickly. Late summer is the best time for a canoe crossing. In some winters one can ski across, but these are rare and one should check locally about the ice conditions.

It is almost exactly 1 mi E from the boat launch to Bullhead Bay, a pleasant, grassy place just S of the old lighthouse where hikers can pull up their boats and find the Perimeter Trail almost immediately. Or they can go NE around the point to Butterfly Bay and pull up on the sandy beach.

A DEC official patrols the island from a boat and gives out maps of the island that show the hiking trails, names of bays, campsites, and rules. Those planning to camp on the island must register with the DEC upon landing or when met at one's campsite.

Kayaking on Lake Champlain near Valcour Island. David Hough

150 Perimeter Trail

Trails Illustrated Map 742: JJ31–32

The following describes a hike around the island on the yellow-marked Perimeter Trail starting S from Bullhead Bay, although the trail can just as easily be hiked in the other direction. Two interior trails create numerous options.

From Bullhead Bay (0.0 mi) walk inland from the beach about 50 ft through the woods to the Perimeter Trail. Turn R, heading S. The trail crosses an open meadow, then a small foot bridge, enters cedar woods and reaches a jct. at 0.3 mi with signs indicating Indian Point R and the Nomad Trail which leads L 0.8 mi to Smugglers Harbor.

A short trail to the R leads to a large, open clearing with two fireplaces, a privy, and several good campsites above lovely Indian Point. Continuing S, the Perimeter Trail enters cool, deep woods of white cedar, white and red pine, maple, oak, ash, spruce, wild grapes, and giant poison ivy. At 0.5 mi a large dead spruce tree bears a sign, "American Revolution, Battle of Valcour, October 11, 1776." On that date a small American fleet led by Gen. Benedict Arnold hid behind the W side of the island and surprised a larger British fleet heading S down the lake, led by Captain Thomas Pringle. The British fleet chased the Americans for two days S to Ticonderoga and destroyed Arnold's brash brigade of boats. Despite this loss, Arnold won a tactical victory by delaying the British, forcing them to return to Canada for the winter. This extra time gave the American troops at Saratoga a chance to build up men and supplies, which resulted in their victory there on October 17, 1777. History buffs revel in the imagined sight of Arnold's tiny, gutsy fleet rounding the S tip of Valcour to ruin what Pringle thought would be an unchallenged trip up Lake Champlain.

From this sign, it is about 50 ft R to a grassy overlook on a cliff with an excellent view of Whiteface Mt. and of interesting fissures in the shoreline limestone rock. Continuing, the trail crosses a footbridge at a little over 0.6 mi and at 0.7 mi reaches campsite 1 (with privy) on Cedar Point. This is a smooth rocky promontory.

The trail onward is over a broad, solid rock incline going into cedar, hemlock, and birch woods. A long elbow-shaped cement dock comes into view on the R through trees. At 0.8 mi, the beautiful old stone "Seton House" with its slate roof offers a path from its front R corner to a pumphouse, dock, and point. One may walk on the dock, or picnic, but mooring a boat here is prohibited.

At 1 mi on the Perimeter Trail, a turn R on a faint track leads to high cliffs with spectacular views S and E of Lake Champlain, the Green Mts., and the Adirondacks. There is loose gravel here, so stay away from the edge and find a firm footing. Now on the E side of the island, at about 1.5 mi, there is a sign to Pebble Beach on the R, a steep trail descending to a cozy beach surrounded by fantastic metamorphic cliffs on either side. Beach stones are rounded and smooth from wave action. This is the closest view of nearby Garden Island. At 1.7 mi there is a turn R off the trail to a SE promontory, and at 1.8 mi there is a 20-ft cliff facing E to Vermont.

The trail now curves W along the shore around a wide cove with shelving rock. There is a good view here of Grand Isle in Vermont. At 1.9 mi the trail reaches small but spectacular Cystid Point, with campsite 18 (cement fireplace, table, and privy). At 2 mi there is a wooden walkway, then a rocky shelf beach, excellent for swimming.

At 2.4 mi, a small foot trail leads R to a rocky overlook above a small cove that offers a good mooring. Just N, at 2.6 mi, there is another campsite; across a wooden walkway is a fenced area around a large beach rock in memory of the captain of the ship Nomad, Gerald Walker Birks, "who sailed these waters many years and found safe harbour in this cove" and of "four members of the crew who fought with Canadian and Imperial Forces 1914–1918."

At 2.7 mi, at a trail jct., a turn R leads to Smugglers Harbor in a few hundred yards, or L to return to Indian Point on the W side of the island via the Nomad Trail in 0.8 mi. Campsites 15, 16, and 17 are along Smugglers Harbor. Hikers may continue along the Perimeter Trail to the next jct. for Tiger Point (0.1 mi), or take a more interesting route 0.2 mi from campsite 15 N along the shore to Tiger Point and back inland to the Perimeter Trail. The strange shape of Tiger Point makes interesting exploring.

From the Tiger Point jct., the Perimeter Trail swings around Sloop Bay, where there is a privy. At 3.2 mi, at another trail jct., it is 0.1 mi straight ahead on a spur to Paradise Bay. Down this spur are an old fireplace and chimney and campsite 13. A larger, more beautiful stone fireplace and chimney on the point suggest that this must have been a site for a house. Campsite 14 overlooks the lake to Spoon Island.

Soon after the Paradise Bay turn-off, the Perimeter Trail descends through cool cedar woods to a jct. at 3.4 mi. A spur R leads to Spoon Bay in a few hundred ft. The Perimeter Trail reaches another jct. in about 250 ft; here the Royal Savage Trail turns L to cross the interior of the island to Butterfly Bay in 1.3 mi.

The Perimeter Trail veers R to continue N, going uphill through hemlocks, then leveling out at 3.7 mi overlooking Spoon Bay. At 3.8 mi there is another overlook, this time over Beauty Bay. The trail turns L and then R downhill over a wooden bridge through giant evergreens to another wooden bridge, then reaches campsites 10 and 11.

Now the trail goes through giant white pines, and at 4.1 mi reaches a sandy beach on the N edge of the island. Crab Island is straight N. On a mainland bluff to the W is Clinton Community College; the large white building was at one time President William McKinley's Summer White House. Just before 4.4 mi there are five more campsites: 5, 6, 7, 8, and 9. This is Island's End.

The trail now heads S. At 4.8 mi there are several giant white oaks, then a large overgrown pasture, then at 4.9 mi a privy. Now the trail turns L under a huge canopy hedge to a "Pioneer Farm Site" sign in a pasture at 5 mi. This is now a huge open pasture with raspberries and goldfinches in summer. From the edge of the pasture one can see the Peru Boat Launch with Whiteface Mt. directly behind.

At 5.2 mi, the trail crosses a wooden bridge surrounded by poison ivy. At 5.3 mi, there is another well-built bridge, then at 5.4 mi a sign, "Island's End," pointing N.

Now the trail enters a lovely mown clearing with shade trees and ten fireplaces and picnic tables on the N edge of the beach on Butterfly Bay. Turn L (E) to find the trail again. The Royal Savage Trail to Spoon Bay (1.3 mi) starts behind the privy on the back of the clearing. The Perimeter Trail returns to its starting point at Bullhead Bay at 5.7 mi, where a trail R (W) leads to a point with an historic 1874 stone lighthouse. (There is also a trail S from Butterfly Beach and W to the lighthouse. At 0.2 mi along this trail, one fork goes L to Bullhead Bay in 0.1 mi and the other goes R to the lighthouse in 0.2 mi).

🚶 Distances: Peru Boat Launch to Bullhead Bay via boat, 1 mi; Bullhead Bay to stone house, 0.8 mi; to Pebble Beach trail, 1.5 mi; to Nomad Trail jct., 2.7 mi; to Royal Savage Trail jct., 3.4 mi; to Island's End, 4.4 mi; to pioneer farm site, 5 mi; to Bullhead Bay, 5.7 mi (9.1 km).

151 Marsh Trail

Trails Illustrated Map 742: HH–II31
see also www.dec.ny.gov/outdoor

An old road within the Ausable Marsh Wildlife Management Area, leads 1.1 mi to the bank of the Ausable River near its mouth with excellent bird watching along the way. Access at DEC sign on US 9 just S of jct. with NY 442.

152 WICKHAM MARSH WILDLIFE MANAGEMENT AREA

Trails Illustrated Map 742: HH31–32
see also www.dec.ny.gov/outdoor

This is one of five State-owned Wildlife Management Areas (WMAs), mostly in the Champlain Valley, within the region covered by this guide. Wickham Marsh WMA comprises about 850 acres near the hamlet of Port Kent on Lake Champlain. It offers a combination of dry uplands, populated by pines and hardwoods, and lower cattail marshes that drain into the lake. Three trails wind through the upper and lower elevations of the preserve, which is managed to improve wildlife habitat, principally waterfowl. This is a wonderful destination for hiking, bird watching, cross-country skiing, nature study, canoeing, fishing, and other quiet outdoor pursuits. Hunting and trapping are allowed on these lands, so be aware of the calendars and locations for these activities.

There are no trail signs and the marking is inconsistent, including red disks, yellow paint blazes, surveyors' ribbons, or nothing. The gated trail along the southern boundary of the preserve has parking access at both ends.

▶ Trailhead: From the center of Keeseville, drive N on US 9 for 2.9 mi. Turn right on NY 373 and drive E 1.3 mi. The Wildlife Management Area sign and parking are on the L just after the intersection with CR 17 (Soper Rd.), which comes in from the R. For the second parking access, drive E into Port Kent, turn L on Lake St., and drive 1.3 mi N to the sign and parking area on the L. ◀

Yellow Gate Trail

This trail is hereby named for the gates at both ends. From the upland parking area (0.0 mi), pass the yellow gate, and walk on the flat, past a log crib, an old shack, and two unmarked intersections to the Red Trail, on the L. (This short connecting trail runs 0.7 mi. along the top of a bluff and has a nice lookout point with a bench near its eastern end.) After the unmarked intersections, the Yellow Gate Trail bears L, down and off the plateau, to the jct. with the North Trail at 0.8 mi. The trail continues R, now following yellow paint blazes, and drops steeply down a bank to the level of the marsh. It proceeds through a wet swampy stretch, occasionally passing "Public Hunting Ground" signs. At the base of a steep hill, the trail heads on a sidehill L between logged-over lands above and the wetland below. It then continues on the flat to a wide clearing at the edge of the cattail marsh. This is a great picnic spot. The trail becomes a gravel woods road leading to the eastern parking area at 1.9 mi.

❄ Trail in winter: Suitable for snowshoeing. Each end is fine and level for skiing.

🐾 Distances: From western parking area to lower level jct. with North Trail, 0.8 mi; to eastern parking area, 1.9 mi (3.1 km).

North Trail

This trail leaves N from the western parking area and heads both on the level and up and down to connect with the Yellow Gate Trail at the latter's midpoint. For half its length it is a pretty woods road along the edge of a bluff with a few glimpses down to the marsh. Despite only sporadic marking, the trail is easy to follow.

From the parking area (0.0 mi), follow yellow and red paint blazes on the property boundary to a jct. with the Red Trail leading R at 0.3 mi. (This short connecting trail runs 0.7 mi. along the top of a bluff and has a nice lookout point with a bench near its eastern end.) Just past the jct. the North Trail descends several steep switchbacks, crosses a stream, and switchbacks up again to the original elevation. It continues along the property line and reaches a posted intersection at 0.8 mi. (The trails to the L are part of the old cross-country network of the Ausable Chasm campground.) Turn R (E) here as the trail becomes a wider woods road. It follows the edge of the bluff until it descends gradually to the lower level and passes two faint trails on the L and three yellow trail markers and a wetland on the R, meeting the Yellow Gate Trail at 2.2 mi.

❈ Trail in winter: Good skiing except for steep switchbacks early in the trail. Excellent snowshoeing.

🏃 Distances: To Red Trail jct., 0.3 mi; to posted intersection, 0.8 mi; to jct. with Yellow Gate Trail, 1.8 mi (2.8 km).

153 Noblewood Park and Nature Preserve

Trails Illustrated Map 742: DD32

Located at the mouth of the Bouquet River, this area offers swimming, camping, and a series of loops that can make for a walk of just over a mile to the end of a long sand bar into Lake Champlain.

SPLIT ROCK MT. AREA

Trails Illustrated Map 742: AA32–33

The Split Rock Mt. area N of Westport on Lake Champlain is a beautiful but little-used region purchased over many years by the state. The most recent acquisition was made in 1993 as the inaugural purchase under New York State's Environmental Protection Fund.

The trails in the area follow a system of old roads built for logging and quarrying. There are signs at most of the trail junctions, but not all, so close attention to this guidebook and its map is advised.

For those interested in viewing wildlife, just NW across the Lake Shore Rd., and slightly N, is Webb Royce Swamp. There are no trails here, but the area is not far from the road and is inhabited by a variety of wildlife. Check the trailhead map for directions.

While most of this area was at one time developed and logged, there are few remnants of that period in the S half of this tract, which was worked for both granite and iron ore over a century ago . The N half has seen more recent timber activities and it is this complexity of logging roads that forms the backbone of the trail system. The forest is characterized by the lower-elevation flora of an open hardwood forest, with oaks and juniper trees on the rocky bluffs and hemlocks growing densely along the cool, moist streambeds. This area is within the historic range of the timber rattlesnake, so it is wise to use caution when traveling over open rocky areas and the densely grassy areas on some of the roads as there are snakes still calling this area home. Never tease or corner a rattler. If you give them a wide berth and leave them alone, they will leave you alone. Eastern timber rattlesnakes are protected under New York State law. It is illegal to kill, take, or possess this species without a special DEC permit.

▶ Trailheads: All of the trails start from Lake Shore Rd., which runs between Westport and Essex. From Exit 31 on the Northway (I-87), head E on NY 9N to the intersection of NY 22 in Westport in 4.2 mi.

Turn L (N) onto NY 22 (0.0 mi) and in 0.4 mi turn R (NE) onto Lake Shore Rd. At 0.9 mi bear R at the Y with Sherman Rd. Continue N past Halds Rd. and Ainger Hill Rd. Trail 155 leaves the road 4 mi N of the jct. of NY 9N/22. All other trails as described start from a parking lot on the R with a Forest Preserve sign at 4.7 mi from the NY 9N/22 intersection.

There are two other access points located 1 mi and 2 mi N of the main trailhead parking area. Coming S from Essex on Lake Shore Rd., the main parking area is 0.4 mi S of the intersection with Clark Rd. or 5.5 mi. S of the jct. of Lake Shore Rd. and NY 22. ◀

155 Calamity Trail

Trails Illustrated Map 742: AA32

An old road, this trail is generally easy to follow, except in two spots where it skirts wetlands. It used to serve as access to the 19th-century granite works at its E end, near Barn Rock Bay; both of these are interesting, unique destinations. This is also sometimes referred to as the Old Granite Works Trail. The name comes from a fatal accident that occurred when the first load of granite was being lowered down a railway to the lake. The operation ceased at that point, which accounts for the numerous cut blocks of granite still evident along this trail.

▶ Trailhead: This trail starts E from the Lake Shore Rd., 4 mi N from the jct. of NY 9N and NY 22 in Westport, in an overgrown field across from a gray farmhouse. Park carefully on the shoulder. One can also approach from the main parking area using the Gary's Elbow and Crossover Trails. ◀

Start by going through an old gate (0.0 mi) on a brushy tractor trail along the S edge of the field. At 0.2 mi the trail heads gradually uphill in pines to a height of land at 0.7 mi. Passing a gate on the R, the trail descends to a yellow-marked jct. with the Crossover Trail going L. [This trail runs N along a sidehill for 1 mi to connect with Gary's Elbow (see below) and the trail leading from the main parking area.] Continuing straight and now with red markers, the Old Granite Works Trail contours R around a wetland, passing a log barricade blocking off the old route. There are views into the swamp on the L, and then the trail bears R at a beaver dam between two arms of the wetland at 1.1 mi. Continuing, the trail skirts a second wetland, sneaking around its S side between grasses and a wooded bank.

The trail quickly jogs N over a small hummock and then E again, before passing some broken granite on the L. It reenters the woods, crosses a swampy outlet, and resumes its road-like character with the outlet stream on the R. There are numerous granite retaining walls on the L, the first signs of the old quarry whose block piles now become obvious everywhere. Keep a careful eye out for snakes if you are tempted to explore these heaps of granite.

The trail steepens down to a T intersection at 2.5 mi. The fork R (S) heads to private property in 0.3 mi. The fork L passes more granite piles and heads N to a jct. with the Barn Rock Trail (trail 159), over a small granite bridge at 2.8 mi. The way R leads to Barn Rock Bay in 0.2 mi. The trail L leads back to the main network of trails and the main trailhead parking lot.

❄ Trail in winter: The trail is mostly wide and smooth for good skiing on less than a foot of snow; there are a couple of fast hills at the E end, but with plenty of room to maneuver. Snowshoeing is fine.

🚶 Distances: Lake Shore Rd. to height of land, 0.7 mi; to first wetland crossing, 1.1 mi; to Barn Rock Trail, 2.8 mi (4.5 km).

156 Split Rock Mountain North Rim Trail

Trails Illustrated Map 742: AA33

This trail traverses the rock ledges over the top of Split Rock Mt. and is one of the more spectacular in the region. It at first climbs gradually and smoothly as a roadway, but soon becomes an undulating exploration of the balds (bare rock areas), wet dips, ridges, open woods, and the several summits of Split Rock Mt. as it winds N to a final lookout at 2.8 mi. It follows old logging road along its entire length and is marked by yellow disks. Combined with the Robins Run Trail (trail 157), it makes a loop trip of just under 6 mi.

▶ Trailhead: The main parking area on Lake Shore Rd., 4.7 mi N of the jct. of NY 9N/22. ◀

From the parking area (0.0 mi) the Split Rock and Louis Clearing Trails are the same to a jct. at 0.3 mi. Bearing L and now with yellow markers, the Split Rock trail climbs to an overgrown jct. on the R at 0.7 mi. One can either follow the yellow markers R on a loop up and over a small bump with a lookout or follow the blue markers 0.1 mi to a jct. with the Robins Run Trail L and the other end of the loop ahead on the R. Continuing E and still with yellow markers, the Split Rock trail winds gradually uphill with occasional wet spots and bowed-over birches as it turns to the N.

At 1.8 mi, a rocky promontory is visible to the R above the trail, as it climbs quite steeply to a jct. R at a small hand-lettered sign, "View", at 2.1 mi. It is a short walk R up and over two bumps to a spectacular lookout over Lake Champlain.

The main trail continues uphill and N to a second lookout on the L over farms, the Jay Range, and Poke-O-Moonshine at 2.2 mi. The trail then continues on a mostly rolling course on the W side of the ridge. At 2.9 mi, the trail meets the N end of Robin's Run Trail coming in from the L. Continuing straight, the trail meanders to a ledge at the end of the trail with views to the N over Whallons Bay and down Lake Champlain that are well worth the side trip.

✲ Trail in winter: The trail is wide enough for skiing and is mostly gentle, though the steep, twisty, and narrow "screamer" hill just S of the two lookouts at 1.8 mi necessitates deep snow and strong skiing skills or a descent on foot.

🏃 Distances: Parking area to Robin's Run Trail, 0.7 mi; to side trail to view, 2.1 mi; to N jct. with Robin's Run Trail, 2.9 mi; to final lookout at yellow markers, 3.1 mi (5 km).

157 Robins Run Trail

Trails Illustrated Map 742: AA33

The trail is a more westerly lowland approach to the N end of the Split Rock Range, climbing significantly only in its last 0.5 mi to the ridge, where it rejoins the Split Rock Mt. North Rim Trail. The two trails can best be combined as a loop, going in either direction.

▶ Locator: This trail starts from the Split Rock Mt. North Rim Trail, forking L from it 0.7 mi from the trailhead. ◀

From the Split Rock Mt. North Rim Trail, the Robin's Run Trail starts L with blue trail markers at a fork (0.0 mi). It is flat along a wet grassy stretch for 0.1 mi and then bears L, heading down on a long sidehill to an old logging clearing on the flat at 0.5 mi. The trail now bears R (N) at the clearing on a grassy path and continues on a rolling but generally rising course to a T intersection in a small hemlock grove at 1.5 mi. Going R, the trail ascends steadily to a jct. with the Split Rock Mt. Trail at 2 mi. The L fork goes 0.2 mi to a lookout, and the R fork heads over the mountain and back to the trailhead parking lot in 2.9 mi.

✲ Trail in winter: This old road is suitable for skiing or snowshoeing, though the hill at the N end can be arduous.

🏃 Distances: Split Rock Mt. North Rim Trail to hemlock grove fork, 1.5 mi; to jct. with Split Rock Mt. North Rim Trail, 2 mi (3.2 km) (2.7 mi/4.3 km from trailhead)

158 Louis Clearing Bay Trail

Trails Illustrated Map 742: AA33

The main access trail, marked by orange snowmobile trail disks, crosses the area and descends to the shore of Lake Champlain with a number of outlooks along the way.

▶ Trailhead: The main parking area on Lake Shore Rd., 4.7 mi N of the jct. of NY 9N/22. ◀

From the parking lot (0.0 mi), the trail heads gradually uphill on an old rutted road. At 0.1 mi a blue-marked spur called "Gary's Elbow" cuts off to the R (S).

(This slightly longer route rejoins the main trail at 0.8 mi. It is also the connection to the Crossover Trail that leads to the Calamity Trail.) The main trail continues on straight ahead and uphill. At 0.3 mi the yellow-marked Split Rock Mt. North Rim Trail (trail 156) branches L. Continuing straight ahead, the trail is mostly level to the second jct. with Gary's Elbow coming in from the R at 0.8 mi. The main trail gradually begins descending and at 1 mi the start of the Barn Rock Trail (trail 159) is on the R (S).

Continuing straight ahead, the trail descends to a jct. at 1.2 mi with a side trail leading R 0.2 mi to Snake Den Bay Lookout. The latter offers a view of the Palisades on Lake Champlain with the shimmering waters of Snake Den Bay about 300 ft below. Bearing L at the jct. the Louis Clearing Bay Trail heads N and then E down a moderately steep grade. The trail is rocky and a bit wet in a couple of places along its descent to the rocky bay, which is reached at 1.7 mi. There are great views to the N, S, and E across the lake to Vermont. Total ascent from Lake Champlain back to the parking lot is about 465 ft (140 m).

❄ Trail in winter: This old road is suitable for skiing or snowshoeing, with gradual grades, until it narrows to a footpath near its end.

🏃 Distances: Trailhead to Split Rock Mountain North Rim Trail, 0.3 mi; to Barn Rock Trail, 1 mi; to Snake Den Bay lookout spur, 1.2 mi; to lakeshore, 1.7 mi (2.7 km).

159 Barn Rock Trail

Trails Illustrated Map 742: AA33

This yellow-marked trail travels through a nice forest of mixed woods, descending to the shore of Lake Champlain and a unique viewpoint over the lake.

▶ Locator: The trail begins at a sharp R turn at 1 mi on the Louis Clearing Bay Trail (trail158) at the head of a small ravine. ◀

From the jct. (0.0 mi.) the trail climbs gradually up the side of the slope. At 0.2 mi the trail levels off, turns and heads in a S and SE direction, then gradually begins descending to a level area at 0.6 mi. The road is level with a couple of wet areas until at 0.9 mi it begins descending again.

Dropping fairly steeply at first over rocks, at 1.1 mi the trail reaches a jct. with the Calamity Trail on the R at a beautiful old stone bridge over a small stream. The Barn Rock Trail stays on the L stream bank and comes to a jct. at 1.2 mi where the yellow markers continue L another 0.3 mi to Barn Rock and its spectacular lookout over Lake Champlain. One may also continue following the now unmarked road, which soon crosses the stream, passes a massive rock wall on the R, and ends at the top of a steep bank down to the lake 0.4 mi from the jct. with the Calamity Trail. A herd path cuts down the steep bank to the L. By following the shoreline back around the head of the bay, one can find a red-marked route that leads up a steep gully to the yellow-marked trail just before its end on Barn Rock.

❄ Trail in winter: At first a gradual and finally a steep descent to the lake, then a long climb back up; great for skis and snowshoes!

👣 Distances: Louis Clearing Bay Trail to stone bridge, 1.1 mi; to end of Barn Rock, 1.5 mi (2.4 km) (2.5 mi/4 km from parking lot). Descent to the lake from the highest point on the trail, approx. 510 ft. (180m)

162 Coon Mt. Preserve

Trails Illustrated Map 742: AA32

The Coon Mt. Preserve is a 246-acre property located in the Adirondack Land Trust's Champlain Valley Farm and Forest Project area. The mountain includes many steep rock faces, small wetlands, and several streams, and the mixed hardwood forest supports a variety of wildlife. From the top are fine views of Lake Champlain, the Green Mountains, and the Adirondack High Peaks rising beyond the farmlands in the valley. In addition to the summit trail described below, the preserve contains the Hidden Valley Trail is a 1-mi loop through a variety of terrain to the L of the summit trail.

The preserve contains most of the higher part of the mountain, and is bordered on all sides by private lands, so be sure to keep your bearings straight to avoid becoming lost and wandering onto private property. This is a preserve. No camping, fires, or the destruction or removal of any plants.

▶ Trailhead: From the hamlet of Wadhams follow NY 22 N for 1.1 mi and turn R onto Morrison Rd. In another mile, cross the RR tracks and bridge over the Boquet River. Bear R, then cross to Halds Rd. There is a small parking lot on the L with Adirondack Land Trust signs, 0.8 mi along Halds Rd. ◀

The trail leaves the N end of the parking lot (0.0 mi) on the level, but soon climbs to the upper jct. with the Hidden Valley Trail at 0.2 mi. It then passes through a hemlock and beech woods on a sidehill with the summit rocks visible up to the L through the trees.

The trail becomes rocky and steeper as it starts up into a ravine at 0.4 mi. At 0.6 mi it reaches a T fork at the base of a rock face. The fork L goes 20 yd to a nice lookout over Northwest Bay of Lake Champlain. Be careful of the drop-off!

Trailhead. Ann Hough

The trail continues up the ravine over many rocks to its head at a trail sign at 0.8 mi. It levels off and turn L past a vernal pool on stepping stones in a small notch before climbing along a lichen-encrusted rock face and up onto the summit at 1 mi. There are two lookouts: one to the W of the High Peaks with farm country in the foreground, and the higher one to the S and E across the lake to the Green Mountains in Vermont.

❄ Trail in winter: Suitable for snowshoeing but not skiing, owing to its steep middle section.

🚶 Distances: Parking lot to summit, 1 mi (1.6 km). Ascent, 610 ft (185 m). Summit elevation, 1015 ft (308 m).

163   Pauline Murdock Wildlife Sanctuary

Trail Illustrated Map 742: AA29

Located near Elizabethtown, this area offers 0.3 mi of trail.

164   Belfry Mt.

Trails Illustrated Map 742: X30

This is a real treat: a short walk and a fantastic view, the lazy hiker's heaven. High Peaks Audubon members come up here to watch hawks fly low over this peak during their fall and spring migrations. At other times it is possible to see a few hawks soaring, so bring your binoculars.

▶ Trailhead: On CR 7C, 1.1 mi N and uphill from the four-way intersection where Tracy Rd. (CR 6), CR 70, and CR 7C meet just N of the hamlet of Wither-bee. This is also 3.5 mi SE of the Lincoln Pond state campground and day-use area on CR 7 and CR 7C. ◀

There is a trailhead sign with red markers next to the bright yellow steel gate. Be sure to park outside the gate, which gets locked daily.

From the gate (0.0 mi), the route follows the ranger access road 0.2 mi to a cabin and radio tower, then at 0.3 mi reaches a clearing and two sheds. The fire tower is in sight. At just under 0.4 mi the trail achieves the summit.

From the fire tower, which can be climbed, there are good views of Lake Champlain, Vermont to the E, the Dix Range to the W, the Great Range, Whiteface to the NW, Rocky Peak Ridge, Giant, and Hurricane Mt. to the N. Mineville and the slag heaps left over from the days of the iron mines can be seen below.

❄ Trail in winter: Suitable for a short ski or snowshoe trip.

🚶 Distance: Road to summit, 0.4 mi (0.6 km). Ascent, 120 ft (36 m). Summit elevation, 1820 ft (558 m).

165 Crowfoot Pond

Trails Illustrated Map 742: W29

This old road is a very pleasant walk. The trees are spectacular and the brook becomes an old friend as you cross and recross it three times before reaching the pond. It is also an excellent cross-country ski run. All of the bridges across Crowfoot Brook are ramped for snowmobiles but that use now appears rare.

▶ Trailhead: At Northway (I-87) Exit 30, drive S on US 9 and make an immediate L turn onto Tracy Rd. Go 1.8 mi down this curving road to a track forking off to the R. This used to be a town road. Park on the shoulder of Tracy Rd. or in the clearing just off the road. ◀

From the start on Tracy Rd. (0.0 mi), yellow trail signs on a dead tree can be seen 50 ft down the old road. The road follows Crowfoot Brook on the R, past a Forest Preserve sign on a tree on the R, and at 0.1 mi crosses a bridge over Crowfoot Brook. After the bridge, the trail turns L and climbs gently through hemlocks and birches. At 0.3 mi, the road passes a spring and at 0.5 mi, the trail bends L and R again around a small, fern-lined streambed. At 0.8 mi there is another bridge over Crowfoot Brook, followed by a climb and descent to a third crossing of the brook at 1.7 mi and then a Forest Preserve marker on the L in a rock cairn at 2.1 mi. At 2.3 mi, the road divides in a small clearing. Continue straight through the clearing (avoid the R track), and at 2.5 mi the W end of Crowfoot Pond comes into view. At 2.7 mi, private camps are visible to the L with the end of public land, and the end of the trail marked by a "POSTED" sign at 3 mi.

❄ Trail in winter: Excellent for skiing or snowshoeing.

🚶 Distance: Tracy Rd. to second bridge, 0.8 mi; to rock cairn, 2.1 mi; to Crowfoot Pond, 3 mi (4.8 km).

167 Clintonville Pine Barrens

Trails Illustrated Map 742: GG28–29

Located N of Ausable Forks, this Nature Conservancy preserve offers a mile of trail through a unique habitat with great blueberry picking in season.

168 Rattlesnake Mt.

Trails Illustrated Map 742: EE31

This locally popular hike, on an unmarked trail on private land, winds gently through the forest and finishes with a steep scramble to a wide summit. The views over Willsboro Point and Lake Champlain to Vermont, are stunning!

▶ Trailhead: From the jct. of NY 9 and NY 22 at Exit 33 of the Northway, drive SE for 5 mi on NY 22 to Long Pond and a dirt turnout on the L. From the jct. with

Skating around Valcour Island. David Hough

Reber Rd. NW of Willsboro on NY 22, it is 0.7 mi to the trailhead. The unmarked trailhead is opposite a small cottage with a large boulder in its yard. ◀

From the trailhead (0.0 mi), the old roadway heads NE on the flat, descends gently, and then at 0.3 mi swings L and up. Bear L twice on this short ascent to stay on the plain trail, after which the trail is again level to a R turn where a new skidder road crosses the trail. Continuing on the flat, at 0.5 mi the trail swings R and climbs toward a notch between the two hills ahead. Just short of the height of land at 0.9 mi, the trail goes L and climbs steeply up to the lookout at the large rocky summit meadow at 1.2 mi. There are additional views to the N and a communications tower further north along the summit ridge.

❋ Trail in winter: An excellent short snowshoe hike.

🏃 Distance: Highway to summit, 1.2 mi (1.9 km). Ascent: 690 ft. (210m). Elevation: 1330 ft (405 m).

169 Big Woods Preserve

Trail Illustrated Map 742: DD32–33

Located just E of Willsboro, this area offers some nice walking through a unique forest on the S bank of the Bouquet River. Approach via the road that goes past the old school and fish ladder.

CHAMPLAIN AREA TRAILS (CATS)

CATS is a not-for-profit organization, formed in 2008, whose mission is to create and maintain hiking and outdoor opportunities in the Champlain Valley. In the winter of 2012, the group designated and began maintenance on twelve trails between Port Henry and Willsboro. These include the trails in the Split Rock Range (155–159), Coon Mountain (162, 162A), and those described below. Many of these trails are on lands protected by the Champlain Valley Conservation Partnership land trust, the Eddy Foundation, and the Northeast Wilderness Trust for inclusion in the Split Rock Wildway. More CATS trails are opened each year. One ultimate goal of CATS is to create a walking trail that connects the villages of Willsboro, Essex, and Westport. This connection is to be known as the Randorf Ramble to honor Gary Randorf, an ardent conservationist and early proponent of such a trail. The sections that have been completed (2012) are the Bouquet Mountain, Homestead, Beaver Flow, and Bobcat Trails, which currently make a 5-mi point-to-point hike. These trails are described below. More information about CATS can be accessed at www.champlainareatrails.com.

172   Rocky Ledges Trail

Trails Illustrated Map 742: CC32

This woodland trail skirts the east and south slopes of North Boquet Mt., and after it forks intersects the Bouquet Mts. Trail (trail 154) at two separate spots. The beginning of this trail is relatively gentle, but both branches are briefly quite steep. The trail borders or crosses hunting club lands, so it is closed September 15–December 15.

▶ Trailhead: At the intersection of NY 22 and Jersey Street, 2.5 mi. W of the village of Essex, turn W onto Jersey St., cross the Bouquet River.and turn L onto Leaning Rd. Dr. S 0.1 mi and park on the shoulder across from two houses. The trail is on the R. ◀

From its start (0.0 mi), the trail climbs gently through pines, old apple trees, and scrubby second-growth until it enters the woods at 0.2 mi. Here it angles L uphill across a small stream and alternates flat and gentle climbs until reaching a large rock face on the R at 0.4 mi. After this large rock, the path bends uphill again, crosses a rock-filled gully, and reaches a fork in a scrubby clearing at 0.7 mi.

The R fork continues uphill, steep in parts, through a leaf-filled gully, and along a private forestry boundary on the R to a crest, after which the trail descends to a jct. with the Boquet Mts. Trail at 1.2 mi. The L fork continues almost level into and through a clearing before climbing along a fairly steep hillside. Beech trees show numerous bear sign before this fork of the trail reaches the Bouquet Mts. Trail at 1.1 mi.

❄ Trail in winter: Good for snowshoeing.

🏃 Distances: Trailhead to Y intersection, 0.7 mi.; to Bouquet Mt. Trail along R fork, 1.2mi. (2 km); to Bouquet Mt. Trail along L fork, 1.1mi (1.9km)

173 Bouquet Mts. Trail

Trails Illustrated Map 742: CC31

This trail passes through beautifully varied woods along the slopes of and between North and South Bouquet Mts. in the town of Essex. Most of these lands are owned by the Eddy Foundation, whose goal is to assemble wildlife habitat in the Champlain Valley. The Foundation works cooperatively with the Champlain Area Trail System, and this trail is part of the proposed hiking connection between Westport and Willsboro. Because the trail borders or crosses hunting club lands, it is closed September 15–December 15. Combining the Bobcat, Beaver Flow, and Homestead trails with the Bouquet Mts. Trail makes for a 5-mi point-to-point hike.

▶ Trailheads: *North trailhead:* At the intersection of NY 22 and Jersey St., 2.5 mi. W of the village of Essex, turn W onto Jersey St., cross the Bouquet River, bear R, and go another 1.3 mi to the trailhead on the L.

South trailhead: From NY 22 in Whallonsburg, go W on Cook Rd., driving N, past a 90-degree L turn and uphill to the end of pavement at the intersection with Leaning Rd. and Black Kettle Farm at 1.7mi. Continue uphill to a green "Wildlife Sanctuary" and trailhead sign on the R at 2.4 mi. There is room to park a vehicle or two here off the road. This is also the N end trailhead for the Homestead Trail. ◀

From the S trailhead (0.0 mi), cross a cable barrier and follow a woods roadway. At 0.25 mi., there is a fork in the trail; the roadway heads L and the trail R; both of these routes continue uphill and rejoin in another 0.25 mi., at a small clearing. Continuing NE on gentle grades into a handsome forest, the trail climbs gradually on a sidehill, crossing several old farm roads. As the path passes through stands of beech trees, there are numerous claw marks and other signs of bear activity on the gray tree trunks. The terrain becomes rockier terrain along the side of South Bouquet Mt., with a ledge offering a nice view toward Lake Champlain.

The trail then takes several curves and descends slightly through scrubby second-growth woods toward the pass between the two mountains. The southerly fork of the Rocky Ledges Trail (trail 172) is reached at 1.5 mi, followed by its northerly fork at 1.8 mi. The trail then crosses several clearings as it becomes the remnant of a logging road and straightens out, still on a gradual downhill, toward its end on Jersey St. at 2.6 mi.

❄ Trail in winter: The entire trail is very suitable for snowshoeing, but too steep and narrow in spots for skiing.

🏃 Distances: To first intersection with Rocky Ledges Trail 1.5 mi; to N end of trail at Jersey St., 2.6 mi (4.2 km).

174 Wildway Overlook Trail

Trails Illustrated Map 742: CC31

This trail is a short hike up the northwest slope of South Bouquet Mt., passing through scrubby cut-over woods along a logging road, to a spectacular view of the Champlain Valley from a summit ledge. The trail's name refers to the jaw-dropping summit vista encompassing much of the newly protected lands in this part of the valley. It will be interesting, over the years, to watch the mountain's forest recover from a zealous logging operation in the 1990s.

▶ Trailhead: On Brookfield Rd, which can be reached by continuing W from either of the Bouquet Mts. Trail trailheads (see above). From the S trailhead, it is 0.3 mi W to Brookfield Rd. and then 1 mi N. From the N trailhead, it is 0.9 mi W to Brookfield Rd. and then 0.7 mi S. The Wildway Overlook trailhead is at a chained woods road on the E side, amidst "Wildlife Sanctuary" signs. Park on the shoulder of the pavement. ◀

From the trailhead (0.0 mi), the trail follows an old logging road uphill through second-growth forest. Brambles abound and will do so until the forest canopy recovers sufficiently to shade the trail. The grade is steeper at the bottom and the top, but never very taxing. The slightly rutted road continues up to a mossy clearing with views NNW through the trees. At this point the trail veers to the S and climbs the summit ridge more steadily. After ten minutes, one rocky lookout and then another offer fantastic views over farm fields, Whallons Bay, and both Split Rock Mt. and Split Rock Pt. to the Green Mountains beyond.

❄ Trail in winter: This makes an excellent snowshoe jaunt. Skiing would be a bit more difficult on the final ascent.

🚶 Distance: From Brookfield Rd. to South Boquet summit, 1.1 mi (1.8 km)

175 Beaver Flow Trail

Trails Illustrated Map 742: BB31

This trail runs between Walker and Cook Rds. and connects with the Homestead (175A) and Bobcat (176) Trails. It is wooded along its entire length, and all beaver activity is out of sight of the trail.

▶ Trailheads: North: On Cook Rd. (see S trailhead for Bouquet Mts. Trail), just past the jct. with Leaning Rd. or 1.8 mi from NY 22. South: On Walker Rd., 1.4 mi W of NY 22 in Whallonsburg. ◀

From the S trailhead (0.0 mi), the trail goes N into oak and beech woods, up along a sidehill and then down into darker hemlock habitat. The route zigs and zags, so keep a close eye on the trail markers. The trail passes a large primeval moss- and fern-covered rocky outcrop on the R, while descending a narrow, steep chute, and proceeds to a jct. with the Homestead Trail (175A) and a stream crossing at

0.5 mi. Bearing R at the jct., it climbs, joins an old logging road, and curves L at another massive oak. The trail flattens out, passes an ancient washing machine and an old trash dump, and reaches its end on Cook Rd. at 1 mi. The Black Kettle Nature Trail is just 0.25 mi downhill to the R, and the Bouquet Mts. Trail is 0.5 mi uphill to the L.

❄ Trail in winter: This trail makes for a wonderful showshoe trip. The twisty, narrow midsection of the route would be quite challenging on skis and would require two or more feet of snow to be skiable.

🚶 Distances: From Walker Rd. to intersection with Homestead Trail (175A), 0.5mi.; to Cook Rd., 1 mi (1.6 km).

175A   Homestead Trail

Trails Illustrated Map 742: BB31

This trail, new in 2011, is an alternative approach to Cook Rd. from the Beaver Flow Trail, of which it is a westerly fork. Its S end begins at 0.5 mi along the Beaver Flow Trail (175) and finishes N opposite the Bouquet Mts. trailhead on Cook Rd. The trail is largely an old woods road, with a few side detours through close trees, to skirt wet areas.

From the Beaver Flow Trail bear L and down a twisting course to a stream at a rock shelf above a small waterfall. From here the trail ascends the far bank and continues on the level to a wide woods road, after which the trail is basically a straightaway route uphill and across a flat section of second-growth woods. On the R (E) here is an old stone wall that the trail crosses twice to avoid muddy areas before reaching Cook Rd. at 0.7 mi from the Beaver Flow Trail.

❄ Trail in winter: Good for skiing and snowshoeing.

🚶 Distances: From intersection with Beaver Flow Trail (175) to Cook Rd., 0.7mi. (1.1 km).

176   Bobcat Trail

Trails Illustrated Map 742: AA31

This path crosses fields, wetlands, and woods with little elevation change on old farm roads and newly cut paths. These varied habitats are biologically and scenically rich, with a hay field, dark forests, a huge beaver-built complex of at least ten ponds, and an overgrown meadow. Wildlife sign is abundant, so bring your binoculars.

▶ Trailhead: At the end of Ferris Rd. off NY 22, 1.7 mi N of Wadhams and 2.1 mi S of Whallonsburg. Turn N onto Ferris Rd. for 0.2 mi to a 90-degree L turn. Pull off on the R at a trail sign for Randorf Ramble/Bobcat Trail, and do not block the roadway into the field. The trail is made possible by an easement with the landowners here. Be sure to respect their privacy and property. ◀

The route heads **N**, passing between the field on the L and "Posted" signs to the R, ascending slightly to the beginning of woods. The trail follows green and white arrow markers along the roadway into the forest. There are occasional twists and turns to the trail, as it narrows and widens before emerging alongside a series of beaver dams and ponds on the L at 0.7mi. Bird and beaver sign abound here.

The path crests a rise that has good views of the wetlands, before it descends to cross an old pasture. The footing is bumpy on this passage, probably owing to former cow traffic in the soft soil of this lowland.

❄ Trail in winter: The route is perfect for skiing and snowshoeing.

🥾 Distances: The trail reaches Walker Rd., downhill from a red brick house on the L, at 1.2 mi (1.9km).

177 Black Kettle Nature Trail

Trails Illustrated Map 742: BB32

Located W of Whallonsburg, this 0.6-mi CATS trail has numbered posts keyed to a pamphlet available at the trailhead.

178 Little Falls Preserve

Trails Illustrated Map 742 AA31–32

Located E of Wadhams, this 15-acre Nature Conservancy preserve is good both as a canoe put-in and a place to swim.

179 Lee Park

Trails Illustrated Map 742: Z31

Located in Westport, this small preserve offers 0.6 mi of trail along Hoisington Brook.

180 Blueberry Hill Trail System

Trails Illustrated Map 742: AA29 | Town of Elizabethtown trail map

This is another of the forward-looking local municipal initiatives to take advantage of resident and visitor interest in trail biking, hiking, and cross-country skiing. Blueberry Hill is an interesting array of paths and woods roads about a mile W of the village of Elizabethtown on land given to the town in the late 1980s by Colonel and Mrs. Holst. The terrain is hilly and includes several lookouts; a cabin, a summit lean-to, and an old sugarhouse, all interesting stops along the way. Some trails are wide, gentle old woods roads while others are narrow scoots and "goat paths." Expect to share the trails with horse riders, skiers, mountain bikers, and the very occasional snowmobile or ATV.

The Town of Elizabethtown trail map shows 22 named trails, and this guide does not try to describe them all. The trail map is crucial for deciphering the entire network and is available at the Elizabethtown Town Hall at 7563 Court Street across from the Champlain National Bank and at the town's website: www.etownny.com. Click on "town maps," and scroll to the bottom of the page. There are two principal points of entry to the trail system, and both have large signs that also include painted maps of the trail network.

▶ Trailheads: *Southerly trailhead:* From the intersection of NY 9 and NY 9N, next to the Cobble Hill Golf Course in Elizabethtown, go W on Route 9N for 1.1 mi. to Lord Rd. on the R. Turn R and look for the Blueberry Hill Trail sign on the L in 0.1 mi. Park well over on the shoulder of the road. *Northerly trailhead* (less well-marked): Continue on Lord Rd. another 0.2 mi. to an intersection with Roscoe R d. Turn L and proceed 0.6 mi. to Bronson Way on the L. Turn in past the only house and find the large trail sign on the R; parking here is also on the shoulder of the road. The map is accurate regarding the overall layout of the network, but it is not drawn to scale, nor are distances included. Trail sections are never longer than 0.5 mi., but close attention should be paid to the map and trail signs at junctions. There are several other unmarked woods roads and trails in the area, and some junctions are lacking signs (autumn 2009). ◀

Blueberry Hill Summit: The best short hike is to the lean-to on the summit of Blueberry Hill. It starts at the Lord Rd. trailhead and follows an old road up to a jct. at 0.3 mi. Both roads lead toward the summit, but the L road is drier. It climbs and curves to the R around to the NW side of the summit where at 0.5 mi a narrower road goes R and up to the summit at 0.6 mi. The rocky summit offers views of Giant Mt. to the SW and the Green Mts. to the E.

Trails in winter: Excellent for snowshoeing and generally fine and wide enough to ski.

181 Tanaher, Mill, Murrey, and Russett Ponds

Trails Illustrated Map 742: Y30

Located just E of Lincoln Pond Rd. N of Witherbee, short trails lead from the road to these ponds that are mostly within a small parcel of Forest Preserve.

182 Cheney Mt.

This new (2012) trail has been constructed by the Town of Moriah with assistance from the Champlain Area Trails System (CATS). on property owned by the town. This effort revives an old route up this small, steep mountain between Port Henry and Mineville. Various ledges offer views of both Lake Champlain and some of the High Peaks. The summit ridge holds a number of large vernal pools and the open hardwood forest allows many wildflowers to bloom in season.

▶ Trailhead: The trail starts on Pelfershire Rd. (CR 54), 1.7 mi E of Fisher Hill Rd. in Mineville, or 1.4 mi W of NY 9N/22 north of Port Henry. The trailhead is a wide turnout marked with a CATS sign at a gate at the base of a hill. The trail is marked with green CATS markers. ◀

From the road (0.0 mi), the trail goes around the gate on the R and begins climbing an old road with a capped landfill soon visible on the R. At 0.2 mi a trail with markers comes in from the R. (This is an alternate approach that comes directly across the capped landfill.) Past this jct. the trail soon swings L and climbs, sometimes steeply, to a jct in a col on the crest of the ridge at 0.6 mi. (Trail L leads 100 yd to a good view to the N.) Swinging R the trail climbs to the summit (no view) at 0.8 mi. Continuing, the trail reaches a jct. in 100 yd. Trail R leads to a series of ledges that provide views of the massive tailings pile plus the Dix Range in the distance. Trail L climbs a bit, passes another ledge on the R, and then descends to a view of the Champlain Bridge at the current end of trail at 0.9 mi. Killington Peak in Vermont is also visible in the distance. One can continue another 150 yd down through open woods to a more expansive lookout that provides a 180-degree view to the E, S, and W.

🥾 Distances: To view at end of trail, 0.9 mi (1.5 km). Ascent from Pelfershire Rd., 500 ft (150 m) 🐾

Glossary of Terms

bivouac: Camping in the open with improvised shelter or no shelter.

bushwhacking: To make one's way through undergrowth without the aid of a formal trail.

cairn: A pile of stones that marks a summit or route.

chimney: A steep, narrow cleft or gully in the face of a mountain, usually by which the mountain may be ascended.

cobble: A small stony peak on the side of a mountain.

col: A pass between two adjacent peaks or between high points of a ridge line.

corduroy: A road, trail, or bridge formed by logs laid side by side transversely to facilitate crossing swampy areas.

cripplebrush: Thick, stunted growth at higher elevations.

dike: A band of different-colored rock, usually with straight, well-defined sides, formed when igneous rock is intruded into the existing rock. Dikes can manifest themselves either as gullies, if the dike rock is softer (as in the Colden Trap Dike), or as ridges.

duff: Partly decayed plant matter on the forest floor. Duff's ability to burn easily has started many forest fires.

lean-to: A three-sided shelter with an overhanging roof on the open side.

lumber road: A crude road constructed for hauling logs.

tote road: A better road constructed in connection with logging operations and used for hauling supplies. Often built with corduroy, many of these roads are still evident after 80 years and are often used as the route for present-day trails.

vlei: A low marsh or swampy meadow (pronounced *vly*).

Highest One Hundred Adirondack Mountains

This list of the highest 100 mountains in the Adirondacks is presented to make hikers aware of the many possibilities for interesting and worthwhile climbs and explorations in all parts of the Adirondack Park. Forty of the listings are presently trailless, and some are privately owned, with permission (which may not be granted) needed to climb.

The 46 High Peaks originally thought to be at least 4000 ft high, based on early twentieth-century surveys, are now listed in order of their actual heights. Midcentury surveys using aerial photography and photogrammetry techniques lowered several of the original 46 peaks while apparently raising one (MacNaughton Mt.) above 4000 ft.

The original 46 peaks, known as the "high" or "major" peaks, are the ones recognized by the Adirondack Forty-Sixers as the requirement for membership. The criteria for these peaks were that each peak rise vertically at least 300 ft on all sides OR that it be at least 0.75 mi distant from the nearest higher summit. In selecting the additional 54 peaks, the criteria used are a 0.75 mi distance AND a 300 ft rise on all sides.

The most recent series of USGS maps for the Adirondacks (the metric series) was created between 1978 and 1990. A number of elevations on the new maps differ from elevations on older maps, the latter created mostly in the 1950s. However, correspondence to date with the USGS has not resulted in sufficient confidence in the "new" elevations to warrant replacing the "old" elevations.

If the new elevations were to be used, Unnamed (Brown Pond) and Sawtooth Mts. No. 4 would be displaced by Wilmington Range high point (Wilmington metric map) at 3458 ft and Bullhead Mt. (Thirteenth Lake metric map) at 3432 ft. Pending further information on elevation data, the list is unchanged from the 1950s with the exception of citing the current metric series map on which each peak is located.

KEY TO ABBREVIATIONS

An asterisk (*) indicates that there is a footnote. The number of the footnote will correspond to the number on the roster.

- A "c" following the height indicates that the elevation shown is that of the highest contour line.
- "Tr" indicates that there is a standard, maintained trail to the summit.
- An extra "T" means that there is a fire tower on the summit.
- A "P" indicates private ownership.
- For peaks not labeled on the map, a map sector (in parentheses) follows the map name.

Rank	Name	Elevation (in feet)	Remark	Topographical Map (metric 7.5' x 15' series)
1	Mt. Marcy	5344	Tr	Mt. Marcy
2	Algonquin Peak	5114	Tr	Keene Valley
3	Mt. Haystack	4960	Tr	Mount Marcy
4	Mt. Skylight	4924	Tr	Mount Marcy
5	Whiteface Mt.	4867	Tr	Lake Placid
6	Dix Mt.	4857	Tr	Mount Marcy
7	Gray Peak	4840		Mount Marcy
8	Iroquois Peak	4840	Tr	Keene Valley
9	Basin Mt.	4827	Tr	Mount Marcy
10	Gothics	4736	Tr	Keene Valley
11	Mt. Colden	4714	Tr	Mount Marcy
12	Giant Mt.	4627	Tr	Elizabethtown
13	Nippletop	4620c	Tr	Mount Marcy
14	Santanoni Peak	4607		Santanoni Peak
15	Mt. Redfield	4606		Mount Marcy
16	Wright Peak	4580	Tr	Keene Valley
17	Saddleback Mt.	4515	Tr	Keene Valley
18	Panther Peak	4442		Santanoni Peak
19	Table Top Mt.	4427		Keene Valley
20	Rocky Peak Ridge	4420c	Tr	Elizabethtown
21	Macomb Mt.	4405		Mount Marcy
22	Armstrong Mt.	4400c	Tr	Keene Valley
23	Hough Peak	4400c		Mount Marcy
24	Seward Mt.	4361		Ampersand Lake
25*	Mt. Marshall	4360		Ampersand Lake
26	Allen Mt.	4340c		Mount Marcy
27	Big Slide Mt.	4240c	Tr	Keene Valley
28	Esther Mt.	4240		Wilmington
29*	Upper Wolf Jaw Mt.	4185	Tr	Keene Valley
30*	Lower Wolf Jaw Mt.	4175	Tr	Keene Valley
31	Street Mt.	4166		Ampersand Lake
32	Phelps Mt.	4161	Tr	Keene Valley
33	Mt. Donaldson	4140		Ampersand Lake
34	Seymour Mt.	4120		Ampersand Lake
35*	Sawteeth	4100c	Tr	Mount Marcy
36	Cascade Mt.	4098	Tr	Keene Valley
37	South Dix	4060	Tr	Mount Marcy
38	Porter Mt.	4059	Tr	Keene Valley
39	Mt. Colvin	4057	Tr	Mount Marcy
40	Mt. Emmons	4040		Ampersand Lake
41	Dial Mt.	4020	Tr	Mount Marcy
42	East Dix	4012		Mount Marcy

Rank	Name	Elevation (in feet)	Remark	Topographical Map (metric 7.5' x 15' series)
43	MacNaughton Mt.	4000c		Ampersand Lake
44	Green Mt.	3980c		Elizabethtown
45	Blake Peak	3960c	Tr	Mount Marcy
46	Cliff Mt.	3960c		Mount Marcy
47*	Peak, unnamed (Lost Pond)	3900c		Ampersand Lake (SE)
48*	Moose Mt.	3899	Tr	Saranac Lake
49	Snowy Mt.	3899	TrT	Indian Lake
50	Nye Mt.	3895		Ampersand Lake
51	Kilburn Mt.	3881		Lake Placid
52*	Sawtooth Mts. (No. 1)	3877c		Ampersand Lake (C)
53	Panther Mt.	3862		Indian Lake
54	McKenzie Mt.	3861	Tr	Saranac Lake
55	Blue Ridge	3860c		Indian Lake
56	North River Mt.	3860c		Mount Marcy
57	Sentinel Mt.	3858		Lake Placid
58	Lyon Mt.	3830	TrT	Lyon Mt.
59*	Sawtooth Mts. (No. 2)	3820c		Ampersand Lake (C)
60	Couchsachraga Peak	3820		Santanoni Peak
61*	TR Mt. (Indian Falls)	3820c		Keene Valley (SW)
62	Averill Peak	3810		Lyon Mt.
63	Avalanche Mt.	3800c		Keene Valley
64	Buell Mt.	3786		Indian Lake
65*	Boreas Mt.	3776	P	Mount Marcy
66	Blue Mt.	3760c	TrT	Blue Mt. Lake
67	Wakely Mt.	3760c	TrT	Wakeley Mt.
68	Henderson Mt.	3752		Santanoni Peak
69	Lewey Mt.	3742		Indian Lake
70*	Sawtooth Mts. (No. 3)	3700c		Ampersand Lake(C)
71	Wallface Mt.	3700c		Ampersand Lake
72*	Hurricane Mt.	3694	TrT	Elizabethtown
73	Hoffman Mt.	3693		Blue Ridge
74	Cheney Cobble	3683		Mount Marcy
75	Calamity Mt.	3620c		Santanoni Peak
76	Little Moose Mt.	3620c		Wakeley Mt.
77*	Sunrise Mt.	3614	P	Mount Marcy
78	Stewart Mt.	3615		Lake Placid
79*	Jay Mt.	3600		Lewis
80	Pitchoff Mt.	3600c	Tr	Keene Valley
81	Saddleback Mt.	3600c		Lewis
82	Pillsbury Mt.	3597	TrT	West Canada Lakes
83	Slide Mt.	3576c		Lake Placid
84	Gore Mt.	3583	TrT	Thirteenth Lake

Rank	Name	Elevation (in feet)	Remark	Topographical Map (metric 7.5' x 15' series)
85*	Dun Brook Mt.	3580c		Deerland
86	Noonmark Mt.	3556	Tr	Keene Valley
87*	Mt. Adams	3540c	TrT	Santanoni Peak
88	Fishing Brook Mt.	3540c		Deerland
89	Little Santanoni Mt.	3500c		Santanoni Peak
90	Blue Ridge	3497		Blue Mt. Lake
91*	Peak, unnamed (Fishing Brook Range)	3480c		Deerland (E)
92	Puffer Mt.	3472		Thirteenth Lake
93*	Sawtooth Mts. (No. 4)	3460c		Santanoni (N)
94*	Sawtooth Mts. (No. 5)	3460c		Ampersand Lake (C)
95	Wolf Pond Mt.	3460c		Blue Ridge
96	Cellar Mt.	3447		Wakeley Mt.
97	Blue Ridge Mt.	3440c		Blue Ridge
98	Morgan Mt.	3440c		Wilmington
99	Blue Ridge	3436		Raquette Lake
100*	Peak, unnamed (Brown Pond)	3425		Indian Lake (N)

25. **Mt. Marshall.** This is shown as Mt. Clinton on the 1953 map but has been corrected on the 1978 *Ampersand Lake* 7.5' x 15' metric map. See MacIntyre Range (p. 101) for history and naming of this peak.

29 and 30. **Upper and Lower Wolf Jaw.** The map reads "Wolfjaw." Because "frog leg" is two words, it is assumed that "wolf jaw" is too. Early mountaineers used a single hyphenated word.

35. **Sawteeth.** This mountain was named for the profile of its several summit nubbles, which were said to resemble the teeth of a great saw. "Sawtooth," as shown on the 1953 map, is incorrect, but has been corrected on the 1978 Mount Marcy 7.5' x 15' metric map.

47. **Peak, unnamed (Lost Pond).** This mountain is easily located because Lost Pond lies practically on its summit. The coordinates are 44°10' N, 74°02' W.

48. **Moose Mt. (St. Armand Mt. on some signs).** Trails to this peak have been reopened. See Shore Owners Association Trails (p. 148) for description and cautions.

52. **Sawtooth Mts. (No. 1).** The Sawtooth Mts. comprise a large, completely wild area SE of Ampersand Mt. It is a region of many knobs, five of which qualify for the list. These have been numbered from one to five in order of

descending altitude. The highest peak (No. 1), elevation 3877 ft, is central to the region. The coordinates are 44°11' N, 74°07' W.

59. **Sawtooth Mts. (No. 2).** The 3820 ft twin knobs of this summit mark the N end of a three-step ridge that lies W of the main 3877 ft peak. The coordinates are 44°11' N, 74°08' W.

61. **TR Mt., formerly "Unnamed (Indian Falls)."** Located to the NW of Indian Falls. In 1999 this peak was named in honor of the centennial of Theodore Roosevelt's tenure as governor of New York State.

65. **Boreas Mt.** With the removal of the fire tower, the trail is now closed and permission (which may not be granted) is needed to climb this peak.

70. **Sawtooth Mts. (No. 3).** Lying 0.5 mi W of the Essex County line, this 3700 ft peak marks the SE threshold of the Sawtooths. The coordinates are 44°10'N, 74°07' W.

72. **Hurricane Mt.** As of 2012, the fire tower is abandoned and unsafe to climb. No longer slated for removal, the tower may be restored.

77. **Sunrise Mt.** The trail to this summit is entirely on private land and is closed to the public. One can approach on public land along the boundary line from the Dix Mt. trail or from the E via West Mill Brook. In recent years permission has not been granted to hikers to use the trail.

79. **Jay Mt.** Both the 1953 and 1978 maps label a 3340 ft peak W of Grassy Notch as Jay Mt. This is the highest point visible from the valley, but the label properly belongs on the 3600 ft summit with the benchmark.

85. **Dun Brook Mt.** This peak is surrounded by private land leased/owned by hunting clubs, whose permission must be obtained to approach it. The summit is on a separate private parcel requiring additional permission.

87. **Mt. Adams.** The fire tower had been restored, but is now closed.

91. **Peak (Fishing Brook Range).** This 3480 ft unnamed peak marks the end of a long ridge leading SW from Fishing Brook Mt., 43°55' N, 74°19' W. It is surrounded by private property owned/leased by hunting clubs whose permission must be obtained before ascending this peak.

93. **Sawtooth Mts. (No. 4).** This 3460 ft peak at the NW end of the Sawtooths lies about 1 mi SSE of Beaver Pond. Nos. 4 and 5 are the same height, but No. 4 is much more massive. Coordinates of No. 4 are 44°12' N, 74°10' W.

94. **Sawtooth Mts. (No. 5).** Also 3460 ft, this summit is found about 1 mi NE of the pass between Ward Brook and the Cold River drainage. Coordinates, 44°11' N, 74°08' W.

100. **Peak, unnamed (Brown Pond).** This 3425 ft peak is found about 3.5 mi ENE of Wakely Dam. Brown Pond lies in a slight depression on its westerly slope. The coordinates are 43°44' N, 74°25' W.

Noonmark. **James Appleyard**

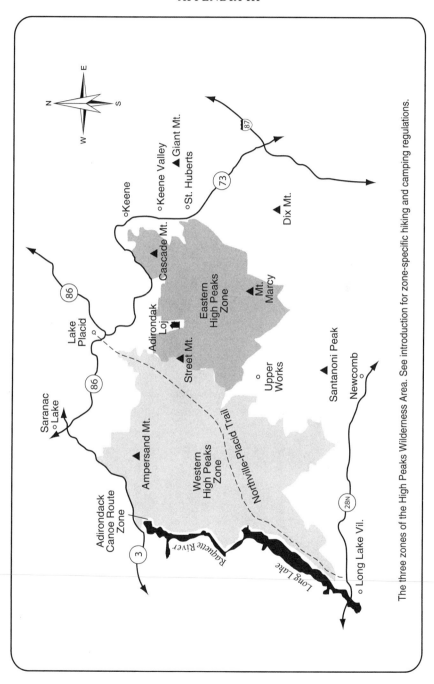

The three zones of the High Peaks Wilderness Area. See introduction for zone-specific hiking and camping regulations.

Heart Lake. **James Bullard**

About the Editors

Tony Goodwin was raised in Hartford, Connecticut, and introduced to the Adirondacks as a child through summers in Keene Valley, New York. He began hiking and skiing at an early age, and ultimately acquired an impressive knowledge of Adirondack trails, particularly those in the High Peaks region.

Goodwin holds a B.A. and an M.A. in History from Williams College and the State University of New York at Plattsburgh, respectively.

His position as venue manager for the Lake Placid Olympic Organizing Committee led to his appointment as manager of Mt. Van Hoevenberg cross-country ski area in 1981. After five years at Mt. Van Hoevenberg, he left to help found the Adirondack Ski Touring Council, which constructed the twenty-four-mile Jackrabbit Trail, and was also named executive director of the Adirondack Trail Improvement Society. He continues to lead both organizations today.

An Adirondack Forty-Sixer, Goodwin has been the editor of ADK's authoritative *Adirondack Mountain Club High Peaks Trails* and of the accompanying map— through several editions and numerous reprintings—since 1984. In addition, he served on the High Peaks Wilderness Citizens Advisory Committee, which provided ideas for that region's Unit Management Plan. He has long filled an informal role as an educator-spokesperson on recreational issues confronting the High Peaks, and has done so with humor and tenacity.

Goodwin is the author of *Ski and Snowshoe Trails in the Adirondacks*, published by the Adirondack Mountain Club in 2003. In addition, he has authored two previous ADK ski touring guides, *Northern Adirondack Ski Tours* (1982) and *Classic Adirondack Ski Tours* (1994), and numerous articles for *Adirondack Life, Adirondack Explorer*, and *Adirondac*.

David Thomas-Train, born in Washington, D.C., has lived in Keene Valley, New York, since 1981. He has a B.A. in English Literature from Kenyon College and an M.S. in Early Childhood Education from Wheelock College. He has been an educator for over thirty-five years, now tutoring students of all ages. He leads canoeing, hiking, and ski trips in the Adirondacks, incorporating environmental education into these activities for various organizations, including the Adirondack Nature Conservancy, Adirondack Mountain Club, Adirondack Ski Touring

Council, Adirondack Trail Improvement Society, Champlain Area Trails, and Natural History Museum of the Adirondacks. He is the Coordinator of The Friends of Poke-O-Moonshine, a grassroots organization dedicated to the restoration of the fire tower and trail on that mountain, and to its use as an environmental education site. He also directs the Adirondack Fire Tower Association, a Park-wide entity dedicated to strengthening private and public initiatives for state-owned fire towers. He has been chair and/or Conservation Coordinator of the Keene Valley Chapter of the Adirondack Mountain Club for over twenty years, and a mapping consultant for the Adirondack Mountain Club and National Geographic Society map series on the Adirondacks. A volunteer for numerous Adirondack scientific and advocacy groups, he contributes his time to fund-raising, invasive species, loon surveys, and mammal tracking.

Join us!

30,000 members count on us, and so can you:
- We produce the most-trusted, comprehensive trail maps and books
- Our outdoor activities take you all around the world
- Our advocacy team concentrates on issues that affect the wild lands and waters important to our members and chapters throughout the state
- Our professional and volunteer crews construct and maintain trails
- Our wilderness lodges and information centers give you shelter and direction

Benefits of Membership include:
- Fun outdoor recreation opportunities for all levels
- *Adirondac* magazine (bimonthly)
- Special rates for ADK education and skill-building programs, lodging, parking, publications, and logo merchandise
- Rewarding volunteer opportunities
- Supporting ADK's mission and thereby ensuring protection of the wild lands and waters of New York State

Lodges and campground
- Adirondak Loj, on the shores of Heart Lake, near Lake Placid, offers year-round accommodations in private and family rooms, a coed loft, and cabins. It is accessible by car, and parking is available.
- The Adirondak Loj Wilderness Campground, located on ADK's Heart Lake property, offers thirty-two campsites and sixteen Adirondack lean-tos.
- Johns Brook Lodge (JBL), located near Keene Valley, is a backcountry facility accessible only on foot and open on a seasonal basis. Facilities include coed bunkrooms or small family rooms. Cabins near JBL are available year-round.

Both lodges offer home-cooked meals and trail lunches. Member discounts are available at all lodges and the campground.

Visit us!
ADK centers in Lake George and on our Heart Lake property near Lake Placid offer ADK publications and other merchandise for sale, as well as backcountry and general Adirondack information, educational displays, outdoor equipment, and snacks.

ADK Publications

FOREST PRESERVE SERIES
1 Adirondack Mountain Club High Peaks Trails
2 Adirondack Mountain Club Eastern Trails
3 Adirondack Mountain Club Central Trails
4 Adirondack Mountain Club Western Trails
5 Adirondack Mountain Club Northville–Placid Trail
6 Adirondack Mountain Club Catskill Trails

OTHER TITLES
Adirondack Alpine Summits: An Ecological Field Guide
Adirondack Birding: 60 Great Places to Find Birds
Adirondack Paddling: 60 Great Flatwater Adventures
An Adirondack Sampler I: Day Hikes for All Seasons
Catskill Day Hikes for All Seasons
Forests and Trees of the Adirondack High Peaks Region
Kids on the Trail! Hiking with Children in the Adirondacks
No Place I'd Rather Be: Wit and Wisdom from Adirondack Lean-to Journals
Ski and Snowshoe Trails in the Adirondacks
The Adirondack Reader
The Catskill 67: A Hiker's Guide to the Catskill 100 Highest Peaks Under 3500'
Views from on High: Fire Tower Trails in the Adirondacks and Catskills
Winterwise: A Backpacker's Guide

MAPS
Trails of the Adirondack High Peaks topographic map
Trails Illustrated Map 736: Northville-Placid Trail
Trails Illustrated Map 742: Lake Placid/High Peaks
Trails Illustrated Map 743: Lake George/Great Sacandaga
Trails Illustrated Map 744: Northville/Raquette Lake
Trails Illustrated Map 745: Old Forge/Oswegatchie
Trails Illustrated Map 746: Saranac/Paul Smiths
Trails Illustrated Map 755: Catskill Park

ADIRONDACK MOUNTAIN CLUB CALENDAR
Price list available upon request, or see www.adk.org.

Contact Us

ADK Member Services Center (Exit 21 off I-87, the Northway)
814 Goggins Road
Lake George, NY 12845-4117
Website: www. adk.org   Information: 518-668-4447
Membership, donations, publications, and merchandise: 800-395-8080

ADK Heart Lake Program Center (at Adirondak Loj on Heart Lake)
PO Box 867
1002 Adirondack Loj Road
Lake Placid, NY 12946-0867
Educational programs and facility reservations: 518-523-3441

ADK Public Affairs Office
301 Hamilton Street
Albany, NY 12210-1738
Public Affairs: 518-449-3870

Adirondack
Mountain Club

The Adirondack Mountain Club (ADK) is dedicated to the protection and responsible recreational use of the New York State Forest Preserve, and other parks, wild lands, and waters vital to our members and chapters. The Club, founded in 1922, is a member-directed organization committed to public service and stewardship. ADK employs a balanced approach to outdoor recreation, advocacy, environmental education, and natural resource conservation.

ADK encourages the involvement of all people in its mission and activities; its goal is to be a community that is comfortable, inviting, and accessible.

The Adirondack Mountain Club is a charitable organization, 501(c)(3). Contributions are tax deductible to the extent the law allows.

Index

Locations are indexed by proper name with Lake, Mount, *or* Mt. *following.*